Radiation Nation

THREE MILE ISLAND AND THE POLITICAL
TRANSFORMATION OF THE 1970s

Natasha Zaretsky

Columbia University Press
New York

Columbia University Press
Publishers Since 1893
New York   Chichester, West Sussex
cup.columbia.edu
Copyright © 2018 Columbia University Press
All rights reserved

Library of Congress Cataloging-in-Publication Data
Names: Zaretsky, Natasha, 1970– author.
Title: Radiation nation: Three Mile Island and the political transformation of the 1970s /
Natasha Zaretsky.
Other titles: Three Mile Island and the political transformation of the 1970s
Description: New York: Columbia University Press, [2018] | Includes bibliographical
references and index.
Identifiers: LCCN 2017038412 | ISBN 9780231179812 (pbk.: alk. paper) |
ISBN 9780231179805 (cloth: alk. paper)
Subjects: LCSH: United States—Politics and government—1977–1981. | Nuclear power
plants—Accidents—Pennsylvania—Harrisburg Region. | Three Mile Island Nuclear Power
Plant (Pa.)—Accidents—Social aspects. | Radiation injuries—United States—Social aspects. |
Political ecology—United States—History—20th century. | Nationalism—United States—
History—20th century. | Conservatism—Environmental aspects—United States.
Classification: LCC E872 .Z37 2018 | DDC 363.17990974818—dc23
LC record available at https://lccn.loc.gov/2017038412

Columbia University Press books are printed on permanent and durable acid-free paper.
Printed in the United States of America

Cover image: © AP Photo/Harrisburg Patriot-News, Martha Cooper

For Jonathan

The accident had ruined a lot of lives. Or, to be exact, it had busted apart the structures on which those lives had depended—depended, I guess, to a greater degree than we had originally believed. A town needs its children for a lot more than it thinks.

—Russell Banks, *The Sweet Hereafter*

CONTENTS

CONTENTS

ILLUSTRATIONS

ILLUSTRATIONS

ABBREVIATIONS

AEC   Atomic Energy Commission
AMA   American Medical Association
ANGRY   Anti-Nuclear Group Representing York
CMCHS   Civilian-Military Contingency Hospital System
DER   Department of Environmental Resources
ECNP   Environmental Coalition on Nuclear Power
EIS   Environmental Impact Statement
FDA   Food and Drug Administration
FEMA   Federal Emergency Management Agency
GPU   General Public Utilities Corporation
MET-ED   Metropolitan Edison
NAS   National Academy of Sciences
NEI   Nuclear Energy Institute
NEJM   New England Journal of Medicine
NEPA   National Environmental Policy Act
NRC   Nuclear Regulatory Commission
NTS   Nevada Test Site
NW   Nuclear Winter
PANE   People Against Nuclear Energy
PCC   Pennsylvania Catholic Conference
PEMA   Pennsylvania Emergency Management Agency

PIRC	TMI Public Interest Resource Center
PSR	Physicians for Social Responsibility
PTSD	Post-Traumatic Stress Disorder
SALT	Strategic Arms Limitation Treaty
SANE	Committee for a Sane Nuclear Policy
SVA	Susquehanna Valley Alliance
TMI	Three Mile Island
UCS	Union of Concerned Scientists
USDA	US Department of Agriculture
WAND	Women's Action for Nuclear Disarmament
YAF	Young Americans for Freedom

PREFACE

Ten years ago I stumbled upon the photograph that graces the cover of this book. Taken in the spring of 1979, it depicts a woman shadowing a toddler, leaning forward and clutching her hand to prevent a fall. This is a familiar moment, one that I have enacted myself many times. But in this case, the cooling towers of Three Mile Island rise up behind the mother and child, introducing a destabilizing element into an otherwise reassuring scene. As a historian of the 1970s who had written about the place of the family in debates about national crises such as the Vietnam War and the OPEC oil embargo, I wondered as I looked at the photograph whether women, gender, and the family might have also played an underappreciated role in the 1979 accident. How did mothers and children, husbands and wives, homemakers and feminists figure into the story of a nuclear crisis? And what might the accident reveal about US political culture at a time of transition, when the intense polarization of our own time first took hold?

This book is the product of my engagement with these questions. It is a cultural history that uses the accident as a lens for examining the shifting political landscape of the late 1970s. Three Mile Island was and remains the site of the worst atomic power plant accident in US history. The near-meltdown confirmed the fears of longtime nuclear skeptics and catalyzed an antinuclear left. From the United States to Australia, from West Germany to the Philippines, the ominous cooling towers became a symbol of atomic

danger, as activists demanded "no more Harrisburgs." However, the immediate actors in the drama were the largely conservative, white, Christian
residents who lived in the shadow of the reactor, especially women who
feared for the health of their babies and unborn children. At Three Mile
Island, the struggle over nuclear energy converged with contemporaneous
struggles over feminism and abortion rights. The crisis thus brought into
relief dimensions of the conservative movement that might otherwise have
remained hidden from view.

Thanks to the cumulative labors of historians, the view of the 1970s as a
sleepy interregnum between the New Left upheavals of the 1960s and the
conservative ascendancy of the 1980s can be laid to rest. In the 1970s we see
the origins of our own time: accelerating deindustrialization and the rise of
global finance capitalism, falling wages and the proliferation of service
work, the shattering of gender hierarchies and the end of the family wage
economy, the resurgence of feminism and the transformation of the public
sphere, the displacement of egalitarianism by meritocracy and the birth of
a neoliberal regime that has (not by coincidence) unleashed economic inequality while feeding off the charismatic currents of feminism, antiracism,
and gay liberation. We also see the roots of the polarization that shapes our
contemporary political landscape, as those who embraced the social and
cultural revolutions of the era squared off against those who opposed them.
It is arguably for this reason that historians often use martial language—
divisions, battlegrounds, wars, blowbacks, standoffs—to portray the decade's
contentious and volatile politics.

But this language, however useful as a heuristic device, presumes that
what fueled the rise of the right above all was reaction and opposition to
the left. The hundreds of letters, depositions, and testimonies written by
Three Mile Island residents after the accident tell a different story. As they
sought to make sense of a nuclear emergency, the men and women who
lived near the plant drew on the protest cultures of the 1960s for inspiration. From the New Left and the antiwar movement, they absorbed a picture
of the US government's duplicity, its secrecy, and its need to maintain its
power without public accountability or deliberation. From ecology, they
borrowed insights about toxicity and contamination. And from the women's
and black liberation movements, they drew on a sense of bodily infringe-
ment and vulnerability that emerged out of a longstanding neglect of health
and community well-being. If by the late 1970s US politics had come to

resemble a warzone, it was one in which concepts, symbols, and insights circulated more widely and moved more freely across the battlefield than most scholars have thus far acknowledged.

This circulation created something new in US politics, what in this book I call *biotic nationalism*. This concept builds on an argument I made in *No Direction Home*, namely, that the 1970s witnessed the rise of an aggrieved nationalism on the right fueled by a sense of injury and violation. This aggrieved nationalism was not without historical precedent, of course. But in the wake of the successive political, military, and economic ruptures of the early 1970s, it functioned like a funhouse mirror, transmuting America's unparalleled geopolitical power into a distorted vision of vulnerability and weakness. In *Radiation Nation*, I expand on this earlier argument by using the term *biotic* to foreground both the role of the body within post-Vietnam nationalism and the influence of ecological thought throughout narratives of national decline and revival in the 1970s. At its core, biotic nationalism is about betrayal: it proceeds from the charge that the nation has callously turned its back on the bodies of its own citizens, leaving the United States itself weakened and sickened. This creates a distinctly embittered strain of US nationalism that can explode to the surface at moments of crisis. "While America keeps a splendid and welcoming house," writes Anatol Lieven, "it also keeps a family of demons in its cellar."[1] One of those demons is nationalism.

The sense of betrayal contained within biotic nationalism originated in the Cold War security state. Throughout the late 1940s and 1950s, the US government willingly (and often knowingly) sacrificed the health, well-being, and life chances of its own citizens in the name of national security. From southeastern Nevada to Hanford, Washington, to Rocky Flats, Colorado, men, women, and children living within patriotic, military communities became sick and died from exposure to radioactive isotopes. The nation's subaltern and dispossessed—descendants of the enslaved, members of the black and brown commons, queers, immigrants, the poor, the homeless, the incarcerated, political radicals and revolutionaries—already knew that theirs were bodies that did not matter to those in power. Nor was this a revelation to the native peoples of the Southwest who bore the burden of uranium mining, milling, and waste. But by the 1970s patriotic white Americans who lived among testing sites and munitions factories were also becoming convinced that their lives had been rendered disposable by the state. Borrowing from the antiwar movement's insights about the Vietnam War, the ecology movement's recognition of the interconnection between biological and environmental health, and the black and women's health movements' insistence that bodily integrity was a stake of social struggle, these patriotic Americans crafted an oppositional politics of their own, one that played a critical and largely overlooked role in the consolidation of late-twentieth-century conservatism.

This politics challenged the logic of the Cold War and in particular a culture of dissociation that sought to isolate a fraught global landscape of nuclear danger from the domesticated and commoditized mores of civilian life. The first chapter traces the creation and breakup of this culture between 1945 and 1979. The second and third chapters turn their attention to Three Mile Island, looking first at the accident and then at the community's ultimately unsuccessful effort to shut down the reactor. These chapters serve as a case study of the interplay between the protest culture, feminism, and conservatism. The final chapter traces the evolution of nuclear fears during the Second Cold War of the 1980s, as the atomic age gave way to the ecological age, an epoch in which all politics is increasingly filtered through the lens of human-made disasters. But even as the atomic age mutated into the ecological one, there remained continuities, not only between the prominence of fear and a collective sense of looming disaster, but also in a vision of the United States as a wounded and vulnerable body.

During the years that I was researching and writing this book, I could not have anticipated the election of Donald Trump, who can be seen among many things as an avatar of biotic nationalism. Trump's victory, propelled by his promise to "Make America Great Again," speaks to the power of the embittered and redemptive strain of US nationalism that I explore here. By promising to build a wall between the United States and Mexico, Trump conjured the *spatial* dimensions of an exclusionary ethnonationalism, but by using the adverb *again* he also made a *temporal* claim; the nation itself—like a human body—is a living organism that can decline or rejuvenate over time. This likening of the nation to a living body has deep religious, philosophical, and historical roots, but after the Vietnam War, it was reborn again and helped to animate an angry, volatile American nationalist current that has always existed alongside civic nationalist aspirations. In the 1970s, this current contested the universalist ideals of the New Left and the early women's movement, and it provides a crucial clue for understanding the triumph of the right.

While *Radiation Nation* focuses on the same period as my prior book, it has taken me down new scholarly avenues. In order to tell the story of Three Mile Island, I have learned much about energy, ecology, technology, and public health. However, like *No Direction Home*, this is a work of cultural history that uncovers gender and the family in surprising places. Ultimately, both books represent my own attempt—however partial and incomplete— to make sense of the paradox that has preoccupied me throughout much of my life, namely, how the New Left revolutions of the 1960s and 1970s transformed US culture and society but failed to halt the nation's rightward political march. The Susquehanna River Valley of central Pennsylvania may seem an unlikely place to puzzle through this paradox, but in the pages that follow I try to make the case that some of the answers might be found there.

RADIATION NATION

At 4:00 AM on Wednesday, March 28, 1979, the most serious accident in the history of US nuclear energy occurred at Unit Two of the Three Mile Island (TMI) nuclear facility.[1] A valve was mistakenly left open, permitting large amounts of water—normally used to cool the plant's core—to escape. As the containment building lost coolant, temperatures and radiation levels rose. The plant began leaking radiation into the surrounding air and water, and a hydrogen bubble formed at the top of the core's container, making it difficult for workers to bring down its temperature and stoking fears of an explosion. Two nights later, CBS news anchor Walter Cronkite warned the nation that it faced "the considerable uncertainties and dangers of the worst nuclear power plant accident of the atomic age. And the horror tonight is that it could get much worse." In fact, the accident did not get worse. No explosion occurred, and plant operators were eventually able to bring down temperatures inside the core. Still, the Three Mile Island accident exposed unresolved safety questions that contributed to an informal three-decade moratorium on the licensing of new plants, making it a watershed in the history of nuclear power.[2]

The accident was more than a technological crisis. It signaled the birth of the ecological age—an era in which political questions are refracted through the fear of environmental disasters caused not by nature but rather by human action. There had been earlier intimations of ecological crisis, including Rachel Carson's warning about DDT and other chemical pesticides in the 1960s, the Santa Barbara oil spill of 1969, and the Love Canal disaster of the 1970s. But Three Mile Island was different in three respects. First, it was a *nuclear* event that evoked the bombings of Hiroshima and Nagasaki in 1945, establishing a historical continuity between an earlier atomic age marked by the fear of nuclear destruction and an emergent ecological age pervaded by the fear of environmental catastrophe. Second, occurring in the late 1970s, when New Deal liberalism had unraveled, the Vietnam War had raised the specter of national decline, and the new right was gaining ground, the accident facilitated the rise of a distinct gender politics that combined women's heightened agency with ecological anxieties about motherhood, reproduction, and species continuity. Finally, the accident revealed that this gender-inflected ecological consciousness could mediate between left and right and, as we shall see, would ultimately infuse the conservative imagination. More than a crisis juncture in the history of nuclear power, the accident in rural Pennsylvania illuminated profound transformations within late-twentieth-century US political culture.

FROM THE ATOMIC AGE TO THE ECOLOGICAL AGE

The ecological age that coalesced in the 1970s had its origins in the nuclear age, which began with the detonation of atomic weapons in 1945. The bombings of Hiroshima and Nagasaki were far more than episodes in World War II's military and geopolitical history. They were also *environmental* ruptures that initiated a new chapter in what geoscientists call the Anthropocene, the moment when human activity began to be traceable in the geological record. While geoscientists continue to debate the question of when the Anthropocene began, the end of World War II was the moment when earth scientists and oceanographers, and then the broader public, realized that radioactive fallout from bomb detonations could—quite literally—change the meteorological, biochemical, even intramolecular constitution of the world.[3] For the first time, the human species was confronted with the prospect of self-induced extinction: not just megadeath, but also the rendering of the planet uninhabitable through alterations in the composition of the atmosphere, the gene pool, and the quantum field of life. Today, almost hourly, a new scientific report suggests that what we once called "human civilization" turns out to have been an enormous, un-regulated, reckless, and potentially catastrophic planetary experiment.[4] But a generation before anthropogenic climate change became the subject of public debate, the atomic bomb introduced the threat of species extinction through the slow, accretive contamination of the air, the land, and the oceans, as well as through the chemical and genetic restructuring of life.

The politics of the atomic age revolved around the revelation that extinction could unfold insidiously. After 1945, the debate about radioactive fallout from atomic weapons testing introduced the specter of an invisible, silent toxin seeping into the air and the food chain, harming human and animal health, and tainting the reproductive gene pool.[5] The stealthy threat of radiation contamination, which can lie dormant within the body for years and even decades before manifesting itself, proved even more devastating than the detonations themselves. This debate receded into the background in the 1960s, but radiation served as the prototype for subsequent warnings about chemical toxicity. Rachel Carson's 1962 classic *Silent Spring* focused on the pesticide DDT, but Carson opened her book with a description of the radioactive isotope Strontium-90's potentially lethal journey from fallout to soil to grass to bones, observing that "chemicals are the sinister and little-recognized partners of radiation in changing the very nature of the world."[6]

By the time of the accident in 1979, radiation still remained shrouded in ambiguity. Utility company employees and government officials at Three Mile Island struggled to both quantify and contain a radiological threat that they could not see, smell, hear, or touch. These challenges were compounded by the fact that no one could see inside the reactor core to assess the damage. Nor could anyone see inside the bodies of residents, who feared that they might be harboring the accident's damage. The crisis thus propelled residents into a state of uncertainty about how much radiological exposure they had sustained and whether they or their family members might get sick at some indeterminate point in the future. Despite official reassurances that the accident had done no harm, these residents feared that radiation from the plant had left behind a "weirded world."[7] Both its invisibility and dormancy made the radiation threat at Three Mile Island an example of "slow violence"—forms of violence that play out across long time horizons, making them difficult to quantify or represent.[8] Such violence leaves behind a sense of strangeness, anticipatory anxiety, and dread about the future that can sometimes shade into paranoia. Seven years after the accident, novelist Don DeLillo immortalized this paranoia in *White Noise*, his fictionalized account of a community transfixed by what De-Lillo called "an airborne toxic event."[9]

The ecological anxiety that emerged at Three Mile Island centered on threats to reproductive futurity and generational continuity, encompassing procreation, birth, maternity, and infancy.[10] This preoccupation also went back to 1945. After the bombings of Hiroshima and Nagasaki, biologists, geneticists, and radiologists determined that radiation was especially dangerous to fetuses, babies, and young children. Exposure in utero posed cancer risks, while children's growing bones, organs, and tissues were more susceptible to the absorption of radioactive isotopes. Radiation exposure could also set in motion cellular mutations associated with birth defects, disease, and premature death. The ecological writings of the 1960s elaborated on the theme of reproduction-under-threat. What rendered the spring silent in *Silent Spring* was the disappearance of robins, starlings, and cardinals in habitats where DDT had been sprayed; the pesticide left a "shadow of sterility" in its wake. Paul Ehrlich's *The Population Bomb*, published in 1968, evoked an equally alarming dystopia: unimpeded human reproduction as the functional equivalent of a large-scale, slow-moving detonation. Arguably the two most influential books of US environmentalism after 1945 oscillated between visions of reproduction-run-aground and reproduction-run-amuck.[11]

Fears, rumors, and speculations of imperiled reproduction were also widespread at Three Mile Island. On the third day of the accident, Pennsylvania governor Richard Thornburgh urged all pregnant women and preschool-aged children living within five miles of the plant to evacuate the area. Expectant mothers called local radio stations, state agencies, and hospitals to find out if their fetuses were in danger. In the months that followed, anecdotal stories of plant and animal mutations and reports of stillbirths, miscarriages, and birth defects circulated through the community. Over and over again, residents expressed the fear that the accident had wrought havoc on the region's reproductive future. As they did so, they brought to the fore a figure that had remained shadowy in 1945 but had become considerably more legible by the late 1970s: the fetus uniquely vulnerable to environmental injury.[12] The unborn could not speak, but it was *the* figure that transmuted the atomic age into the ecological age, and Three Mile Island was where it happened.

The fear of contamination that erupted at Three Mile Island also reflected a wider crisis in political authority, one linked to the place of science and technology in society. Throughout the 1950s and 1960s, would-be nuclear experts had insisted that dangerous levels of radiation could emanate from weapons, but not from power plants. This insistence was part of a postwar culture of dissociation, which sharply demarcated bombs from power plants, splitting off the destructive elements of atomic weaponry from its civilian uses. Central to this culture was the claim that radiation was a part of—rather than a threat to—the natural world. Revising a turn-of-the-century fascination with radium as an elixir, promoters of nuclear power portrayed radiation as ordinary and benign. In their attempts to separate nuclear energy from its destructive wartime purpose, promoters also placed great faith in plant design. Redundant safety systems, they had maintained, made a serious accident impossible. The Three Mile Island crisis undermined these arguments and shattered the culture of dissociation, which had always been part of a larger dissociative logic that sought to suppress Cold War military violence and deny its inextricable relation to the domestic, civilian realm. This logic unraveled during the Vietnam War. That war not only exposed the considerable costs and failures of policies of containment and rollback; it also raised dire questions about the technocratic experts responsible for the disaster. At first, the near-meltdown redirected these questions toward the utility company that operated the plant. Part of what made the accident so shocking was that residents who lived near the reactor had been assured that it would never happen. Soon, however, for reasons we will explore, the initial mistrust of the utility would be transformed into mistrust of the state.

The dual threat of a meltdown and an explosion at TMI unleashed the fears that the industry and the government had tried to allay: power plants *could* behave like bombs. They could explode, they could poison people and animals, and they could contaminate the land. State and federal officials rushed into the Susquehanna River Valley, handed out Geiger counters and gas masks, conducted full-body scans of local residents, and stockpiled potassium iodide, which can block the thyroid's absorption of Iodine 131, a radioactive isotope. Americans watched the crisis on the evening news, and polling conducted at the time revealed that the public believed a plant explosion would replicate a bomb attack. The dissonance between earlier assurances about nuclear safety and the escalating crisis at the plant created a credibility gap that resonated with the Vietnam War and Watergate. But unlike these emergencies, the accident at Three Mile Island centered on a potential assault on the civilian population's biological health and unfolded within a new reproduction-centered ecological imaginary.[13]

POLITICAL REALIGNMENT AND THE SUFFERING BODY

This new ecological imaginary took shape against the backdrop of the dramatic political transformations that were underway in the United States by the late 1970s, often described reductively in terms of "the rise of the right." The problem with this description is not that it is untrue, but that it is incomplete. It neglects the considerable cross-pollination between left and right that took place during the 1970s and overlooks what both sides shared: waning public confidence in governmental institutions and rising skepticism vis-à-vis official truth-claims. The accident simultaneously deepened this loss of confidence and brought into relief its atomic age origins. The culture of dissociation, always precarious, supplied the field within which realignment germinated. At Three Mile Island, local citizens and outside observers accused Metropolitan Edison (Met-Ed), the utility company that owned the plant, of lying to the public about the accident's severity. Could they trust official reassurances that radiation releases posed no threat to public health? If plant conditions had deteriorated, were state and local officials prepared to evacuate the surrounding population? Could they trust the government at all?

Throughout the 1960s, the antiwar movement had charged the US government with obfuscation and deception. Now, however, the accident occurred in a region of Pennsylvania well known for its political and cultural conservatism: the predominantly rural Susquehanna River Valley, an area of pastoral landscapes and small towns dominated by agriculture, manufacturing, tourism, and government. Most residents were descendants of German and Scotch-Irish immigrants, and the majority were Christians. The Valley was a Republican Party stronghold where respect for God and country was well established. This is not to suggest that there was no dissent. There had been some opposition to the Vietnam War, especially among the region's college students, and by the early 1970s, the antinuclear movement had established a modest presence in the area. But prior to the accident, most men and women who lived near the plant considered themselves conservative patriots. They supported nuclear power, were grateful for the employment opportunities that the state and private industry provided, and—above all—had supported the war in Southeast Asia.

The accident shattered the community's confidence in Met-Ed, the Nuclear Regulatory Commission, the public officials who had been blindsided by the partial meltdown, and ultimately the federal government itself. Skeptical of the official story, many residents became convinced that the plant posed an ongoing public health threat and should be shut down. After the accident, they wrote letters to officials, provided testimony at public hearings, formed protest groups, filed class-action lawsuits against the utility, passed referendums calling for the decommissioning of the plant, and traveled to the nation's capital to participate in antinuclear protests. Far from being untouched by the upheavals of the 1960s, then, the region had been transformed by them. The movement against the Vietnam War had instilled an appreciation of the power of protest. Men and women who had never participated in antiwar activism nonetheless grasped the opening it had breached. Thus at a hearing in Harrisburg in 1982, conservative businessmen and housewives stood and cheered when an activist warned that if the reactor was restarted, residents would occupy company headquarters and block access to the plant. In a demonstration at the plant gates in 1983, the first lines of protestors were Republican Party Committee women. These actions drew on indigenous features of the region's conservatism, such as antagonism toward big government, populist skepticism vis-à-vis experts, and communitarian appeals to local control, but wove them into a new post-Vietnam interrogation of authority. Local residents extended this interrogation to the nuclear industry, which they now saw as representing an unholy alliance between the utility company, the Nuclear Regulatory Commission, and public officials who, in their view, had failed to protect citizens from harm.

The fear of derailed reproduction structured the community's response. Coursing through letters, testimonies, speeches, and lawsuits was the claim that the accident had cast doubt over the viability of the region's biological future. Residents contended that radiation from the plant had imperiled their reproductive health by leading to infertility, miscarriage, or stillbirth; by risking disability and sickness among their children; or by unleashing runaway mutations that would later appear in their offspring. Throughout the 1960s and 1970s, the ecological imaginary had remained within the provenance of the political left.[14] But after the accident, TMI residents drew on its visions of imperiled fetuses, degraded environments, and debased, contaminated bodies to construct themselves as a "community of fate," or a community under threat. In the process, they created a new hybrid politics, a *conservative ecological politics*, which established an affinity between somatic and environmental injury, fortified the image of the fetus as uniquely vulnerable, cast the struggle at TMI as one between local and federal authority, and tethered a biotic conception of a community-under-threat to the specter of sickened, irradiated bodies. As a result, a growing mistrust of authority combined with a new ecological awareness to produce a body politics on the right that provides a missing piece of the puzzle of how and why conservatives gained ground after 1980.

This politics indexed the heightened visibility of the suffering body over the twentieth century. The advent of ever-more-lethal forms of weaponry, fire bombings, and atomic weapons had generated photographic and other visual images of irradiated, contaminated, mutilated, and broken bodies. But within the United States, the Vietnam War marked a turning point in which the body became charged with meaning. In the 1960s, Americans watched as college students were shot down by the National Guard, soldiers came home in body bags, Buddhist monks immolated themselves, and the bodies of Vietnamese men, women, and children were seared with napalm. By the early 1970s, as the Vietnam War wound down, other social movements turned their attention to bodily pleasure, health, and injury. Feminists insisted that control over their own reproductive and sexual lives was essential to women's pursuit of freedom. *Our Bodies, Ourselves*, a primer published in 1971 that stressed women's control over their own bodies, became a best-selling classic. After 1969, gay men celebrated their bodies as sites of pride, sexual pleasure, and excitation. These transformations spilled well beyond the boundaries of the New Left. Throughout society, there was a heightened awareness of the body's capacities, pleasures, and vulnerabilities, as well as of the social agents that monitor, survey, and police bodies, including doctors and scientists.[15]

At Three Mile Island, this heightened awareness of bodily vulnerability took the form of what I call a post-Vietnam *patriotic body politics*.[16] This was a politics that linked physical illness (both actual and potential) to a collapse of trust in authority; it combined a fear of bodily injury with wounded patriotism and deepening suspicions of government duplicity. Like women's and black healthcare activism (and later AIDS activism), the body politics that emerged at Three Mile Island focused on a potential assault on health. But in contrast to feminist, black, and gay activism, which viewed medical discrimination as part of a wider capitalist, racist, patriarchal, and heterosexist power structure, TMI residents were self-described patriots whose encounters with illness created in them something new: a profound breach of trust in their relationship with the state. Rather than being fueled by party loyalty or partisanship, this politics was fueled by what historian Michael J. Allen has described as a "politics of loss" rooted in the conviction that the state had abandoned its most patriotic citizens.[17] Patriotic body politics located physical illness and the suffering body at the center of a politics that hinged on the belief that the government had turned against those who had been most loyal to it.

Patriotic body politics drew inspiration from the era's social movements. From pacifism it borrowed the insight that militarization permeated every aspect of life; from ecology it took the warning that human health could be threatened by environmental assaults; from the black and women's health movements it drew on the awareness that sickness could have political meaning; and from feminism it took the recognition that the body could be a site of contestation. But above all, it took from the antiwar movement the revelation that the government could deceive its own people, even in matters of life and death. Indeed, it was the Vietnam War that provided the crucial historical backdrop for patriotic body politics. The call to military service was the moment when men were asked to give up their lives—to sacrifice their bodies—on behalf of their nation.[18] The failures of the war, combined with divisiveness on the home front, raised the question of whether that sacrifice had been for nothing. This question haunted not just the families of dead and returning servicemen, but also the relatives of prisoners of war and MIAs, disabled veterans, and US soldiers exposed to Agent Orange. Narratives recounting the suffering of these men tethered physical illness to lost patriotism and disillusionment. Within these narratives, somatic suffering emerged as a symptom of national injury inflicted not by a foreign enemy, but by the US government.[19] As the country hovered between left and right in the late 1970s, an ambiguous body politics incorporated the legacy of the social movements of the 1960s *and* facilitated the nation's rightward shift.

Occurring six years after the signing of the Paris Peace Accords, which formally ended the war in Vietnam, the accident at Three Mile Island relocated threats of bodily injury and premature death away from the warfront to the domestic realm, and from the masculine, martial body to the reproductive female body, the young child's body, and the fetal body. This relocation positioned women—specifically in their capacities as mothers, nurturers, and custodians of health—at the center of the struggle over the fate of the reactor. At Three Mile Island, it was primarily mothers of young children who rejected the official claim that the accident had done no harm and who demanded the decommissioning of the plant. In the shadow of the nuclear reactor, patriotic body politics became women's reproductive politics. The accident thus crystallized the centrality of women to the conservative ecological imaginary. To be sure, this was not wholly new. The call for a ban on weapons testing in the 1950s, for example, had been spearheaded largely by white, middle-class women who mobilized hegemonic conceptions of motherhood and domesticity in order to critique Cold War militarism and deflect red-baiting. This movement had allowed women to carve out a public space for themselves before the resurgence of feminism while enabling them to surpass the limits of Cold War politics.[20] Women's activism at Three Mile Island resonated with this earlier mobilization, but it occurred against a radically different political backdrop: the feminist revolution of the 1970s.

The women's politics that emerged at Three Mile Island stood in complex relation to this revolution. On the one hand, the women who lived near the plant drew on the feminist insight that women's reproductive health was a political issue, and that state and medical experts could not be trusted. On the other hand, they appealed to an earlier maternalist tradition that valorized motherhood and familial obligation in ways that many (though not all) women's liberation activists were rejecting. While late-twentieth-century feminism was multidimensional, a primary goal was to free women from the claim that women's biological capacities should delineate their place in society; thus women's reproductive rights encompassed the right not to have children at all.[21] The politics of reproduction at Three Mile Island was very different, centering not on how to protect women from the reproduction imperative, but on how to protect reproduction from external threats. If the culture wars were waged over the fate of women's reproductive rights, these wars played out against a broader, more diffuse backdrop animated by ecological questions over the fate of reproduction writ large. At Three Mile Island, then, conservative women articulated a new politics that drew simultaneously on post-Vietnam critiques of expert authority, a feminist politicization of the body, and a biologically based rendering of community peril. At the center of this politics was the figure of the unborn, which first took shape within the atomic-cum-ecological imaginary and only later assumed prominence within the culture wars over feminism, gay liberation, and reproductive rights.

Radiation Nation thus makes two interrelated moves. It places reproduction at the center of the ecological imaginary, and it places the ecological imaginary at the center of post-1968 conservative politics. By doing so, it revises our understanding of the conservative counterrevolution in four ways. First, this book complicates an account of the conservative resurgence that interprets it exclusively as a backlash against the perceived excesses of the 1960s and 1970s—against the antiwar movement, which it condemned for its elitism and antipatriotism; against the liberal welfare state, which it saw as a benefactor of racialized largesse; and against the feminist and gay revolutions, which it construed as a threat to traditional familial and gender roles.[22] These accounts all proceed from the premise that the upheavals of the 1960s and 1970s gave rise to a divide between those who endorsed and those who rejected multiculturalism, feminism, and gay liberation. Thus we have the metaphor of the culture wars. Accordingly, historians characterize the 1970s *either* as a period of conservative reaction (for example, in the creation of right-leaning think tanks and political action groups) *or* as a time when the legacies of the left-inflected social movements of the 1960s endured, even as national politics moved rightward (for example, within local community organizing and institution building).[23] But such characterizations are partial and incomplete. What happened at Three Mile Island makes clear that the strength of post-1968 conservatism hinged less on an overt rejection of the antiwar, ecology, and feminist movements and more on its capacity to appropriate and retool their insights that a deceptive, callous government could turn its back on its most loyal citizens and that women's bodies could be sites of political struggle. Yet as these insights were integrated into post-1968 conservatism, their meanings shifted, often in ways that stripped them of their earlier ethical content. If the culture wars are associated with polarization, the ecological age is animated instead by a culture of suspicion that blurs the line between left and right and places the imperiled body at the center of eroding trust.

Second, by contending that the imperiled body played a constitutive role in the rise of the right, this book attends not to policy-making, but rather to the structures of feeling and affect that animated post-1968 conservative politics. To be clear: one argument that I am *not* making is that the attention to suffering bodies that found expression in patriotic body politics translated into tangible policies and practices that protected bodily health and safety. On the contrary, in recent years, the political right has often advanced highly *disembodied* arguments that champion abstract principles such as the "free market" and "personal liberty" over the protection of biological health. Examples include the staunch advocacy of gun ownership rights, opposition to a perceived "nanny state" that seeks to use public policy as an instrument for promoting wellness, and the shredding of federal regulations that place public health and environmental protection above corporate profit. What mattered historically about patriotic body politics, in other words, was not that its preoccupation with suffering bodies somehow became concretized or codified within conservative policy-making. Rather, it mattered because, at a crucial moment of transition in the nation's political life, it provided a potent field of imagery and emotion that shaped the affective regime of post-Vietnam conservatism. This regime was structured above all by a profound sense of betrayal.[24]

Third, the conservative ecological politics that came to the fore after the accident was not based on an electoral or demographic realignment, of the sort classically described in works like Lisa McGirr's *Suburban Warriors*, Kevin Kruse's *White Flight*, and Elizabeth Tandy Shermer's *Sunbelt Capitalism*.[25] This story is *not* one of voters shifting their party allegiances or one of a redrawing of the political map in central Pennsylvania. On the contrary, the region had been a Republican Party stronghold in the state before 1979 and remained one afterward. This is instead a story of a transition *within* conservatism, as local actors at Three Mile Island incorporated elements of the protest culture into their ideological and strategic arsenal, a move that at once deepened the region's long-standing suspicion of big government and populist skepticism toward expertise and extended them into intimate spheres of bodily illness, sickness, and death. If the body politics that emerged at Three Mile Island reflected the reach of social movements like feminism, it also captured the extent to which, by the late 1970s, the core insights of these movements—contrary to being blockaded by post-Vietnam conservatism—had been folded into the conservative imaginary. Rather than being displaced, the region's conservatism underwent a change or—to borrow from radiation's own lexicon—a *mutation*, one that made it stronger rather than weaker.

Finally and in its broadest implications, this book complicates the view of the United States as a quintessentially liberal nation founded on the principle of individual rights that has become more inclusive over time.[26] According to this civic nationalist account, the story of the nation is one of gradual inclusion of historically excluded groups into the liberal fold and the continuing extension of political and civil rights: first to immigrants, then to African Americans, and then, in the 1970s, to women and gay people. But this version of history neglects an alternative vision that runs alongside the liberal one and often undercuts its promise: an ethnonationalism that mobilizes images of community endangerment, demarcates sharp lines between insiders and outsiders, and creates a climate of paranoia, fear, and distrust. This US ethnonationalism began in the colonial era, spanned the history of western settlement, gave shape to ideologies of racial and ethnic hierarchy, underwrote nativism and xenophobia, reached a fever pitch during the Cold War, and resurfaced amid the political, economic, and military ruptures of the 1970s.[27]

My thesis is that in the late 1970s, this second nationalism became shot through with ecologically derived images of the vulnerable bodies of mothers, babies, and fetuses, creating a *biotic nationalism*. *Radiation Nation* draws on the story of Three Mile Island to illuminate this process. I use the term *biotic*, which refers to living and organic systems, in order to stress the new, enhanced role of the body within an aggrieved nationalism that took hold on the political right in the wake of military defeat in Vietnam. As we shall see, biotic nationalism did two crucial things at once: it compelled many Americans to imagine the nation as a weakened body, feeding into a narrative of national decline, and it cited the suffering body as evidence of betrayal, propelling the rightward turn. The near-meltdown at Three Mile Island thus revealed both the endurance of ethnonationalism and its ecological adaptation within late-twentieth-century American politics.

Chapter One

THE CULTURE OF DISSOCIATION AND THE RISE
OF THE UNBORN

The political realignment of the 1970s had its roots in the early Cold War. The dropping of the atomic bomb in 1945 unleashed what peace advocate Norman Cousins described as "a primitive fear, the fear of the unknown [which] has burst out of the subconscious and into the conscious, filling the mind with primordial apprehensions."[1] In the United States, this fear intensified with the acceleration of nuclear testing that accompanied the Cold War arms race. That race transformed the nation's infrastructure, as the government built plutonium factories, uranium mines, enrichment facilities, and testing sites across nearly all fifty states. Physicist Niels Bohr predicted to scientist Edward Teller that building the atomic bomb would require remaking the United States into one huge factory.[2] Between 1946 and 1963, this factory kept busy: the government conducted nearly six hundred atomic tests (many above ground), produced more than seventy thousand nuclear warheads (more than all the other nuclear states combined), and set in motion a series of slow-motion disasters in the form of cancer epidemics at testing sites and munitions factories.[3] Meanwhile, the possibility of the deployment of atomic weapons never went away. Between 1952 and 1969, the US military considered such deployments in Korea, French-Indochina, Cuba, and Vietnam.

The atomic presence was at once ubiquitous and hidden from view, a slight of hand achieved through the creation of a culture of dissociation, a

Cold War cultural logic according to which US civilians could supposedly be shielded from danger while its military wielded a nuclear arsenal comprising bombs, missiles, submarines, and doomsday devices. This culture aimed to defuse or tamp down what political and policy elites saw as the greatest danger posed by the atomic age. This was not atomic weaponry itself, but rather the unleashing of irrational, extreme emotions that could take a variety of forms: populist mass movements such as Nazism, Communism, and McCarthyism on the one hand, or the widespread panic and hysteria that civil defense planners imagined might ensue in the event of a nuclear attack on the other.[4]

Drawing on this culture, postwar promoters of atomic power insisted that the dangers of nuclear bombs did not extend to power plants. At the same time, atomic power's role as a source of cheap household electricity aligned it with the normative ideal of the white, middle-class domestic sphere of the 1950s. The "peaceful atom"—to borrow from President Eisenhower's famous "Atoms for Peace" speech—would power the myriad household appliances flooding the US consumer market: refrigerators, air conditioners, televisions, washers, dryers, and vacuum cleaners. If the bomb symbolized the instability of the atomic age, then power plants would be associated with the opposite: a tranquil domestic space that provided white, middle-class consumer-citizens with safety, health, cleanliness, and abundance. Within the atomic imaginary, an ostensibly apolitical, consumption-oriented, feminized domestic realm provided cover for a technocratically managed war machine.

This culture of dissociation was always fragile. Haunting it was the specter of radiation. When Marie Curie first discovered radium in 1898, chemists and biologists heralded it as an elixir with vitalizing properties. But the bombings of Hiroshima and Nagasaki in 1945 remade radiation (released when radium decays) into a symbol of death, and in the United States, the subsequent acceleration of nuclear testing incited fear that radiation could seep into the atmosphere and harm human health. Throughout the 1950s, radiation scares became a routine, if also unnerving, feature of everyday life. The testing of atomic weapons sickened and killed livestock, spread radioactive ash and rain, and deposited Strontium-90 in wheat and milk. In 1959, President Eisenhower created a federal radiation council, and biologists singled out young children, infants, and "the unborn" (a term that referred to both developing fetuses and those not yet conceived) as vulnerable to radiological dangers.

The culture of dissociation fell apart in the late 1960s. The protest movements of the era challenged a Manichean Cold War logic that relied on isolating the foreign and domestic realms—that is, maintaining militarization abroad and peaceful consensus at home. Meanwhile, as the licensing of power plants sped up, radiation fears once centered on weapons testing were redirected toward nuclear power plants. In the 1970s, two social movements reflected the shift: an antinuclear movement that insisted that nuclear weapons and plants were part of one interconnected system, and a community of radiation sufferers from every stage of the nuclear fuel cycle. Three Mile Island alone did not undo the culture of dissociation. But the accident shattered the dissociative logic by challenging the distinction between plants and bombs, undermining the official claim that American citizens would be protected from radiological harm, and propelling the symbol of the irradiated body to the center of a crisis in authority. Before turning our attention to the accident itself, we need to look first at the history of the culture of dissociation between 1945 and 1979—how it was assembled, how it came apart, and how it was haunted by the figure of the unborn.

STRIPPING THE MILITARY CASING: CREATING THE CULTURE OF DISSOCIATION

Both the drive to integrate atomic energy into a peaceful, consumerist economy and the difficulties inherent in that process became evident soon after World War II. In August 1946, Congress transferred atomic weapons and energy research from military to civilian control when it created the Atomic Energy Commission (AEC). From now on, this federal agency would oversee the diffuse web of government laboratories, university-housed programs, and production plants established as part of the Manhattan Project. At the time of the AEC's creation, this web included thirty-seven installations located in nineteen states and Canada, and it employed thirty-eight thousand contract workers, almost four thousand government workers, and two thousand military personnel.[5] The aim of the AEC would be to continue the wartime work of research into atomic weaponry, while turning attention to the civilian applications of atomic power. While the new agency ostensibly brought atomic energy under civilian jurisdiction, the military retained a firm practical and psychological hold over the new technology. The 1946 legislation created a powerful military liaison committee, and both civilian elites and military officers in the commission remained fixated on the issue of national security. Because military and civilian atomic power would now be housed under the same administrative umbrella, the latter could never fully shed the aura of secrecy associated with the earlier Manhattan Project.

While the internal structure of the AEC reflected the inseparability of the military and nonmilitary applications of atomic power, the agency worked tirelessly to make the case that civilian atomic energy had nothing to do with war. As President Eisenhower explained in 1953, atomic power needed to be "put into the hands of those who will know how to strip its military casing and adapt it to the arts of peace."[6] Doing so required that a hypermilitarized, on-edge society behaved as if it were at peace. In modern psychology, the term *dissociation* is used to describe the ways victims of trauma protect themselves from pain by splitting off the trauma from their other experiences. The trauma becomes something abstracted: it exists "out there" and cannot be coherently integrated into the victim's own life story. A similar process attended the promotion of the "peaceful atom" throughout the late 1940s and 1950s. The trauma in question was the dropping of the atomic bomb. But here, it was the perpetrators rather than the victims who sought refuge in dissociation. The peaceful atom had to be shorn of its painful associations with wartime violence, and the atom's civilian applications had to be split off from the extraordinary destruction wrought at Hiroshima and Nagasaki. Many years later, nuclear power critics like Helen Caldicott would accuse industry promoters of self-servingly celebrating the promises of the peaceful atom in order to assuage their own sense of guilt over the bombings.[7] But AEC members were in fact candid about the reparative function of civilian atomic power. As the first AEC chairman David Lilienthal explained, commission members wanted to "prove that the atom has a peaceful nonmilitary promise of high importance, that somehow a weapon so destructive [had] humane applications."[8] In the simplest terms, something bad had to be remade into something good. This required both a celebration of the atom's generative potential and an amnesic suppression of its dangers, which periodically threatened to resurface throughout the Cold War, as the US military considered the deployment of nuclear weapons in the Korean War (1952), the Battle of Dien Bien Phu (1954), the Berlin Blockade (1961), the Cuban Missile Crisis (1962), and Vietnam (1969).[9]

This dissociation did not begin with the dropping of the atomic bomb. During the Spanish-American War in the Philippines, William James insisted that the scale and anonymity of the modern corporate-state made it difficult to penetrate what he called the "invisible molecular moral forces that work from individual to individual."[10] This difficulty deepened during World War II, which was a "highly rationalized, bureaucratized, compartmentalized undertaking" that relied on high levels of abstraction.[11] This abstraction was necessary because most military men never met their enemies face to face, and carpet and saturation bombing meant that pilots dropped incendiaries on civilians from high above ground.[12] The construction of the atomic bomb also relied on mechanisms of denial, abstraction, and distancing. Those who worked on the bomb did so "thousands of miles" away from the deaths that they eventually enabled, and with the exception of atomic scientists, few of the tens of thousands of employees who worked on the bomb even grasped that they were building a nuclear weapon.[13] The dropping of the bomb was the culmination of a process that had brought civilians into the orbit of military risk on a wholly unprecedented scale.

The culture of dissociation also shaped the Atoms for Peace program. Initially, the program advanced a technological utopianism that encompassed visions of planetary engineering (the use of atomic technology to alter the global terrain) and predictions of the peaceful atom's miraculous, soon-to-be-tapped potential. Industry promoters predicted that civilian atomic energy would one day ameliorate a range of social and economic ills, from bodily sickness to world hunger to natural disaster. General Leslie Groves, who had overseen the Manhattan Project, imagined that atomic energy would eventually raise "the curtain on vistas of a new world."[14] If the wartime atom constituted an unprecedented threat to humanity, the peaceful atom was the opposite: a magical, almost talismanic gift. Promoters speculated that barren deserts could be transformed into nuclear-powered food factories, that radiation could breed new crop strains, that nuclear power could be harnessed for the propulsion of ships, barges, and submarines, that radioactive isotopes could cure cancer, that nuclear explosions could alter the course of ocean currents and dissipate the destructive effects of hurricanes and tornadoes, and, finally, that nuclear energy could provide clean, cheap electricity to people from the Arctic to the Sahara.[15] An article in the *Saturday Evening Post* described the heady range of possibilities: "In spite of its lethal potentialities, atomic energy has become for small nations and large, the new symbol of the more abundant life, the radioactive key to industrial independence. It has been seized upon as the all-purpose tool, suited to any task—from moving mountains to curing cancer. It can power factories, light homes, drive ships, find leaks in pipelines and trace underground water sources."[16]

These utopian ambitions for atomic energy evoked an earlier fascination with radium's magical and vitalizing properties. While many elements are relatively inert, radium displayed a special capacity for transmutation. After its initial discovery in 1898, physicists, biologists, and botanists saw radium as an elixir that held the "secret of life." "Atomic literally meant that which could not be subdivided," writes historian of science Luis Campos. But radium was different. It was "a substance that had all the hallmarks of an element, that fit an empty spot on the periodic table, and yet came apart, spontaneously."[17] Radium's unique capacities to ferment, spark, glow, and generate heat established a powerful metaphorical and experimental link between the living and the inert, the animate and the inanimate, and the biological and the physical. Indeed, radium was the "rock star" of the periodic table. In 1903, crowds flocked to New York City's Museum of Natural History to see 125 milligrams of radium on display behind a protective glass casing, part of the turn-of-the-century radium craze. Yet scientists soon discovered the dangers of both radiation exposure and radium ingestion. Physicians observed that extended X-ray exposure could burn their patients, and in the 1920s, young women factory workers who painted radium dials on watches and clocks fell fatally ill. The 1930s witnessed two high-profile deaths from radium poisoning. In 1932, a wealthy socialite died after ingesting large quantities of a popular radium tonic called Radithor. And in July 1934, radium discoverer Marie Curie succumbed to aplastic anemia, caused by years of working with radioactive material without adequate safety precautions.[18] Even before World War II, radium's earliest association with vitality and life was corroded by its association with danger and death. But the bombings in 1945, followed by the acceleration of weapons testing in the late 1940s, facilitated the transformation of both radium and radiation into objects of fear.

And yet radiation's association with magic never completely disappeared. It was instead granted an afterlife within postwar predictions of civilian atomic energy's potential, one that could be realized only through American stewardship. The capacity of the United States to bequeath the gift of atomic power to other states enhanced the nation's unprecedented military, economic, and political hegemony after World War II, while appearing to affirm that the United States alone possessed the maturity—a trait that likened the nation to a living being—required to oversee such a powerful technology. The AEC included a foreign aid program, the commission showcased atomic energy at international trade fairs and exhibits, and, by the end of 1957, US firms had sold twenty-three small research reactors abroad.[19] In contrast to atomic weapons, atomic research was promoted as something that could rise above the Iron Curtain and rally international cooperation. When Eisenhower gave his speech in 1954, he called on the world's nations to share atomic information (the International Atomic Energy Agency was created three years later), implying that the peaceful atom might somehow transcend US-Soviet hostilities. In reality, of course, civilian atomic energy was closely bound up with Cold War competition. Turning their gaze to the global South, science writers predicted that atomic energy would turn deserts and jungles into "new lands flowing with milk and honey," and that Africa would be transformed "into another Europe."[20] William Knox, the president of Westinghouse Electric (the company that opened the first nuclear power plant in the United States), believed that atomic energy was destined to become the safest and cheapest source of power in the developing world: "it is in these vast expanses of desert and jungle where atomic energy will . . . play its most important economic and social role. In these areas of our shrinking world, demands will not wait for gradual evolutionary developments. We must help them leapfrog many stages of progress and endeavor to telescope into the next twenty to thirty years much of what it has taken a century or more to realize in the United States or Europe."[21] These narratives about the gift implied that the magical capacities of atomic power, when paired with American stewardship, could enable developing nations to defy sluggish, evolutionary time by leapfrogging into late modernity. Simultaneously, such accounts elided the labor-intensive role played by the global South (and Africa in particular) in the making of the atomic age as a crucial extractive source of uranium, the heavy metal that enabled the industry to flourish. Throughout the Cold War, between one-fifth and one-half of the Western world's uranium came from Congo, Niger, South Africa, Gabon, Madagascar, and Namibia, making it (along with oil) what historian Penny von Eschen has dubbed a "quintessential cold war commodity."[22]

Yet even as promoters aligned atomic power with magic, they fretted over whether this association might inhibit public acceptance of the new technology. A report commissioned by the World Health Organization in 1958 (in which the AEC participated) made clear that the atomic age posed new kinds of threats to both biological and psychological health. The "shattering possibilities" contained within atomic power, the report warned, could trigger "strong psychological reactions" and provoke "irrational phantasies." Such fantasies, the report continued, "may well be related to those of early childhood—of magical power, the casting of spells, the working of miracles, and so on—dreams by which children compensate for their felt smallness and weakness. Being of very early origin in the emotional life, these childhood phantasies are normally hidden in the unconscious mind, but are likely to arouse strong emotional reactions, the origin of which remains largely unknown to the conscious mind, whenever they are triggered off by actual experiences of a psychologically similar nature."[23] Indexing the considerable cultural and political authority of psychiatry at mid-century, the report mobilized the psychoanalytic concept of the unconscious in the service of crafting what would turn out to be an enduring claim about atomic age citizenship: the extraordinary capacities of nuclear power could trigger regressions and pathologies that threatened to infantilize all citizens. This perceived threat would place the psychological management of the citizenry at the center of Cold War–era governance, a mode of management that would reappear at Three Mile Island.

By 1960, the most utopian ambitions for atomic energy had receded and engineers were turning their attention to the construction of civilian nuclear reactors.[24] Two pieces of congressional legislation in the mid-1950s facilitated this change. In 1954, Congress passed the Energy Act, which granted private utility companies greater access to atomic energy research. Three years later, in 1957, it passed the Price-Anderson Act, which both limited industry liability to $560 million in the event of a single nuclear accident and committed the federal government to footing almost 90 percent of the bill. That act emerged out of growing concern within the nascent nuclear industry about legal liability in the event of a worst-case accident. The first AEC-sponsored risk assessment revealed that such an accident could kill three thousand people and injure forty thousand more, while also inflicting seven billion dollars in property damage.[25] Recognizing that private utility companies would never assume such a high liability, the federal government pushed for legislation that would effectively shield the nuclear industry from the fluctuations of the insurance market. Breaking with free market principles, the Price Anderson Act represented, in sociologist Christian Joppke's words, the "partial abolition of market controls" and a "pampering of risk taking"[26]—moves that would set the nuclear industry on an anomalous path. The first American nuclear power plant went online at Shippingport, Pennsylvania in 1957, and soon there were plants in the Midwest (Illinois, Michigan, and Nebraska) and along the eastern seaboard (New York and Massachusetts). The 1960s witnessed a boom in plant construction, with companies like General Electric expanding their nuclear divisions and new plant orders peaking in 1967.[27]

As the licensing of new plants took off in the 1960s, the earlier logic of dissociation crystallized around one claim: that nuclear power plants could not behave like bombs. In 1959, one atomic scientist likened nuclear power stations to obedient children, observing favorably that, at least so far, they had been "docile and well-behaved."[28] The descriptors *docile* and *well-behaved* implied that power plants were not simply unlike bombs, but were the *opposite* of bombs—predictable rather than volatile, stable rather than erratic. The emphasis on atomic docility was not new. From its beginning the AEC had aimed to domesticate the atom, that is, to convince the public that atomic energy, while endowed with near-preternatural capacities, was nonthreatening and even familiar, something whose powers could be harnessed and controlled.[29] An AEC coloring book marketed to young children provided a paradigmatic example. It featured an animated character named Reddy Kilowatt who was portrayed as at once magical and chummy: "I'm a Busy Little Atom / I Split Myself in Two / I Multiply As Many Times / As I Have Jobs to Do / In Summer, Winter, Spring or Fall /I'm Ready Every Hour / Just Flip a Switch and Watch Me Zip /With Heat or Light or Power!"[30] A personified figure like Reddy Kilowatt was meant to fill the void left by the atom's invisibility, a characteristic that the AEC was convinced compounded public fears of atomic technology. The cartoon also represented an attempt to demystify atomic science, which the AEC believed was necessary in order to build public trust. A commission-sponsored newspaper series in the early 1950s noted: "We must get over the dangerous delusion that laymen cannot understand atomic energy as well as they understand automobiles and radios . . . one does not need to be a scientist to grasp the fundamentals of atomic energy."[31]

The cartoon—which featured Reddy Kilowatt entering and exiting a house through an electrical outlet-turned-portal, zipping excitedly from room to room, and cheerfully powering everyday household appliances—also brought into relief atomic power's close alignment with the domestic sphere. The domestication of the atom thus referred not just to taming the atom but also to a historically specific model of white, middle-class domesticity. Unlike oil, which was associated with the automobile and spatial mobility, nuclear power—with its promise of cheap and limitless electricity—was associated with the middle-class home in ways that exceeded its comparatively modest share of household electricity generation. Foundational to the faith in nuclear power was the myth that a ramped-up energy regime could supply something for nothing—electricity that, in one famous prediction, would be "too cheap to meter." Reddy Kilowatt, then, was the conduit through which atomic power's mythical qualities entered the middle-class home, where electricity would effortlessly circulate in and out of wall outlets, vitalizing and charging commodities, dissolving the boundary between the living and the inert. At once magical and mundane, Reddy Kilowatt advanced a fantasy that underwrote the tremendous capitalist expansion of the postwar period: energy could be forever secured on the cheap, ensuring the endless replication of a high-consumption way of life.[32]

Despite such PR efforts, the AEC's task of domesticating the atom remained daunting. By the mid-1960s, when Metropolitan Edison (the utility that operated Three Mile Island) decided to construct a nuclear power plant, the company predicted that it would face a mammoth task of educating the local community about its turn to nuclear technology. In 1965, Met-Ed drafted a public relations plan that identified several goals: to change public perceptions of the atom "from that of 'The Bomb' to that of peaceful uses," to convince the public that nuclear power was safe and economical, to highlight "the scientific, cultural, and prestige" advantages of

FIGURE 1.1. Reddy Kilowatt Coloring Book. Courtesy of National Archives II, University of Maryland, College Park.

having a plant in the region, and to show the public how the plant operated. In a move that revealed the company's simultaneous awareness of and contempt for the still-inchoate environmental movement, the plan predicted that opposition would come from three constituencies: citizens groups, comprising residents in downstream communities and dominated by "uninformed mothers" and members of "garden clubs"; "ban everything groups," spearheaded by frustrated scientists and "do-gooders"; and finally, "beauty and blight groups"—conservation activists—who would "protest almost any sight for almost any reason" because "everything is hallowed these days." Conceding that there were a few radicals within each constituency who would remain intransigent, Met-Ed predicted that it could win over most current skeptics through a well-conceived PR strategy.[33]

At the heart of Met-Ed's plan was the goal that had structured the AEC's publicity from the beginning: to dissociate nuclear power plants from atomic bombs (indeed, the word *nuclear* was chosen over the word *atomic* with this aim in mind).[34] The most-pressing publicity challenge, as the plan presented it, was that "The Atomic Age was born with the atom bomb. The public has a vivid vision of destruction when they think of atomic energy."

The company would have to counter this vision by convincing the public through advertising that a plant could not explode. One proposed radio spot featured a dialogue between two men: "Couldn't your nuclear reactor blow up like an atomic bomb if something went wrong?" one man asks. The other replies: "It is physically impossible for a reactor to behave like a bomb."[35] As one utility company spokesman asserted, "We feel there is no more connection between nuclear power and the bombing of Hiroshima than there is between electricity and the electric chair."[36] Met-Ed would also need to address the fear of a serious accident, as well as the concern that the plant, even during normal operations, would emit radiation via the electrical grid. On this latter point, the plan stressed that the public would need special reassurance that "electricity generated at the nuclear plant will not transmit radiation into the homes via the electric wire." The company appeared unaware of how the industry itself had contributed to this worry through its own widely disseminated images of "busy little atoms" zooming in and out of electrical outlets. The way to ameliorate such fears was to liken atomic energy to other natural forces that were Janus-faced in their effects, such as fire (conflagration vs. fireplace), wind (tornado vs. windmill), water (flood vs. hydroelectric generation), and electricity (lightning vs. electric power). Met-Ed believed that "the forces of nature can be destructive, but man has learned to control them."[37] Thus humans could harness atomic power, just as they had harnessed fire, wind, and water. For Met-Ed, this power source was a part of—rather than a threat to—the natural world.

The identification of atomic power with nature was a constant motif in promotional literature. Brochures featured illustrations of plants in pastoral settings, surrounded by butterflies, trees, and birds.[38] Designed to blend into park-like landscapes with power lines buried underground, in marked contrast to the ugly slag heaps and smokestacks associated with the industrial age, the aesthetics of power plants were meant to convey harmony with their environmental surroundings. According to Glenn Seaborg, nuclear plants were "as close to an extension of nature as any human enterprise."[39] Aligning atomic power with a benign view of nature was premised on the notion that while the atomic age may have been historically new, atomic power itself was ageless, as was the radiation it emitted. "Radiation is not new to the world; it is not new to Met-Ed," one company brochure explained. "Radiation is part of our natural environment. We have always lived in its presence. Natural radiation . . . comes from cosmic rays reaching

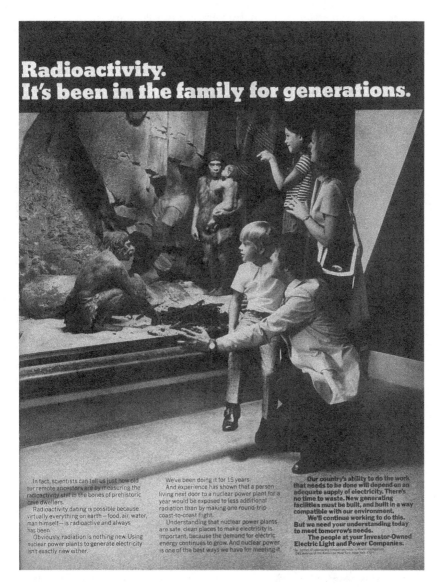

FIGURE 1.2. "Radioactivity. It's Been in the Family for Generations." Advertisement for Investor Owned Electric Light and Power Company. Reprinted from *Life* magazine, October 13, 1972.

earth from outer space and naturally radioactive substances present in commonplace materials in our bodies."[40] This emphasis on the ubiquity of radiation was meant to efface its toxicity. One Met-Ed brochure even urged readers to take a personal radiation inventory questionnaire to estimate how much radiation they harbored internally. Throughout its safety reassurances, the industry oscillated back and forth, sometimes emphasizing that radiation could be safely contained inside the walls of power plants, while at other times insisting on its ubiquity. "There is not a nook or cranny of the ocean, the earth, or space . . . that is free of radiation," one industry brochure proclaimed. "There is not a living thing upon our earth that has not been subjected to radiation throughout its existence . . . there is not a single ancestor of any of us that has not been subjected to radiation throughout his or her lifetime."[41] As one proposed Met-Ed radio spot reassured listeners: "You're exposed to more radiation on one sunny afternoon at the beach than by living next door to a nuclear power plant for a whole year."[42] Turn-of-the-century scientists had looked upon radium as possessing magical properties, but by the mid-1960s, industry promoters were taking pains to convince Americans that radiation was everywhere and ordinary.

A CRIME AGAINST THE FUTURE: THE RADIATION SCARES
OF THE 1950s AND 1960s

Industry efforts to construct radiation as ordinary were countered by a growing public fear of atomic testing. Testing was endemic to the Cold War era. Between 1945 and 1976, the military tested 588 nuclear and thermonuclear weapons, nearly a third of them above ground.[43] In the years between 1946 and the signing of the Limited Test Ban Treaty in August 1963, the AEC oversaw multiple test series, including Operation Crossroads (July 1946), Operation Greenhouse (May 1951), the Ivy-Mike nuclear test (November 1952), Castle Bravo (March 1954), Operation Teapot (1955), Operation Redwing (May 1956), Operation Plumbob (May 1957), Operation Hardtack I and II (April–October 1958), Operation Argus (August 1958), and Operation Dominic (May 1962). Anthropologist Joseph Masco writes of this period: "Nuclear devices were exploded on towers, dropped from planes, suspended from balloons, floated on barges, placed in craters, buried in shafts and tunnels, launched from submarines, shot from cannons, and loaded into increasingly powerful missiles."[44] These tests were conducted in either the Pacific Proving Grounds (an umbrella term that referred to sites in the Marshall Islands and other parts of the Pacific), or the Nevada Test Site (NTS), a 1350-square-mile range located ninety miles north of Las Vegas.[45] Nuclear testing thus established a connection between the water-bound atolls of the Pacific Ocean and the arid desert of the US Southwest. Both sites were remote and relatively depopulated. But they were not empty, and residents of the Pacific atolls and the US Southwest bore the brunt of atomic dangers disproportionate to their populations.

One problem was that fallout from testing did not follow a predictable path. Between 1951 and 1962, fallout drifted from test sites over one hundred times. In 1951, scientists detected radioactive fallout in snowfall as far away as Rochester, New York. The same year, the AEC began receiving letters reporting that fallout was disrupting weather patterns around the world.[46] In March 1953, stockmen in Utah blamed nuclear testing in neighboring Nevada for the deaths of over one thousand ewes and lambs. The following year, the Castle Bravo explosion spread radioactive ash over seven thousand square miles of the Pacific, exposing over 250 Marshall Islanders to radiation poisoning. A Japanese fishing boat was in the plume's path, and twenty-three fishermen suffered radiation illness. One of them, Aikichi Kuboyama, died. In 1954 and 1955, radioactive rain fell in Troy, New York, and Chicago, two cities located well over a thousand miles away from the NTS. As oceanographers and earth scientists began monitoring these radiation releases, they confronted an epistemological dilemma. Because they initiated surveillance of radiation levels *after* weapons testing had commenced, they had no way of knowing what constituted a baseline radiation level. Scientists thus found themselves tracking a planetary radiological experiment that was already well underway by the time their observations began.[47]

Strontium-90, an isotope that mimics calcium and can lodge in the bones, posed a special problem. In 1957, traces of Strontium-90 were detected in wheat and milk, suggesting that fallout had entered the food chain through cows grazing on exposed pasture. A government study published in June 1959 found that in some parts of the country, the Strontium-90 content in milk approached the proposed maximum permissible dose.[48] This finding was troubling not only because exposure to Strontium-90 increased the risk of bone cancer, but because the isotope had a half-life of twenty-eight years (a half-life refers to the time it takes for 50 percent of an isotope to dissipate), thus posing a long-term danger. Throughout the late 1950s, Congress received letters from thousands of citizens worried about the milk supply, scientists warned that radiation could cause leukemia and blood disorders, citizens groups conducted local studies on radiation exposure, and the *Saturday Evening Post* named radioactive fallout "the silent killer."[49] At precisely the moment that promoters of civilian atomic power were honing their claims about its ordinariness, radiation was being transformed into a symbol of slow death.

A moniker like "the silent killer" offers a clue to why this transformation occurred: radiation defied all modes of sensory perception. Sociologist Kai Erikson cites radiation as one example of "a new species of trouble"—forms of toxicity and contamination symptomatic of late industrial modernity that inflict harm surreptitiously. "They penetrate human tissue indirectly," Erikson writes, "rather than wound the surfaces by assaults of a more straightforward kind."[50] Invisible and silent, radiation could penetrate the body, lie dormant for decades, and then violently return to the surface, producing premature death. As we will see, radiation's invisibility in particular would pose a thorny phenomenological challenge at Three Mile Island: In the absence of visual cues, how could the boundary between safety and danger be determined? The invisibility of radiation placed a heavy burden on technological fixes, such as Geiger counters, that might fill the void.

The scare was also amplified by a lack of scientific consensus about whether there was such a thing as a safe threshold below which radiation did no harm.[51] By mid-century, there was no doubt that high levels of radiation exposure could produce toxicity, illness, and death, but the effects of low-level radiation remained elusive. As the National Academy of Sciences explained in 1960, "many aspects of the [radiation] problem are too little understood to permit more than tentative conclusions," including whether there was "a radiation threshold."[52] Some scientists contended that below a certain level, the effects of radiation were so negligible as to pose virtually no health risk, meaning that there was what they called a permissible dose of radiation. But others advanced what was called the linear no-threshold dose hypothesis, according to which there was a directly proportional relation between radiation and risk all the way down to the lowest levels. The public thus encountered confusing and contradictory reports. For its part, the AEC consistently reassured residents living near the NTS that the amount of radiation emitted from fallout was slight and did not add significantly to what it called "normal background radiation," that is, radiation emitted from earth, rocks, and the sun. When confronted with the findings of geneticists who warned that *any* radiation exposure could do harm, the AEC minimized the risk by framing it in the broadest possible statistical terms. At one point, AEC chairman Lewis Strauss explained that radiation exposure from testing "would be only a small fraction of the exposure that individuals receive from natural sources and medical x-rays during their lives."[53] "It's not dangerous," echoed anchorman Walter Cronkite in reference to a radioactive dust cloud during a televised Nevada test explosion in 1953.[54] But several studies conducted in the mid-1950s by scientific bodies like the National Academy of Sciences and the UN Scientific Committee on the Effects of Atomic Radiation broke with the commission, warning that even low-level radiation from fallout could be dangerous.[55] Thus throughout the 1950s, reassurances from the AEC often appeared alongside more somber assessments. Atomic physicists who felt confident that radiation levels could be controlled often clashed with biologists and geneticists who were more alarmed by the potential danger. And international bodies like the International Committee on Radiation Protection tended to be more conservative than their US counterparts when making recommendations about what constituted an acceptable maximum dosage of radiation.[56] Confusion surrounding low-level radiation illuminated both the considerable cultural and social authority of postwar science and the limits of that same authority (as radioactive fallout filtered into the environment).

This debate about radiation thresholds registered a historically new way of thinking about the human body and its relationship to the environment. This encompassed a proto-ecological awareness of the body's permeability by its outside, and it prompted the question of whether there was such a thing as a permissible toxic load that this body could bear. That question had its origins in the theory of homeostasis, first popularized in 1932 by physiologist Walter Cannon, which posited the idea of the body as a self-regulating system.[57] As historian Linda Nash argues, industrial toxicologists drew on the model of homeostasis to develop the concept of "biologic thresholds—that is, the assertion that there is always a level of exposure below which the body can absorb and adjust to pollutants without sustaining permanent harm."[58] The permissible dose theory of radiation reflected an influential method of risk assessment according to which the threat of disease or injury from chemical toxicity was correlated to the amount of exposure. This toxicological principle was captured in the formulation "the dose makes the poison."[59] Emerging out of the debate in the 1950s was what scholars have called the ecological body.[60] This body was defined not simply by its more porous relationship to its environment, but also by the presumption that some kind of chemical and toxic load was both inevitable and sustainable. Haunting the ecological body, though, was a series of tricky, elusive questions about dosage: At what point might toxic exposures push the homeostatic system beyond its tipping point? When might the dose of any toxin become a poison? And when might somatic resilience and adaptation give way to vulnerability, decomposition, and death?

The realization that radioactive isotopes from fallout could infiltrate bodily organs and tissue—not unlike the way they seeped into land and oceans—established an intimate association between somatic and planetary risk.[61] The mounting concern in the late 1950s over the presence of Strontium-90 in milk provides the most salient example. Milk is a unique food in two senses. First, it is what is called an indicator commodity, in that it is one of the first places where radioactive isotopes are detected (irradiated milk is often a tip-off that other staples are contaminated).[62] Second, milk is a deeply symbolic commodity because of its primal associations with motherhood, nursing, and infancy. Fallout could travel a circuitous but recognizable path through the food chain, from an ostensibly remote test site to a farm pasture where cattle grazed, then from the body of a cow into a bottle of milk, then from a bottle of milk onto a kitchen table, and then from a kitchen table into children's bodies. In 1960, the Committee for Nuclear Information collected baby teeth—the final stop on the chain—in order to gauge children's exposure to Strontium-90.[63] In a St. Louis living room, women volunteers gathered around card tables, meticulously sorting through tens of thousands of baby teeth donated to the committee in order to gauge the presence of Strontium-90 in the young.[64] The presence of a mobile, radioactive isotope in milk and baby teeth suggested that despite the trappings of domestic tranquility, the atomic age contained destructive elements that could not be purged from either the homes or the bodies of American civilians. A sanctified, feminized domestic realm was at the heart of Cold War ideology, and the radiation threat undermined that ideology by suggesting that weapons testing might constitute a graver threat to Americans than any Communist enemy.

The story of Strontium-90 is also significant because of the figure at its center: the child.[65] While postwar scientists argued about a permissible dose, all agreed that babies and young children were especially vulnerable to radiological injury. This consensus suggested that the *amount* of the dosage alone was insufficient for assessing risk; the *timing* of radiological exposure also mattered. Still-growing bones, organs, and tissue were more susceptible to the absorption of radioactive isotopes like Strontium-90, and children's life spans meant that they simply had more time than adults to process radiation's cumulative effects. One of the first suspected civilian casualties of nuclear fallout in the United States was a young boy named Martin Laird, who had been three years old when testing began seventy miles away from his home in Carson City, Nevada. He died of leukemia four years later. His mother was convinced that fallout from testing had caused his death. "We are forgotten guinea pigs," Martha Laird would later charge at a congressional hearing in Las Vegas, "We were feeding our children and families poisons from those bombs." Nevada Republican senator George Malone accused her of pedaling "Communist-inspired scare stories."[66] But a number of studies conducted in the late 1950s and early 1960s found that children living near the NTS had been exposed to Iodine-131, another radioactive isotope that can lodge in the thyroid gland and cause thyroid cancer.[67] These findings filtered into magazines ranging from the *New Republic* to the more middlebrow *McCall's Magazine*, where articles appeared with titles like "Our Irradiated Children" and "Radioactivity Is Poisoning Your Children." In 1958, a critic of the AEC appeared on Edward Murrow's nationally syndicated television show and recounted the story of Martin Laird's leukemia.[68] In 1961, a Public Health Service official in Albany, New York, received a worried phone call from a mother who had heard from a news report that there had been a tenfold increase in airborne radioactivity near her home. Her first question for the official was whether it was "safe to send her children to school."[69] By the late 1950s, the specter of white, middle-class children endangered by an invisible threat hung over atomic weapons testing. This undermined the culture of dissociation by implicitly evoking the terror of Hiroshima and Nagasaki. The utter decimation

Your children's teeth contain Strontium-90

All children's teeth now contain radioactive Strontium-90 from nuclear weapons tests.

Radioactive Strontium is a potential cause of leukemia, as pointed out in the United Nations report on radiation. Early signs of leukemia appear in the mouth, and dentists are familiar with them.

Scientists can tell how much radioactive Strontium-90 is in children's bones by measuring the radioactive material in their teeth. A recent analysis of baby teeth shows a 16-fold increase in Strontium-90 over the past five years.* Unlike baby teeth, however, the permanent teeth and bones retain Strontium-90 throughout their existence.

As dentists, we deplore the buildup of radioactive Strontium-90

in children's teeth and bones. It is a measure of the sickness of our times. Even if nuclear weapons tests cease today, the accumulation of Strontium-90 will continue for years.

We oppose nuclear weapons testing by all nations not only because of the contamination of bones and teeth of our children and patients, but because it is a direct stimulus to the runaway arms race. The testing race only multiplies mistrust and tension, and increases the chances of nuclear war.

Therefore, as dentists, our responsibility to promote life and health compels us to make this public appeal to all governments to cease nuclear weapons tests and to develop those international agreements which would eliminate the nuclear arms race.

*Committee for Nuclear Information St. Louis Baby Tooth Survey

FIGURE 1.3. "Your Child's Teeth Contain Strontium 90," SANE Advertisement, 1963. Copyright Held by SANE, Inc. Courtesy of Swarthmore College Peace Collection.

of those cities meant that there were very few photographs of fractured, gutted buildings—the images often associated with European carpet-bombed cities like London and Dresden. Instead, as historian John Dower has observed, images of mothers and children served as visual proxies for Japanese cities where there were no buildings left to photograph. Indeed, "the victimized Japanese mother and child became perhaps the most familiar symbol of the horrors of nuclear war."[70] The smiling children featured in an advertisement from the Committee for a Sane Nuclear Policy (SANE) appeared thousands of miles away—both spatially and emotionally—from the Japanese mother and child at Hiroshima in 1945. But the potential for radiological injury merged the biological fates of children otherwise divided by geography, race, class, and circumstance.

Further fueling such fears were the somatic and genetic injuries associated with radiation exposure. The most serious threat was cancer. Radioactive isotopes like Strontium-90 and Iodine-131 could cause bone and thyroid cancers, and by the 1950s, researchers were observing elevated rates of leukemia among Hiroshima and Nagasaki survivors, as well as among children who had been exposed to X-rays during infancy. The cancer threat was thus a constitutive feature of the radiation scare, and the radiation scare, in turn, arose amid a constellation of mid-century fears surrounding cancer. As oncologist and writer Siddhartha Mukherjee has argued, cancer occupied a unique place in the postwar American cultural and social imaginary.[71] At a time when new wonder drugs like penicillin were saving lives, cancer—its causes, treatments, and cures—remained a stubbornly enigmatic puzzle. As breakthroughs in immunology and bacteriology lengthened the lives of many Americans and as infant and child mortality rates fell, the persistence of cancer and its maddening refusal to be definitively cured once and for all illuminated the limits of modern medicine. At the same time, researchers of the 1950s were discovering that exposure to certain industrial pollutants, namely carcinogens, posed serious cancer risks. During the postwar years, in other words, cancer came to play an anomalous and even defiant role in modern epidemiology. It was elusive to any single cure or treatment and was a hallmark of (rather than something eradicated by) industrial modernity. The specter of a young child stricken down by a radiation-induced leukemia amplified the singular horror of cancer, while cancer research brought into relief the scientific debate about the differences between low and high levels of radiation exposure. After all, in the field of oncology, radiation was a double-edged sword: high doses of radiation could cause cancer, while low doses could help cure it. Radiation was both carcinogen *and* weapon in the growing arsenal of cancer treatment, a paradox that captured its dual identification with death and rebirth, sickness and health.

A second constellation of threats posed by radiation exposure revolved around reproductive and fetal health. Here, scientists and clinicians issued three warnings. First, they cautioned that the risks of radiation exposure were even more acute for the developing fetus than they were for the young. "A living organism is more sensitive to radiation damage in the early embryonic stage than at any other time in the entire life cycle," explained one radiology expert.[72] Geneticists and biologists in the late 1950s warned that fetal exposure to radioactive isotopes like Tritium and Cesium-137 could cause birth defects like microcephaly and mental disability, both of which had been diagnosed in Japanese babies who had been in utero at the time of the bombings in 1945. The second warning was that both male and female reproductive organs were especially sensitive to radiation. Thus exposure could lead to sterility and infertility. Finally, scientists warned that radiation could unleash multigenerational genetic mutations that might not appear at first, but could manifest at some indeterminate future point. After the Bravo test in 1954, A. H. Sturtevant, a geneticist at the California Institute of Technology, predicted that the explosion alone would eventually exact a "genetic toll" on eighteen hundred children. This figure was based in part on evolutionary biologist Thomas Hunt Morgan's famous *Drosophila* experiments, in which radiation had been used in the laboratory to induce mutations in fruit flies.[73] "Every new bomb exploded will result in an increase in this ultimate harvest of defective individuals," Sturtevant warned in baldly eugenicist language. In 1956 and 1958, the genetics committee of the National Academy of Sciences and the UN Scientific Committee on the Effects of Atomic Radiation issued similar warnings. While the NAS study was tentative about the carcinogenic effects of low-level radiation, the findings of its genetics committee were less ambiguous: "radiation causes mutations or harmful changes in the genes or germ cells of the reproductive organs." These mutations could shorten life spans and eventually lead to an increase in what the Academy called "deformed or freakish children." A follow-up UN report stressed that once a genetic mutation occurred, the process was irreversible: "Even if the mutation is in one gene, there is some harmful effect and that mutation will go through every generation until the line that bears it becomes extinct."[74] The report stressed that in contrast to somatic injuries, genetic injuries were intergenerational. "Man's actions," it argued, "can damage the genetic inheritance . . . once the genes have been altered, there is no changing them back."[75]

These warnings placed genetic injury at the center of a widening public debate about atomic weapons testing. In November 1958, chemist and test critic Linus Pauling predicted that every year of continued testing could eventually lead to fifty-five thousand "defective births" and one hundred thousand stillbirths.[76] By causing premature death, radiation-induced cancers imperiled the presumably protected realm of childhood, but a pediatric cancer—as horrific as it was—went to the grave with its victim. Genetic damage was different. It could upend the reproductive process altogether, either through bringing it to a halt through sterility or infertility, or through setting in motion runaway mutations that divorced reproduction from the logic of generational continuity on which it ostensibly relied. As the National Academy of Sciences explained, a genetic injury would only fade out with the extinction of the genetic line. "Mutant genes," it warned, "can only disappear when the inheritance in which they are carried dies out."[77] Anticipating a dawning anthropogenic consciousness, Danish biologist Mogens Westergaard grimly concluded that humans had entered a new era in which their mistakes were now irreversible, drastically altering "the course of man's biological evolution."[78]

Like oncology, genetics occupied a central place in US postwar science. The federal government greatly increased funding for genetics research after 1945, in part because it wanted to better understand the hazards of low-level radiation exposure. But as historian Luis Campos has shown, the links between radiation and genetics went back much further.[79] As we have seen, radium's vitality—its role as a "mutant" among the elements—had convinced turn-of-the-century scientists that the element contained the secret of life. Thus the discovery of radium prefigured, and would eventually be displaced by, the subsequent claim that the origin and nature of life were encoded within the gene. In the 1950s, radiation propelled some of the most significant advances in genetics, including the first photographic image of the DNA molecule, which relied on X-ray diffraction and laid the groundwork for the discovery of the double helix two years later. In addition, evolutionary biologists and botanists enlisted radium, radiation, and

X-rays as mutagens in the life-sciences laboratory—that is, as agents that could artificially induce mutations. Radium and radiation thus provided life scientists with the metaphorical, material, and experimental supplies required for the eventual development of a genic theory of mutation. The work of evolutionary biologists in particular yielded a corrective to the Darwinian theory that species change could only occur over a long time horizon. Mutations could occur abruptly, even within a single generation.

This fear of mutation, and the prospect of a "weirded" reproduction contained within it, propelled the figure of the unborn to the center of the radiation scare and facilitated the transformation of the fetus into an object of intensified visual and legal scrutiny. This was something new. Before 1945, human fetuses had been displayed only at museums, exhibitions, and world's fairs. But between 1946 and 1953, photographs of the developing fetus were featured in *Newsweek*, *Time*, and *Life*, allowing millions of Americans to "see" it for the first time. In 1946, the same year that *Newsweek* printed a photograph of a three-month-old fetus, the District Court of the District of Columbia heard the case of Bette Gay Bonbrest, a girl born in 1939 who had sustained serious injuries during her delivery by forceps. Her father sued the obstetrician for negligence, and the court established "the right of a child to recover from harm incurred when it was a viable fetus *in utero*." Establishing that "a child *en ventre sa mere* is regarded as a human being from the moment of conception," the case overturned six decades of legal precedent and was quickly emulated by other courts. By 1960, eighteen states had awarded damages for prenatal injury.[80] The growing legibility of the fetus became entwined with the rise of atomic power.[81] A volume published in 1959 titled *Atoms and the Law* devoted over twenty pages to radiation and prenatal injury and the *Hibakusha*, the Japanese term for the community of bombing victims, included babies who had been in utero at the time of the explosions.[82] The postwar cultural, scientific, and legal construction of the fetus, in other words, emerged in a proto-ecological field psychologically saturated with radiation.[83]

The unborn was thus an atomically charged figure before it became caught up in the coming abortion war. And it was the growing movement against atomic weapons testing, in which mothers played an outsized role, which helped to suffuse this figure with new political meaning. The coalition calling for a test ban that took shape in the late 1950s and 1960s was diverse. It included pacifist organizations like the American Friends

Service Committee, religious organizations like the World Council of Churches and the Lutheran World Federation, and prominent public scientists-cum-activists like Linus Pauling and Albert Schweitzer. But the shock troops of organizations like SANE (1957) and especially Women Strike for Peace (1961) were white, middle-class women who appealed to hegemonic conceptions of motherhood and respectability in order to legitimize their role in a male-dominated public sphere.[84] In the wake of McCarthyism, when dissent was seen as almost treasonous, the appeal to motherhood—sometimes referred to as maternalism—provided test ban activists with political cover while also helping to give the movement a religious inflection. The Catholic Church was especially vocal in its opposition. In his 1955 Easter Sunday address, Pope Pius XII condemned nuclear testing on the grounds that it threatened "that mysterious something which is deep down in every living thing" and warned of the "horrors of monstrous offspring."[85]

As activists honed their arguments, they increasingly appealed to "the rights of the unborn." Insisting that testing constituted an ethical Rubicon for the nation, they contended that it produced two distinct but parallel crises of political representation. First, because fallout did not follow any predictable path, it posed a threat to citizens beyond the territorial bounds of the United States. In 1958, Albert Schweitzer presented the dilemma clearly: "Bomb testing harms peoples far from the sovereign territories of the nuclear powers—endangering the lives and health of distant peoples."[86] From this, Schweitzer concluded that nuclear testing fell under the jurisdiction of international rather than national law, a claim that captured how traditional political boundaries were becoming attenuated within the Anthropocene. "No nation has the moral right to take risks for other people without their consent," explained a SANE pamphlet, "No nation has the moral right to contaminate the air and water and the food that belong to other people. The air does not belong to the US alone, or the Soviet Union alone, or Great Britain alone."[87] Because testing posed a physical danger to peoples who had never consented to it, activists claimed, it constituted a form of what they called annihilation, extermination, or contamination without representation. One SANE advertisement placed the question of consent at the center of the testing crisis: "we have every right to take such risks to ourselves as we wish in the pursuit of our own security. But we do not have the right—nor does any nation—to take risks, large or small, for other people without their consent." "If we persist in an act that is actually or potentially hazardous to other peoples," the advertisement continued, "we have the obligation to give them the complete right to participate in the processes of government and public debate inside our own nation."[88]

The testing crisis was not only spatial. It followed a temporal course as well, and it is here that the unborn entered. Unlike somatic traumas, radiation's genetic harms stretched into the future, ensnaring successive generations in its web. This meant that fallout posed a threat not only to living humans, but also to those who had not yet been conceived. As one *Newsweek* reader put it, "once upon a time, war affected only those in the line of fire, now it reaches into the third and fourth generations."[89] The claim that fallout constituted a form of contamination without representation thus established an affinity between non-US citizens and the unborn. Neither had political voice, and both were being placed at biological risk without their consent. In May 1958, Albert Schweitzer published an essay titled "The Rights of the Unborn and the Peril Today" in which he singled out the dormancy of radiation as its "most sinister aspect" precisely because of its repercussions for those not yet here: "Years may pass before the evil consequences appear," he wrote. "Indeed, incipient injuries may manifest themselves, not in the first or second generations, but in the following cycles. Observers in generation after generation, for centuries to come, will witness the birth of ever-increasing numbers of children with mental and physical defects."[90] Citing French biologist Jean Rostand, who had condemned weapons testing as a "crime against the future," Schweitzer insisted that the living had obligations to the not yet born: "Only those who have never been present at the birth of a deformed baby, never witnessed the whimpering cries of its mother, could dare to maintain that the present risk of nuclear tests must be taken."[91] Similarly, Indian delegate Krishna Menon told the UN General Assembly during a debate about nuclear testing that the United Nations had an obligation not "only to represent ourselves but to represent . . . the generation that is unborn."[92] In April 1958, *Time* magazine featured a photograph of prominent SANE supporters with the caption "Defenders of the unborn . . . or dupes of the enemies of liberty?"[93] The magazine went with the later theory, but the caption indexed just how prominent the figure of the unborn had become.

The movement also deployed this figure in its visual iconography in order to convey a sense of urgency. The earliest SANE advertisements had been densely worded position statements that contained no photographs or illustrations. But in July 1959, SANE member Lewis Mumford wrote to founder Norman Cousins, warning that these well-intentioned advertisements would come up short: "The facts you list are properly horrifying, but they won't be read . . . and they won't lead to action . . . I'd rather see four quarter page advertisements that would hit the reader like a blow between the eyes."[94] To that end, Mumford suggested simple, hard-hitting sentences accompanied by photographs of children, since, as he put it, "the people who will have the most cause for complaint against our nuclear policy are our descendants."[95] By the early 1960s, the architects of SANE's publicity campaigns were taking his advice. The famous "Dr. Spock Is Worried" campaign, launched in April 1962, featured a photograph of the prominent pediatrician standing over a toddler girl. The following July, another SANE ad featured a single milk bottle stamped with a skull and cross-bones, provoking outrage from the milk industry.

No less alarming was a SANE advertisement from August 1962 that showed the silhouette of a woman in the final weeks of pregnancy, her hands clasped over her pregnant belly, her hair done up in a tidy bun. The caption that accompanies the photo reads: "1 ¼ Million unborn children will be born dead or have some gross defect because of Nuclear Bomb testing." The power of the advertisement resides precisely in what it does not show. There are no grotesque images of dead or deformed fetuses, and there is no window into this woman's womb. Instead, the caption asks readers to imagine what *might* be happening inside this woman's impregnated body. It alerts them to the frightening possibility that this seemingly healthy pregnancy has been compromised, perhaps fatally, by weapons testing. The refined, manicured outward appearance of the pregnant woman stands in implicit contrast to something unpredictable and terrifying that could potentially be unfolding within. The ultimate crime of testing, the advertisement suggests, is that it transports the reproductive process from the domain of the natural, the universal, and the predictable into that of the liminal, the volatile, and the uncanny.[96]

The radiation scare undermined the Cold War logic of dissociation that relied on stark distinctions between the foreign and the domestic, safety and danger, and war and peace. The possibility that radiation from atomic testing could infiltrate the most intimate interstices of life (baby teeth, chil-

FIGURE 1.4. "1 ¼ Million Unborn Children Will Be Born Dead," SANE Advertisement, 1960. Copyright Held by SANE, Inc. Courtesy of Swarthmore College Peace Collection.

dren's bones, milk, the womb) meant that atomic danger transgressed all boundaries: the political boundary between the soldier and the civilian; the territorial boundary between nation-states; the biological boundary between the body and its environment; and the temporal boundary between the living and the not yet born. The scare was a by-product of the atomic age, but it prefigured the centrality of the imperiled body to the coming ecological age: the emergence of a body permeable to stealth assaults; the fear of cancer as a nimble disease of late industrial modernity; an elusive set of questions surrounding the human body's capacity to carry toxic loads; the advent of risks that relayed back and forth between the somatic and the planetary; and an ambiguity surrounding whether it was the dosage or the timing of exposure that rendered the body vulnerable to toxic injury. The question of timing located the figure of the unborn at the center of the radiation scare in a way that fueled the construction of the fetus as a legal person susceptible to environmental harm.

But even as the scare haunted the Cold War, the line between plants and bombs remained intact throughout the 1950s and 1960s. Because anxieties centered on fallout from weapons testing, civilian nuclear power remained removed from it. That the first nuclear power plant went online in 1958 at the height of the scare suggests that promoters of civilian atomic energy were at least partially successful in their efforts to distance reactors from bombs. But their success was also the result of historical timing. With the signing of the Limited Test Ban Treaty in 1963, the radiation scare receded from view; the licensing of new plants was taking off just as public fears of radiation were subsiding. The suppression of this fear would prove short-lived, however. By the late 1960s, the debate over radiation resurfaced, and this time, nuclear reactors would be at the center of the controversy.

THE CULTURE OF DISSOCIATION COMES APART

The culture of dissociation had always been fragile, but by the late 1960s, it was unraveling amid political, social, and cultural upheaval. The movement against the Vietnam War shattered the Cold War consensus, as antiwar activists insisted that militarization could not be cordoned off but instead violated the entire society. Over the course of the 1970s, the antiwar impulse and the antiauthoritarianism of the prior decade were extended to the nuclear power industry. Three intersecting forces proved especially crucial:

dissident scientists who broke ranks and publicly voiced concerns about plant safety; a burgeoning antinuclear movement that fought to decommission existing reactors and halt the building of new ones; and a politicized community of radiation victims and their families who sought recognition and redress for their suffering. Together, these actors placed the irradiated body at the center of the political realignment of the 1970s.

By the late 1960s, the debate about low-level radiation—earlier confined to the fallout controversy—was pivoting to civilian nuclear power safety. With the AEC licensing new plants at a steady clip, a handful of scientists and engineers began to warn that the industry's radiological safety standards were inadequate. Among the most prominent were Arthur Tamplin and John Gofman, two researchers at the University of California's Lawrence Livermore Laboratories who had received AEC funding to study the health risks associated with low-level radiation exposure. The commission had enlisted the two men in the hopes that they would dispel allegations about radiological risk that were circulating at the time, in particular those leveled by Ernest Sternglass, a professor of radiation physics at the University of Pittsburgh. In specialized journals like the *Bulletin of Atomic Scientists* and more popular outlets like *Esquire*, Sternglass estimated that fallout had caused approximately four hundred thousand infant deaths and an incalculable number of fetal deaths. He maintained that the danger extended to nuclear power plants, claiming that infant mortality rates were statistically higher in communities where reactors were situated.[97] While Gofman and Tamplin refuted Sternglass's direst estimates, their own findings were sobering. In 1969, they warned that the maximum radiation dosages permitted by the Federal Radiation Council were far too high and could lead to over thirty thousand annual cases of fatal cancer. Rejecting the concept of a safe radiation threshold, they insisted that there was a direct proportional relationship between radiation and adverse health effects "right down to the lowest doses." The dosages permitted by the AEC amounted to, in their words, "trading human lives for some supposed benefits of technology."[98] The AEC froze Gofman and Tamplin's research funds and terminated their staff.[99] The experience of University of Pittsburgh researcher Thomas Mancuso followed the same trajectory. Mancuso had received AEC funding in 1964 to study the health effects of workers' radiation exposure at Hanford, Washington, the site of the world's first full-scale plutonium production reactor. In 1977, he concluded that Hanford workers had suffered disproportionately high rates of fatal cancer, even when exposures had not exceeded permissible doses. Like Gofman and Tamplin, Mancuso found his research funds withdrawn.[100]

Joining these dissident scientists were three middle-management nuclear engineers who resigned in protest from General Electric's Nuclear Division in February 1976. The men distributed copies of their resignation letter to the *San Francisco Chronicle*, the *New York Times*, and the *Los Angeles Times* and were soon campaigning on behalf of a ban on nuclear power plant construction in their home state of California. When they had joined GE's nuclear division, they recalled, they had been hopeful about the "promise of a virtually limitless source of safe, clean, and economic energy," but the nuclear industry had become, as they put it, "an industry of narrow specialists, each promoting and refining a fragment of technology, and with little comprehension of the total impact on our world system." The dangers of compartmentalization compounded the likelihood of error. "It's human fallibility that's the chink in the whole nuclear armor," they later told Congress. "You cannot expect these things to run flawlessly for forty years. With as many people as have to be involved with them—in fuel manufacturing, fuel distribution, reprocessing, transport. There are too many people, too many steps, too many weaknesses in the whole chain." Gofman and Tamplin had challenged the notion of a safe threshold of radiation, and now the three engineers exposed the presumption of human infallibility on which the industry relied.[101]

As the debate about low-level radiation pivoted from the dangers of weapons testing to those of nuclear reactors, an antinuclear movement coalesced that aimed to stop entirely the expansion of nuclear power. This movement had roots in both pacifism and a legal activist public interest tradition, but it also took its cues from the upheavals of the 1960s and 1970s.[102] From the black freedom movement, it borrowed the tactic of nonviolent direct action. From the antiwar movement, it took the directive to question authority. From the cultural feminist wing of the women's movement, it drew on a celebration of an essential female culture that cast women as natural opponents of both nuclear power and war, while from the liberal and radical feminist wings, it took the insight that women were independent citizens and actors in the public world. And from the New Left as a whole, it appropriated the concept of participatory democracy, which called on citizens to play an active role in democratic decision-making.[103]

But even as the movement reflected the endurance of the left, it simultaneously indexed a growing conservative influence in a way that foretold the realignment of the 1970s. This was not a simple movement from left to right, but rather one that melded earlier categories, creating a new politics that would gradually tilt in an antistatist (rather than anticorporate) direction. The attempt to slow down or halt plant construction attracted libertarians who opposed the government's support of the nuclear industry on the grounds that it violated free market principles. It drew into its orbit national security hawks who feared that more plants would lead to weapons proliferation. And the centralized nature of the industry placed the question of community control at the center of the fight. By accusing federal regulators of placing local communities at risk, the antinuclear movement tapped into long-standing localist and communitarian impulses that, by the late 1970s, were being harnessed by grassroots activists throughout the country in battles over desegregation, schooling, and taxation. The antinuclear movement of the 1970s represented a mash-up that drew together disparate and even contradictory political elements.

These disparate elements created a movement that aimed not only to halt the spread of nuclear power plants, but also—borrowing a metaphor from the era's gay liberation movement—to out them.[104] By physically occupying a nuclear power plant at Diablo Canyon or a nuclear weapons facility at Rocky Flats, activists brought the atomic age out of the shadows and exposed the scope of a vast nuclear complex that had been hiding in plain sight. Consider Kristin Iverson's memory of growing up near a plutonium weapons factory at Rocky Flats, Colorado, in the 1960s. When, as a young girl, she wondered aloud what went on at the plant, her mother told her that it manufactured cleaning supplies, while her father stated that it represented "the defense of our country."[105] One answer was a lie and the other a euphemism. When activists protested at places like Rocky Flats in the late 1960s, they were, through the physical act of occupation, challenging the mechanisms of concealment and distortion on which the Cold War relied and that a young child unknowingly confronted when she posed the seemingly innocuous question: What happens there?

By engaging in what political theorist Timothy Pachirat has called a "politics of sight," which pulls back the curtain on those places that society hides from view in the service of domination,[106] activists constructed an alternative geography of North America. This was a nuclear geography that mapped out uranium mining, weapons manufacturing, power plants, atomic testing, and nuclear waste and showed how they were part of a single interconnected system. Movement pamphlets, leaflets, and newsletters included maps of the nation that outlined the multiple stages of the nuclear fuel cycle, from the mining of uranium to the detonation of bombs to the disposal of nuclear waste. A SANE pamphlet featured one such map depicting a vast network of facilities that by the late 1970s had reached into "nearly every state of the union": 130 uranium mill sites, three enrichment facilities, three reprocessing centers, twenty waste disposal sites, thirty reactors operated by the Department of Defense and the Department of Energy, 148 naval reactors, and fifty-one weapons storage and deployment sites.[107]

This new geography demanded a revised atomic history. Attempting to expose what the Clamshell Alliance described as the "malignant connection" between plants and bombs, activists revisited the bombing of Hiroshima. A nuclear power plant, they argued, was a "silent bomb" that housed enough nuclear material "to flatten dozens of Hiroshimas." A nuclear reactor could produce as much high-level waste as two thousand Hiroshima-sized atomic bombs. Within each nuclear reactor was a "potential Hiroshima." The same force that had claimed thousands of lives at Hiroshima and Nagasaki was "stirring in your backyard."[108] Industry promoters had gone to considerable lengths to portray the power plant as the antithesis of the bomb; it was placid where bombs were explosive, predictable where bombs were dangerous. Activists countered by warning that destruction lay dormant beneath the plant's calm veneer and that every community where a plant was located could find itself transformed into the very place that the AEC had tried to make the public forget: Hiroshima.

In addition to arguing that power plants were *like* bombs, activists pointed out that plants, full as they were with nuclear materials, could be converted *into* bombs. One nuclear reactor produced enough plutonium each year for the construction of ninety nuclear warheads. By placing tons of plutonium into commercial circulation, activists warned, nuclear power plants could lead to the creation of a black market in the metal that could end up in the hands of "terrorists, gangsters, and maniacs." India, Israel, and South Africa had become part of a nuclear monopoly by diverting plutonium from their own civilian nuclear power programs. Activists

FIGURE 1.5. "The Peaceful Atom Is a Bomb." Copyright Held by SHAD Alliance. Courtesy of Swarthmore College Peace Collection.

contended that the industry was thus trapped in a vicious circle: "The arms industry has used the power plants as a shield to legitimize their technology," proclaimed the Clamshell Alliance in its Declaration of Nuclear Resistance, "and the reactor industry has spawned nuclear bombs to nations all over the world."[109] The nuclear cartography aimed to expose this symbiotic relationship.

FIGURE 1.6. Map of Manmade Radiation Hazards, SANE WORLD, May 1979. Copyright Held by Women Strike for Peace. Courtesy of Swarthmore College Peace Collection.

What made this cartography innovative was that it combined land and soma. As they mapped the nuclear fuel cycle, activists simultaneously traced radiation's somatic journey through the human body. A widely distributed movement flyer titled "Ionizing Radiation" showed a drawing of a woman's naked body that tracked how radioactive isotopes of Iodine, Cesium, and Strontium became lodged in specific organs (the liver, the thyroid, the ovaries).[110] This mapping was meant to concretize the bodily violence that accompanied abstract talk of radiation thresholds and permissible doses, but it also established an affinity between bodily vulnerability and a contaminated national landscape.[111] As the atomic age gave way to the ecological age in the late 1970s, the geographies of land and body became enmeshed. Radiation—because it was so insidious, because it could travel so easily from one site to the next, because it could mutate and jump between generations, because it could create monstrous new species along the way—had sutured together a new world, establishing a relay between somatic and planetary injury, between the individual (often woman's) body and the land.

This homology between body and nation was not new, of course. The metaphor of the "body politic" envisions a political community as an entity

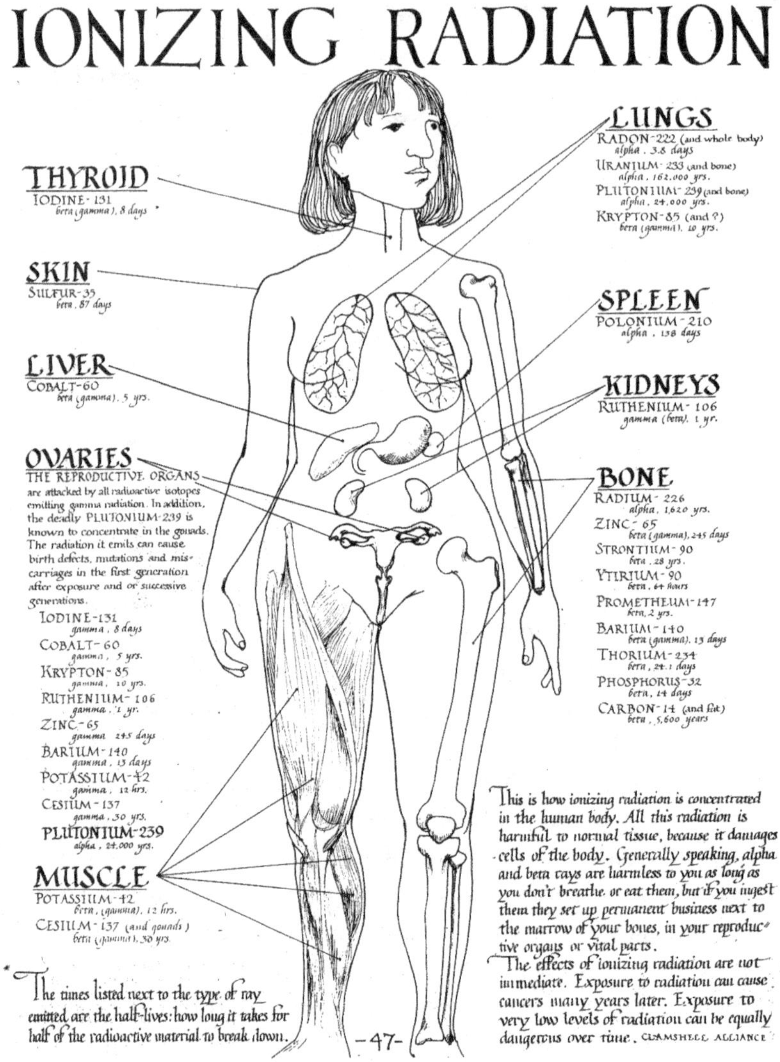

IONIZING RADIATION

THYROID
IODINE-131
beta (gamma), 8 days

SKIN
SULFUR-35
beta, 87 days

LIVER
COBALT-60
beta (gamma), 5 yrs.

OVARIES
THE REPRODUCTIVE ORGANS
are attacked by all radioactive isotopes
emitting gamma radiation. In addition,
the deadly PLUTONIUM-239 is
known to concentrate in the gonads.
The radiation it emits can cause
birth defects, mutations and miscarriages in the first generation
after exposure and in successive
generations.

    IODINE-131
      gamma, 8 days
    COBALT-60
      gamma, 5 yrs.
    KRYPTON-85
      gamma, 10 yrs.
    RUTHENIUM-106
      gamma, 1 yr.
    ZINC-65
      gamma, 245 days
    BARIUM-140
      gamma, 13 days
    POTASSIUM-42
      gamma, 12 hrs.
    CESIUM-137
      gamma, 30 yrs.
    PLUTONIUM-239
      alpha, 24,000 yrs.

MUSCLE
POTASSIUM-42
beta (gamma), 12 hrs.
CESIUM-137 (and gonads)
beta (gamma), 30 yrs.

The times listed next to the type of ray
emitted are the half-lives: how long it takes for
half of the radioactive material to break down.

LUNGS
RADON-222 (and whole body)
alpha, 3.8 days
URANIUM-233 (and bone)
alpha, 162,000 yrs.
PLUTONIUM-239 (and bone)
alpha, 24,000 yrs.
KRYPTON-85 (and ?)
beta (gamma), 10 yrs.

SPLEEN
POLONIUM-210
alpha, 138 days

KIDNEYS
RUTHENIUM-106
gamma (beta), 1 yr.

BONE
RADIUM-226
    alpha, 1,620 yrs.
ZINC-65
    beta (gamma), 245 days
STRONTIUM-90
    beta, 28 yrs.
YTTRIUM-90
    beta, 64 hours
PROMETHEUM-147
    beta, 2 yrs.
BARIUM-140
    beta (gamma), 13 days
THORIUM-234
    beta, 24.1 days
PHOSPHORUS-32
    beta, 14 days
CARBON-14 (and fat)
    beta, 5,600 years

This is how ionizing radiation is concentrated
in the human body. All this radiation is
harmful to normal tissue, because it damages
cells of the body. Generally speaking, alpha
and beta rays are harmless to you as long as
you don't breathe or eat them, but if you ingest
them they set up permanent business next to
the marrow of your bones, in your reproductive organs or vital parts.
    The effects of ionizing radiation are not
immediate. Exposure to radiation can cause
cancers many years later. Exposure to
very low levels of radiation can be equally
dangerous over time. CLAMSHELL ALLIANCE

-47-

FIGURE 1.7. Flyer of Ionizing Radiation in the Female Body. Copyright Held by SANE, Inc. Courtesy of
Swarthmore College Peace Collection.

whose members are united in a corporate whole. The origin of the term is medieval: the king's body signified the realm. After the Enlightenment, the metaphor incorporated elements borrowed from modern medicine, giving rise to the use of anatomical concepts to describe politics, such as *circulation* and *political anatomy*. Throughout modern history, the metaphor appeared across diverse landscapes, from seventeenth-century England and prerevolutionary France to Nazi Germany.[112] Its rhetorical power lay in its endowing the nation with an organic lifecycle; the nation is born, has a youth, a stage of maturity, and a decline. In the US political culture of the late 1970s, this link between body and nation became newly fortified by ecological insights about somatic vulnerability and land contamination. These insights had first originated on the political left. But at a post–Vietnam War moment when many conservative policymakers perceived national decline, they jumped the political track.

Nowhere was this track-jumping (and the body's decisive role within it) more evident than in the radiation activism of the 1970s. This movement was made up of radiation sufferers and their relatives who created a community of illness by bringing together those who worked, lived, and died along the nuclear fuel cycle. These were the people who populated the nuclear geography—Native American uranium miners in the US Southwest, workers in Rocky Flats, Colorado, and Hanford, Washington, who toiled in nuclear enrichment, fuel, and weapons facilities, civilians who lived downwind from the Nevada Test Site, and Marshall Islanders who had been exposed to fallout from testing at the Pacific Proving Grounds. The community also encompassed military veterans who had participated in nuclear weapon detonations and the Japanese victims of Hiroshima and Nagasaki.[113] While all of these groups were united by anger and a sense of betrayal, two constituencies came to dominate radiation activism: downwinders and military veterans. Over and over again, downwinders (people who lived downwind from testing sites), veterans, and their relatives recounted how officials from the AEC had assured them that radiation exposure posed no danger to health, assurances belied by the appearance of cancer years or decades later. As a consequence, a once-steadfast faith in government had been shattered. Radiation victims thus elaborated a patriotic body politics that linked physical illness to a growing conviction that the state had abandoned its most loyal citizens. This belief would prove critical to the rise of biotic nationalism in the 1970s.[114]

Several factors fueled the politicization of this community. First, by the late 1960s, the Cold War's toxic toll was coming into fuller view. As early as the mid-1950s, residents of southern Nevada and southwestern Utah had begun hearing rumors about friends and neighbors stricken with cancer. But between 1960 and 1970 several medical studies confirmed what residents had intuited: in their communities, as Republican senator Orrin Hatch later put it, "cancer borders on being the rule rather than the exception."[115] A study conducted in 1963 concluded that infants and children living downwind from the NTS had received hundreds of roentgens of Iodine-131, which can accumulate in the thyroid and cause cancer. Two years later, a study found higher-than-expected rates of cancer in two Utah counties downwind from the site. Another study conducted in 1969 revealed a fourfold increase in thyroid cancer in Utah, primarily among people between the ages of twenty and twenty-nine.[116] By the late 1960s, then, scientific findings confirmed that certain populations exposed to radiation had suffered disproportionate rates of leukemia, thyroid cancer, bone cancer, multiple myeloma, lymphoma, and aplastic anemia.[117] Over the next decade, still more information came to light. Although some of the most damning studies on the dangers of low-level radiation had been completed in the 1960s, they were not released by the AEC until 1978 and 1979 after investigative journalists filed FOIA requests with the Department of Energy.[118] What this meant was that by the late 1970s, downwinders were armed with mounting evidence of radiological injury.

This evidence was crucial to the formation of a community of radiation sufferers. But the politicization of this community can only be understood in light of the Vietnam War. The credibility gap created by that war—the revelation that the government could deceive its own people—had shifted the terrain of the political culture, not simply among activists who had fought to end the war, but also among patriots who had at first defended it. As Hannah Arendt observed in 1971, "the policy of lying was hardly ever aimed at the enemy . . . but was destined chiefly, if not exclusively, for domestic consumption, for propaganda at home."[119] The gradual realization over the course of the 1970s that the United States had blundered and lied itself into a war, which it then lost, generated a symbol that resonated powerfully with downwinders and other radiation victims: that of the young patriot whose body the government viewed as disposable and whose death was meaningless. As a result, the figure of the radiation sufferer could shade into that of the veteran. As one downwind activist put it, "We were used as fodder, the same as our young men were used in Vietnam."[120]

In the shadow of Vietnam, these men and women entered into political struggle not out of partisan loyalties, but rather because of a perceived threat to their own families and communities. These "accidental activists" crafted a politics that revolved around the sickened body.[121] They provided healthcare services within their communities through locating sufferers, conducting mobile health screenings, ensuring adequate care, disseminating medical information, and providing referrals and assistance. They worked to keep the radiation issue alive through newsletters and letter-writing campaigns, responding to newspapers whenever an article or editorial on the topic appeared. They also held conferences and hearings and provided congressional testimony. Finally, they fought to incorporate radiation suffering into the fabric of Cold War commemoration by holding candlelight vigils at the Nevada Test Site and calling for a National Radiation Victims Day.

Activists also fought for financial redress through class-action lawsuits. Former atomic workers demanded that the Veterans Administration recognize radiological injuries as a legitimate form of war-incurred disability, while downwinders relied on tort litigation. Within the legislative and legal arenas, the essential line of argument was the same. The AEC had failed to level with citizens about the risks of radiation exposure, and as a result, people had sickened and died. As one atomic veteran explained at a hearing in April 1980, "Although our claims are difficult to prove because we cannot feel, taste, hear or smell radiation, it is more deadly than bullets or shrapnel."[122] Victims, who frequently labeled themselves as "radiation fodder," felt they should no longer be asked to prove that their illnesses had been caused by radiation exposure sustained years in the past (an impossible task). Instead, it was time for the government to acknowledge what it had long denied: that certain groups had shouldered the burdens of the atomic age without their consent.

In their activism, radiation sufferers elaborated the geography mapped by the antinuclear movement. Many had witnessed the hypervisible displays of the atomic age: the flashing lights, the blasts, and the mushroom clouds from bomb detonations, what scholars have called "the nuclear sublime," a term used to describe the sense of awe and terror such scenes can evoke.[123] Appearing before Congress, one downwinder recalled the ritual trip she and her father took to the desert when she was a teenager: "I was fourteen when they started doing the testing, and I tell people that I went out on the desert with my Dad and I watched the blasts. I have seen mushroom clouds."[124] But activists also testified to what was *not* visible, namely, the pain unleashed by radiation exposure. A 1980 national conference for radiation sufferers was called "Invisible Violence," and over and over again activists commented on radiation's stealth quality. According to a *Las Vegas Sun* editorial on the plight of NTS workers, "Radiation kills silently. No blood gushes from open wounds. Often the body from the outside shows no signs of mutilation. Instead, radiation penetrates cells, often attacking the core of life itself—genes, the carriers of life. Sometimes it takes only days or weeks. In other individuals, the damage won't show for years."[125] As psychiatrist Robert Jay Lifton testified, the fear "doesn't go away for years . . . the sense of having something left in your body, a fear of a poison that may take effect at any time."[126] Radiation sufferers were witnesses in a dual sense. They had watched atomic spectacles up close, but they also testified to what could *not* be seen—the internal suffering unleashed by radiation-induced cancers and blood disorders.[127]

This atomic activism bespoke the wider politicization of illness over the course of the 1970s. Throughout that decade, feminist and black health activists indicted mainstream medicine and created their own institutions to meet the healthcare needs of their communities.[128] They challenged the authority of the medical establishment and sought to provide vital services. Like these activists, radiation victims challenged the monopoly of experts and cited illness as evidence of injustice. Yet while women's and black health activists viewed medical discrimination as symptomatic of a wider nexus of inequality, radiation sufferers were self-described patriots whose encounters with illness created a breach of trust in their relationship with the state. Radiation activism was populated by "people from America's heartland," observed a SANE newsletter, "the soldiers, the housewives, the workers. Not protestors, not skeptics—to begin with. But their bruising encounters with government irresponsibility . . . have worked a remarkable transformation. They have become activists, researchers, one-person investigating teams."[129] A disillusioned widow in the National Association of Radiation Survivors raised what for many activists had become the crucial question: "How could the government of the greatest nation in the world be so irresponsible, unconscionable, and unconcerned towards the fighting men of our country?"[130] A psychiatrist affiliated with Physicians for Social Responsibility coined a new term, *atomic veterans syndrome*. "A healthy man," he explained, "becomes an unhealthy man, an unquestioning patriot becomes angry at the government, and focuses his life on that anger."[131] By the early 1980s, anger and disillusionment fueled the movement: the government had betrayed its citizens by downplaying or concealing the dangers of radiation.[132]

With the mobilization of radiation sufferers in the 1970s, the mistrust of government—first voiced by a relatively small group of testing critics in the 1950s and then by a mass movement of antiwar activists in the 1960s—migrated to patriotic, military communities. Yet as this mistrust migrated, it also mutated. Radiation activism borrowed from the antiwar movement the revelation that the state could transform bodies into fodder, but it broke with the earlier movement when it came to which bodies were worth grieving. Those who had opposed the war mourned not only the soldiers coming home in body bags, but also the Vietnamese men, women, and children who were killed. The latter were the "collateral damage" that the US government disowned through pseudo-objective, deceptive, and distancing reportage. Antiwar activists thus rejected a nationalist logic that saw American lives alone as worth mourning. Radiation activists moved in the opposite direction. The government's crime, they suggested, was not that it had devalued human bodies in a universal sense, but that it had turned *American* bodies into fodder. Where the antiwar movement had brought questions of moral culpability to the fore, radiation activists were animated by a sense of victimization, at once rooted in the body and reverberating beyond it.

Thus even as radiation sufferers drew on the earlier antiwar movement for inspiration, they distanced themselves from it. They often described themselves as "reluctant activists" whose encounters with illness had left them with no alternative but to embrace an antagonistic stance vis-à-vis the state. They found this new position uncomfortable; it was anathema to their true political proclivities, which ran in the opposite direction. This appeal to reluctant activism simultaneously acknowledged and disavowed the protest culture that had supplied its language and sense of outrage. The motivations of antiwar activists had been specious and self-seeking, radiation sufferers now began to argue, while their own motivations were pure, precisely because their activism had been arrived at only with great ambivalence. The radiation sufferers' repeated claim that they had turned to activism as a last resort drew an implicit line between good and bad activism. The latter embraced radical politics without apology, hesitation, or qualification.

Ultimately, what made the radiation sufferer such a powerful mediating figure was the bodily trauma he or she had sustained. At a moment of political interregnum, this sense of trauma established a homology between somatic and national injury. The injury had not come from an external enemy, but rather from within, which was why it constituted a form of betrayal. The New Left had sought a more self-critical direction for US foreign, military, and economic policies after Vietnam, but the emerging right sought something else: the restoration of a lost patriotism and the reconstitution of national power. This call for restoration took diverse forms throughout the 1970s, including the push for a return to market fundamentalism, the steady drumbeat of law and order, the championing of traditional family values, and the demand for the renewal of the nation's military strength on the world stage. But amid a political realignment, the radiation sufferer provided something indispensable: a sickened, betrayed body that could serve as the proxy for a wounded American nation. This body would surface again at Three Mile Island, the site of the worst nuclear accident in the nation's history.

Chapter Two

THE ACCIDENT AND THE POLITICAL
TRANSFORMATION OF THE 1970s

Accidents can function like X-rays, revealing tears and fissures in the so-cial fabric, subterranean streams and pathways, and structural weaknesses and breaking points. They can also reveal hidden forms of resistance and resilience, including powerful—if also ephemeral—forms of communal solidarity.[1] The Three Mile Island accident functioned in this way. On the surface, it appeared nothing more than a dramatic episode in the history of nuclear power. But it occurred against the backdrop of the political, so-cial, and economic transformations that were underway in the 1970s and that were restructuring late capitalism.[2] The decade witnessed the end of New Deal liberal egalitarianism, the decline of the Keynesian-Fordist wel-fare state, and the beginning of a neoliberal era of financial domination, antistatism, and widening inequality. The crisis at the reactor brought into relief five features of this transformation.

First, it afforded a glimpse into one patriotic, largely working-class com-munity at a moment when its way of life was under pressure. The decline of the auto and steel industries, the shift to corporate agriculture, the pro-liferation of service and information-based work, the rise of the two-earner family, the influx of women into wage labor, and the growing dominance of the Sunbelt: all of these upheavals were upending the lives of workers and farmers throughout the Northeast. These transformations eroded the institutions that had undergirded Fordism—the male-breadwinner family, a sanctified domestic sphere, local support networks, and the church. Si-multaneously, feminism and sexual liberation sought to dismantle the gen-der and sexual hierarchies on which those institutions had relied. The Three Mile Island region was more economically stable than other areas of Pennsylvania, but it was very much part of this world-in-transition. Before the crisis at the plant, most residents were Republican Party loyalists, had supported the Vietnam War, and prided themselves on their love of family and country. The accident not only challenged their worldview, but it oc-curred as the region's older Fordist institutions were giving way to a new order dominated by a professional managerial class. These new elites as-signed a crucial role to public relations, the terrain on which much of the drama at Three Mile Island would play out.

Second, the accident illuminated how a growing mistrust of the govern-ment was filtering into patriotic communities by the 1970s. Hostility to-ward the government had been a long-standing, recurring feature of US political culture, of course. But throughout much of the New Deal era, many Americans viewed private corporate power with suspicion and looked favorably to the government for countervailing remedies. This was reversed during the 1970s. In the era of Vietnam, Watergate, and energy shortages, the government itself became an object of public distrust and derision, because it was seen as either deceptive, ineffectual, or both. Com-ing toward the end of a decade in which it seemed that nearly everything had gone wrong, the accident contributed to this reversal. After all, the in-dustry had promoted nuclear power as an essentially risk-free technology, and now, overnight, central Pennsylvanians found themselves confronting the worst accident in the history of the reactor program. As we shall see, while residents would initially blame the accident on the utility, they would later redirect their anger at the state, a shift that captured the broader turn against government in the neoliberal age.

Third, the accident located the *body* at the center of a crisis of authority. At a moment of eroding public trust, both locals and outsiders questioned the official story about what had happened at the plant. That story would prove remarkably consistent. It maintained that however frightening the partial meltdown, it had never endangered public health. Many residents, however, were convinced that both the utility and the state were downplay-ing the accident's severity and that they had suffered latent biological injury. Because it threatened to trigger a radiological health emergency among civilians, in other words, the accident assigned a critical role to the imperiled human body—indeed, the *irradiated* human body—within the political realignment. This body helped give shape to a biotic nationalism that interpreted the key crises of the decade—defeat in Vietnam, the energy crisis, productivity lag, and stagflation—as symptomatic of national decline. Within this nationalism, the nation itself was imagined in biological terms as an enervated body. Simultaneously, a steady attention to the suffering bodies of patriots rerouted a politicization of the body from the 1960s into a conservative politics of betrayal.

Fourth, Three Mile Island made clear that it was the woman's body—and more specifically, the maternal body—that animated biotic nationalism. It revealed how gender was displacing class within US society and politics in the 1970s. The irradiated body that exploded to the surface after the accident was not just any body. Rather, officials singled out three bodies as uniquely endangered: that of the pregnant woman, the young child, and the fetus.[3] As a consequence, the region's conservative, patriotic, white women emerged as central protagonists, articulating not merely a critique of authority, but an ecological, reproduction-centered critique. In public testimonies and private letters, mothers who lived near the island voiced their suspicion that the accident had induced infertility, miscarriage, and stillbirth, raised the risks of birth defects among their babies, and transformed their sons and daughters into carriers of "damaged genes" that might one day be transmitted to their own offspring.[4] For nuclear engineers, the TMI accident constituted a technological crisis. For the state, it constituted a crisis in governance. For the utility that operated the plant, it constituted a public relations crisis. But for the women who lived near the plant, the accident constituted a crisis in reproductive futurity. At Three Mile Island, then, the figure of the unborn would reappear, where it tied the earlier atomic age to the emergent ecological one, highlighted the centrality of reproduction to the realignment, and revealed how fears of biological injury were becoming knitted into the cultural fabric of one patriotic community.

Finally, the accident offers a vital clue as to how conservatives were able to establish hegemony after 1980; the new conservatism was shaped in part by an ecological consciousness that could not in itself be described as left or right. This consciousness had its origins in dissent, but over the 1970s, it pivoted rightward. The political history of the 1970s was thus one of creative appropriation as much as polarization. From the antiwar movement and the New Left, conservatives borrowed a distrust of state authority. From feminism, they took the idea that women's bodies were sites of political contestation. From evangelical Christianity and Catholicism, they appropriated a "grammar of life" that they operationalized not merely to curtail abortion rights, but to condemn the nuclear industry for making bodies into fodder—or, as local residents put it, turning them into "guinea pigs." By the late 1970s, insights about bodily illness and disposability that had originated on the political left were being folded into the conservative counterrevolution.

THE ACCIDENT

What occurred at TMI Unit Two in the early morning hours of Wednesday, March 28, 1979, was what nuclear engineers call a "loss of coolant accident." A relief valve that was supposed to close remained open, permitting large amounts of water—normally used to cool the plant's core—to escape. For several hours, operators did not realize that the valve was open, and as the containment building lost coolant, temperatures and radiation levels began to rise. If the reactor core was exposed for too long, it could overheat and eventually melt, releasing radioactive material into the environment. The most dangerous potential consequence of the accident was a meltdown, popularly known as "the China Syndrome," a term that referred to the possibility that reactor core materials could dissolve and bore through the earth. Short of that, the accident posed several immediate threats to public health. First, because of damage to the reactor's core, there was a radiation leak in the plant's auxiliary building. Second, beginning on Wednesday morning, plant operators began releasing steam into the air that, because of a leak in the primary cooling system, contained detectable amounts of radiation. Third, on Thursday, plant operators discharged water containing small concentrations of xenon, a short-lived radioactive gas, into the Susquehanna River. Finally, by Friday, a large hydrogen bubble had developed in the top of the core's container, making it difficult for workers to bring down the core's temperature and stoking fears of an explosion.[5]

This was an accident that was never supposed to have happened. As we have seen, as orders for nuclear plants peaked in the mid-1960s, the AEC had waged an ambitious public relations campaign to convince Americans that nuclear technology was not only safe, but essentially accident-proof.[6] In the winter of 1966, when the utility company Metropolitan Edison (a subsidiary of the General Public Utilities Corporation) announced its plan to build two reactors on Three Mile Island, it embarked on its own public relations campaign. The utility published brochures that reassured residents that the plant posed no danger, contending that the amount of radiation released from the plant during normal operations would be negligible and that radiation was a benign product of nature. The company opened a public observation center on the island, where visitors could acquire an elementary understanding of nuclear power, and local officials and opinion-makers were routinely invited to tour the plant.[7] In 1975, a year after the opening of TMI Unit One, these publicity efforts were bolstered by the release of the Rasmussen Report, an NRC-sponsored study that concluded that a citizen was more likely to be killed by a meteor than by a reactor accident.[8] The report reflected a culture of overconfidence that pervaded the industry throughout the 1960s and 1970s. As the NRC's director of nuclear reactor regulation, Harold Denton, later recalled, "within the NRC, no one really thought you could have a core meltdown. It was more a Titanic sort of mentality. This plant was so well designed that you couldn't possibly have serious core damage."[9]

This institutional overconfidence trickled down to the local community. Robert Reid, the mayor of nearby Middletown, remembered that "Everyone was assured by the federal government and by Met-Ed that this plant was safe, and there would never be an accident."[10] One survey found that 75 percent of the local population had been either neutral or positive about TMI before 1979. This is not to suggest that there had been no resistance. By the early 1970s, two statewide environmental groups, Citizens for a Safe Environment and the Environmental Coalition on Nuclear Power, had declared their opposition to the planned plant.[11] In 1977, three years after the opening of Unit One and a year before Unit Two began operations, members of the local community formed TMI-Alert (TMIA) to voice safety concerns.[12] But despite some protest, the community had welcomed the plant. As Carol Pfeiffer, a fifty-three-year-old grandmother who could see the towers from her bedroom window explained, "I don't think hardly anybody in town realized the danger before the accident. We were just plain stupid about it. We didn't understand. We were so pleased about the prosperity it brought to the town."[13]

The community's confidence in the plant was a product of the nuclear industry's promotional efforts, but it also took shape against the backdrop of the political economy of south central Pennsylvania in the 1970s. With an economy that combined agriculture with manufacturing, tourism, medicine, and government, the Susquehanna Valley was made up of rural landscapes dotted with small towns. In contrast to other parts of the state, devastated by the precipitous decline of the steel industry, the area largely weathered the deindustrialization of the 1960s and 1970s.[14] Some people worked at Bethlehem Steel in Steelton (located ten miles north of the island), but there were other sources of employment. The largest city, the state capital of Harrisburg, provided government jobs. Penn State University's Hershey Medical Center, a medical hub, was just over ten miles from the island. Tourists flocked to the chocolate factory in Hershey and to the Pennsylvania Dutch Country. Lancaster County, located south of the reactor, had some of the richest farmland in the nation. Because of the diversity of the economy, the region had a stable population and lower unemployment rates than the state as a whole.

Still, just as in many parts of the industrial northeast, people worried about whether the region could sustain itself as the country's economic center of gravity shifted toward the Sunbelt. In November 1964, the Department of Defense announced that it was closing Olmstead Air Force Base, a major employer in the area. When Met-Ed went public with its plans for Three Mile Island two years later, residents predicted that the plant would help fill the void. Once in operation, the plant would be a modest employer, providing only about five hundred jobs. But in the short term, the plant required an army of builders and construction workers. The plant was also seen as a cleaner, healthier alternative to an old coal-fired plant in Middletown that dumped soot and dust over the town's cars and front porches. In addition, Met-Ed promoted the plant as an antidote to rising energy costs. Although the electricity produced by the plant would be outsourced to other parts of the state, it would benefit local residents by keeping utility costs down. Thus as employer, source of tax revenue, nonpolluter, and provider of low-cost electricity, the plant appeared to be a boon for the local community.

The community's faith in the plant also reflected the extent to which the area had remained largely—although not entirely—insulated from the social, political, and cultural upheavals of the 1960s and 1970s. Dauphin

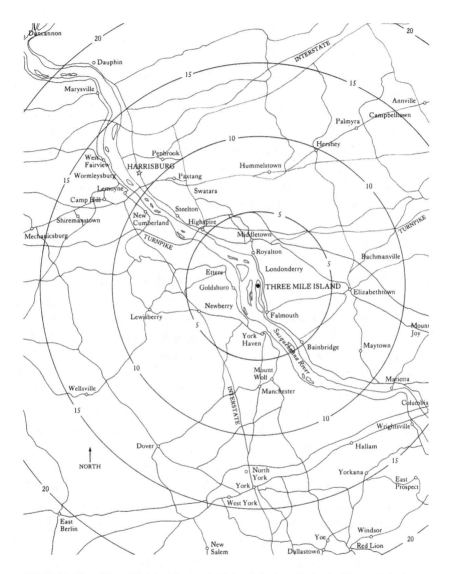

FIGURE 2.1. Map of Three Mile Island. Reprinted with Permission from *The People of Three Mile Island*. Copyright Held by Robert Del Tredici. Courtesy of Robert Del Tredici.

County, where TMI was located, had a predominantly white, rural population.[15] Many of the families who lived in the towns and farms near the
plant could trace their ancestry back to the German and Scotch-Irish immigrants who had settled the region in the mid-eighteenth century. Susquehanna Valley was a Republican Party bastion in the state, and the people
who lived there were politically and socially conservative, possessing a
paradoxical worldview that combined patriotism and respect for authority
with an indigenous folk culture of suspicion. Harrisburg journalist Paul
Beers described the culture this way: "For two centuries the Harrisburg
area had an old-world Dutch hypersensitivity to fear and rumor."[16] Yet this
culture of suspicion coexisted alongside a collective deference to authority.
One syndicated columnist went so far as to declare the region around TMI
"the confidence in authority capital of the country."[17] Many local residents
were also religious Christians. Dauphin County alone was home to 130
Catholic, Evangelical Lutheran, and United Methodist congregations.[18]

Of course like any place dominated by conservatism, there were pock-
ets of dissent. There had been some antiwar mobilization in the cities of
Lancaster and Harrisburg, as well as on the college campuses that dotted
the region. And the antinuclear movement had established a foothold in
the area by the early 1970s. Local residents would also have been familiar
with the Catholic radical pacifist tradition. In 1972, priest and antiwar activist Philip Berrigan, along with six others, was charged with twenty-three
counts of conspiracy, including plans to raid federal offices, bomb government property, and kidnap national security advisor Henry Kissinger.
Their trial was held in the Pennsylvania capital, where the accused—who
came to be called the Harrisburg Seven—were acquitted of all charges.
Thus the region had not been wholly sequestered from the upheavals of the
era. But before the accident, the patriotic men and women who lived near
the plant were loath to question either the veracity of the utility company
or the effectiveness of government safeguards regarding nuclear power. As
one Middletown resident ruefully observed of his neighbors, "They think
everything the government says is the gospel, Middletown people. Wave a
flag in front of them and they'll march off with you anywhere."[19] Confidence in the nuclear industry, the hope that the plant would secure the
region's economic viability, and a homegrown conservatism were all knitted into the Cold War culture of dissociation, which began to unravel as
the coolant flowed out of the reactor core.

If there were a single word to describe the first forty-eight hours of the accident, it would be "confusion." The confusion began in the control room during the first minutes when over one hundred alarms went off simultaneously. Without a mechanism for turning off less important alarms in order to concentrate on the crucial ones, operators quickly became overwhelmed by the control panel. Multiple, redundant safeguards were built into the reactor, but these safeguards had the unintended consequence of bombarding operators with too many signals, increasing the likelihood of human error. This made Three Mile Island a paradigmatic case of what Charles Perrow calls "normal accidents"—accidents that emerge out of the failures and vulnerabilities inherent in any complex technological system.[20] As one operator later told the Kemeny Commission (appointed by President Carter to investigate the accident): "I would have liked to have thrown away the alarm panel. It wasn't giving us any useful information."[21] Plant operators had received extensive emergency training, but they found themselves blindsided. "We did not have a procedure to cover these conditions," recalled Edward Frederick, who was there that morning. "We had no guidelines by which to operate."[22]

The confusion inside the control room soon migrated beyond the plant. Met-Ed first contacted the Pennsylvania Emergency Management Agency (PEMA) at 7:02 on Wednesday morning, three hours after the problems began, but immediately after the crew declared an emergency. Within twenty minutes, PEMA officials had contacted the state's Department of Environmental Resources (DER), as well as the Civil Defense coordinators for Dauphin, Lancaster, and York counties. Between 7:45 and 9:00, PEMA director Oran Henderson called the governor and the lieutenant governor, the NRC was notified, and it relayed the news to the White House. At 9:02, the first AP bulletin reported a general emergency at Three Mile Island, and at 10:55, the governor's office held its first press conference about what was then being called an incident.[23] "Everything is under control. There is and was no danger to public health and safety," William Scranton, the state's lieutenant governor, told reporters.[24] Scranton then explained that Met-Ed had been monitoring the air in the plant's vicinity, and while there had been a small radiation release, there had been no increase in normal radiation levels in the area. While reassuring, his statement provoked a troubling question: Where was the Department of Environmental Resources, the state agency responsible for radiation monitoring? When this question was posed to William Dornsife, a nuclear engineer who worked with the DER's Bureau of Radiation Protection, he answered that the DER lacked mobile monitoring equipment and was relying on Met-Ed's readings. Indeed, the DER did not even have the legal authority to enter the plant.[25] However calm in tone, this first press conference revealed the disturbing extent to which officials were reliant on the utility for information about a crisis that had potentially serious implications for public health.

Over the next two days, the state's dependence on Met-Ed emerged as a problem, as the utility issued statements that were contradictory, vague, and overly optimistic. As fragmentary information traveled from the utility to the state to the NRC and back again, local residents were subjected to an unnerving game of telephone. Met-Ed first reported that there had been "no recordings of significant levels of radiation" outside the plant, but clarified a few hours later that in fact there had been a "low level release of radioactive gas beyond the site boundary." When Met-Ed vice president Jack Herbein arrived at the island on Wednesday morning, he minimized the situation, describing it as a "minor fuel failure." Later that day, he clashed with state officials over the utility's decision to vent radioactive steam to relieve pressure on the damaged reactor. Officials expressed anger that they had not been consulted, and the exchange left them convinced that Met-Ed could not be trusted.[26] On Wednesday afternoon, Scranton expressed his growing frustration with the utility, telling reporters: "This situation is more complex than the company first led us to believe. . . . The company has given you and us conflicting information." While he still believed that there was no immediate danger, Scranton now acknowledged that detectable amounts of radiation had been released.[27]

Worries intensified over the next forty-eight hours. As of Wednesday night, conditions seemed to be improving as operators worked to cool the core. At a press conference, NRC representative Charles Gallina announced that there was no significant core damage (a groundless claim) and predicted that the reactor would be in a cold shutdown within a day.[28] On Thursday morning, Jack Herbein and Met-Ed president Walter Creitz exuded confidence, telling television viewers that the radiation releases were too small to pose a danger. As Herbein snapped to an ever-growing press corps, "I can tell you that we didn't injure anybody through this accident, we didn't overexpose anybody, and we certainly didn't kill a single sole [sic]." The levels of off-site radiation were "absolutely minuscule."[29] But later that day, industry critic Ernest Sternglass flew into the area and announced that his portable monitor showed radiation levels fifteen times the norm. He urged pregnant women and young children to leave immediately.[30] That afternoon, Governor Richard Thornburgh spoke publicly for the first time about the accident, assuring residents, and explicitly pregnant women and children, that there was no cause for alarm.

But by Thursday night there were two more worrisome developments. First, as operators struggled to bring down temperatures, they realized that the damage was far more extensive than anyone had first grasped. Bringing the reactor to a state of cold shutdown was not going to be as simple as the utility had predicted. Second, officials learned that Met-Ed had discharged slightly radioactive water into the Susquehanna River earlier in the day.[31] The utility had asked NRC regional officials for permission to dump the wastewater, which was granted on the grounds that the water's radiation levels remained within regulatory limits. But both Thornburgh and upper NRC officials were angry when they learned of the decision. They feared that there would be an impression that the company had endangered public health. Indeed, neither the press nor those living downstream from the plant had been informed that the utility was releasing contaminated liquid into a river that provided drinking water and fish to local communities.[32]

By Friday both plant conditions and communications were deteriorating. Early that morning, operators vented radioactive gas out of the reactor's auxiliary building as a way to relieve pressure, and a helicopter showed a very high radiation reading.[33] The emission had been planned, but both PEMA and the NRC erroneously thought that the crippled reactor was now leaking dangerous amounts of radiation into the air. Because of this faulty information, the NRC headquarters in Bethesda advised Governor Thornburgh to issue an evacuation order. For the first time, civil defense authorities in Dauphin, Lancaster, and York counties were informed that an evacuation was likely, and Dauphin County's civil defense director announced on local radio that an evacuation might be necessary. But both Thornburgh and officials at the plant were confused by the evacuation recommendation, which seemed unwarranted based on the reactor's relatively stable condition. To Thornburgh, who was ultimately responsible for the evacuation decision, the recommendation seemed rash, even reckless. The confusion captured the difficulties involved in gathering consistent information, sustaining clear lines of communication between those who were working on- and off-site, and coordinating a coherent response to the accident. As NRC chairman Joseph Hendrie complained, "We are operating almost totally in the blind: his [the governor's] information is ambiguous, mine is nonexistent and—I don't know—it's like a couple of blind men staggering around making decisions."[34]

On Friday came another dire concern: a large hydrogen gas bubble had developed in the container that housed the core. If workers could not reduce the bubble, they would not be able to cool the reactor. On Friday afternoon, officials began speaking publicly for the first time of a possible core meltdown. At the same time, if oxygen levels rose inside the vessel, the mixing of hydrogen and oxygen could cause an explosion. Central Pennsylvania now appeared to be at risk for the two catastrophes that the nuclear industry had said could never happen: a meltdown and a detonation. Indeed, the NRC had been so unprepared for this second contingency that, during the crisis, commission members had called "all around the country to find out whether a hydrogen bubble could or could not blow up in the reactor."[35] And while a hydrogen explosion was not the same as a weapon detonation, the distinction mattered little to a public that still associated plants with bombs. "The world has never known a day quite like today," Walter Cronkite announced on the CBS evening news that Friday night. "It faced the considerable uncertainties and dangers of the worst nuclear power plant accident of the atomic age. And the horror tonight is that it could get much worse."[36] The fear of an explosion persisted until Sunday night, when Met-Ed and the NRC learned that the size of the bubble had diminished. At that point, five days after the accident, the worst of the crisis appeared to be over.

THE BREAKDOWN OF TRUST

The confusion during the early days of the accident created a serious credibility crisis for Met-Ed. The fact that the company had waited several hours to contact government officials, combined with its early overconfidence about the state of the reactor, left some convinced that the utility was whitewashing what had happened. That theory resonated with the Vietnam War, which had exposed patterns of dissemblance characterized not simply by the deliberate withholding of information, but also by the careful *titration* of information with the aim of emotionally containing the population. Secretary of State Dean Rusk later recalled of the Vietnam era: "We made a deliberate decision not to stir up war fever among the American people. . . . We felt that in a nuclear world it's just too dangerous for an entire people to become too angry. That might push the situation beyond the point of no return."[37] Thus when reporters asked him what Met-Ed was doing in response to the accident, Jack Herbein could retort with impunity: "We have more important things to do than to tell you every little step we take." Such comments fed into a growing suspicion that the utility was engaging in a cover-up.

This cover-up theory resonated not only with the Vietnam War debacle but also with the Watergate scandal, another crisis of authority that had exploded five years earlier. A man from New Jersey described his experience of watching the Watergate hearings in 1973 in a letter to the *New York Times*: "One of the frightening effects . . . is the feeling that we can no longer trust in the reality of our experience. We have witnessed so much façade, contrivance, and deception in our political and economic processes . . . that one has the sensation of living in a kind of movie-set society where the people and the buildings look real but are actually hollow." The most fatal damage inflicted by Watergate, he continued, was that it had undermined the concept of "face value—that reality is what we perceive it to be."[38] The accident was suffused with the same air of unreality, fueled by speculation that those in positions of authority were lying. As Curtis Wilkie, the Washington bureau reporter for the *Boston Globe* recalled: "The guys from Met-Ed looked conniving, looked like people with something to hide. They had the look of Richard Nixon in '74."[39] For the first time, too, local residents had realized how dependent they were on the utility for leveling with them about their own safety. As one man put it, "I believe that we as citizens have been lied to about many things that have happened."[40] Another resident described what he called "a Watergate cover-up feeling," and a twenty-year-old folk singer poked fun at Met-Ed's efforts to downplay what had happened, penning a song with the line: "We're top of the news for the entire week, because of what they call a minor leak."[41]

At a moment when national opposition to nuclear power was growing, then, Met-Ed executives grasped that the accident constituted a public relations crisis of considerable proportions. And if Watergate was on the minds of local residents and reporters, Met-Ed executives were also thinking about the political thriller *The China Syndrome*, released only twelve days before the accident. The film told the story of a reporter and camera-man (played by Jane Fonda and Michael Douglas) who join forces with a plant operator (played by Jack Lemmon) to expose safety problems at a nu-clear power plant in Ventana, California. In the film, the owners are un-ambiguous villains: deceptive, reckless, profit-driven, and willing to resort to violence to hide safety problems. Met-Ed president Walter Creitz later told the Kemeny Commission that he had seen the film before the accident and that it loomed over him as he prepared to talk with reporters: "Because of the credibility gap that developed in *The China Syndrome*, I wanted to be able to tell the news media, the people, exactly what happened." But be-cause "exactly what happened" inside the reactor remained elusive, Creitz could not do this. He instead found himself preoccupied with striking the appropriate tone. "I must admit I was nervous," he told the commission. "I didn't want to make a statement accredited to the company that might have been over-pessimistic as well as over-optimistic. I was concerned about cre-ating panic. At the same time, I didn't want to indicate that everything was in good shape or good hands, and yet looking back at it I guess there were times when we were more optimistic than we should have been."[42] More than anything, Creitz had wanted to distance himself from the film's depiction of the shady company executive who had "tried to hide the facts."[43] But in his eagerness to appear unlike a villain, Creitz ended up resembling one. Met-Ed's vice president Jack Herbein noted the irony. During a congressional tour of the plant soon after the accident, a con-gressman asked Herbein if he had seen the film. Herbein answered that he had. When the representative asked him what he had thought of the film's portrayal of the company's deceitful public relations man, Herbein answered, "I didn't like him at all. . . . But you know, a week later, I was doing the same damn thing."[44]

If Met-Ed had sustained the most serious damage to its credibility, the NRC did not emerge unscathed. The poor communication between the plant, the commission's regional offices, the governor's office, and the Bethesda headquarters demonstrated just how weak the NRC was as a command center during a crisis.[45] TMI was, in the words of NRC engineer Harold Denton, "the most serious accident in the life of the reactor pro-gram," and it had taken the commission by surprise.[46] The combined causes of the accident—mechanical malfunction, design flaws, and human error—had exposed a fallacy built into the Cold War culture of dissociation: the

belief that reactor design could be perfected to the point that it could eliminate human error. As Denton later recalled, there had been a pervasive
belief that machines could be so well designed that they "would not place a
lot of demands on operators."[47] At the time of the accident, there was no
NRC office devoted to the interface between machines and human beings.
It was an oversight that, according to the Kemeny Commission, revealed
"a persistent assumption that plant safety is assured by engineered equipment."[48] More broadly, the accident had punctured a hole in the modern-
izing, Cold War image of a sophisticated, high-end technology. Carolyn
Lewis, who served on the commission, recalled her postaccident tour of
TMI. "I was rather horrified," she testified, "to find we had these large pipes
with rags around them and yellow markings on the floor which said 'Contaminated Water.' I had had an image of a high, clean technology that was
well looked after and well run, and I found something that really, frankly,
looked like the underside of a 100-year-old house that I once owned. . . . It
was not high technology."[49]

The accident also exposed the dependency of elected officials on un-
elected technological experts. From the time he learned about the accident, Governor Thornburgh had sought to create what he called an "island
of credibility" to which citizens could look for reliable advice.[50] But this
proved to be extraordinarily difficult. The poor communication between
the utility, the state, and the federal agencies meant that Thornburgh was
confronted with what he called a "kaleidoscope of signals." Not unlike the
operators in the TMI control room, the governor found himself inundated
with uncoordinated information fragments. As the accident emerged as the
biggest news story of the year, media reports coming into the governor's
office grew alarming. The real problem, as Thornburgh later described it,
was "sifting out fact from fiction, hyperbole from analysis, cant from can-
dor, and guesswork from solid reporting."[51] The challenge was compounded
by the fact that neither the governor nor the lieutenant governor knew
much about nuclear power. Prior to the accident, Thornburgh's only source
of information on the topic was *We Almost Lost Detroit*, a book that
detailed a 1966 accident at Fermi-1, the first commercial breeder reactor in
the United States.[52] Neither Thornburgh nor Scranton understood either
the workings of nuclear reactors or the health risks posed by radiation. "I am
not a nuclear engineer," Scranton responded to reporters when asked to
explain the reactor's alarm system.[53] When Thornburgh was questioned

three days later about why children and pregnant women were more vulnerable to radiation exposure than adults, he answered, "I'm not a medical doctor."[54] Furthermore, Thornburgh did not have the medical resources he needed. Gordon MacLeod, the state's secretary of health, later recalled, "There was not even a book on radiation medicine in the department. Worse yet, the medical library had been completely disbanded two years previously for budgetary reasons. There was no bureau of radiation health in the health department."[55]

Thus the three organizations directly involved in the accident—the utility, the NRC, and the governor's office—appeared unreliable and unprepared. Underlying the confusion was a more elemental problem that captured the opacity surrounding the nuclear issue: no one could see inside the reactor core to assess either the nature or the extent of the damage. Nuclear engineers had relied on instrumentation to gauge the core's temperature, and they could analyze water samples to determine approximate radiation levels. But because both temperatures and radiation levels were so high within the core, the containment building was too dangerous for inspection. Indeed, it would not be until late July 1980—almost sixteen months after the accident—that two engineers, clothed in protective gear and breathing through respirators, would enter the building to get the first look at the core.[56]

The accident thus created a crisis of visibility in which engineers, public officials, reporters, scientists, and the public were hungry for information about something that they could not see. One reporter was reminded of the Attica prison uprising, where "there was a story going on inside [the] walls and you couldn't really see any evidence."[57] This is one hallmark of the Anthropocene. Ecological crises cannot always or easily be captured through visual means. The inability to see the evidence—that is, to see into the damaged core of the reactor—simultaneously intensified the public's hunger for certainty and eroded their confidence in official sources. Meanwhile, as the crisis unfolded, new knowledge workers and public relations specialists arrived on the scene in order to manage it.

INVISIBILITY AND THE EMERGENCE OF BIOLOGICAL CITIZENSHIP

There was a crisis of visibility in a second sense. The most serious threat posed by the accident—the release of radioactive material into the environment—was not detectable to the eye. As the NRC's public affairs officer, Karl Abraham, recalled, "You can't see radiation, you can't smell it, you can't feel it, you don't know when it's coming."[58] Officials, journalists, and residents commented on this dimension of the crisis over and over. In contrast to the dangers posed by natural disasters, the damage from a nuclear accident could not be instantly assessed. Unlike floods, fires, and earthquakes that abruptly upend the landscape and claim lives, the accident left no evident destruction in its wake. One reporter described it as "a continuing drama, but not a drama you could pinpoint—there were no flames, no people dropping like flies."[59] Invisibility could mean ubiquity, exacerbating the fear because the danger could not be quantified. Some equated the risks of living near a nuclear reactor with those of living near a flood-prone river. As one woman reflected, "It's just like the river. I've been through five floods at my cottage on the river across from the plant, and I've always gone back."[60] But most residents felt that the dangers posed by the plant were different from those caused by the flooding of the Susquehanna River during Hurricane Agnes (1972) and Hurricane Eloise (1975) because the release of radiation provided no visual or auditory warning.[61] As one government document put it, the danger was one that "normal body senses are incapable of detecting."[62]

Precisely because radiation eluded sensory perception, monitoring emerged as an urgent task. Initially, it was Met-Ed alone that was tracking radiation releases (a point that would assume significance later as some contended that exposure levels had been higher than the company claimed). But as the seriousness of the accident came into view, officials from the NRC, the Environmental Protection Agency (EPA), the US Department of Energy, the Food and Drug Administration (FDA), PEMA's Bureau of Radiation Protection, and the state's Department of Health and Department of Environmental Resources all began tracking radiation. In the process, the pastoral landscape of south central Pennsylvania was transformed as local residents confronted the possibility that their bodies had become repositories of radiological contamination. One reporter described the scene as something out of a science fiction story.[63] Civil defense coordinators handed out yellow Geiger counters to volunteers, the FDA, Met-Ed, and the NRC placed approximately two hundred thermal luminescent dosimeters within a twenty-mile radius of the plant, the Department of Energy sent up helicopters to take aerial measurements, and respirators were shipped into the area for everyone coming and going from the island. In addition, both the NRC and the state's Department of Health brought in portable detectors for the full-body counting of local residents, officials took samples of soil and milk from farms near the plant and tested them for Iodine-131, residents traveled to nearby Hershey Medical Center to have their thyroids checked, and the FDA ordered the shipment of 259,000 bottles of potassium iodide, which can block the thyroid's absorption of Iodine-131.[64]

Meanwhile, hundreds of news reporters descended on the scene. Because radiation did not discriminate, these reporters became players in the story that they were covering. Journalists wore dosimeters on their lapels and hung Geiger counters from their car windows, editors provided their correspondents with radiation exposure badges, reporters were rotated in and out of the area to protect them from overexposure, and the Associated Press shipped in breathing devices and protective clothing for its staff. As John Emshwiller, an energy reporter for the *Wall Street Journal* recalled, "You feel you were in a crisis, but it was a crisis you couldn't see, and you

FIGURE 2.2. Worker in Gas Mask Driving to Three Mile Island. Reprinted from *Three Mile Island: A Report to the Commissioners and to the Public, Volume I.*

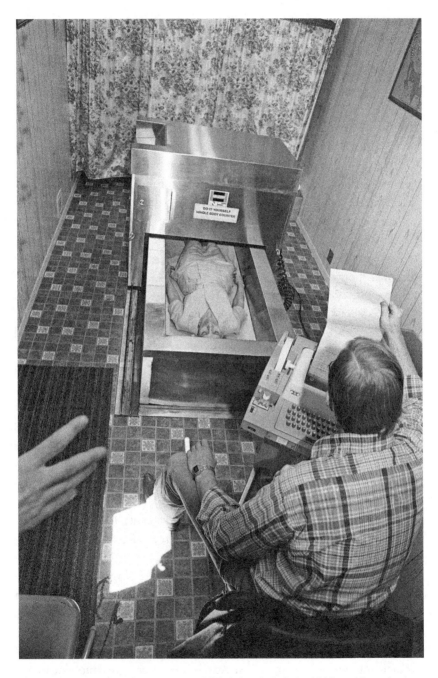

FIGURE 2.3. A Red Cross Volunteer Receives a Full-Body Scan for Radiation, Middletown, Pennsylvania, April 11, 1979. Courtesy of AP Photo/Vathis.

couldn't quite be sure whether you were in a danger or non-danger area. I remember vividly standing in the observation center where the NRC had set up its command post—and I walked over to the river and looked across at this thing, and then the wind changed and it started blowing across at us, and I was thinking, 'what's it doing, and why am I standing here?'"[65] National Public Radio's Nina Tottenberg claimed to know reporters who had spent a year in Saigon and had refused to cover the TMI story because of the danger.[66]

Extensive radiation monitoring meant that both residents and journalists were subjected to protocols normally confined to nuclear industry workers. Every TMI worker who entered a contaminated area of the plant wore a personal dosimeter, a device used to measure the absorbed dose of ionizing radiation. Everyone who worked on the island was also issued a thermal luminescent badge, which gave off radiation-level readings when heat was applied to it.[67] These safety procedures transformed the bodies of workers into objects of routine surveillance. Every industry employee had what was called a radiation bank. In any given year, the worker was permitted to absorb a total of five rems of radiation. If the worker absorbed less than that amount, the balance could be carried forward into the future, just as, in the words of a New York Times article, "an investor on Wall Street carries forward a long term capital loss."[68] Because low-level radiation exposure had become such a routine part of their lives, some plant workers shrugged off the danger. One TMI worker who had been exposed to a large dose of radiation during the crisis boasted to a reporter, "I never felt a thing."[69] Another equated the risks of working in a nuclear plant with those of "a miner going into a coal mine." We're exposed to this all the time," he noted with aplomb.[70]

The same could not be said for most local residents. For them, the accident constituted a breach. They had trusted the safety assurances of the nuclear industry, only to be faced with a near-disaster. They had seen the plant as a source of cheap electricity; overnight, it became ominous. They had to confront the possibility that radiation—something they assumed would remain sequestered within the reactor's containment building—was now entering their farms, their homes, their food supply, and, most frighteningly of all, their bodies. The accident thus transformed local men and women into what anthropologist Adriana Petryna calls "biological citizens," that is, citizens whose relationship with the state is mediated by a set of concerns about biological health and illness.[71] While this citizenship mode becomes more acute during states of emergency, it arguably applies to all citizens in the atomic-cum-ecological age.[72]

Biological citizenship revolves around access to information. In the first days of the accident, the men and women who lived near the plant were hungry for credible reports. Very quickly, both the governor's office (where a citizen information and rumor control center had been established) and local radio stations were deluged with phone calls. At its peak, the rumor control center was fielding several hundred calls an hour.[73] Should people leave their homes? If they did, would they ever be able to return? What were the symptoms of radiation sickness? If there were a meltdown, would the fallout be as bad as at Hiroshima? How long would food and water supplies be contaminated? Rumors circulated. Would a meltdown render the area uninhabitable for one hundred years? How would people retrieve money from their savings accounts? Had radiation contaminated the gasoline supply?[74] For many residents, the greatest fear was that they would leave their homes and not be able to return. One man recalled, "the worst mental anguish was suffered over the weekend—time spent wondering if the situation would be stabilized or if we were going to be faced with a meltdown, have to leave our homes, valuables, and property behind and most likely never return."[75] The fear was compounded by the fact that officials had few answers. As one local recalled, what worried her most was "the fact that they didn't seem to know what was going on. They were the so-called experts, and they couldn't seem to handle it and that's what started getting me nervous."[76]

EVACUATION, THE PANIC MYTH, AND THE REHABILITATION OF THE STATE

The state's ultimate response to the accident propelled pregnant women, young children, and the unborn to the center of the Three Mile Island story. On the third day of the crisis, Thornburgh advised—but did not require—all pregnant women and preschool-aged children under the age of five living within a five-mile radius of the plant to leave the area.[77] How did he arrive at that decision? From the time they first learned of the accident, both Thornburgh and Scranton realized that an evacuation might become necessary. Because of the flooding of the Susquehanna River in 1972 and 1975, local residents were no strangers to evacuations, and civil defense personnel had experience coordinating them. But in the case of a nuclear accident, the issue of evacuation was complicated by several factors. First, the twenty-mile radius around the island was jurisdictionally complex. It encompassed no fewer than seven separate counties, each of which contained dozens of municipalities.[78] In addition, individual counties and municipalities were at different stages of emergency planning at the time of the accident. While the state had a general evacuation plan for people living within five miles of the island, as mandated by the NRC, the nearby towns of Middletown and Royalton lacked completed evacuation plans.[79]

Indeed, the Kemeny Commission later recalled that it found "an almost total lack of detailed plans in the local communities around Three Mile Island."[80] This meant that as the accident was unfolding, local civil defense planners were filling in gaps in preexisting ones or crafting new plans on the fly. At the height of the crisis, the NRC warned that an evacuation of everyone living within the twenty-mile ring might be required. With that warning, officials found themselves planning for a large-scale removal of 650,000 people, thirteen hospitals, and a prison. Like Met-Ed and the NRC, civil defense coordinators were blindsided. As a police officer remembered, "This was something that nobody had ever thought would happen! Nobody was [ready for it], really. They could say they were, but where the hell would the decontamination centers be? What hospitals would treat as many people as were in this area if they were exposed to radiation, to combat the loss of white blood cells? What hospitals in the area would have anywhere from 100,000 to 500,000 pints of blood for transfusion? There were no answers. There is no way in hell that [we] could have been prepared properly to deal with such a large contamination."[81] The state was caught off guard as well. Gordon MacLeod, the state's secretary of health, recalled that Pennsylvania's health department, which lacked a specialist in radiation medicine, had done no planning for this scenario.[82]

Both the jurisdictional complexity of the area and the lack of preparation were obstacles in the way of evacuation, but there was a third complication that gave Three Mile Island its paradigmatic character: the elusive nature of the radiation threat. Radiation exposure would not follow the cartographic path of five-, ten-, and fifteen-mile radial rings around the plant recommended by evacuation planners. If a plume of radiation escaped, its path would depend on wind direction, a simple fact that was nonetheless overlooked in evacuation planning. One man who lived in Carlisle, located approximately forty miles west of the reactor, mocked the notion that radioactive emissions could somehow be contained within a twenty-mile radius. "What are they going to do?" he asked. "Have people stand up on the border with fans and blow it back?"[83] The NRC's Harold Denton, who recommended evacuation at one point, later told the Kemeny Commission that he had not realized the challenges it entailed. It was only after meeting with the governor that he learned how difficult it would be to evacuate areas downwind of the plant. "Their plans weren't set up for downwind areas," he recalled. "They were set up to remove people from certain blocks of property."[84] The realization led Denton to question evacuation as a defense-in-depth measure,[85] and it underscored a point that industry critics had long been making: whatever their claim to the contrary, the state could not protect citizens from a nuclear accident.[86]

But evacuation was complicated by another factor. Governor Thornburgh presumed that it would be accompanied by a panic. He described his dilemma thus: "I had to weigh the *potential* risks of TMI against the *proven* hazards of moving people under panic conditions."[87] The movement of the elderly and the sick, the transport of babies in incubators, and the traffic on highways could all lead to deaths and injuries that Thornburgh hoped to avoid.[88] He was also worried that it would be impossible to confine an evacuation to a circumscribed area. "It is not a big deal if you can control it to a five mile evacuation," he later explained, "but if you can look me in the eye and tell me that nobody within the ten mile, twenty mile, or fifty mile area is going to on their own begin to evacuate . . . I would doubt it."[89] Thornburgh also took no comfort in the region's prior experience with evacuations. As he saw it, in the case of "flood or hurricane or tornado . . . you can always look out and say, 'Well, the river is rising, it's coming up to 10 feet, and when it gets to 20 feet, we will have to move these folks and those folks.'" The TMI accident, in contrast, was "an event that people are not able to see, to hear, to taste, and to smell."[90] He assumed that the invisibility of the accident, coupled with the elusiveness of the radiation danger, would make local residents more rather than less prone to panic.

The governor's preoccupation with panic can be traced back to the early 1950s, when Cold War civil defense planners predicted that mass panic would ensue in the event of a nuclear attack.[91] According to one planner who served under President Eisenhower, panic prevention was *the* primary goal of 90 percent of all emergency measures developed under the purview of civil defense.[92] Thornburgh's predictions of public panic thus indexed the extent to which the emotional management of the population—indeed, the *containment* of emotional volatility—had been incorporated into Cold War visions of civil defense. What is more surprising than Thornburgh's assumption is that state officials pushed back against it. PEMA director Oran Henderson openly disagreed with Thornburgh. "I tried to discourage the Governor in this aspect," he recalled. "I've been able to find no authoritative documentation of any of the surveys that have ever been taken or the studies that have ever been made since the British evacuated over one and a half million of their children on the first, second, and third of May in 1939. And then two million Londoners voluntarily evacuated. I know of no incidents of this kind of mass panic, and I had to sort of take exception to my Governor on this." An evacuation would be accompanied by frustrations, delays, and accidents, Henderson clarified, but he did not believe there would be a panic.[93] Henderson's skepticism is consistent with disaster research. One of the most robust, consistent findings of the field is that if people are convinced that they can get out of the path of danger, evacuations tend to be orderly, and panic is exceedingly rare. So rare, in fact, that some scholars think the term *panic* should be dropped as a social science concept altogether.[94]

Given this lack of evidence, how do we explain Thornburgh's fears? In part, what has been called the panic myth allowed Thornburgh to reassert the state's authority at a moment when it had been severely compromised. We may recall how disempowered Thornburgh was during the first two days of the accident. He knew little about nuclear power, had no idea what was going on inside the reactor, possessed no real knowledge about the threat posed by radiation, and was struggling to assess the credibility of conflicting information he was receiving from Met-Ed, the NRC, and the press. In this context, Thornburgh drew a distinction between the "potential" risks posed by the reactor and the "proven" risks associated with evacuation. If he was unsure of how to protect citizens from the reactor, he could at least protect them from themselves. He could serve as a protector at the precise moment that the accident had called into question the state's capacity to keep citizens out of harm's way. At a time when the state was increasingly desperate for sound information and the local population was displaying remarkable equanimity, the panic myth created an imaginary dichotomy between a desperate, out-of-control population and a sober-minded state.[95]

But Thornburgh's actions also evoked a chivalric ideal of the state as a protector of women, children, and the unborn. Thornburgh insisted that his advisory to pregnant women and preschool-aged children was precautionary and that there was no imminent threat. But if the situation did deteriorate, those citizens most vulnerable to radiation exposure needed to be removed from the path of danger. Thornburgh issued the advisory on the recommendation of NRC chairman Joseph Hendrie, who had reported that morning that conditions on the island remained worryingly unclear. "If my wife were pregnant and I had small children in the area," he told Thornburgh, "I would get them out because we don't know what is going to happen."[96]

The governor's advisory, in combination with Sternglass's warning the day before, incited pregnant women to take action. On Thursday, worried expectant mothers began calling local radio stations, state agencies, and hospitals to find out if their fetuses were endangered. The calls were so persistent that one regional NRC administrator quipped, "We have heard from every pregnant woman in the area."[97] Photojournalists began documenting young mothers and children fleeing their homes. Appearing in newspapers and on television screens throughout the country, these images would soon take on iconic status: mothers holding towels and blankets over their children's faces in a makeshift effort to protect them from radiation exposure; pregnant women temporarily housed in the mass care centers established by the Red Cross; and mothers loading their children into station wagons and driving away, with the reactor's towers looming ominously in the distance. Although by all accounts the voluntary evacuation was orderly, there were a few reports of mothers frantically picking up their children from the region's schools on their way out of town.[98] One young mother recalled, "I had seen cars, bumper to bumper, filled with women and children leaving the countryside."[99]

Why did the bodies of women, children, and fetuses take on such a freighted symbolic role? The answer lies with the enduring centrality of women, children, and the unborn to the formation of political community and perceived threats to security. Throughout the nation's history, the policing of community boundaries was justified on the grounds of defending the bodies of women and children. From Puritan captivity narratives that

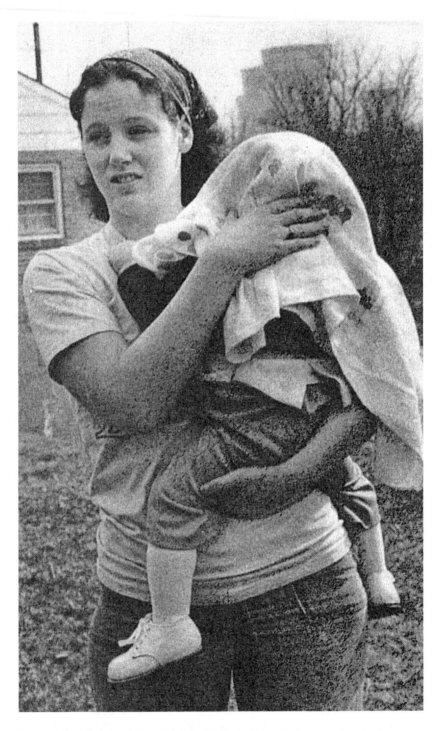

FIGURE 2.4. Mother with Child. Reprinted from *Washington Post Special Report*. Courtesy of Dick Thornburgh Papers, University of Pittsburgh Special Collections.

FIGURE 2.5. A Neighbor Helps a Mother and Child Evacuate Three Mile Island Area, March 30, 1979. Courtesy of AP Photo/Paul Vathis.

pitted the fates of colonial Christian women and children against hostile native peoples to the displacement of indigenous communities along the Western frontier, and from the white male chivalric ethic of the antebellum South to the breadwinner family ideal of the Cold War, the ostensible protection of white, Anglo-Saxon women and children aimed to establish who belonged (and who did not) to any given community. With its steady preoccupation with the safety of women and children, the accident tapped into these earlier moments of perceived community endangerment. But it modified them by introducing a new threat that could not be so easily projected onto an imagined foreign enemy: the debased, contaminated environment created by the Cold War atomic state itself. At Three Mile Island, then, the bodies of mothers and young children captured what was most deeply at stake in the debate over nuclear power, the question of generational continuity.[100] These bodies evoked questions about the destructiveness of the US global order that had surfaced with the bombings of Hiroshima and Nagasaki, but that had remained largely suppressed throughout the Cold War.

But the symbolic centrality of women and children at Three Mile Island also captured how working-class identity was dissolving and being displaced by identities along axes of gender, race, and sexuality in the 1970s.[101] In rural Pennsylvania, as elsewhere, the New Deal–era category of the industrial working class was melting away in an increasingly globalized, financialized, and service-based economy. This new economy would require a neoliberal workplace that was at once more inclusive and less equal, one in which, according to historian Thomas Borstelmann, the "clearly artificial hierarchies of race and sex" would be replaced by "a new hierarchy considered more natural: the sorting out of people in what were seen as their natural socioeconomic levels by the operation of the free market."[102] At the same time, new political fault lines appeared that could not be reduced to the struggle between capital and labor: between a "silent majority" that retained a commitment to patriotism and militarism and an antiwar left that demanded a total reappraisal of American power; between feminists and gay liberationists who expanded the bounds of political citizenship and those who sought the restoration of the traditional, heteronormative family; between a black freedom movement that called for political and economic justice and those who fought to maintain their hold on racial power; and between Americans who saw the *Roe v. Wade* decision as a linchpin of women's equality and others who saw it as a declaration of war on the innocent. The eviction of class from the political field by the end of the decade helps make sense of why an accident that might have once been interpreted primarily as a crisis of workplace safety instead came to center on women and children.

This shift away from class did not go uncontested, however. On the contrary, after the accident, unionists fought to remind the public that it was nuclear plant workers who were most imperiled by lax safety standards. Both rank-and-file union members and union leaders traveled to an antinuclear demonstration in Washington, DC, in May 1979, where the International Association of Machinists president William Winpisinger reminded the crowd, "Workers slowly die of radiation making nuclear fuel and operating nuclear power plants. Workers transport the fuel. [They] are frontline economic, health, and safety casualties whenever nuclear accidents and mishaps occur."[103] At a New York City rally the following September, David Livingston, speaking on behalf of the United Auto Workers, observed that there were "growing forces in the labor movement ready to join hands in this fight against nuclear power."[104] And on the two-year anniversary of the accident, the Labor Committee for Safe Energy and Full Employment organized a commemorative protest march in Harrisburg that was sponsored by nine international unions.[105] The labor movement's growing opposition to nuclear power was propelled by two forces: concern with workplace safety issues and worry that nuclear power would displace other energy industries, and coal in particular, thus eliminating jobs. Both concerns made unionists key players in the struggle over nuclear power, yet their role was often obscured or overlooked as media outlets identified women and children as the frontline victims of the radiological threat.

The displacement of class by gender placed the latter at the center of a contest between two US nationalisms in the 1970s. The great feminist strides of that decade—heightened awareness of sexism, the growing demand for women's equality, the democratization of the workplace—were assimilated into a vision of the nation as a land of individual opportunity becoming ever more meritocratic and inclusive. This was a postfeminist adaptation of a long-standing civic nationalist tradition that championed American pluralism. But women, and in particular mothers, also loomed large in an alternative biotic nationalism that figured the nation as a living body (in which soil, land, air, and water functioned as dynamic systems), as possessing a lifecycle, as capable of death and rebirth, and as dependent for its survival on a protected healthy sphere of reproductive continuity. This was an adaptation of an earlier exclusionary ethnonationalism that relied on spatial metaphors of boundaries and borders. Biotic nationalism shared certain features with ethnonationalism, but it relied primarily on a temporal conception of the nation. This conception took hold on the political right in the second half of the 1970s, as conservatives perceived a nation weakened, even existentially threatened, by military defeat, economic recession, energy shortages, and challenges to patriarchal authority. The accident amplified their collective sense that older systems of order were no longer working, while affirming that gender was at the center of the story. At Three Mile Island, women, children, and the unborn emerged as the avatars of a biotic nationalism that imagined the nation as a living, organic entity. The crisis at the plant endowed this nationalism with something new: an ecological dimension.

Simultaneously, the preoccupation with women and children at Three Mile Island aimed to rehabilitate the state's authority. Despite the fact that the vast majority of evacuees chose to stay with family and friends during the crisis, widely reproduced photographs of pregnant women and children camping out at a mass care center implied that the state was tending to its most vulnerable citizens.[106] As Thornburgh recalled after touring the center, "this was a stark reminder of the responsibility of governing." Walking through the stadium, he saw "young children, mothers carrying babies, and their bewilderment and confusion over a technology they clearly didn't understand, seeking reassurance that the situation had been handled."[107] A photograph of an African American toddler sleeping peacefully under a Civil Defense–issued blanket seemed to suggest that the state had risen to the occasion.

Governor Thornburgh lifted the evacuation advisory for pregnant women and preschool children on April 9, twelve days after the start of the accident. By then, the hydrogen bubble had disappeared, temperatures in the core had gone down, and the reactor was in stable condition. By the time the crisis passed, approximately 144,000 people who lived within fifteen miles of the plant had left the area, almost 40 percent of the total population. Thornburgh's predictions of panic never materialized, but he had been right about one thing: residents who lived beyond the plant's five-mile ring evacuated along with those who lived within it.[108] Women had

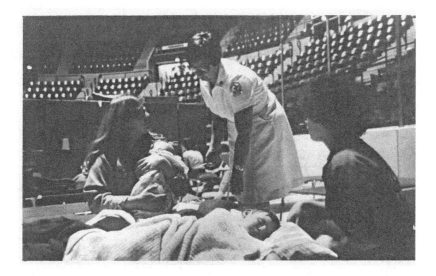

FIGURE 2.6. A Nurse Administers to Women and Children at the Hershey Center, Hershey Park. Reprinted from *Three Mile Island: A Report to the Commissioners and to the Public, Volume I.*

been more likely to evacuate than men, and a full 90 percent of pregnant women living in the area relocated. On April 6, Governor Thornburgh appeared on television and spoke directly to the people of central Pennsylvania. "We sustained, and we continue to absorb, psychological and financial injuries the extent to which may never be fully identified. They're the kind of injuries that will live with us for years—perhaps generations." For Thornburgh, the pregnant woman embodied the community's suffering. "It's not easy for a child-bearing young woman to pack up her belongings, in a rush of fear, and move to the floor of a stadium during the most anxious month of her life. Not all the comfort in the world can erase that memory from this woman's consciousness—nor perhaps even that of her unborn son or daughter."[109]

Beyond his appeal to the pregnant woman as the most apt symbol of the community's ordeal, Thornburgh's statement is meaningful in two ways. First, his emphasis on psychological—as opposed to physical—suffering anticipated a claim that local residents would mobilize in the years ahead as they fought to decommission the reactor, namely, that they were the victims of a psychological trauma that could only be overcome by the closing

FIGURE 2.7. A Red Cross Volunteer Feeds Children at the Hershey Center, Hershey Park, April 4, 1979.
Courtesy of AP Photo/Rusty Kennedy.

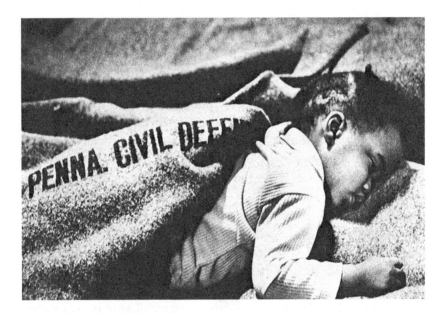

FIGURE 2.8. Child Sleeping Under Civil Defense Blanket, Hershey Center, Hershey Park. Reprinted from
Washington Post Special Report. Courtesy of Dick Thornburgh Papers, University of Pittsburgh Special
Collections.

of the plant. As we shall see, this claim built upon and repurposed a Cold War preoccupation with psychology that would live on in the post–Cold War era. Second, Thornburgh implied that the tumultuous experience of evacuation would be forever seared not only into the memory of the expectant mother, but also into the memory of the unborn. This depiction of the unborn as both innocent victim and active subject had powerful roots in the political culture of the local community and would soon reappear.

COMPETING ASSESSMENTS AND CONSERVATIVE ECOLOGICAL POLITICS

The accident shattered the trust that had held the community together. In the weeks and months that followed, local men and women described a breach that divided their lives into a before and an after. Previously, they trusted the experts to protect them from harm and believed the claim that there would never be a serious accident at the reactor.[110] In the words of one woman, "I was trusting so I stayed. My faith outweighed my fear. I barely knew the plant was there. All I cared about was that it would produce power so cheaply they wouldn't have to read the meter."[111] The accident tipped the scale in the other direction, with fear outweighing trust. Fear was often accompanied by a sense of betrayal, rooted in the conviction that the utility and the NRC had downplayed the seriousness of the accident during the first forty-eight hours. One father recalled that his children had been playing outside, "sucking up radiation—just because those bastards didn't tell the truth about releases."[112] Friday, March 30, as one woman stated, was "the last day in my life I'll ever trust the utility or our government to do the right thing for me."[113]

This erosion of trust hinged on one question: Had residents been exposed to levels of radiation that threatened their health? For federal and state officials, the answer was an unequivocal no. After analyzing data gathered from a range of monitoring devices, officials were convinced that while radiation levels had soared inside the reactor's containment building, they had never reached dangerous levels beyond the plant perimeter. The full-body counting of over seven hundred citizens showed no internal contamination. The USDA and the FDA found only minute traces of radiation in the hundreds of food samples they collected throughout April. The Department of Agriculture detected Iodine-131 in only a small number of the two hundred milk samples they took from farms within an eighteen-mile radius of the plant. And those few samples contained levels three hundred times lower than the level at which the FDA recommended removing cows from pasture. This finding was particularly reassuring because of milk's status as an indicator commodity. As one Department of Agriculture official explained, "milk is one of the first places you are going to see it [Iodine-131]. If you don't find it in milk, you're not going to find it anywhere."[114] The cumulative data was so reassuring that in May 1979 a team of experts projected that statistically, off-site radiation exposure would lead to approximately one case of fatal excess cancer and approximately two cases of excess health effects (including fatal cancer, nonfatal cancer, and genetic injury) among the population living within fifty miles of the plant.[115] They concluded that in the worst conceivable scenario, an individual had received a radiation dosage of less than one hundred millirems, a figure significantly less than the five hundred millirems considered the permissible annual dose.[116]

The community's response to these findings ranged from acceptance to wariness and skepticism to outright rejection. On one end of the spectrum were those who insisted that they were more likely to be killed by an oncoming car than by a nuclear reactor. On the other end were those who accused the state of a whitewash, contending that the monitoring had been inadequate (particularly during the accident's first forty-eight hours) and that radiation exposure had been far worse than officials claimed.[117] But most residents found themselves somewhere in the middle. Neither wholly dismissive of the radiation threat nor convinced of a cover-up, most believed that no one knew what the accident's long-term health effects would be.

This uncertainty stemmed from several sources. First, it emerged out of radiation's dormancy, which made it impossible to assess injury. As one study observed, "people did not know whether they had been harmed; they were aware that the effects of radiation may be delayed many years and are uncertain." If residents chose to leave the area, the study continued, they feared that "they might be taking personal damage with them rather than leaving it behind." Residents thus found themselves confronting an ambiguity that conjured the experiences of veterans who had been exposed to chlorine gas during World War I and Agent Orange during the Vietnam War.[118] As one woman put it, "It's like having those time bombs in your body. Not knowing how long it will be before you pay the price . . . I think we all have, to some extent, that time bomb in our bodies."[119] Industry critics like Helen Caldicott pointed out that it is the "latency period that allows the industry to say no one died at Three Mile Island. We don't expect anyone to have died *yet*."[120] Locals produced posters and T-shirts that read: "I Survived TMI, I Think."[121]

Uncertainty also stemmed from the fact that the scientific debate about low-level radiation remained unresolved. While some scientists continued to insist that low levels of exposure posed little or no health risk (a claim embraced by the nuclear industry), others remained convinced that there was no safe threshold. As Harvard biologist and nuclear industry critic George Wald warned on the second day of the accident, "Every dose of radiation is an overdose. There is no threshold. A little . . . radiation does a little harm, more of it does more harm."[122] Compounding this uncertainty was mounting controversy surrounding disproportionate cancer rates among populations who had lived and worked at nuclear facilities. Only ten days after Thornburgh lifted the evacuation order in Pennsylvania, several members of Congress traveled to Salt Lake City to hear testimony from NTS residents who had either fallen ill or lost loved ones to cancer. Central Pennsylvanians followed the hearings, expressed their identification with downwinders as fellow "guinea pigs," and voiced their fear that they would confront the same fate.[123] Reports coming out of Utah and Nevada raised doubts about whether people could trust the official account of the accident. As an editorial in the *Washington Post* asked: "who could trust a government that in the past had—perhaps knowingly—allowed members of the armed forces and citizens of Utah to be exposed to clearly dangerous levels of radioactivity?"[124] Was this yet another case, asked one mother, "of the traditional cover-up elaborately maneuvered against the local ranchers' complaints in Utah and Nevada?"[125] Growing doubts were apparent in the TMI region, where residents, no longer convinced that they could rely on official reports, began buying their own radiation monitoring equipment and government-surplus Geiger counters.[126] One woman wrote President Carter in July 1979, bitterly informing him that she had given her husband a dosimeter as a Father's Day gift.[127]

Mistrust of the state exacerbated the uncertainty. The governor's precautionary advisory struck some residents as inadequate and arbitrary. People questioned why the governor limited the order to pregnant women and preschool-aged children within the five-mile radius. What if you lived within the five-mile radius but had children who were six, seven, or eight? What if you lived six miles from the plant, but were pregnant or had children under the age of five? A local dairy farmer explained her confusion: "They advised that preschool children and expectant mothers get out of the area but how could they know the radiation wouldn't harm the eight year old son when they were concerned with kids six and under?"[128] And what about women who only learned they were pregnant after the accident? At a public hearing in May 1979, one man recalled a woman who had not evacuated and later learned that she had been pregnant when the accident occurred. "Now she is scared to death that her child is going to be a genetic defect [sic]. Now how are you going to tell her to have that child and take a chance on having a genetically defective child?" The fact that the evacuation was voluntary rather than mandatory placed an unfair decision-making burden on this woman, he maintained. "They didn't demand that we leave," he recalled. "You talk to the mother about it, and she starts crying. She breaks right down, because she doesn't know whether to have this child or whether to have an abortion."[129]

This woman was hardly alone. While state officials were trying to gather credible information about plant conditions and nuclear engineers were attempting to bring temperatures down inside the core, pregnant women in the region were trying to decide whether to have abortions. Obstetricians later reported that throughout late March and early April they had been deluged by phone calls from pregnant women asking whether they should abort their fetuses, and the office of Three Mile Island Alert (TMIA) fielded the same question.[130] One obstetrician recalled that the phone calls were so constant that routine office business was derailed.[131] Although almost all pregnant women evacuated the area by Friday afternoon, they feared that their fetuses had been endangered during the early hours of the accident, when public officials had not yet grasped how bad plant conditions were. The American College of Obstetrics and Gynecologists and the American College of Radiology went so far as to issue a joint press release advising women in the TMI area not to terminate their pregnancies.[132] Meanwhile, local nurses urged pregnant women who were planning on breastfeeding to drink powdered milk until they had determined the extent of radiation exposure.[133]

One might assume that these fears were alleviated in the months that followed. After all, the government's report in May 1979 suggested that radiation releases had been too small to cause fetal injury. A year later, the Pennsylvania Department of Health announced that it had seen no spike in infant mortality, congenital abnormalities, or miscarriages.[134] But because the Three Mile Island crisis had punctured a layered set of beliefs about atomic-era citizenship, the community's fears surrounding reproductive health could not be easily assuaged. In the months and years ahead, women continued to express dread about the accident's health consequences, especially for future generations. Some mothers focused on radiation's carcinogenic effects, wondering whether their children would one day get radiation-induced cancers. A mother of a nine-month-old girl and an eight-year-old boy who lived a mile and a half from the plant asked state officials if her children "are going to be alright or are they going to develop cancer or leukemia as young adults?" She recalled that her son had asked her if he was going to get cancer and die. "What do I tell him?" she wondered.[135] Another mother had decided to have a second child after the accident because she wanted to ensure that her son would have a sibling who could serve as a donor if he eventually developed a radiation-induced cancer.[136]

Other women feared that their outwardly healthy children had sustained genetic damage that might one day manifest in children of their own, a fear that was fueled by reports of mutations among animals. As local dairy farmer Jane Lee reported at a public hearing in May 1979: "We are experiencing problems in reproduction. We are experiencing problems with fowls. We are experiencing mutations. The young animals seem to be the most vulnerable—rabbits, cats. The newly born of any size seem to be very vulnerable, including the calves." Lee went on to detail the devastating human toll. Afraid of the accident's future effects on pregnancy and childbearing, young women in her community had told her, "I can't have any children now," or "I'm thinking about having my child aborted." "This, to me, is a horrible situation, because I am a woman," Lee declared. "I have four children and I know what it means and how a woman feels to reproduce. This is her highest achievement and to be denied this achievement, to me, is a horrendous prospect."[137] Local women took seriously the warning that ionizing radiation was most damaging "to future unborn generations."[138] One mother queried about her children: "are they going to have damaged genes that could cause them to have defective children?"[139] Another instructed her daughter to warn whomever she married that she had lived near the reactor at the time of the accident. "Isn't it terrible," she asked, "to have to worry about damage to unborn children from that monstrous plant?"[140] Several women told the commission that the most searing aspect of the accident was the question their daughters had asked in its wake: "Will I still have healthy, normal children someday?"[141] The National Institute of Mental Health interviewed over three hundred mothers who lived near the plant and found that, despite official reassurance, almost 43 percent of them believed that the accident would unleash health problems in future generations.[142]

These fears projected the invisibility of radiation onto an indeterminate future. While the accident left no visible signs of damage, many local women suspected that it would wreak generational havoc by triggering runaway mutations. For this betrayal, they blamed both Met-Ed and the state. One fifty-eight-year old woman who lived near the plant explained that the accident had shattered her trust in both the utility company and public officials: "I don't believe anything they say because they lied to us in the first place." But her anger was on her grandchildren's behalf. "I've lived my life, but I'm worried about my grandchildren." One of her grandsons lived across from the plant, and she worried about him constantly.[143] Another woman who lived eight miles from TMI told a reporter that there was always a question in the back of her mind: "In twenty years, will it affect my children?"[144] In May 1979, one local woman wrote a letter to the Kemeny Commission in which she explained that she had always had faith in government leaders and what she termed "so called professionals." But the accident changed that: "after this monster was released on us all I have is cynicism and mistrust." Since the accident, she continued, "I live in dread of the future for my two teenage children." She ended with a warning: "The tyranny of forever learning by trial and error will cost us our lives."[145]

This was patriotic body politics, but now centered on women and children. Patriotic body politics had often been mediated through men's relationship to the military. Narratives recounting the suffering of injured and sickened military men indicted the state for having turned its back on those most willing to sacrifice on its behalf. The accident rerouted this insight from warfront to home front, from the martial arena to the familial one, and from men to women. At Three Mile Island, patriotic body politics centered not on the debilitated bodies of male warriors, but on the threatened reproductive female body, the child's body, and the fetal body. More than any other constituency, it was mothers with young children who expressed both skepticism toward the official claim that the accident had done no harm and fear that radiation exposure had imperiled their reproductive futures. At Three Mile Island, patriotic body politics *became* women's reproductive politics.

As a consequence, the unborn displaced the soldier as the central animating figure. The unborn, already made more legible during the postwar years, became even more charged in the 1960s and 1970s, as advances in obstetrics led to both unprecedented levels of visual information about the fetus and growing vigilance surrounding fetal health. In the early 1960s, ultrasound exams were introduced as a routine obstetrics practice. In April 1965, *Life* magazine published "Drama of Life Before Birth," a sixteen-page photo-essay by Swedish medical photographer Lennart Nilsson that charted the development of the human fetus. The issue sold eight million copies in its first four days on newsstands.[146] This new, visually mediated attention to the human fetus went hand in hand with the growing perception that it was vulnerable to environmental assault. In 1973 the University of Washington first identified fetal alcohol syndrome as a cluster of physical and mental birth defects associated with the expectant mother's consumption of alcohol, and in 1981 the surgeon general's office issued its first official warning about the risks of drinking alcohol during pregnancy.[147] In 1977 the American Cancer Society used fetal sonogram images to reinforce the warning that smoking endangered public health.[148] If the reactor core at Three Mile Island was concealed from view, the fetus now occupied the inverse position. It was hiding in plain sight.

This casting of the fetus as visible and vulnerable had profound political implications. This was the era of an escalating war over abortion, and Pennsylvania was home to an active grassroots movement against expanding abortion rights. As early as 1969, Pittsburgh activists started People Concerned for the Unborn Child, the state's first prolife group. In 1970 the Pennsylvania Catholic Conference (PCC) launched Pennsylvanians for Human Life, an educational group designed to rally support for abortion restrictions. The PCC adopted the Second Vatican Council's definition of abortion from 1965 as the functional equivalent of infanticide.[149] By the early 1980s several organizations had formed the Pennsylvania Pro-Life Federation, a state affiliate of the National Right to Life committee. Together, these groups put the state on the vanguard of the fight to roll back abortion rights.[150] This was more than a legislative battle. It was a struggle over the question of what constitutes life itself, one that hinged on a new fetal imagery. As one popular prolife slogan put it, "If there were a window on a pregnant woman's stomach, there would be no more abortions."[151] Throughout Pennsylvania, antiabortion activists fought to gain a discursive monopoly over a term—*life*—that appeared to transcend politics altogether.

How did this struggle over abortion shape the community's response to the accident at Three Mile Island? There is no question that it was a salient feature of the Susquehanna Valley's political landscape by 1979, as activists from throughout the state traveled to Harrisburg to meet with legislators and to protest on the steps of the capitol building. The three largest religious denominations in the region —Catholicism, Evangelical Lutheranism, and United Methodism—all condemned abortion (albeit to varying degrees). The Republican Party dominated the area, and by the late 1970s, grassroots activists were trying to make abortion a centerpiece of the party's national agenda. At the same time, it would be wrong to assume based on the conservative Christian complexion of the region that the women who lived near the reactor had a unified or consistent position on the issue. On the contrary, even if they claimed to oppose the practice, a sizeable number of pregnant women considered obtaining abortions when they feared that their fetuses had been harmed from radiation exposure, at least according to local obstetricians' reports about being deluged with phone calls from expectant mothers. If anything, the searing experiences of pregnant women at TMI affirmed rather than undermined the prochoice principle that women should control their reproductive lives.[152]

What is clear, however, is that after the accident, women at Three Mile Island drew on the prolife movement's grammar of sanctified human life and deployed it against the utility that owned the plant, against the government, and—in some cases—against the nuclear industry writ large. As one woman who had been pregnant at the time put it, "I am still unable to forget the total violation I felt when I realized my trust and faith in the Government had been betrayed." She had come to believe that her unborn baby had been imperiled by an industry that was reckless and profit-driven. "Growing inside me was God's most precious gift," she recalled, "and growing outside was an industry that lost sight of that precious life."[153] Her statement evokes what anthropologist Faye Ginsburg identifies as a central prolife motif: "the violation of the boundary of the impregnated womb by male figures representing the profit motive."[154] In the years ahead, local women would mobilize this motif in their fight to decommission the plant. Five years after the accident, a photograph appeared in the *Pittsburgh Post-Gazette* of a woman holding up a protest sign featuring a baby picture. The message beneath read, "Make a Grave for TMI, not my baby."[155] Thus at TMI, a grammar of life appealed to the figure of the unborn, not in the service of rolling back abortion rights but to condemn the profit motive and the state.

Of course, part of why women at Three Mile Island were able to do this was because the unborn had begun its political life as an atomic creation and never stopped being one. Throughout the 1970s, this figure routinely shuttled between the prolife and antinuclear movements. The abortion war was fueled by the horrific image of the fetal body made into trash, but it hardly had a monopoly on that image.[156] Antinuclear activists often portrayed the human fetus as the industry's most vulnerable, voiceless, and defenseless victim. Helen Caldicott carried a baby casket at antinuclear marches—a symbolic act that might have just as easily appeared at a prolife rally.[157] The shadow of endangered or discarded fetal life hung over both movements. This helps to explain why at Three Mile Island, the unborn could play such a capacious, flexible role. It was a symbol of injuries that could play out across long time horizons, a cord that tethered the atomic age to the ecological one, a synecdoche for collective suffering, an accusatory weapon against the nuclear industry, and a political lubricant that eased the transition of some conservative Christians in their turn against nuclear power. The political power of the unborn was decades in the making. Before it animated the abortion war, the unborn had embodied questions about reproductive futurity that haunted the Cold War nation.

Yet there was no question that when women at Three Mile Island spoke of God's most precious gift, they were borrowing rhetoric from the prolife movement. But even as they did so, they drew on the feminist movement, propelled by the view that what happened to women's bodies—including assaults on health from invisible streams of toxicity from a debased environment—had political meaning. But contra feminists who often critiqued the family as a locus of patriarchy, these women positioned themselves as *defenders* of the family. They thereby crafted a hybridized conservative ecological politics in which a prolife championing of the fetus, a feminist attention to the body, and a defense of the traditional family coexisted in sometimes uneasy but unmistakably powerful accord. During the 1950s and 1960s, mothers had cultivated this proto-ecological figure in order to push back against Cold War repression. Now, it would help propel the pendulum toward the political right.

Ultimately, what made this politics *conservative* was that it routed the decade's politicization of the body into an incipient biotic nationalism. This nationalism was structured around the conviction that the United States, while it might have still appeared strong, had sustained a series of wounds over the 1970s that left it weakened, not unlike an irradiated body. These included military defeat in Vietnam, growing dependency on foreign oil, a slowdown in economic productivity, and energy shortages, along with the challenges to patriarchal authority embodied in feminism and gay liberation. As the conservative movement gained momentum, its leaders responded to this perceived weakness by calling for the reinvigoration and restoration of American power, both on the world stage and at home. Meanwhile, the protest movements of that decade had placed the human body at the center of political, cultural, and social revolution. From the women's health movement to the feminist movement against sexual violence, from black power's condemnation of police brutality to the Afrocentric slogan that "black is beautiful," from the gay liberation movement's cataloguing of homophobia's depredations to its demand for sovereignty over sexuality, these movements all identified the body as a site of discrimination and violence *and* as a locus of liberation and pleasure. But conservatives folded the body into a discourse of decline and betrayal, creating a body politics of their own. Bringing together somatic suffering, environmental risk, and national injury, biotic nationalism reinvigorated post-1968 conservatism in a deeply affective way.

At Three Mile Island, women injected something crucial into this new nationalism: the theme of imperiled reproduction and the devaluation of young life. "Nuclear power is downgrading and shortening human life," one local woman told legislators. "We can buy other forms of energy but where are we going to buy a human life?"[158] If nuclear power continued to spread, another wrote to the commission, then "we are as expendable as German Jews."[159] For the subaltern and dispossessed, this insight about expendability was not new. But for the largely traditional, patriotic, white, middle Americans who lived near the reactor, it was the televised Vietnam War that made it tangible. South central Pennsylvania was no hotbed of antiwar mobilization, but its residents had watched as the war remade bodies into fodder. For them, the war revealed that those in power could lie to the public, that the bodies of patriots could be cast aside, and that they could die meaningless deaths. The accident brought these insights home, rerouting them from the martial to the reproductive arena, displacing the soldier for the unborn along the way. As one man pleaded with public officials, the plant should be shut down because "an unborn child is more important than those towers over there."[160] Riffing on the antiwar term *cannon fodder*, TMI residents feared they had been remade into the "radiation fodder" of the nuclear age.

On May 6, 1979, less than six weeks after the accident, a woman named Carolyn Walborn traveled from central Pennsylvania to Washington, DC, to participate in a collective action for the first time in her life: a national antinuclear rally organized by activists who believed that the Three Mile Island accident had been a catastrophe that could turn the public tide against the industry for good. This was her first march, but "if the American Government doesn't wake up," she wrote to the Kemeny Commission, "it will not be my last." She estimated that about half of the seventy thousand marchers were "first timers" like her: "They were concerned Americans. They weren't radicals or nuts." She described her own participation as an expression of her motherhood, her patriotism, her Christianity, and her status as a TMI evacuee. "I marched, as a mother for my children's children; as an American citizen, because I love America, and I would like to see it stop poisoning the people, land, air, water, animals, etc, by the whole nuclear power cycle; as a Christian, because it is spiritually and morally wrong; as a TMI evacuated person with a 17 yr. old & a 19 year old along with my family members who are unfortunate enough to live in Middletown." Walborn concluded the letter by reminding the commission of the trauma sustained by her community. Because no one really knew the effects of low-level radiation, the people in the area did not know whether "they survived without cancers or mutations." She ended by writing in all capital letters: "WE ARE THE GUINEA PIGS."[161] The accident had left behind no death toll or visible destruction in its wake, but rather something else: the specter of future harm. Between 1980 and 1985, as a struggle ensued over the fate of Three Mile Island, this specter would hang over the Valley as residents painted a portrait of an irradiated landscape populated by the mutated bodies of plants, animals, and humans.

Chapter Three

CREATING A COMMUNITY OF FATE
AT THREE MILE ISLAND

On August 8, 1984, Mary Osborn, a mother of two who lived six miles from Three Mile Island, stood on trial in the Dauphin County courthouse. Almost fifteen months earlier, Osborn and nine others had been arrested for blocking traffic onto the island. Osborn justified her civil disobedience on the grounds that the plant, if reopened, would pose a public health threat. Throughout her testimony, she mobilized two strategies to make her case. First, she recalled the accident. The morning of March 30, she had been playing outside with her son when she noticed a metallic taste in her mouth, a burning in her eyes, and a reddening of her skin—all symptoms, she maintained, of radiation exposure. Second, Osborn presented the court with physical evidence of radiological damage to the local landscape. She held up deformed plants she had discovered in her own backyard, including "pinched-looking daisies with two or more heads fused and growing from one stem." As she told the court, "I don't want more radiation from an operating plant, especially when we've already had more than this area can take."[1]

This chapter traces the cultural, social, and political fallout from the accident between mid-1979 and October 1985, when TMI-Unit One resumed operations. TMI-Unit Two had sustained too much damage from the partial meltdown to ever reopen. But during the first half of the 1980s, a struggle ensued over the fate of Unit One, the unit of the plant untouched by the accident. On one side of the struggle were the NRC and General Public Utilities (GPU, of which Met-Ed was a subsidiary). Both expressed confidence in the reactor's safety and wanted it back in operation. On the other side were people like Mary Osborn, who had come away from the accident convinced that the plant should be permanently decommissioned. Over six years, these citizens became politically mobilized, many for the first time in their lives.

The fight to shut down the plant presented them with the same challenge that confronted Mary Osborn in court—how to prove that if reopened, the reactor would threaten public health. Establishing this would not be easy. As we have seen, a constitutive feature of the accident was its invisibility. Whatever damage it had wrought was not discernible to the naked eye. Furthermore, state and federal officials maintained that the amount of radiation released at the time of the accident had been lower than initially feared. How could local residents establish that the reactor was dangerous in the absence of any incontrovertible evidence of injury? Residents attempted to meet this challenge by constituting themselves as a community of fate—that is, a community formed through duress and social emergency.[2] They did this in two intersecting but distinct ways. First, just as Mary Osborn had done in her testimony, they sought to make the accident visible by insisting that, contrary to the official claim, it had wrought physical and biological damage on the people, animals, and plant life of the region. And second, they insisted that they were victims of a psychological trauma that could only be overcome through the shuttering of the plant. Taken together, both arguments advanced a portrait of central Pennsylvania as a locus of deep somatic and psychological injury.

This construction of a community of fate tracked closely what literary scholar Lawrence Buell identifies as a toxic discourse, "an expressed anxiety arising from a perceived threat of environmental hazard due to chemical modification by human agency." This discourse relies on four motifs: a sense of a disrupted pastoral or destroyed Eden, totalizing images of a contaminated world, a morality play between the strong and the weak, and gothic descriptions of deformed bodies and polluted landscapes.[3] This toxic discourse would be operationalized at Three Mile Island, where it would prove politically contradictory. At one level, it reflected how the protest cultures of the 1960s had extended their reach into a pocket of the country where most residents identified as rural, conservative, and traditional. But this same discourse ended up deepening rather than overturning the political conservatism of the region, which remained a Republican Party stronghold. How did this happen? After all, the community's initial response to the accident seemed to hold out other possibilities. At first, many residents had blamed Met-Ed for the crisis and expressed their unease with a privately owned company overseeing a technology that had dire implications for public health. The accident appeared to endorse a core principle of Progressivism and New Deal liberalism, that corporations required strong government regulation and oversight. But between 1979 and 1985, local anger was redirected away from Met-Ed and toward the NRC, the federal agency that would decide whether to reopen the plant. This shift meant that the struggle over the fate of the reactor would be recast from a fight against corporate malfeasance to a fight against federal power. Along the way, core insights from the left were rerouted into an incipient conservative ecological politics that placed psychic trauma and victimhood at the center of a story about an aggrieved local community squaring off against a tyrannical centralized authority. Throughout the 1970s, this same story appeared over and over again as grassroots struggles ensued over property taxes, bilingualism, sex education, zoning, desegregation of public spaces, and busing. But at Three Mile Island, the fight for local control integrated ecological risk into the conservative counterrevolution. Critical to this integration was a shift in the enemy from private corporate power to the state.

RELUCTANT ACTIVISTS AND THE FIGHT TO SHUT DOWN TMI

Between 1980 and 1985, the crisis of authority that first erupted in 1979 came to center on whether the undamaged unit of the reactor should resume operations. At the time of the accident, Unit One had been shut down for routine refueling, and it remained out of commission as officials assessed what had gone so wrong in the reactor core of Unit Two. Not surprisingly, GPU was eager to get Unit One back in operation, as the company had sustained financial damage from the accident and was losing money every day that the plant remained closed. Shortly after the immediate crisis passed, the utility asked the NRC to green light the restart of Unit One, promising to implement any new safety recommendations made by the federal agency. But in June 1979, Governor Richard Thornburgh asked the state's Department of Justice to petition the NRC for a suspension of GPU's operating license, and in early July, the agency complied. The NRC announced that it would hold a series of restart hearings in order to determine the ultimate fate of the reactor.[4]

In May 1985, six years and dozens of hearings later, the federal agency's board voted four to one to allow GPU to return Unit One to service, and the plant reopened in October of that year. TMI had lain dormant over those six years, but in the meantime, local men and women, convinced that the plant posed an ongoing threat, fought to shut it down permanently. Once a symbol of regional prosperity, the reactor had been transformed into a symbol of danger. Rejecting the NRC's and the utility's promises to heed the accident's lessons, residents now maintained that they were no longer willing to incur the risk. As they saw it, the industry had oversold the safety of nuclear technology and had lulled the community into a false sense of security, thus breaking an implicit social compact. As the Dauphin County commissioner told the NRC, "We are just plain folk from central Pennsylvania. We work hard and worship. We parent and play. We aren't hysterical. We are quite sane and our judgment is that we would rather live without TMI."[5]

The six-year fight over the plant activated and mobilized citizens throughout the region. Antinuclear groups like Three Mile Island Action Alert (TMIA) and the Environmental Coalition on Nuclear Power (ECNP) established before the accident saw their membership rolls grow, but residents also launched new organizations. These included the Middletown-based People Against Nuclear Energy (PANE), the Campaign to Stop the Restart, the Newberry Township Steering Committee, Concerned Citizens of Londonberry, the Anti-Nuclear Group Representing York (ANGRY), and the Lancaster-based Susquehanna Valley Alliance (SVA). These groups also formed umbrella organizations like the TMI Coalition, the TMI Public Interest Resource Center (PIRC), and the Stop the Restart Campaign to coordinate their activities, which were extensive and diverse. Citizens went door to door gathering signatures on antirestart petitions, circulated newsletters, launched letter-writing campaigns, and withheld a percentage of their utility bill. Some, like Mary Osborn, trained in civil disobedience and got arrested. They kept the TMI issue in the public eye by publishing letters and editorials, protesting on the steps of Harrisburg's capitol building and at Metropolitan Edison's headquarters, and organizing annual vigils to commemorate the accident. They placed nonbinding referendums on three county ballots, all of which passed by a two-to-one margin in May 1983.[6] Finally, they pursued litigation. In 1981, over 150 lawsuits filed by over two thousand local residents claiming accident-incurred financial and medical damages were moved to federal court, where a twenty-five-million-dollar settlement fund was established.[7]

Residents crafted several arguments against the restart. They contended that the risks of radiation exposure outweighed the plant's economic benefits, that the utility company was incompetent, and that it was citizens themselves—rather than a federal commission—who should have control over the final decision.[8] Underlying these arguments was the erosion of trust between the local community and both the utility company and the NRC. This was reflected in a number of claims: radiation exposure from the accident had been worse than official reports, GPU lacked the integrity to run a power plant, the NRC cared more about protecting industry than redressing local grievances, evacuation was an inadequate response to a radiological hazard, and the centralized nature of nuclear regulation undermined democratic decision-making.

This erosion of trust transcended political affiliation. One study of nearby Middletown found that whether someone was "liberal or conservative" was no predictor of how they felt about the restart issue.[9] In fact, one organizer described TMI activists as middle-class, predominantly Republican, moderate to conservative property-owners.[10] "The majority of us are 30–45 year old family oriented conservatives," one woman wrote to the NRC.[11] This transcendence of partisanship created scenes of protest that defy the left-right polarization often ascribed to American political culture during this period. For example, at a TMIA-organized demonstration at the plant gates in 1983, Republican Party Committee women were on the front lines. And at a NRC hearing in Harrisburg in 1982, businessmen, housewives, and their children cheered when an activist warned that residents would engage in civil disobedience if the reactor ever reopened.[12]

If party affiliation could not predict who became active in the restart fight, then what did? The Middletown study found that the single factor that determined whether a local resident became involved in the struggle to shut down the plant was whether he or she had children. "Parents with children at home are more likely than others to oppose nuclear power and the Unit 1 restart," explained a news article about the study. "That cannot be said of any other group in the Middletown population."[13] Local men and women routinely appealed to NRC commissioners in their capacity as parents, explaining as one woman did that she would "worry till [her] death about the genes and chromosomes" of her children and her grandchildren.[14] Men and women often brought their children to NRC hearings and city council meetings, pointing to them as flesh-and-blood embodiments of how high the stakes were in the fight over the reactor. One man held up his young son at a Middletown council meeting in June 1979. "How many watts is that kid worth?" he asked the council. "How many jobs is that kid worth? We're here because we feel endangered."[15]

This sense of endangerment was catalyzed by a post-Vietnam loss of confidence in technocratic expertise and state authority. As the disastrous outcome of that war came into view, antiwar activists had blamed a Cold War–era cult of managers, engineers, and technocrats—ironically dubbed "the best and the brightest"—for creating a misguided blueprint for disaster. Now, the same accusations were leveled against the nuclear industry. "What are they going to say a year from now about how high the level of radiation was?" one man asked. "It's like Vietnam. Now we're finding things out about Vietnam we didn't know."[16] What frightened them most

FIGURE 3.1. Middletown Council Meeting, June 20, 1979. Reprinted with permission from *The People of Three Mile Island*. Copyright held by Robert Del Tredici. Courtesy of Robert Del Tredici.

about the accident, residents recalled, was that the "so-called experts" were thrust into a state of confusion.[17] Another resident emerged from the accident with a "skeptical point of view about government commissions, government preparedness, scientific expertise; it just goes on and on."[18] The people of the region, as the TMI Coalition portrayed it, were "confused by the conflicting claims of government officials, utility representatives, and scientific experts" and were left to "struggle virtually alone to find the truth."[19] In a newsletter of the Susquehanna Valley Alliance published in March 1980, a contributor noted that residents were being terrorized by technology. "Not even the experts," he wrote, "can agree on how it should be handled. . . . no one, not even the experts or the government, has devised a clear or safe plan to handle the hot bed of radioactivity which now rests on Three Mile Island."[20] As one NRC commissioner lamented, "there was complete mistrust of anyone who was in an official position."[21] A pamphlet published by the Stop the Restart Campaign captured the mood. It showed the plant's cooling towers in the background and crossed fingers in the foreground. The caption below read: "Do You Trust GPU to Run Three Mile Island—Again?"[22]

This mistrust intensified as the community deliberated the best way to clean up Unit Two. The accident had left large amounts of radioactive water and gas in its auxiliary and containment buildings, and the reactor's core remained radioactive.[23] The cleanup effort was inseparable from the restart of Unit One, since the restart would first require the disposal of radioactive waste left behind by the partial meltdown. The accident had transformed the plant into a "hazardous waste site" and a "de-facto waste dump," a transformation that had racial and class connotations.[24] Historically, nuclear power plants were often (though not always) built in white, middle-class communities, precisely because of the industry's overconfidence regarding safety. By contrast, toxic incinerators and solid-waste transfer stations were disproportionately located in poorer, low-income communities populated by people of color.[25] The accident at TMI muddied this distinction as a nuclear power plant *became* a hazardous waste site. Residents had to confront the fact that there was a defunct reactor full of radioactive waste in their neighborhood. A new bumper sticker commented bitterly, "TMI: Our own Love Canal," a reference to the infamous working-class neighborhood in Niagara Falls, New York, devastated by toxicity and environmental illness.[26]

The response revealed a collective sense of anger and distrust. Both the NRC and Met-Ed agreed that the best method for cleaning up the plant was venting, by which krypton-85 (a radioactive noble gas) would be released into the atmosphere in a series of planned emissions. Because this process would be controlled and incremental, NRC and Met-Ed insisted, the radiation released would be lower than the amount emitted from the plant during normal operations.[27] Local residents rejected the plan, in part because they recognized it as a step toward the reopening of Unit One.[28] But their rejection also revealed their complete loss of confidence in the utility and the NRC. As one woman explained, "The past year has been difficult for me and my family as we struggled to find out about the painful truth of TMI. One important lesson I learned is it is absolutely essential to seek the facts rather than just accept the facts because they come from experts."[29] Many local residents simply did not believe industry assurances about the safety of the venting process. As one protest sign put it: "The NRC is sure krypton won't hurt us, just as they were sure that there wouldn't be an accident."[30] If the industry failed to level with the public about the risks of an accident in the first place, the logic went, how could the community trust it to level with them now about the removal of radioactive waste?

Residents were also convinced that they already bore too heavy a radiological burden. As state representative Stephen Reed Carter wrote in a letter to President Carter, the people of central Pennsylvania "do not volunteer their bodies and their children's bodies to be receptors."[31] This sense of somatic vulnerability was palpable throughout the spring of 1980 as the debate over venting escalated. At an NRC hearing held in Middletown that March, five hundred residents gathered at the town's fire station to express their disapproval of the plan. Inside the hall, residents stood up and angrily denounced the NRC with shouts of "liar" and "murderer," while outside others denied entry because of overcapacity banged on the doors and windows in protest. One woman told NRC administrator Reginald Gotchy, "You hurt my child." Gesturing toward the boy in her arms, she recalled that at the time of the accident, he "was throwing up long, slimy stuff that I'd never seen come out of a baby's mouth before." Then she added: "The calves were throwing up! In twenty years those farmers never had calves throw up!" When Gotchy responded that a state veterinarian had investigated similar reports and found no correlation between the accident and subsequent illness in animals, the woman replied, "I don't trust the state, as I don't trust you."[32]

Ultimately, the venting proceeded as planned, but the angry protests illuminated how the accident had ushered new elements into the region's political culture: distrust in the utility and the NRC, suspicion toward expert authority, and a heightened sense of somatic vulnerability. Officials, meanwhile, went to considerable lengths to pacify residents. Governor Thornburgh, for example, enlisted the Union of Concerned Scientists, a prominent group of scientists critical of nuclear power, to study the venting issue. The UCS concluded that while venting posed no radiological hazard, it would exacerbate the "psychological stress" of people living near the plant. Emotional suffering was becoming critical to the community's self-understanding. For his part, Thornburgh recognized that the repeated assurances of neither the governor's office nor the NRC nor Met-Ed would suffice.[33] As he explained to the Kemeny Commission, "All of us in one way or another are trying to earn back that fragile connection of trust."[34]

When they challenged authority, residents were borrowing from both the antiwar and antinuclear movements. But there was a crucial difference. Conservatives viewed leftist activists as having made a free moral choice to protest for what seemed misguided, fanciful, or even perverse reasons, such as opposition to imperialism, solidarity with third-world struggles, or some pie-in-the-sky commitment to protecting the earth. By contrast, residents at Three Mile Island saw themselves as *reluctant* activists, driven to protest by their organic relationship to the land. The fact that they had no choice, that their activism was something forced upon them, compelled them to disavow the political left, even as they recognized its role in creating the preconditions for protest. As one York County woman recalled, "I had never protested, attended a rally, or admonished an NRC commissioner. Since the accident, I've done all those, and much more."[35] Or as another seventy-year-old man wrote, it was hard for him to believe that he was writing his very first letter of protest.[36] As a newsletter explained it, "We really don't like doing this. We would rather be mowing the grass, cutting the hedge, coaching boys/girls baseball, spending more time with our families, not attending TMI meetings."[37] The implication was that residents were "typical, Middle Americans," not "crazy, anti-nuke kooks," as one woman derisively called them.[38] Local residents took pains to label themselves "concerned citizens" rather than activists, emphasizing that the restart was not a "pro or anti-nuclear issue" but rather one of "integrity, health and safety."[39] "I'm not a radical person," qualified a salesman to Middletown's city council as he demanded that the reactor be shut down.[40] One woman from Mechanicsburg (located twenty miles west of the plant) later recalled that "Prior to TMI, I looked upon political activists as ivory tower intellectuals or malcontent hippies." "I would certainly not categorize myself as an intellectual or a hippie," she continued. But the woman was, by her own admission, now "full of anger, doubt and fear," and she felt that protest was "the way to work those feelings out."[41] Another woman closed an angry letter to the NRC by listing all of her family members who lived within a fifteen-mile radius of the island. "I only list my family," she wrote, "so you know I am not a professional protester."[42] The motivations of professional protesters were suspect, she implied, but her motivations were pure, because they were tethered to the community rather than to some abstract ideal. As the *Philadelphia Inquirer* observed in 1980, the people of central Pennsylvania were "good, solid, skeptical, tax-paying citizens without an anti-nuke activist among them." These were people "to whom protesting does not come naturally or easily."[43]

Expressions of reluctance vis-à-vis protest went hand in hand with affirmations of the traditional family, especially as women emerged as the most visible and vocal opponents of the restart. The transformation of women into outspoken critics of Met-Ed, the NRC, and the state mirrored a national trend. Women everywhere were more apprehensive than men when it came to nuclear power, more likely to oppose the building of plants and the siting of a nuclear power plant where they lived, more worried about the dangers posed by radiation, and more inclined to evacuate their homes in the event of an accident.[44] As women became involved in antinuclear organizing, they sometimes cited nuclear power as a feminist issue. At places like Seabrook and Diablo Canyon, for example, women antinuclear activists articulated connections between gender liberation and their opposition to nuclear power, insisting that the nuclear threat was symptomatic of a global pattern of masculine hubris.

Women at Three Mile Island adopted one key aspect of this feminist critique of nuclear power: its challenging of the distinction between expert and lay knowledge. Local activist Beverly Hess leveled a charge that just as easily might have come from a feminist at the time: "[We] have been variously ignored, dismissed, inaccurately labeled as being 'emotional' in a pejorative sense, and characterized as being just ill-informed lay people, and as being trouble-makers, needlessly agitating about issues which had best be left to 'the experts.'"[45] But residents often diverged from feminists when it came to the family. While feminists emphasized how women had been constrained by traditional familial roles, Three Mile Island women proudly flagged their status as wives and mothers and linked this status to their reluctant activism. Before the accident, a Middletown mother remembered, "I was totally ignorant of nuclear power and quite content to bake cakes, clean the house, care for my family, and essentially live in my own little world."[46] A local group called Concerned Mothers and Women echoed the same sentiment. Before March 1979, their biggest concerns "as mothers were PTA meetings and baking oatmeal cookies. That is no longer true. We now have committed our energies to protecting the health and safety of our families and community."[47] Joyce Corradi, a Middletown mother of five, described herself as "a person who is very home and family-oriented (sewing, canning, flower arranging). Until the accident at TMI my biggest problem was looking for a new moneymaker at my children's school PTA. My days have drastically changed since that time. My biggest problem now is finding the time to go to the meetings, seminars, and public hearings concerning Three Mile Island."[48] Another local woman complained that the round of hearings disrupted the rhythm of family life: "Every weekend is tied up with hearings or marches or other activities to close TMI (forever!)." But the sacrifice and disruption were necessary, she maintained: "Sometimes a little boy must sacrifice some of his childhood so he can have an adulthood. Sometimes he must sacrifice a fishing or camping weekend so he can have fish and parks."[49] An article in the *Washington Post* distinguished the women activists at TMI from the "usual nuclear protesters." "They are not peripatetic intellectuals out to save the world from the mushroom cloud," the article observed. "They are working class women who want to save their children."[50]

Residents also presented their protest as an affirmation of, rather than a departure from, their Christian identities. The most predictable example of this was Quakers, who had long been on the front lines of activism. For example, SVA leader Beverly Hess was a devout Quaker, and Quaker institutions provided the organization with funding and office space. "I'm filled with joy at being a member of a Society which struggles to know God's will, and then DO IT," Hess wrote to the Philadelphia Yearly Meeting after the organization gave the SVA five thousand dollars. "I now feel a responsibility to God's spirit," she continued. "I feel driven, pulled, and led to deal with the dangers of nuclear power in a struggle for the safe preservation of the earth and the human race."[51] But Lutherans, Methodists, and Roman Catholics also rooted protest in religious conviction. Lancaster resident Charlotte Dennan was one of several hundred people who traveled from central Pennsylvania to Washington, DC, in May 1979 to participate for the first time in a national antinuclear protest. "I have two wonderful children," she wrote to the Kemeny Commission, "Jessica is thirteen, and Rick is fifteen. We all marched together in Washington D.C. in the anti-nuclear rally. We are a family who shares a belief in God. We feel we are taking a Christian stand on the issue of nuclear power."[52] It was her Christian beliefs, another woman wrote to the NRC, that "enabled me to cope and know in my heart and mind that Nuclear Energy in Middletown is wrong."[53]

Many local churches backed the protest. One pastor gave a sermon the Sunday morning after the accident in which he creatively revised Psalm 23: "Nuclear power is my provider. I shall not want for energy. It maketh me to lie down in potentially hazardous green pastures. It leads me beside potentially contaminated waters. . . . Even though I am constantly assured that I may walk through the valley of the shadow of Three Mile Island and fear no evil, Thy uncertainties art always with me."[54] Throughout the crisis, church offices had been inundated with worried phone calls. "I shall not forget those three hectic days," a pastor at Trinity Lutheran Church remembered, "when young families and older people called around the clock for guidance and counsel; and those long hours of my own wrestling in prayer and critical thought concerning what counsel to give, and what to say at the Sunday services when the outcome of events remained unclear."[55] In the years that followed, area churches provided meeting space for anti-restart organizations and participated in interfaith services on the anniversary of the accident, where they led call-and-response prayers that included lines like "I ask God's love to make us sensitive to the pain and terror which has come and will come to our brothers and sisters through the abuse of nuclear power."[56] Several Christian councils and synods formally declared their opposition to the restart of the plant until all safety concerns had been addressed.[57]

Christian arguments against the restart often evoked the organic basis of the protest. Ministers insisted that God mandated Christians be stewards of the land. As the York County Council of Churches explained, the accident brought "us face to face with the question of whether our life styles as we have defined it [*sic*] is compatible with our stewardship responsibilities both for human life and for the rest of the natural world."[58] More often, clergy cited opposition to nuclear power as part of a broad Christian reverence for life. Human beings make mistakes, the National Council of Churches observed in May 1979, but in the case of nuclear power, those mistakes could do "irreversible damage to . . . the human gene pool."[59] Christians recognize that "human beings are not cheap commodities" and are called upon to "resist forces that destroy life."[60] Sometimes, they transformed the TMI story into a cautionary tale about the inevitability of sin. "Sin is not a popular word these days," proclaimed Wallace Fisher, the pastor of Trinity Lutheran Church in Lancaster, during a Sunday sermon in November 1979, but the accident had exposed its ubiquity. Taking aim at the nuclear industry's (now-debunked) claim that redundant backup systems made accidents virtually impossible, Fisher deployed the industry's own terminology against it, concluding that "human beings are not fail-safe."[61]

Reluctant activists' appeals to the traditional family and Christianity were often accompanied by expressions of patriotism, or, more precisely, *wounded* patriotism. "When your government subsidizes an industry that commits murder," explained Sue Shetrom, "your patriotism gets bruised."[62] In May 1979, a woman who lived less than a mile from the reactor appeared before the Kemeny Commission. She deliberated in what capacity she should speak—as a mother who feared that her child had sustained genetic injury, as an angry victim who suffered from swollen lymph glands, laryngitis, and a chronic sore throat that she attributed to radiation poisoning, or as a property owner who could see the towers from a home that she feared had become a financial liability. But what was not up for deliberation was her patriotism. "I'd like to say, I love this country," she told them. "I'm one of those minorities whose eyes still fill with tears when I hear 'The Star-Spangled Banner.' But I sit here in total loathing and disgust for the legislators, all parties."[63] Her patriotism had not disappeared, but the accident had redirected it away from the nation-state and toward a localized community of sufferers.

MAKING THE CASE FOR PHYSICAL INJURY

At the heart of the effort to shutter the reactor was a dire claim, that if the plant were put back in operation, it would pose a radiological threat. This argument placed a heavy evidentiary burden on restart opponents, who had to prove that the plant, if reopened, would be dangerous. Part of what made this burden challenging was that the state's assessment of the accident's health effects had been so reassuring. While radiation levels within the containment building soared and the reactor core sustained severe damage, monitoring devices indicated that radiation releases beyond the plant had been minimal. While much of the public interpreted the accident as an exposé of the technology's dangers, nuclear industry supporters were in one respect heartened by what had happened: a reactor core partially melted down but did not breach containment. The state's initial findings were bolstered after 1979. In April 1980, the Pennsylvania Department of Health and the Centers for Disease Control released a study indicating that neither fetal mortality nor infant mortality nor birth defects had risen within a ten-mile radius of the plant in the six months after the accident.[64] The state's health department also conducted a cancer study within a twenty-mile radius of the plant between 1974 and 1983 and found that rates had remained unchanged. A subsequent study between 1982 and 1989 among people living within a five-mile radius of the plant came to the same conclusion, and a follow-up study conducted in 2000 affirmed the earlier findings. The cumulative data suggested that while the accident had been frightening, no one had been physically hurt.[65]

Thus one aim of restart opponents was to debunk the official findings about radiation releases. They argued that radiation monitoring had been inadequate during the crucial first seventy-two hours and that dosimeters tracked certain kinds of radioactive isotopes and not others. They insisted that the NRC underestimated individual exposure levels and that a radioactive plume from the plant touched down on some communities where there had been no dosimeters at all.[66] These claims were meant to cast doubt on official findings by insisting that the crucial question about the accident remained unanswered. As a TMIA-PIRC flyer from 1985 put it: "TMI's neighbors still have no answer to the major question surrounding the accident and its aftermath: How much radiation was released into the environment and what does that mean to our health?"[67] Fliers like these circulated widely throughout the community and suggested that the accident had consigned residents to a permanent state of uncertainty. As one man explained, "The residents of this area continue to live with a life-threatening situation not knowing which experts to believe or not to believe. Will they get cancer in twenty years? If not them, what does the future hold for children growing up in this area?"[68]

But restart opponents needed to do more than cast doubt on the official story. They also had to advance an alternative account. Between 1979 and 1985, local residents provided testimonies, granted interviews, and wrote letters in which they documented the accident's effects on the animal life, plant life, and people of the region. Along the way, they challenged the monopoly of experts over scientific and medical knowledge, questioned the ties between scientific authority and state power, and participated in what sociologist Phil Brown has called "popular epidemiology," a practice by which laypeople gather knowledge and draw their own conclusions about the causes and prevalence of disease.[69]

By cataloguing the accident's physical and biological damage, local residents were challenging its defiance of the senses, especially its invisibility. Some echoed Mary Osborn's courtroom argument by claiming that they had experienced physical symptoms of radiation exposure the morning of the accident, before they even knew of the crisis at the plant. These included a metallic taste in the mouth, dryness in the throat, sunburns, tearing and burning of the eyes, diarrhea and nausea, tingling sensations, and skin rashes. One man recalled that "there was a taste of metal in the air," and a woman remembered that a wave of heat had engulfed her as she stood on her farmhouse porch that morning.[70] Ruth Hoover, the wife of a dairy farmer in nearby Bainbridge, described what she called white fallout—"it looked like fine snow, real tiny."[71] Others recalled that the air had turned orange that day, while still others remembered a grayish or bluish haziness in the sky.[72] Radiation released from the plant, it now turned out, had been tasted in the mouth, felt on the skin, and seen with the naked eye. This counternarrative cast local residents not only as victims but as witnesses of an ecological disaster.

Residents extended this cataloguing of injury to the landscape. They culled their backyards for evidence, reporting flowers with doubled blooms and freakishly long petals, weeds with thickened and leathery stems, dandelion leaves as long as one's arm, raspberry bushes twenty-eight feet high, mushrooms one hundred times their normal size, a four-foot-wide cabbage, and trees whose leaves were experiencing all four seasons at once.[73] Reports of such botanical oddities became frequent enough that Johnny Carson poked fun at them on *The Tonight Show* in November 1979, joking that the Thanksgiving dinner table at Three Mile Island featured a fifty-pound cranberry.[74] "Before TMI," one reporter observed, "such giant vegetables were saved for the farm show, or they at least merited a picture in the local paper. Now they have become fuel for the health effects controversy. Mutated plants, the theory goes, are precursors of mutated people."[75] A local paper even featured a story on what it dubbed "Boy George corn," a reference to the gender-fluid singer-songwriter who headed up the 1980s new wave band Culture Club. "[Normally] the tassel is the male organ," the article explained. "The ear is the female organ. The tassel sheds pollen on the ear, and the ear makes baby kernels." But now the male tassels were changing sex and producing their own miniature ears with kernels. It appeared that the region's corn, like Boy George, had undergone some sort of mutation.[76] An article from 1985 described how Mary Osborn's garden, once a source of pleasure for her, had become an unnerving laboratory of radiological damage. Convinced that officials had underestimated radiation releases, Osborn routinely went out to her garden in search of proof. She found mutated flowers, which she placed in Tupperware containers with a drying agent, and grotesquely oversized maple leaves that she pressed between the pages of newspapers. "I don't really like to garden anymore," she told a reporter, "because I'm afraid to see what comes up."[77] "There are many intangible losses such as peace of mind and the pleasures we once had in our gardens and trees," Charles and Helen Hocker of Etters, a town twenty-five miles from the plant, wrote to the NRC. "The berries and bushes that we planted for the enjoyment of our whole family are now a source of worry. We ask ourselves if it is really safe for our grandchildren to be picking and eating fruit. Should they be visiting us at all?"[78]

And then there were the animals. In the months after the accident, farmers reported animals born with missing limbs and eyes, as well as higher rates of stillbirth, miscarriage, and spontaneous abortion among livestock. One woman reportedly discovered dead rabbits in the bushes around her house, and a man claimed to have found dead birds on his front lawn the morning after the accident.[79] Jane Lee compiled a long list of illnesses she had observed among the cattle, cats, rabbits, and guinea pigs on her farm since 1979. It included arthritis, bone fractures, brittle bones, muscle deficiency, blindness at birth, missing eyeballs, sterility, premature births, spontaneous abortions, hermaphroditism, stillbirths, and a failure to dilate during labor. One farmer recalled the deformed calves born the spring

FIGURE 3.2. Illustration of Sex Reversal in Corn. Copyright held by Mary Osborne. Courtesy of Dickinson College Archives and Special Collections.

after the accident. "The calves' heads hung to one side until they were six months old. Their necks appeared twisted."[80] These reports of mutation and deformity could become fodder for gallows humor, as in one editorial cartoon that featured a turkey from a regional poultry farm with a third drumstick.[81] But for the region's farmers, cattle were valuable commodities, and sickness among animals was serious business (the cost of a good dairy cow averaged between eighteen hundred and two thousand dollars at the time). As Mary Osborn had done with her plants, Lee sought to chart the damage among animals. "I am not a qualified scientist, and I am aware that my work lacks scientific credibility," she explained in an interview, "but somebody must keep track of these events. I have sent my report to the governor of Pennsylvania and to my representatives, both state and federal; I have sent it to the NRC and to the president of the United States. But not one word, not one single word has leaked out about what is going on with these animals."[82]

Lee believed that what she was seeing among the animals was a harbinger of the accident's eventual human toll. "As far as I am concerned, this is the key that is going to open the door. Because what is happening to the animals is going to happen to us—it's just going to take longer."[83] This predictive logic cast animals as augurs. Antinuclear activist Helen Caldicott recalled that a veterinarian had told her to "watch the animals. They will manifest signs first, because their noses are closer to the ground." Disease among animals, Caldicott speculated, "may mean something more to come in the human population. We don't know."[84] Others mobilized animal metaphors in order to depict local residents as involuntary subjects of a nuclear experiment. "My four year old son and my baby will have to be the guinea pigs," one mother lamented.[85] Oblivious to the nuclear danger before the accident, another woman recalled, the people who lived near the reactor had "been led like sheep to the slaughter."[86] At Three Mile Island, animals played a triplicate role. They were commodities owned *by* humans, predictors of future disease *in* humans, and metaphors for radiological experimentation *among* humans.

While some catalogued animal illness and deformity, others reported the disappearance of animals that had populated the valley. One dairy farmer contended that the local birds had gone away after the accident: "we saw only one robin last summer. No blue jays, hummingbirds, finches, cardinals, or red-winged blackbirds; and I saw only six swallows. And the starlings, which have always plagued the area by the hundreds of thousands, never showed up at all."[87] As a local Republican committeeman recalled in an interview, "it was amazing here after the accident. There were no bees or other insects, no birds for months."[88] A woman who lived in Annville, a town twenty miles northeast of the plant, described a landscape emptied of animal life. "It was like the world came to an end. There was nothing there. It's still like that now, you're lucky if you see a rabbit on this mountain. The hunters are really complaining about it because there's no game."[89] No one died at Three Mile Island, but as these witnesses understood it, the crisis left the valley denuded and hollowed out. These accounts distinguished between a superficial normality and an underlying devastation. At first glance, the region appeared undisturbed by the accident, but if one looked closer, the Susquehanna River Valley had been transformed into a quasi-apocalyptic world reminiscent of Rachel Carson's silent spring. There were trees without birds, gardens without insects, and landscapes devoid of life. As one woman from Etters explained, "So many times since the accident I've been struck by the incongruity of the peaceful countryside and the nightmare that hangs over it."[90]

State officials refuted these accounts of animal and plant mutation, sickness, death, and disappearance. The Pennsylvania Department of Agriculture commissioned veterinarians to sample livestock feedstuffs for radioactivity and perform autopsies on animal corpses. It found no correlation between herd health problems and radiological exposure. In May 1979, the department investigated one hundred farms within a five-mile radius of the reactor. In this case, it found five farms where there were unusual health problems among the livestock but attributed the cases to viral infections and poor nutrition.[91] Penrose Hallowell, the state's secretary of agriculture, explained in an interview in 1980 that animal illness and death had always been a routine part of rural life, but that the accident "has raised the anticipation level . . . of farmers looking for or being on the alert for any kind of problem that they can relate to radioactivity." Hallowell was adamant that the state had uncovered no evidence of radiological injury, but the rumors proved persistent.[92] One woman told the Kemeny Commission that she had heard about the dying livestock and the mysterious animal illnesses and remained "scared to death."[93] The reports persisted because many residents suspected that officials had not come clean about the accident—either because they did not know the full truth or because they were concealing it.

These accounts of biological injury suggested that the radiological threat was now mediating the community's relationship to the environment. Anthropologist Joseph Masco refers to this mediated relationship as the "nuclear uncanny." The term considers the Freudian idea of the uncanny in relation to an atomic age in which nuclear materials, precisely because they "travel an unpredictable course through ecosystems and bodies," have the capacity to "render everyday life strange."[94] At Three Mile Island, the nuclear uncanny centered on the region's plants, trees, flowers, and animals and their imperiled reproduction. As Beverly Hess told Senator John Heinz,

"Our Eden has changed; perhaps most notably in our *perception* of it."[95] The accident was so grievous because it had remade home into an ominous, spooky, and unfamiliar place. One local Middletown activist wondered why his region, famously celebrated as the country's "garden spot," had been the target. "Why Middletown? And Londonberry? And Goldsboro? Lancaster is the richest farmland in the United States of America. In fact, in the world. And they damn near wiped it out with their machine. The big machine."[96] These appeals to an agricultural Eden indicted the nuclear industry for recklessness, but they were also shot through with nostalgia for a way of life that was sharply contracting. By 1980, just over 5 percent of Lancaster residents were still employed full-time in agriculture, forestry, fishing, and hunting, and the figure was even lower for the other counties surrounding the plant.[97] Thus when restart opponents spoke of an "agricultural Eden" and a "garden spot," they were talking about a world that was disappearing.

Reports of botanical mutations, dead and deformed animals, and an eviscerated landscape raised the question of the human toll. Although impossible to prove, many residents believed that such symptoms as swollen lips, recurring rashes, burning and blistering of the skin, metallic taste in the mouth, hair loss, diarrhea, rectal bleeding, kidney problems, swollen lymph glands, and sore throats were caused by plant emissions, not only from leaks during the accident, but also by the venting being done to decontaminate Unit Two and by routine releases.[98] This final charge was significant because it aimed to establish that the plant posed an ongoing health risk, even under ostensibly normal conditions. As Mary Osborn explained, "My skin burns sometimes. I don't know, maybe the radiation is in the soil, or maybe I'm just very sensitive if TMI has a small release—they have them all the time, you know, and they always say it's just the normal background levels."[99]

Others were convinced that there was a cancer cluster in the region. Among them were Marjorie and Norman Aamodt, a married couple who owned a farm in Coatesville (approximately forty-five miles from the plant) and who had been named official intervenors in the restart hearings. One journalist described Marjorie Aamodt as a "farmer, Cub Scout Den Mother, and housewife" whose life as a mother of three had been upended by the accident. Since March 1979, she had written thousands of pages explaining why the plant should remain closed. Along with her husband, she had gone door to door gathering data to establish that cancer rates were seven times higher than normal in communities near the plant.[100] Her theory was that at the time of the accident, a radioactive plume had behaved like a tornado, randomly touching down only in some spots.[101] As a result, cancer rates were normal in some areas and disproportionately high in others, a pattern, she asserted, that state and federal investigators had missed. Sickened bodies had to compensate for the state's oversight. As Aamodt put it, "the only dosimeters left to us now . . . are the human dosimeters in our study."[102] The Aamodt findings were made public in June 1984, and the following September, the state's Department of Health rejected them as invalid. The editors of the *Harrisburg Patriot* backed the department: "It may be emotionally and, for some, financially satisfying to blame the TMI accident for life's misfortunes, but it is also intellectually dishonest. The accident was bad enough in reality without imagining or inventing harms that no reliable and independent authority can verify."[103] Marjorie Aamodt viewed the situation differently. "We were all victims," she wrote, "and we had to do something about it. It would be like coming onto a hit and run accident and seeing a body lying in the street bleeding. You don't just walk away from it."[104] For her, this meant doing whatever she could to prevent the restart. "We don't want them to ever start that plant again," she said. "People have been very badly hurt, physically and psychologically. I don't think people should have to live with that kind of terror."[105]

The cancer-cluster theory appeared plausible in light of the history of atomic testing. Helen Hockers of Etters wrote to President Carter that "We are old enough and sophisticated enough to know that we are no different from our fellow Americans who were given deadly doses of radiation at the same time that they were being assured that they were not being harmed."[106] The Carter Administration anticipated that residents would make the link. On the second day of the accident, President Carter's deputy assistant, Les Francis, wrote a memo to congressional liaison Frank Moore in which he explained that a "perfect storm" was brewing around radiation, fueled by growing distrust of the government: "The revelations coming out of southern Nevada and Utah, coupled with the Harrisburg incident, are turning skepticism into open hostility. The government is viewed, by the way, not as a neutral observer in all of this, but rather as an active co-conspirator (probably with considerable justification)."[107] TMI residents saw in downwinders people much like themselves—patriots who had trusted the government but who were now facing the prospect of radiation-induced illness years or even decades in the future. As one young mother put it at a meeting in Middletown in May 1981, "If I live to be a grandmother or great-grandmother and see normal children, grandchildren, and great-grandchildren, then I'll believe we were lucky enough not to have been permanently harmed. . . . The feds probably don't know either, but if they did, do you think they'd ever tell us the truth?"[108]

Concerns surrounding fetal and infant health persisted amid the generalized distrust. Ernest Sternglass and Gordon MacLeod were convinced that rates of infant hypothyroidism in three nearby counties had increased in the months after the accident, indicating exposure to radioactive iodine. State officials investigated and found no link, and they also rejected a separate claim that there had been a postaccident spike in infant mortality. The state's health department released data showing that thirty-one infants had died within a ten-mile radius of the plant in the six months after the accident, a figure that appeared high compared to the twenty infant deaths in 1978 and the fourteen in 1977. But because the total number of live births had also risen, the rate of infant deaths had remained constant.[109]

Still, some residents remained convinced that babies were dying from the reactor. An Annville woman told an interviewer in 1980 that "the ladies [near the plant] are having babies, and they're being stillborn and God, it makes you wonder. It scares you. They're not telling the truth."[110] A woman from Hershey who had gotten pregnant soon after the accident chose to have an abortion: "I couldn't handle having a baby that would either develop leukemia or be deformed or deficient in any way. I just didn't believe that I could have a child that would suffer like that."[111] Another woman explained it at a public hearing, "My three children are all daughters, and I am very concerned about what is going to happen to them as potential child-bearers. After working in state hospitals, I don't want to see them have brain damaged children."[112] One restart activist had her daughter carry a sign at rallies that read "What Have They Done to My Genes?"[113] Meanwhile, what came to be called "flipper baby jokes" circulated throughout the community: "What's red and has a hundred flippers? Answer: The maternity ward in Harrisburg."[114]

As the restart fight heated up, concerns about *male* reproductive health also came to the fore. Nuclear physicist-turned-critic John Gofman contended that the nuclear industry was "irradiating the sex cells—in the gonads—of the nuclear workers." "Many of these workers," he predicted, "are going to have children, and thanks to the extra radiation, some of these children are going to have defective genes. And these defective genes will be passed into the whole population when these children have children of their own."[115] Between 1979 and 1985, this figure of the irradiated or mutated male nuclear worker became ubiquitous in visual culture. Sometimes, he glowed in the dark, a property that circled back to the turn-of-the-century fascination with radium. After the accident, residents jokingly told one another, "You're glowing," or "You look radiant today."[116] A *Dallas News* cartoon from 1979 depicted a plant worker as a translucent skeleton, levitating off the ground and emitting light. He hovers in his bedroom doorway and assures his terrified wife, "I'm home, dear. . . . that nuclear reactor malfunction kept us busy through th' night. But I think we've got everything under control now."[117] At other times, the figure was presented as a mutant—half-human, half-animal. An editorial cartoon from December 1982 showed a conversation between two men standing in front of Three Mile Island in the year 2079. In the first three frames, the men are shown from the neck up, and they speak admiringly of the plant. "I can hardly believe it! Here it is 2079, and the ol' nuclear power plant is still going strong after 100 years!" one says to the other. Scoffing at the protests and the "silly fears" and "blind mistrust" of the past, they conclude: "it just goes to show how wrong you can be." But the final frame of the cartoon reveals that the men are species-crossing mutants—they have bat wings, dinosaur tails, and elephant feet.[118]

Whether evoking radium's magical properties (radiance) or radiation's scarier potential (mutation), the gothic humor of the cartoons derived from their rendering of a collision between the domestic and the horrific. There was a dissonance between the captions, which offered up bland reassurances of nuclear safety, and the graphics themselves, which revealed radiation's sublime and terrifying capacity to remake human bodies. In these cartoons, the Cold War culture of dissociation unraveled. The claim that "everything is under control" was revealed not simply as fallacious, but as dangerously unmoored from reality. The subjects were not simply mutants; they were dolts who did not realize that they had undergone mutation. The message was clear: those in positions of authority could not be trusted. If

FIGURE 3.3. Mutant Editorial Cartoon. JIM BORGMAN © Cincinnati Enquirer. Reprinted with permission of ANDREWS MCMEEL SYNDICATION. All Rights Reserved. Courtesy of Dickinson College Archives and Special Collections.

the men who defended the industry did not recognize that their own bodies had been reconstituted by radiation, then how could they be expected to protect others from danger?

On April 7, 1979, *Saturday Night Live* posed this very question to a mass television audience. "The Pepsi Syndrome" sketch opens in the control room of a nuclear power plant called "Two Mile Island," where an operator named Matt (played by Bill Murray) casually hands out sandwiches and drinks to his two coworkers beneath a conspicuous sign reading "No Soft Drinks in Control Room." When Matt spills his soda all over the control panel, the room descends into chaos. The panel sparks flames, an alarm bell begins to ring, and panicked workers shout that there is water loss and an explosion in the reactor core. The scene then switches to a press conference, where the plant's upbeat PR man assures a room full of reporters that the situation is under control. He offers a quick primer on nuclear power, pointing to a flow chart that connects a plant to an icon titled "energy" to a kitchen toaster. When a reporter asks him how much radiation they are being exposed to at that moment, the PR man gropes for an analogy. It's like a chest X-ray that your doctor has to give you over and over again, he explains. Or, it's like falling asleep under a sun lamp for a week or two, he continues. Or, it's like drying your hair in a microwave oven. To signal that there is no danger, he announces that the president will visit the site the following day.

We next see President Carter (played by Dan Akroyd) and first lady Rosalind Carter (played by Laraine Newman) in the control room twenty-four hours later. Against his wife's worried objections, Carter insists on entering the reactor core in order to assess the damage. He confidently points to his feet swathed in plastic, boasting: "I know how to handle myself around a nuclear facility. Besides, I'm protected. I've got my little yellow boots on." After Carter enters the core, the first lady expresses her relief that they did not bring their daughter Amy along for this particular trip. She had school, she explains, "and besides, what if one day Amy wants to have children?" The president soon emerges from the core, where he has been visibly irradiated; his body emits a pulsing, bluish light. "Don't touch me," he commands Rosalind. "I am a nuclear engineer, and I am pretty worried right now." And not without reason. The president has been exposed to such a high dose of radiation that he soon morphs into a ninety-foot giant, "the Amazing Colossal President." In the skit's final scene, Carter's oversized head is seen outside the window of a tall building, King Kong–style, as reporters gather inside. "This experience has not changed my commitment to nuclear power," he insists. Yet while his physical transformation has not eroded his support for the technology, he feels he can no longer be with Rosalind. He announces that he is going to leave her and marry Violet, an African American woman maintenance worker at the plant (played in drag by Garrett Morris) who, like him, grew in size after entering the core. The skit closes with reporters frantically running for cover at the spectacle of the president, now a naked, irradiated behemoth.

Like the editorial cartoons, the skit relied on a series of disconnects: between the glaring sign on the control room wall and Bill Murray's casual disregard for its warning; between the PR man's cheerful tone and the situation's direness; between the severity of the contamination threat and the paltriness of the safety measures to contain it; and between the president's radiation-induced metamorphosis and his unwavering support for nuclear power. Airing only days after the accident, "The Pepsi Syndrome" advanced a knowing commentary that would have resonated with SNL's audience, made up largely of white, urban viewers who had entered political maturity in the era of Vietnam and Watergate. Plant workers flouted safety rules, PR men lied to the public, and nuclear industry boosters stuck to their guns, even when confronted with overwhelming evidence of danger. In an age of declining trust, the sketch was hardly unique in satirizing compromised political authority, technological hubris, and corporate smugness. But its humor was also infused with a pervasive anxiety about mutations that threaten to derail reproduction through setting in motion irreversible changes at the cellular level. This danger was rendered fantastically when the Amazing Colossal President took up with a metastasized African American woman janitor, thereby linking mutation to racial and class transgression. But the danger was also alluded to when Rosalind Carter explained that she has kept her daughter Amy away from the plant because she might want to have children one day. This line was met by conspicuous silence from the SNL audience.

The construction of a community of fate at Three Mile Island brought into relief the contested place of scientific authority, gender and reproduction, and the ecological imaginary within the political realignment of the late 1970s and early 1980s. By rejecting the official story about the accident, residents were challenging the state's monopoly over scientific expertise and seeking to accrue their own body of knowledge about radiological illness. They read books on the topic, brought scientists into the area to lecture, accumulated documents and evidence, and traveled door to door to confer with neighbors about the accident's health effects. Women in particular engaged with the key scientific and medical questions at the heart of the nuclear power debate, something they were unlikely to have done before the accident.[119] Mary Osborn began by reading about radiation in her daughter's school textbook and eventually compiled mountains of documents stacked throughout her home. She described herself as a "dippy housewife" who was nonetheless convinced that "these cancer and animal deaths should be looked into."[120] Anne Trunk, a local woman appointed to the Kemeny Commission, recalled that before the accident, she had known nothing about nuclear power, not even "the difference between a millirem and a reactor vessel." But she had since learned a great deal. "If a housewife can understand it, anybody can," she told a reporter. "That way, we won't be afraid anymore."[121]

These local efforts indexed a larger attempt to democratize science in the 1970s. As Phil Brown has argued, popular epidemiology does not reflect an antipathy toward science, but rather an alternative conception of what science is and who should control it.[122] The decline in public confidence in science in the late 1960s and 1970s did not represent a loss of confidence in science writ large, so much as it represented a critique of the trajectory of scientific knowledge since World War II, when science became embedded in what Stuart W. Leslie has called the "military-industrial-academic complex."[123] One TMIA newsletter argued that the medical community was locked in its "sterile laboratories" without access to real "human beings." "They accept totally inadequate data from GPU and the NRC, extrapolate meaningless projections on health effects, and find it unforgivably rude of people to get sick in spite of their computations."[124] Local residents suspected an unholy collusion between medical authorities, the utility company, and the NRC, and they responded by crafting an alternative narrative of what had happened in 1979. This was a formidable conceptual task that required mastering a new vocabulary and acquiring an elemental understanding of a technology that had once seemed too complex to grasp. But many residents felt they could no longer remain in the dark. As the Union of Concerned Scientists explained, the debate over nuclear power "is not a question just for experts—each citizen must make an informed choice."[125] "What is going on here is the test of American democracy," asserted ecologist Barry Commoner, who traveled to the region in 1980. "You people are doing your best to make democracy live under difficult conditions."[126]

The cataloguing of radiological damage to plant, animal, and human life provided a window into the cultural unconscious of the Cold War by referencing several key events in US and global history. Accounts of burns, blistering skin, and "waves of heat" circled back to the suffering of the Japanese victims of the bombings of Hiroshima and Nagasaki, while fears of cancer conjured the experiences of leukemia-stricken residents of the US Southwest who had grown up near atomic testing sites in the 1950s. The specter of a valley evacuated of birds and other animals evoked Rachel Carson's exposé of industrial pesticides and the war-inflicted defoliation of the jungles of Southeast Asia. And reports of mutations among plants and animals took inspiration from both science fiction films like *Them!* (a film from 1956 in which atomic testing transforms carpenter ants into giant mutants) and popular comic book series such *The Incredible Hulk*, in which radiation had the sublime power to rearrange genetic and biological material.

Claims of injury also evoked darker, suppressed moments in the history of reproduction. The flipper baby jokes referenced the birth defects associated with thalidomide, a sedative prescribed to pregnant women from 1957 to 1961. If the thalidomide disaster, in which the medical establishment failed to protect pregnant women and their children, seemed far removed from the nuclear question, it nonetheless resonated within a community whose members felt that the experts had derailed their reproductive health. And while the charge that radiological exposure had unleashed an epidemic of sterility might have appeared far-fetched, there *had* been state-sponsored sterilization campaigns throughout the nation's history, directed first at the "feeble-minded" and later at African American women and other women of color, who were accused of sapping the welfare state's resources by having too many babies. Residents did not make direct reference to these campaigns, and in all likelihood they were not even aware of them. But the suspicion that the nuclear industry had derailed reproduction tapped into a racialized and class-based history of state intervention into women's bodies.

Finally, the community's response revealed something crucial about conservatism by the late 1970s: how images culled from ecology were becoming woven into a vision of the nation as a soil-based biotic system that possessed a reproductive life that could go awry. This biotic, reproduction-centered nationalism captured how an emergent ecological consciousness could go in any number of different political directions. Throughout the 1970s, many environmental achievements—from the passage of key pieces of legislation like the Clean Air Act and Clean Water Act to the creation of the first Earth Day—were integrated into a liberal civic nationalism that called for greater regulation and rational planning with the aim of safeguarding natural resources and redressing the crisis of industrial pollution. But at Three Mile Island, a new ecological consciousness conjured a more ominous national vision of an eviscerated landscape in which the "natural order" of things had been turned upside down. Within this landscape, the cycle of plant life becomes torqued and twisted, monsters and mutants have colonized the animal kingdom, and political authority is at once outsized and absurd. While many features of this landscape germinated during the atomic age, they came into full view at Three Mile Island as the culture of dissociation came apart. What gave ecology its power within the post-1968 conservative imaginary was its steady preoccupation with the threat of reproduction-under-assault. This preoccupation did two things at once. It fortified the condemnation of a domestic culture upended by feminism, abortion rights, and gay liberation (all perceived by conservatives as threats to the traditional reproductive order), and it underwrote the conviction that the nation, not unlike a living body, had sustained wounds that threatened the reproduction of its power on the world stage.

TRAUMA AND FEAR AT THREE MILE ISLAND

Alongside the claim of biological damage, restart opponents operationalized a vocabulary of collective *psychological* trauma. There was in fact broad consensus that the accident's most palpable effects on the community were stress, depression, and anxiety. George Tokuhata, a researcher with the state's health department, felt that the accident's psychological reverberations were more measurable than its physical ones.[127] This marked yet another way that the accident upended conventional logic. Typically, symptoms associated with physical illness are readily apparent, while psychological symptoms are elusive. But at Three Mile Island, it was the opposite. The biological effects of radiation exposure remained out of reach, while the psychological effects could be observed and diagnosed. In fact, the accident's physical and psychological effects could be difficult to distinguish.[128] As a press release from TMIA maintained, "the stress and trauma suffered by the residents is [sic] as important to us as any physiological symptom. . . . the two are often inseparable."[129] For many residents, these symptoms surfaced during the accident and had abated quickly. However, research suggested that they persisted with one particular group: women, and especially mothers of young children, who lived in close proximity to the plant. This group was at the greatest risk for anxiety and depression up to one year after the accident.[130] The Kemeny Commission attributed this mental stress to the confusion during the early days of the crisis, when the public had been subjected to contradictory information about both the severity of the radiation threat and the likelihood of an evacuation order.[131] The ambiguity surrounding long-term health consequences continued to fuel the stress, especially for mothers living near the plant. "The nuclear facility at TMI," as a TMIA press release explained it, "just may be the most efficient generator of stress ever engineered and thrust upon a host population."[132]

While researchers identified clusters of behavioral and somatic symptoms, local residents drew on popularized psychological language to describe their condition. In their words, they had been the victims of a trauma. As TMIA member Joanne Doroshow wrote to Governor Thornburgh in August 1982, "the people in this area . . . have experienced the trauma of the worst commercial nuclear accident ever. They have read and studied the documents telling what really happened that day, and remember the misleading press statements issued by the utility and the state. They have no confidence in the company at all. They are alienated by the NRC and have lost confidence in government's concern for their health and safety."[133] The accident had been a nuclear nightmare, explained a local advertisement: "Over 140,000 of us fled our homes. Our children still have bad dreams. We'll never forget the terror of that time."[134] In his public statements, Governor Thornburgh also characterized the accident as a trauma.[135] A woman from Mechanicsburg recalled that before March 1979, she had never had strong feelings about nuclear power and had taken her children to the plant's observation tower. But seeing the cooling towers for the first time after the accident had been distressing. "I guess the closest analogy," she wrote, "would be the feeling inside the rape victim when she comes face to face with the attacker."[136] Even the acronyms for local organizations—PANE, ANGRY—were meant to convey deep emotional and psychological distress.

What made the language of trauma so powerful was that it introduced a temporal horizon. The psychoanalytic concept of trauma is bound up with the idea of repetition—if a traumatic wound does not heal, it can fester and continue to inflict psychic harm. In the unconscious of its victim, an unresolved trauma repeats itself over and over again. The claim of collective trauma thus amounted to a prediction that if TMI remained open, the traumatic experience of the accident would be repeated ad infinitum. Larry Hochendoner warned the NRC that the restart of Unit One would consign the community to a permanent state of suffering. "Our judgment," he wrote, "is that we don't want to live with TMI. If you make the wrong decision, our nightmare will go on and on. We will literally be perpetual victims."[137] Radiation could not be confined by space and time. No evacuation plan could outpace a radioactive plume, and

FIGURE 3.4. Protesters Carrying a "Thank You, Met Ed" sign. Copyright Held by SHAD Alliance. Courtesy of Swarthmore College Peace Collection.

there was no statute of limitations on when a radiation-induced cancer might appear. Like a true trauma, then, the accident had "never really stopped."[138] As a TMIA pamphlet from 1980 presented it, "The accident is not over. Our lives are still in great danger. We face another spring knowing that our children may be irradiated when we go out to play. We do not know whether our air will be safe to breathe, our water safe to drink, our land safe to farm."[139] The accident was ongoing and could only be stopped with the permanent closing of the plant.

The concept of trauma also established an affinity between residents and war combatants. This was because at the time of the accident, the term *trauma* was associated with the new diagnosis of posttraumatic stress disorder (PTSD). The term *PTSD* was coined in the mid-1970s and first appeared in the *Diagnostic and Statistics Manual of Mental Disorders III*

Have you forgotten about Three Mile Island? _We_ haven't.

Above, left to right: Jane Perkins, SEIU, Coordinator GHA Labor Committee for Safe Energy and Full Employment; Morris Roth, P.I.P.; Suzanne and Aja Patton, Veronica Callendar, P.I.P.; Marian Horton, P.I.P.; Rev. Greg Harbaugh, Lakeside Lutheran Church; Dave Nack, ILGWU; Andy Stern, PSSU Local 668; Joan Grimsley, ILGWU; Earl Keihl, United Furniture Workers, Susan Barley, RCTWU; Local 464; Howard Snyder, Pa. Association of Older Persons; USWA Ret.; Ed Clinch, District 98, IAM; Ed Womer, IUOE Local 452; Susan Shelcomb, TMI Public Interest Resource Center, Project Director (Organizational affiliations are for identification purposes only.)

ON MARCH 28, 1979 we awoke to a nuclear nightmare they told us would never happen. Over 140,000 of us fled our homes. Our children still have bad dreams. We'll never forget the terror of that time.

Now, two years later, they want to restart the twin of the crippled Three Mile Island plant. They also want to dump 700,000 gallons of their radioactive waste from Plant #2 in our water.

Now, two years later, the industry pretends the accident didn't happen. But _we_ remember because it's *still* happening. We are workers, farmers, students, and parents from the Harrisburg area. With your help, we'll never have to go through this nightmare again.

March on Harrisburg
Saturday, March 28
Keep Three Mile Island shut down!

Labor Committee for Safe Energy
Information: **and Full Employment**
1037 Maclay Street, Harrisburg, PA 17103   Washington, DC
(717) 232-0396   (202) 797-2371

–over–

FIGURE 3.5. Have You Forgotten About Three Mile Island? Courtesy of University of Pittsburgh Special Collections.

(the DSM-III) in 1980. Although the diagnosis of PTSD would become increasingly diverse in its applications, in the late 1970s its primary association was with war and specifically with the conflict in Vietnam. While reports of battle-associated stress reactions (for example, shell shock) had existed as long as modern warfare, US soldiers returning from Vietnam were the first to receive a formal PTSD diagnosis, and their struggles with trauma became a synecdoche for the national struggle to come to terms with the failed war. The ubiquity of trauma in discussions of the accident invited a host of military analogies. Residents compared themselves to prisoners of war on the grounds that, like POWs, their predicament could remain unresolved for years. The ambiguity surrounding radiological injury also invited comparisons to chlorine gas victims and Vietnam veterans who had been exposed to Agent Orange.[140] One researcher argued that TMI residents were suffering from "radiation response syndrome," a condition seen in atomic veterans convinced that they were suffering from radiation poisoning (regardless of whether they were or not).[141] Taken together, these analogies suggested that the accident had remade central Pennsylvania into a kind of combat zone, and that its civilian residents were suffering in ways—in both degree and kind—normally confined to war.

Residents used one final analogy to convey the suffering of the residents: the hostage. The accident had been the biggest news story of 1979, but it was superseded the following November by the Iranian hostage crisis. That crisis began when sixty-five Americans, most of them State Department officials, were taken hostage by Iranian students who hoped to foment a break between the United States and Iran in the wake of the fall of the shah. Thirteen of the hostages were freed within weeks, but the other fifty-two remained in captivity for 444 days. The hostage crisis emerged as a media obsession and unleashed feelings of American nationalism that had been suppressed over the previous decade.[142] It also became a vivid point of reference for local TMI residents, who insisted that, like the hostages, they had been consigned to a state of permanent uncertainty. On the accident's one-year anniversary, a local TMIA activist who stood vigil at the plant told the crowd, "I stand before you as a hostage. There are not fifty of us, but a million of us . . . and no one is negotiating for our release."[143] "We feel like hostages," a woman who lived in Hershey told an interviewer in March 1980, "People are very concerned about the hostages in Iran, and nobody is concerned about us at all."[144] References to the hostage ordeal conveyed both identification and frustration. There was a feeling of kinship with the hostages on the grounds that, like them, their situation remained painfully unresolved. But there was also a sense of frustration that their own story had been eclipsed by the dramatic plight of the captives in Iran.

Above all, residents referenced the emotion of fear in their depictions of posttraumatic life. They contended that as long as the plant remained in operation, they were going to "live with some kind of fear."[145] According to the *Harrisburg Patriot*, one mother who resided near the plant "lives in fear, and every time a siren sounds she thinks, God please let somebody's house be on fire, instead of an emergency at the plant."[146] A Middletown resident explained to the same newspaper what went through his mind every time he heard the sirens. "It may be just another alert, which turns out to be harmless," he wrote in a letter to the editor, "or it may be the evacuation of our homes forever! What other forms of energy impose this sort of fear upon the thousands upon thousands who live in its environs?"[147] Dauphin County commissioner Larry Hochendoner described a "communal convulsion" every time there was an incident at the plant. "People stop, they anticipate the worst, hold their breaths, and then they go on. And that's one hell of a way to live."[148] A Hershey Medical Center study found a sharp increase in sleeping pill and tranquilizer use among residents.[149] These accounts advanced a vision of a community in the collective throes of PTSD, with men and women on the edge, suffering from jangled nerves, self-medicating, and always bracing themselves for the next radiological emergency. Exacerbating the fear was the fact that residents could no longer turn to the authorities for guidance. As one local woman explained it, "I don't believe anything they say because they lied to us in the first place. The people that work there, they say it's all fine, but I think they've all been brainwashed. I don't believe the government either. You just don't know who to believe anymore."[150] For central Pennsylvanians, the story would not be over until the plant was shuttered. The reactor should be sealed up forever, in the words of one local grandmother, "as a monument to the folly of the twentieth century."[151]

But a debate about the origins of this fear reflected community divisions. One survey found that Middletown was roughly split down the middle on the question of restart.[152] As one person observed, there was a divide between the "people who believed that everything was under control and the people who believed that everything was not under control."[153] As residents fought to close the reactor, others—in particular those whose economic livelihoods were tied to the plant—fought to restart it. They too organized groups, wrote to public officials, and sent letters to local newspapers. They also produced TMI merchandise to promote the plant, which had the paradoxical effect of memorializing the accident within the realm of material culture kitsch. Coffee mugs and lamps were shaped like cooling towers, key chains were carved into miniature containment buildings, and T-shirts were emblazoned with the slogan "Unit One, Let It Run."[154] These pro-TMI activists attempted to counter the image of a community gripped by fear. One TMI supporter addressed Governor Thornburgh in February 1982, debunking the charge that mothers in particular had been shaken by the accident. "I am a mother," she wrote. "I have been blessed with six fine, healthy children. . . . I live about one mile up the road from TMI; however, I am not afraid of TMI. I am here today to let you know that there are many, many mothers in this area who aren't afraid either."[155]

More often, however, rather than denying the presence of fear, TMI supporters placed the blame for it on a sensational national media that had overblown the accident, exaggerated its dangers, and alarmed the public. A Middletown man asserted that it was media (rather than radiation) overexposure that had inflicted the real harm on his community. "I felt that the only overexposure to which I was subjected . . . was the overzealous and rude photographers, and the television people who wanted to hear negative comments from area citizens."[156] It was reporters, he argued in a newspaper guest column, who had first stoked fear in the community and then overstated its prevalence in their coverage. In her testimony before the Kemeny Commission, Anne Trunk contended that reporters had placed too much emphasis on the "what if" rather than the "what is." Because of the speculative nature of the reporting, she argued, "the public was pulled into a state of terror, of psychological stress." And more than any other news form, it was the national evening news that "proved to be the most depressing, the most terrifying."[157] A local reporter with the *Harrisburg Evening News* also discerned a difference between the local and national coverage: "I've had people tell me that they would go home and read the *Patriot* or the *Evening News*, then turn on the national news at 6:30 and get all scared because it sounded so much worse than it was. The farther away you got from Harrisburg, the more sensational the coverage seemed to get, the

FIGURE 3.6. Antinuclear and Pronuclear Protestors in Front of a GPU Meeting, Johnstown, Pennsylvania, May 10, 1979. Industry Supporters Are Carrying Signs That Read "Energy not Darkness." Courtesy of AP Photo/Bob Donaldson.

more dire the situation looked." One resident later learned that in Germany there had been reports that Pennsylvania had been wiped off the map.[158]

These critiques were not without merit. There was no question that local and national news outlets approached the story from different angles. Jeff Blitzer of WHP-TV, a Harrisburg-based local television station and a

CBS affiliate, later told the Kemeny Commission that the accident had brought home to him the "old premise that a well-informed public will make the right decision." "We were dealing with a community that was unusually hungry for any scrap of information it could get," he remembered. "This was a case where people were making real decisions based on what they were hearing minute to minute on the radio or on TV." With this in mind, Blitzer sought to provide local viewers with accurate information while adopting a tone that was reasoned and cool. He recalled that there had been much soul searching among staff members who felt a sense of responsibility to their local community. This differed from the journalists who flooded into the area after the accident. Blitzer, who worked alongside many of them, observed favorably that they worked hard on their reports and aimed for accuracy. But he also felt that they were pressured by their editors to produce a "harder story." "So often, they would say on the phone, 'But it's just not that bad here.'"[159] The drive among national and international reporters to transform the accident into what one journalist called "the news story of the year" overshadowed the more mundane but more vital imperative to provide news that would empower residents to make well-informed decisions.[160]

But attempts to shift the blame for psychological distress away from the nuclear industry and to the news media were ultimately spurious. This constituted a form of blaming the messenger, suggesting that it was the journalists themselves—rather than the nuclear industry—that had inflicted harm. This same conflation had occurred during the Vietnam War, when journalists were accused of *causing* the content of their own reporting, namely, the collapse of morale among US military forces. It also neglected journalists' good faith efforts to understand what was happening inside the reactor. Throughout the accident, reporters were spotted on the streets of Middletown, gathered around science writers who held up diagrams of the reactor's feed water and primary cooling systems. Reporters were trying to grasp the basics of nuclear technology on the fly, what one observer called "learning in the streets."[161] Finally, the charge that journalists had stirred up fear reiterated the same accusation leveled against antinuclear activists that outsider agitators were responsible for the community's distress.

By constituting themselves as collective trauma victims, residents established an affinity between themselves and other kinds of national "victims," from the hostage to the war combatant to the POW. Along the way, they fostered a broader tendency to interpret disaster exclusively through the lens of trauma. This tendency is a problem, Rebecca Solnit argues, not because people do not sustain trauma during states of emergency, but because the trauma lens obscures other dynamics that can take place in those moments, including heightened solidarity and mutual aid.[162] At the same time, by mobilizing the language of trauma and psychological suffering, residents were shrewdly repurposing the Cold War security state's own long-standing preoccupation with the containment of extreme emotions (fear, panic, hysteria) and redeploying it in their effort to decommission the plant.

But did this repurposing work? That question would ultimately be answered in court. A broad coalition, including several local groups and the governor's office, asked the NRC to consider psychological issues throughout the restart hearings. The NRC rejected the request, contending that such issues fell outside their purview and had already been addressed. "Congress has already decided that the country is to have a nuclear power program," NRC chairman Joseph Hendrie explained, "even if it makes some people uneasy."[163] The Middletown-based PANE disagreed, and the group took the NRC to federal court to compel the agency to consider psychological questions throughout its deliberations. PANE made two arguments. First, it contended that the renewed operation of the plant would cause distress, anxiety, tension, and fear among residents. If the plant reopened, "PANE's members and other persons living in the communities around the plant will be unable to resolve and recover from the trauma from which they have suffered. Operation of Unit 1 would be a constant reminder of the terror which they felt during the accident." The NRC needed to consider these damaging psychological consequences in its Environmental Impact Statement (EIS), the study required by the National Environmental Policy Act of 1969 (NEPA) for all major federal actions affecting the human environment. PANE maintained that the plant's psychological consequences on people—no less than its radiological consequences on air, water, and land—fell under the purview of environmental health as defined by the NEPA. The group's second contention was that the accident had turned the reactor into a community liability, and that the NRC needed to consider that as well: "The perception, created by the accident, that the communities near TMI are undesirable locations for business and industry, or for the establishment of law or medical practice, or homes compounds the damage to the viability of the communities."[164]

In January 1982, the court agreed that health encompassed "psychological health" and ordered the NRC to take up the issue. "Americans have never before experienced the psychological aftermath of a major accident at a nuclear power plant," the court observed, "one that aroused fears of a nuclear core meltdown and led to a mass evacuation from the surrounding communities."[165] Environmental law did not encompass economic concerns or political disagreements, explained circuit judge J. Shelly Wright. But it did extend to "post-traumatic anxieties accompanied by physical effects and caused by fears of recurring catastrophe."[166] Circuit judge Malcolm Wilkey dissented on the grounds that the ruling extended the NEPA's reach "far beyond its intended scope." The contention of PANE, Wilkey insisted, was not that the resumption of operations of Unit One would endanger human health, but rather that "fears of an accident at the plant, combined with [a] lack of confidence in the NRC, will lead to an extension of the psychological stress allegedly caused by the accident."[167] Instead of assessing literal risk, Wilkey argued, the NRC was now being asked to "assess how people perceive and react to the risk."[168] In his view, this was irrational. "We have thus come a long way in fifty years," Wilkey observed, "when the president of the United States was widely and enthusiastically applauded for declaring: The only thing we have to fear is fear itself. Now the fear itself necessitates an environmental assessment."[169]

In April 1983, the US Supreme Court overturned the lower-court decision. The court found that the NEPA guidelines did not encompass psychological health but applied only to "air, land, and water." When Congress designed the law, Justice William Rehnquist explained, they were talking "about the physical environment—the world around us." The court did not intend to minimize the community's fears, he maintained, but it supported the NRC's original contention that they fell outside the agency's scope.[170] An editorial cartoon mocked the decision, depicting members of the Supreme Court shielded by their own hazmat suits as they declared the case closed. PANE was defeated in court, but its legal effort had illuminated how psychological trauma permeated the political culture of the 1980s, as well as how the construction of a community of fate could go in any number of different directions. While PANE was attempting to hold the nuclear industry accountable specifically, the claim of psychological suffering could be mobilized in other struggles, especially those over race and class. The broader implications were not lost at the time. The *Philadelphia Inquirer*

FIGURE 3.7. Case Closed Cartoon. © Tribune Content Agency, LLC. All rights reserved. Reprinted with permission. Courtesy of University of Pittsburgh Special Collections.

characterized the Supreme Court ruling as a "victory for the federal government, which feared that the appeals court's rationale, if allowed to stand, would subject proposals for prisons, military bases, low income housing and other projects to extensive assessments of psychological impact."[171] "How long can it be," asked an article in *Harper's* in 1982, "before someone's citing studies to show the alleged adverse psychological impact of busing for desegregation on white communities?"[172]

THE SHIFTING OF BLAME

In the end, the creation of a community of fate ultimately reinvigorated rather than deposed the region's homegrown conservatism. How did this happen? After all, the accident at first appeared to affirm foundational liberal principles of early-twentieth-century Progressive and New Deal–era reform. A private utility company had jeopardized the health and safety of local citizens, suggesting the need for greater regulatory oversight of the nuclear industry. Yet on the whole, the community responded not by calling for more extensive government regulations, but by moving in the opposite direction—that is, by developing an intense mistrust of the state. Indeed, between 1979 and 1985, there was a gradual shift in blame at Three Mile Island away from Metropolitan Edison and to the regulatory commission itself. With this shift, an earlier critique of corporate power fell from view and was replaced by a critique of centralized power, and the community's fight was recast as a struggle between local autonomy and federal authority.

This transposition was not a foregone conclusion. The accident had created a credibility crisis for three parties: the utility company, the NRC, and the state. However, it was Met-Ed that initially came in for the lion's share of public criticism. The charge that it had delayed reporting the escalating situation, combined with its contradictory statements to the press, left some convinced that the utility had engaged in a cover-up. For the first time, many asked whether a profit-making corporation responsible to its shareholders could be trusted with something as potentially dangerous as nuclear technology. The NRC, on the other hand, had played a largely calming role throughout the crisis. To be sure, the accident had exposed both the commission's limitations as a command center and its overconfidence about safety. But on the third day of the crisis, President Carter dispatched NRC director Harold Denton to supervise staff at the plant, communicate with state officials about conditions, and field questions from reporters. From the moment he arrived on the scene, Denton—an unassuming, forty-six-year-old nuclear engineer—appeared honest and straight-shooting, especially in contrast to utility spokesmen who came off as prevaricating. If there was anyone who approximated a heroic role during the crisis, it was Denton. The local community trusted him. One Middletown resident described Denton as "someone who looks like an ordinary guy. Not like those goddamn know-it-all snobs they got down there at Met-Ed."[173] After the accident, residents wore T-shirts that read, "Thank you, Harold Denton," and local schoolchildren wrote him and expressed their gratitude for his having let "the air out of the bubble."[174]

But the restart fight revised the terms of the struggle. It focused not on Met-Ed but on the NRC, the federal regulatory body that would decide whether to reopen or decommission Unit One. That decision resided exclusively with the NRC, a sign of the highly centralized nature of civilian atomic power in the United States.[175] As the months passed, Denton's quasi-heroic role faded from view, the NRC replaced Met-Ed as the community's prime adversary, and government control displaced corporate malfeasance as the most formidable threat facing the community. This is not to imply that hostility toward Met-Ed disappeared. Throughout the early 1980s, the utility was accused of a string of abuses, including falsifying data, concealing documents, destroying monitoring records, intimidating whistleblowers, violating testing requirements, tolerating managerial incompetence, and mishandling cleanup operations.[176] But during the same period, the General Public Utilities Corporation embarked on a low-key but well-coordinated publicity campaign to rebuild its reputation, increasing its public relations budget tenfold in the region.[177] In the five years after the accident, Met-Ed, the original target of public suspicion, quietly reintegrated itself back into the local community, while the NRC became the embodiment of hostile, distant authority, callous toward residents' physical suffering and psychological distress. Marjorie Aamodt vented her rage at the NRC. "It is nothing short of criminal," she wrote, "for this small group of men safely ensconced in well-appointed offices in Washington D.C. to deliberately inflict further stress on the families . . . by restarting Three Mile Island after what has already been done to them. This will turn out to be the environmental Watergate of our time."[178]

This charge of governmental indifference was accompanied by a second accusation, that the decision-making process had been a sham. Despite the hundreds of hours they had spent writing testimony and attending NRC hearings, many restart activists suspected that in the end their efforts did not matter. As one local woman put it, "I resent five men in Washington holding the fate of my life in [their] hands."[179] "Have you ever had the feeling that you were crying for help and no one was listening—Well, I do now!" wrote one woman to the NRC in August 1981. She saw the commission hearings as a complete waste of time: "We feel that the decision to restart TMI Unit 1 is a FOREGONE CONCLUSION and nothing we have said or will say will make any difference." The NRC was not simply guilty of callousness, in her view. It had perpetrated a fraud against the people of the region by creating an ersatz show of democracy that had deluded residents into believing that they "had any voice in [their] own lives and futures where nuclear power is concerned."[180] On May 29, 1985, the NRC voted four to one in favor of the Unit One restart. More than three hundred local opponents had traveled to Washington for the final hearing. As the four commissioners called out their affirmative votes, shouts of "murderer" were heard from the floor. Meanwhile, back at Three Mile Island, eighty-two protestors were arrested at the plant gates.[181]

The community of fate at Three Mile Island revealed something crucial about the political transformation of the late 1970s that gets lost in narratives of culture war, polarity, and division. In the shadow of the reactor, self-identified patriots culled insights from the protest cultures of the 1960s and rerouted them into a new post-Vietnam conservative imaginary. These insights included a generalized suspicion of authority, a heightened politicization of the body, a drive to debunk false claims of expertise, an ecological awareness that air, water, and land could be contaminated, the power of collective psychology and the concept of trauma, and the value of local autonomy over federal authority. Weaving these insights into the conservative imaginary was no easy task. It took considerable time, commitment, creativity, and labor, much of which was performed by the region's women, who drew on their traditional roles as wives, mothers, and Christians. All the while, residents identified themselves as *reluctant* activists who had been conscripted into the political arena by their wounds, in contrast to the rootless cosmopolitan activists seemingly driven instead by abstract, hazy principles. In the end, the construction of a community of fate failed not only as a legal strategy, but as a political one as well. Its reliance on a status of injury precluded other affective stances—like empathy and solidarity—that might have laid the groundwork for other possibilities. Left behind instead was a transpartisan culture of suspicion that revolved around a post-1968 politicization of the imperiled body, but one ethically unmoored from the very protest movements that had first brought it into being. Between 1980 and 1985, this imperiled body would appear yet again as the revival of Cold War militarism reintroduced the threat of nuclear war.

Chapter Four

THE SECOND COLD WAR AND
THE EXTINCTION THREAT

On November 20, 1983, almost five years after the Three Mile Island accident, one hundred million Americans switched their television channels to ABC and watched as an imagined Kansas City—described as the epicenter of the nation's heartland—was blown to smithereens in a Soviet nuclear attack. Combining genre elements from family melodrama, "social issue" television, and disaster films, *The Day After*'s plot centered on husband, father, and physician Russ Oakes (played by Jason Robards), who witnesses the detonation from the highway. Realizing that his home is gone and his wife and children are dead, he returns to his workplace, a campus hospital in nearby Lawrence, where he attempts to administer to the burned, the injured, and the dying. Viewers are introduced to other stock characters: a farmer and his family who initially survive the blast in their cellar-cum-shelter; a woman who is nine-months pregnant with her first child; and a young premed student at the University of Kansas.

Before the attack, the farmer and his wife are planning to marry off their eldest daughter, the pregnant woman is awaiting her baby's arrival, and, when viewers first see Dr. Oakes, he is staring at an ultrasound image, lit from behind, that reveals a fetal heart defect in an unborn child. Characters go about their tasks, at first paying only scant attention to an escalating military crisis along the German border, where NATO and Soviet forces have amassed. They recall earlier Cold War scares like the Cuban Missile

Crisis and express confidence that cooler heads will again prevail. They hear snippets of radio and television reports. East German soldiers have rebelled, West Berlin has been blockaded, and the United States has detonated three tactical warheads over Soviet troops. At first these events feel far away, but in a nuclear world, "far away" no longer exists. "What's the chance that something will happen way out here in the middle of nowhere?" a young man asks nervously as he sits in a barbershop in Lawrence. "There's no nowhere anymore," another customer responds. "You're sitting next to the Whiteman Air Force Base right now. That's about 150 Minutemen silos spread down the state of Missouri. That's an awful lot of bulls-eyes."[1]

Representing nuclear war and its aftermath created certain challenges for the creators of *The Day After*. First, they were depicting an event that, not unlike radiation, shattered all logics of representation. The detonation itself—featured in the film—would instantaneously blind if not incinerate any observer. As writer and disarmament activist Jonathan Schell wrote, a film that showed the full consequences of a nuclear holocaust would fail to attract either sponsors or spectators. It would "have to display nothingness on the screen, and last forever."[2] Director Nicholas Meyer agreed, noting that "if you told this story accurately, there would be no story."[3] A second challenge was that the film's subject, a full-scale nuclear war, had never occurred. Thus the film was inherently speculative, compelling its creators to rely on government-sponsored studies like the Office of Technology Assessment report *The Effects of Nuclear War* (1979), antinuclear tracts like Helen Caldicott's *Nuclear Madness* (1978), and writings by organizations like Physicians for Social Responsibility (PSR) that imagined the probable biological and medical effects of a nuclear attack.[4] Throughout the early 1980s, these thought experiments made nuclear war appear both possible and imminent. Indeed, a Gallup poll conducted in 1982 found that almost half of all respondents (47 percent) believed that such a war would likely occur within five years.[5]

At a time of heightened Cold War tension, the film courted controversy. Although its creators denied that *The Day After* contained an overt critique of US and Soviet military policies (the plot was ambiguous on the question of blame), critics on the right branded the film an alarmist piece of Soviet-inspired propaganda, one that, in William Rusher's words, had inspired "an ignorant public hysteria."[6] The show aired shortly before the NATO

FIGURE 4.1. Film Still from *The Day After*, ABC Circle Films, 1983.

deployment of Cruise and Pershing II missiles in Western Europe, and critics like Rusher interpreted the film as an implicit condemnation of the planned action. "Why is ABC Doing Yuri Andropov's job?" asked the cover of the *New York Post*.[7] Another accusation was that the film threatened to derail rational policy-making by sowing panic. When asked for his response to it, Henry Kissinger wondered, "are we supposed to make policy by scaring ourselves to death?"[8] But the film also came under fire from critics who lamented its reliance on melodramatic conventions and in particular its tendency to filter an urgent geopolitical problem—perhaps *the* most urgent problem in planetary history—through the lens of domestic, familial, and romantic liaisons and dalliances. The first half of *The Day After* moves from one domestic scene to the next as clichéd rituals of heterosexual love, courtship, romance, and sex play out against the backdrop of escalating crisis. As film critic Kim Newman derisively put it, the problem with *The Day After* was that it treated nuclear holocaust as one "giant *coitus interruptus*."[9]

CIVIL DEFENSE, THE BODY-UNDER-ASSAULT,
AND THE PHYSICIAN-ACTIVIST

The revived fear of nuclear war in the early 1980s marked another moment of transition as the atomic age was reconfigured into the ecological one. The previous decade had witnessed the rise of an environmental consciousness within the United States. The first Earth Day was organized in 1970 in response to the oil spill off the Santa Barbara coast one year earlier. In 1971, Greenpeace was founded on the belief that ecological threats could not be remediated through policy-making and political legislation alone; civil disobedience would be necessary. Satellite images of the earth from space fostered a new planetary awareness of the globe as a small, solitary, and fragile entity. Meanwhile, as we have seen, the antinuclear movement hitched this expanding environmental consciousness to a critique of the Cold War complex. It gained momentum over the course of the 1970s, as direct actions and occupations contributed to plant closures at Shoreham, Yankee Row, Millstone I, Rancho Seco, and Maine Yankee. The Three Mile Island accident had immediate consequences for the industry, as activists throughout the United States and Europe seized on the island's cooling towers as a global symbol of the nuclear threat. In May 1979, 125,000 people attended an antinuclear demonstration in Washington, DC. The following September, almost two hundred thousand people gathered in New York City's Central Park to protest nuclear power. Faced with growing popular opposition and declining investor confidence, the NRC stopped licensing new plants. As a consequence, by the early 1980s, the fear of nuclear power receded and was supplanted by the fear of nuclear annihilation with the reescalation of the arms race. The accident at Three Mile Island had transformed central Pennsylvania into a site of radiological emergency. In its aftermath, every community in the country reimagined itself in a state of acute crisis, this time brought on by nuclear attack. Fears of radiation and atomic energy were thus rerouted away from nuclear power and channeled back into their original source: nuclear weaponry and war.

The wider backdrop of this rerouting was the Second Cold War of the 1980s. Between 1979 and 1984, détente collapsed, the second Strategic Arms Limitation Treaty (SALT) died in the Senate after the Soviet invasion of Afghanistan in 1979, and a new, even more lethal generation of nuclear weapons was brought to life. In 1979 NATO installed intermediate-range missiles in Britain, West Germany, the Netherlands, Belgium, and Italy. This was widely condemned as a unilateral act of provocation and sparked massive protests across the European continent. The US Pershing II missiles stationed in West Germany were capable of hitting Soviet targets within six to nine minutes. Between 1980 and 1984, the defense budget in the United States grew by 80 percent, and by 1980, the global nuclear stockpile comprised over sixty thousand weapons, the equivalent of over one million times the bomb dropped on Hiroshima.[10] The research, development, and deployment of new kinds of weapons—the Pershing II missile, the MX cruise missile system, the Trident Submarine, the B-1B Bomber—reflected a strategic shift away from deterrence toward counterforce and first-strike capabilities.

Throughout the globe, this reescalation sparked fears of nuclear catastrophe. But within US policy circles, it went hand in hand with a claim that nuclear war could be limited, survivable, and even winnable. This claim was first elaborated in Presidential Directive 59, the "Nuclear Weapons Employment Policy," a confidential directive signed by Jimmy Carter in July 1980 (the contents were subsequently leaked) that aimed to give the president more latitude in nuclear war planning. Unlike a policy of deterrence, which assumed that the lethality of nuclear weapons effectively deterred either side from using them, Directive 59 articulated a doctrine of first-strike willingness and a reliance on counterforce weapons, which were designed to disable an adversary's military capabilities. It imagined several options beyond a massive strike, including using high-tech intelligence to strike nuclear weapons targets on the battlefield and then assessing damages (what was called a "look-shoot-look" capability). The directive assumed that a nuclear war could be both controlled and contained.[11]

The concept of a limited, winnable nuclear war received considerable support after the election of Ronald Reagan in 1980. In press interviews and statements before Congress, key players in the new administration predicted that the nation could survive and even emerge victorious in a nuclear war. When in January 1980 George Bush (who would soon be selected as Reagan's running mate) was asked by journalist Robert Scheer how you win a nuclear exchange, he replied: "You have a survivability of command and control, survivability of industrial potential, protection of a percentage of your citizens, and you have a capability that inflicts more damage on the opposition than it can inflict upon you. That's the way you have a winner."[12] National Security Council member and détente-critic Richard Pipes speculated that in a nuclear war the "country better prepared could win and emerge a viable society."[13] William Chipman, the director of the Federal Emergency Management Association's (FEMA's) Civil Defense division, conceded in the *Los Angeles Times* that a nuclear war would be depressing and miserable, but that in all probability, people would "rise to the occasion and restore some kind of a country that would fairly be called the post-attack United States."[14] When asked on the floor of the Senate in June 1981 whether the country could survive a full-scale nuclear exchange, Eugene V. Rostow, who at the time was being considered for the directorship of the Arms Control and Disarmament Agency, reflected that "the human race is very resilient."[15] Taken together, these statements painted a picture not simply of a more confrontational Reaganesque military policy, but of an administration that was entertaining nuclear war as a rational possibility. This notion struck critics as deranged. As Bernard Feld, an MIT Physics professor and the editor of the *Bulletin of the Atomic Scientists*, put it, reports of a nuclear strategy based on a limited counterforce exchange "raise the serious question of whether our leaders have taken leave of their senses."[16]

Adding to mounting public anxiety was a fear that Ronald Reagan's alliance with evangelical Christianity had led him to view nuclear war as inevitable, even scripturally preordained within an eschatological worldview. The Old Testament's Book of Revelations predicted an Armageddon—a final battle between good and evil emanating from the Middle East that would end with God taking charge of human history through the second coming of Christ. Some evangelical Christians saw the escalating arms race as one of several prophetic signs that the "end days" were fast approaching, and throughout the early 1980s, Reagan implied that he might share this view. During his presidential campaign, Reagan had confided to evangelical leaders like Jerry Falwell and televangelist Jim Baker that he "sometimes saw Armageddon coming up very fast."[17] In a phone conversation with AIPAC executive director Tom Dine, Reagan reportedly said, "I turn back to your ancient prophets in the Old Testament and the signs foretelling Armageddon, and I find myself wondering if we're the last generation that's going to see that come about. I don't know if you've noted any of these prophecies lately, but believe me, they certainly describe the times we're going through."[18] The concept of limited nuclear war had proceeded from the premises that a nuclear exchange could resemble conventional warfare and that life would go on after an attack. Talk of Armageddon moved in the opposite direction, implying that if a nuclear war came to pass, it would be the result of divine rather than human intervention and would constitute a millennial rupture in time. Despite the differences, however, the military's embrace of a limited nuclear war doctrine and the evangelical discourse of Armageddon reinforced each other by making the prospect of nuclear war appear more rather than less likely.

The concept of a limited nuclear war circled back to the early Cold War by resurrecting the issue of civil defense, whose viability hinged on the survivability of a significant portion of the population. The Reagan Administration also saw a vigorous civil defense as crucial to restoring the nation's military strength and maintaining the overall balance of power. Several members of Reagan's foreign policy team were convinced that the Soviets had gained the upper hand in civil defense planning, and in March 1982, the administration proposed a 4.3 billion dollar, seven-year civil defense program that had two components: crisis relocation (the physical relocation of 150 million Americans from higher-risk to lower-risk locations) and protection in the form of shelters that would save lives, preserve major industries, and allow for the continuity of government after an attack. The scenario for crisis relocation went like this: At a time of escalating crisis, US satellite intelligence would detect that the Soviets had initiated their own defense measures, indicating that preparations were underway for an attack. The president would then identify the areas and urban centers within the United States to be evacuated. Evacuees would be moved to the countryside, where they would be sheltered in host communities outside the range of immediate destruction. The implementation of the evacuation plan would take approximately one week, and assuming that it had sufficient warning, FEMA predicted that it could protect 80 percent of the US population (a figure that sounded impressive until one realized that this translated into 46.3 million fatalities). "It would be a terrible mess," FEMA head Louis Giuffrida acknowledged to ABC News, "but it wouldn't be unmanageable."[19]

A second component of the plan assumed that properly designed shelters could provide adequate protection from a nuclear blast and the radioactive fallout that would follow. In an interview in January 1982, the deputy undersecretary of defense for strategic and nuclear forces, T. K.

Jones, explained that shelters could work, as long as there were enough shovels for distribution. "Everybody's going to make it if there are enough shovels to go around. . . . Dig a hole, cover it with a couple of doors and then throw three feet of dirt on top. It's the dirt that does it."[20] Jones was called before Congress to explain the quotation (he never appeared), and the *New York Times* jokingly wondered whether he was a peace movement mole who had infiltrated the Reagan White House in order to discredit it.[21] But while Jones's reckless statement made him an easy target for ridicule, he was hardly an outlier in his contention that civil defense, if properly implemented, could work. On the contrary, the vision of an effective civil defense was fundamental to Reagan's reassertion of the nation's military strength vis-à-vis the Soviet Union after a decade of perceived American retreat and decline.

Reagan's vision did not go uncontested. In the early 1980s, a broad, transnational movement emerged that condemned both the reescalation of the nuclear arms race and the talk of "winnable war" that accompanied it. In 1980, arms control advocate Randall Forsberg wrote *A Call to Halt the Nuclear Arms Race*, which appealed to both the United States and the Soviet Union to halt the testing, production, and deployment of nuclear weapons.[22] The idea was to "freeze" the nuclear arms race in place and only then turn to the thornier work of disarmament. Building on the earlier movement to stop the spread of nuclear reactors, the simple call for a mutual and verifiable freeze—precisely because it cut through military and technocratic jargon—proved remarkably effective as a tool of political mobilization throughout the United States.

Like the fight over the restart at Three Mile Island, the freeze movement transcended the divide between left and right, not in the name of bipartisanship, but rather through a shared sense of emergency. By the summer of 1982, freeze resolutions had been endorsed by state legislatures, city councils, and at town meetings throughout the country. Working in thirty-seven states, twenty thousand volunteers collected over two million signatures in support of a freeze, and in the November midterm elections, twelve million Americans voted for a bilateral freeze on referenda at the ballot box. In June of that year, 750,000 people gathered again in Central Park to demand an end to the arms race, the largest protest rally in US history up until that time. Fanning out across the country (including into regions like the South that tilted promilitary), freeze activists helped to create what historian Lawrence Wittner has described as "the largest, best-financed, and most popular disarmament campaign in American history." In partnership with their transatlantic allies—who recognized that the European theater would be ground zero for any nuclear war between the superpowers—these activists constituted what, according to Wittner, was the most dynamic, international citizens movement of the modern era.[23]

A constitutive aim of this movement was to dismantle the concept of a limited nuclear war. In order to do this, the freeze movement had to appropriate a technique from the Cold War national security state—futurology—and repurpose it for its own ends. The post–World War II national security state had devoted vast resources toward predicting and planning for a nuclear war. Convinced that the advent of nuclear weapons rendered earlier military history irrelevant, Cold War policymakers relied on intelligence estimates, war plans, role-playing exercises, and technology forecasts in order to both predict and shape specific outcomes.[24] With the reescalation of the Cold War in the early 1980s, freeze activists came to believe that the only way to generate massive support for a freeze was to compel the public to imagine repeatedly a full-blown nuclear attack. This required activists to take the security state's own forecasting techniques and remake them into weapons against the arms race. "We are forced in this one case to become historians of the future," wrote Jonathan Schell in 1982, "to chronicle and commit to memory an event that we have never experienced and must never experience."[25] Since no one would be left to bear witness to a nuclear-induced extinction, Schell contended, "We must bear witness to it before the fact."[26] Nuclear war was a scenario that, in the words of astronomer Carl Sagan, could only "be treated theoretically." Recognizing that the problem transcended science, he explained that such a war was "not amenable to experimentation."[27]

As freeze writings, speeches, and films routinely invited their audiences to envision what would happen if the places where they lived, loved, and worked came under nuclear attack, every locale became its own version of central Pennsylvania, with nuclear bombs replacing power plants as the primary existential threat. Freeze activists detailed the decimation of buildings and infrastructure, stressing how iconic American cities would be rendered unrecognizable at the moment of detonation. But the buildings were only the surface of the disaster. To counter the official discourse of survivability and to incite citizens to take action against the arms race, the movement called attention to the multiple assaults—biological, physiological, radiological, epidemiological—that would bear down on the human body in the event of a nuclear attack. Thus at the center of the freeze movement was the same vulnerable, irradiated body that had exploded to the surface at Three Mile Island.

Yet there were differences. TMI residents had expressed dread about the dormant and accretive effects of radiation over months, years, and even decades. With the threat of a nuclear war, however, the slow violence of low-dose radiation exposure was displaced by images of immediate and acute radiation poisoning: gastrointestinal distress, bleeding, hair loss, open skin sores, and severe fatigue. If an attack occurred, tons of irradiated soil and debris would drift away from the blast area, and between one and two hundred rads of radiation would produce nausea and vomiting in up to half of those exposed. A dose of four hundred and fifty rads of radiation would kill off 50 percent of the population, assuming the best-case (and highly unlikely) scenario of adequate medical care.[28] In other words, as radiation fears were rerouted away from power plants and toward weaponry, and as the threat of low-dose exposure was eclipsed by that of rapid, high-dose exposure, the symptomatology of radiation was transformed from something slow-moving and stealthy into something acute and visible on the body.

In addition, in the event of a nuclear attack, radiation exposure would be only one of *several* traumatic assaults on the human body. People in a targeted city, if not incinerated or crushed to death right away, would be vulnerable to multiple injuries caused by flying glass and debris. They would sustain internal injuries to the chest and abdomen, broken limbs, skull and spinal cord fractures, ruptured lungs and eardrums, lacerations, hemorrhaging, and bleeding. Many would suffer retinal damage and blindness, creating scenes of "disarray as billions of blinded beasts, insects, and birds began to stumble through the world."[29] But by far the most serious assault on the human body in the event of a nuclear attack would come from burns. A booklet published by San Francisco's Department of Public Health predicted that over half of the people living between 1.5 and 5 miles from that city would be killed from third-degree flash burns.[30]

What would make such injuries so dire was the unparalleled medical manpower required to treat them. In New York City alone, the number of burn victims from an attack would exceed by a thousand the capacity of all burn care centers throughout the entire country. Howard Hiatt, the dean of Harvard University's School of Public Health, predicted that whatever remained of the medical system after a nuclear war would "choke completely on burn victims."[31] This staggering list of injuries did not even take account of the utterly transformed postattack landscape. The pharmaceutical industry would be wiped out, and any remaining vaccines and antibiotics would need to be carefully rationed. There would be no sanitary water supply, no sewage system, and no waste disposal. Any remaining stocks of food would be rapidly depleted, and there would be no refrigeration. There would be hundreds of thousands of decomposing corpses, and there would be no means of disposal. These conditions would lead to hunger, famine, and cold among survivors, as well as to the likely return of epidemic diseases (typhus, cholera, meningitis, hepatitis, tuberculosis, polio) that had been largely eradicated throughout the developed world by advances in modern medicine. In its enormous capacity to alter *space*, a nuclear war would also amount to a form of *time* travel for any survivors— what the *New England Journal of Medicine* in 1962 had called an "atavistic return." "It is one matter for man to have evolved from living deep in a Paleolithic cave to the city apartment or the garden home in the suburb," the article observed, "but an entirely different matter to consider whether he can successfully return to the cave. The question of whether an abrupt return along this evolutionary path is psychologically possible will hopefully remain a metaphysical issue."[32]

Freeze activists often relied on documentary photographs and film footage of Japanese bombing victims as real-world approximations of the victims of a full-blown nuclear war. Footage of burned and irradiated sufferers at Hiroshima was spliced into Physicians for Social Responsibility's film *The Last Epidemic*, a documentary that imagined the effects of a nuclear detonation on San Francisco. The film's narrative describing the hypothetical nuclear destruction of that city was accompanied by footage showing actual victims from 1945. Fictionalized films like *The Day After* and *Testament* (another film released in 1983 that centered on the postattack lives of a mother and her three children in a small northern California town) also invoked Hiroshima as a point of reference. Panoramic shots of postattack Kansas City in *The Day After* took their inspiration from photographs of Hiroshima, and in *Testament*, the lone nonwhite characters in the film are a Japanese father and his son, pointedly named Hiroshi, who is mentally disabled. Thus throughout the freeze movement, the victims at Hiroshima and Nagasaki emerged as proxies for nuclear war–induced bodily injury. Film footage of Japanese burn victims was meant to do more than flag the inaugural event of the atomic age. By providing a window into one possible future, they prefigured an ecological age in which emergencies constituted the rule rather than the exception. "The Hiroshima people's experience . . . is of much more than historical interest," wrote Jonathan Schell. "It is a picture of what our whole world is always poised to become—a backdrop of scarcely imaginable horror lying just behind the surface of our normal life, and capable of breaking through into that normal life at any second."[33]

This vision of the environment as a scene of somatic vulnerability and bodily trauma required a new politics of health. Noting the many doctors and psychiatrists who had come out in support of a bilateral freeze, Schell observed that the movement was animated by people "ordinarily concerned not with politics but with disturbances in the body, the psyche, and the soul."[34] Once confined to the task of relieving individual suffering, psychiatrist Robert Jay Lifton explained, the physician's mandate now extended to "threats to the human species."[35] Physicians for Social Responsibility gave organizational legitimacy to this new mandate. Originally founded in 1960 by a group of Boston-based doctors who successfully advocated for the limited test ban treaty, PSR was revived in 1978 and grew rapidly over the next five years. The group had gained a national constituency in the wake of the TMI accident, and at the time of its revival, PSR was committed to the issues of both nuclear power plant safety and atomic weaponry. But in 1980, the organization chose to focus on nuclear arsenals alone, a decision that signaled how the escalation of the arms race was consigning the nuclear power issue to the periphery. Over the next decade, PSR convened conferences and symposia on the medical consequences of nuclear weapons, produced and distributed documentary films like *The Last Epidemic*, engaged in dialogue with its Soviet counterparts, and encouraged its members to publish on species threats in the *New England Journal of Medicine* and similar venues. It organized "bombing runs," in which physicians toured the country and told audiences what would happen if a one-megaton bomb were dropped on the city or town where they were speaking. Placing the nuclear threat at the center of an emergent anthropogenic consciousness, the organization imagined the planet itself as a sickened hu-

FIGURE 4.2. Physicians Marching for Disarmament, New York City, June 1992. Copyright held by Physicians for Social Responsibility. Courtesy of the State Historical Society of Missouri.

man body whose future hung in the balance. PSR leader Helen Caldicott described opposition to the arms race as "the ultimate form of preventive medicine. If you have a disease, and there is no cure for it, you work on prevention."[36]

This proto-ecological vision, based on a circulation between somatic and planetary injury, was widely shared among physicians. Throughout the early 1980s, the American Medical Association, the American Public Health Association, the American Psychiatric Association, and the National Medical Association all passed resolutions urging physicians to become involved in the campaign to prevent nuclear war. Articles on the health consequences of such a war appeared regularly in medical and scientific journals, and the nation's leading medical schools offered courses on the topic. Meanwhile, PSR chapters spread quickly throughout the country. As Harvard cardiologist James Muller observed, "This is not just some fringe group, it's now the mainstream."[37] Glen Geelhoed, a physician who worked with the American Red Cross, explained that he would not

have joined PSR "if it were a 'kook' movement for fear of injury to my career." In his words, he had "no truck with idealism."[38]

Where PSR broke with traditional organizations, however, was on the
crucial question of politics. PSR leaders like H. Jack Geiger and Bernard
Lown believed that physicians were obligated to do more than detail the
medical effects of a nuclear attack. They were also obligated to speak out
against federal civil defense planning for nuclear war, which the organization condemned on psychological grounds as delusional, on strategic
grounds as provocative, and on ethical grounds as a "travesty of morality."[39] In the closing minutes of *The Last Epidemic*, Geiger, who at the time
was a professor of community medicine at the City University of New York,
receives loud applause when he tells his audience, "any physician who even
takes part in so called emergency medical disaster planning specifically to
meet the problem of nuclear attack . . . is committing a profoundly unethi-
cal act."[40]

PSR's opposition to civil defense reflected a new ecological awareness of
the planet's fragility and inescapability. The organization rejected the effi-
cacy of both shelters and relocation, the two prongs of Reagan's civil defense plan. During the World War II–era bombings of Hamburg and
Leipzig, they recalled, those who had remained in shelters had died from
intense heat and carbon monoxide poisoning. Something similar would
happen in the event of a nuclear attack, PSR predicted: the firestorms would
turn shelters into crematoria.[41] The organization also took aim at crisis
relocation plans. In a booklet published in 1982, PSR asked what relocation
would mean from an epidemiological perspective: "Crisis relocation," it
wrote, "serves merely . . . to substitute immediate death in the cities for a
more protracted but nonetheless certain death in relocated areas."[42] Like
the radiation threat at Three Mile Island, nuclear war had the capacity to
render meaningless the boundaries between soldiers and civilians, between
illness and health, between danger and safety, between war and peace.

But for PSR activists, the problem was not limited to any one particular
civil defense plan or another. They found delusional the very concept of
survivability embedded in *all* civil defense planning for nuclear war. Like
those who lived at Three Mile Island, PSR members were concerned about
the future of reproduction, but now it came down to the question of survival itself. "To evaluate that concept," explained the booklet, "we must
stretch our understanding of what existence may or may not mean . . . our

cities in rubble, our land burned and contaminated, our friends and relatives gone, our future grimly foreshortened by prospects of famine and disease. Civil defense cannot change what the weapons can do."[43] What made the concept of survivability so perverse, in their view, were not only the massive biological traumas, but also the near-total collapse of medical services, since most hospitals and treatment centers were located in cities.[44] In the *New England Journal of Medicine*, Bernard Lown imagined how such a scenario might play out in Boston. Out of approximately sixty-five hundred physicians who worked in the city, nearly 74 percent of them would immediately be killed in an attack, and another 16 percent would be injured.[45] The wounded would receive no morphine for pain relief, no intravenous medicine or fluids, no emergency surgery, no antibiotics, no dressings, no nursing, and little food and water.[46] It was not that a nuclear war would place an excessive burden on doctors. Rather, it was that such a war would eviscerate medical services altogether. The point was vividly made in *The Day After*, when after the attack, the campus hospital is transformed into a morgue.

By challenging the concept of survivability central to civil defense planning, PSR anticipated the ecological insight that there were some disasters that could not be outrun. This reality prompted some city councils to push back against federal disaster planning. After PSR hearings, city councils in Boston, New York City, Philadelphia, Seattle, San Francisco, Boulder, and Boston came out against crisis relocation. In San Francisco, the Board of Supervisors rejected any federal nuclear attack contingency plans involving relocation on the grounds that such planning heightened the likelihood of war by deceiving citizens into thinking that evacuation would save them. In Greensboro, North Carolina, the director of the region's Emergency Management Assistant Agency not only refused to sign on to relocation planning, but removed the city's fallout shelter signs to protest what she saw as their misleading claim of protection. In March 1981, the city council in Cambridge directed its civil defense director to cease distribution of evacuation plans and instead circulate a publication that would inform citizens that the one thing that could truly protect them from nuclear war was worldwide disarmament.[47]

Not all physicians agreed that civil defense fell within their purview. Some felt that civil defense was a *political* issue that dovetailed with strategic nuclear policies, an arena where physicians had, in the words of *NEJM* editor Arnold Relman, "no special competence or authority."[48] This divide within the medical community came to a head in 1981 in a debate over a Department of Defense proposal that called on civilian healthcare providers to supplement military ones in the event of an overseas war. The goal of the plan, called the Civilian-Military Contingency Hospital System, or CMCHS, was to secure approximately fifty thousand civilian hospital beds that could be used by the military "for the treatment of casualties from a future large-scale overseas war that might begin and end very rapidly and might produce a great many casualties."[49] The AMA, along with the American Hospital Association, supported the plan, signaling the organization's reluctance to take a critical position vis-à-vis federal civil defense planning. But others were alarmed by the proposal, which they interpreted as a de facto endorsement of the concept of a limited nuclear war. As Kathryn Bennett, a medical administrator in California, explained in a letter to the assistant secretary of defense, John H. Moxley, her hospital staff was "particularly disturbed by the kind of war anticipated by this plan. The proposals' language, emphasizing the expectation of an unprecedented number of casualties in a short period of time, indicates the likelihood and acceptance of 'limited' nuclear war."[50] A month later, Archbishop John Quinn of San Francisco called on all Catholic hospitals to oppose it, contending that the plan fueled the delusion that there could be an effective medical response to nuclear war. In a letter to the British medical journal *Lancet*, fifty physicians from Oakland, California, condemned CMCHS, noting its perverse prioritization of hypothetical future need over so much actual need in the present. "Public hospitals," they wrote, "are being asked to expend manpower and resources in preparation for human slaughter, while patients are denied basic medical needs because of lack of funds."[51] The deans of seven medical schools in New York City called on the city's hospitals to reject the plan, and PSR urged hospitals throughout the country to do the same.[52] The controversy captured how effective PSR had been at reframing civil defense as an issue that fell within the medical establishment's purview.

Again, some doctors felt that PSR and its allies had gone too far. Jay C. Bisgard, a physician within the Defense Department, contended that a doctor's highest obligation was to care for casualties, regardless of whether they were military or civilian. In his view, those who rejected the CMSHS proposal were reneging on that obligation. "My sacred vow as a physician was to use my skill to save life and alleviate suffering," he wrote in April 1982, "It would be a moral outrage for a physician to withhold care from any human being in need."[53] Writing more broadly about the proper role of the physician within antinuclear activism, *NEJM* editor and doctor Arnold Relman drew a sharp distinction between the medical and the political-strategic dimensions of the nuclear issue. Physicians possessed special insights when it came to the medical consequences of nuclear war, Relman observed, and they had a responsibility to share those insights with the public. But they possessed neither special knowledge nor a single, unified position when it came to nuclear strategic policies. If physicians spoke out publicly on *those* policies, he warned, they ran the risk of undermining solidarity within the profession, eroding public confidence in their authority, and confusing personal conviction with professional expertise.[54]

In contrast, PSR leaders contended that the nuclear threat had blurred the line between the medical and the political-strategic. This was because nuclear war planning was qualitatively different from other kinds of disaster planning. In contrast to a flood, a fire, or an earthquake, preparing for nuclear war could actually make such a war *more* likely to occur. The planning itself, in other words, produced outcomes and shaped futures. "We are far likelier to approach [nuclear war] step by step . . . in a process that escalates risk to the breaking point," Geiger wrote in 1982.[55] In his view, plans like CMCHS, which treated limited nuclear war as a viable possibility, were one step along the path of escalation. Consequently, they confronted the physician with an ethical dilemma. If the physician gave her assent to such a plan, she would be providing the public with false assurance while promoting the dangerous myth that there was no real distinction between conventional war (in which medicine can relieve suffering) and nuclear war (in which it could not).

With the reescalation of the Cold War in the 1980s, the fear of nuclear power that had dominated the political landscape over the previous decade was eclipsed by the fear of nuclear war. As the threat of an attack displaced the threat of an accident, radiation was transformed from something stealth and slow-acting into something that could inflict visible and immediate injury. By calling attention to an attack's medical and biological consequences, doctors placed the imperiled human body at the center of disarmament politics, elaborated a portrait of a vulnerable planet, and conjured images of a disaster that could not be escaped. In the process, they helped to translate the atomic age into the ecological one. But what was the freeze movement's relationship to the political realignment of the 1970s? The answer resides in the contradictions and tensions contained within disarmament activism.

THE FREEZE MOVEMENT AND POLITICAL REALIGNMENT

Three Mile Island captured how the protest culture of the 1960s had migrated into regions of the country removed from the epicenters of social upheaval. Freeze mobilization offers an inverted version of the same story; it demonstrates how local varieties of conservatism were transforming national politics. Playing out at the same moment, the fight over the restart and the fight over the freeze were very different. One centered on a localized threat, the other on a planetary emergency. But despite the differences, there were revealing resonances. Both embraced a centrist politics of respectability, both appealed to traditional gender and family roles, religion, and patriotism, and both aimed to distance themselves from the earlier antiwar movement. Thus like the local fight at Three Mile Island, the freeze movement registered not only how key elements of left and right were combining and reconstituting themselves in the 1970s and 1980s, but also how a biotic nationalism, centered on the vulnerable human body, helped to tip the balance of national politics rightward.

The defining accent of freeze activism was its appeal to the supposedly bipartisan center of American politics. Indeed, the very concept of a bilateral freeze—in its specificity, its simplicity, its accessibility, and its plea to both superpowers—was meant to transcend partisanship. As National Freeze Campaign director Randy Kehler told Congress in March 1982, the campaign "is broad-based and non-partisan. It includes both conservatives and liberals, young and old, whites and non-whites. While it has recently found an enthusiastic response in the halls of Congress, the campaign is rooted in town halls, union halls, and parish halls in hundreds of communities all across America."[56] Polling conducted at the time indicated that this strategy was very effective. One poll conducted in 1983 found that 70 percent of the public favored a freeze.[57] In a report on American politics for Cambridge Survey Research, pollster Patrick Caddell observed that the freeze represented "the first potential centrist mass movement in our lifetime." He described it as "a self-generated middle class movement, consisting of yeomen, burghers, and housewives, who, normally politically passive, [have] reacted spontaneously to the rhetoric and actions of the Reagan Administration."

Much like the restart fight, freeze activism defined itself against the earlier antiwar movement. In contrast to the movement against the Vietnam War, Caddell explained, the freeze was not "a student/activist effort at the fringe of the body politic." In fact, it almost transcended conventional politics. Rather than an attempt to achieve a specific or concrete goal, it should be interpreted as "an expression of concern" that had activated what he called "the normally dormant center." Caddell praised the sheer numbers that the movement had mobilized, but he was even more impressed with the way the movement rose above the familiar, stale political divisions. No comparable national cause, he wrote, can match "the centrist middle-class nature of those activated."[58]

Caddell was right about the movement's breadth, but by associating it with moderation and centrism, he missed what was driving freeze activists in their efforts to win the center: a deep sense of planetary urgency. Simply put, many were convinced that they were running out of time. Two California-based freeze activists insisted that this was why the movement needed to eschew any wider political debate about US Cold War militarism and instead focus on one clear message. "The differences are too deep," they wrote, "the time too short. We need consensus in three to five years, not three to five decades. We have to focus on this single narrow option, the Freeze. And we have to promote it, however urgently, in such a non-offensive, non-partisan way that any faction—for any ideological or political reason whatsoever—can not fail to see that it is this or doomsday."[59]

Winning the center entailed a bid for respectability and an accompanying attempt to attract professionals. The freeze signaled a new politics within late US capitalism as deindustrialization, globalization, and the rise of an information- and service-based society devastated the industrial working classes, creating a larger, more ostensibly meritocratic professional-managerial class that would displace them within the political arena. The freeze sought to woo this new class. In addition to physicians, other constituencies were well represented throughout the movement, including educators, lawyers, social workers, nurses, psychologists, and musicians. Such professionals either formed groups to support the freeze or endorsed the freeze resolution at their annual meetings.[60] Freeze organizers believed that the visibility of these professionals would not only reinforce the campaign's nonpartisan character, but also endow it with legitimacy. Steve Ladd, a field director for the Northern California Freeze Initiative and a cochair on the national campaign, urged his fellow organizers to line up "credible and respected people" who could "speak to the moral, scientific, medical, or economic aspects of the issues."[61] Part of what made these professionals so highly valued was that they defied popular expectations of what an activist was supposed to be. "Chances are the words 'anti-nuclear activist' do not bring to mind your high school physics teacher, family doctor, or local attorney," commented the *Nuclear Times* in 1983, "But over the last two years, dozens of professional groups, combining expertise with enthusiasm, have brought sizable constituencies to the movement."[62] The *New York Times* argued that the participation of these groups distinguished freeze activism from the antiwar demonstrations of the late 1960s: "The leaders are not bearded radicals but middle aged and middle class men and women, many accustomed to positions of responsibility and prestige."[63]

Like the coverage of the local fight over the restart at Three Mile Island, such commentaries were as much about the legacy of the 1960s as about their ostensible subject. In this case, the *New York Times* not only derided "bearded radicals," but also neglected the considerable scope of antiwar activism at high tide. After all, by the late 1960s, there *were* many middle-class men and women (as well as doctors, nurses, scientists, and priests) who had come out against the war. The careful demarcation of freeze activism from antiwar activism, in other words, relied on two related moves: denial of the freeze movement's roots in earlier forms of social protest and a degradation of an unapologetic leftist politics. And while it is tempting to pin these gestures on the media alone, it was freeze leaders themselves who sought to ward off the stigma of radicalism. Antinuclear activist Helen Caldicott told audiences that there was "nothing left wing or radical" about opposition to nuclear war. Quite the opposite; in her words, it was "the ultimate in conservatism."[64]

The appeal to a bipartisan center, the prominent role assigned to professionals, and the attempt to distance itself from the antiwar movement all combined with a distinct gender politics. Women, specifically in their capacities as mothers, were central to freeze activism, just as they had been at Three Mile Island. The terrifying scenarios of nuclear attack all came down to the fact that most mothers would never see their children again, and those who did would watch them die excruciating deaths. This prediction placed mothers at the heart of the freeze, not simply as advocates of disarmament but as guardians of children, reproduction, and the planet as a whole. In an interview in 1983, actress and freeze supporter Joanne Woodward echoed the widely held view that motherhood endowed women with innate sensitivity to the nuclear threat. Women, she declared, "are the ones who raise children, who give birth to the children. It's our children who will be destroyed along with us."[65] In 1982, Helen Caldicott helped to launch Women's Action for Nuclear Disarmament (WAND) after observing that it was women in her audiences who responded to her message with the greatest sense of urgency.[66] Above all, it was pregnant women who embodied the escalating danger. In preparation for a rally to be held in May 1984, WAND wrote a letter to supporters urging anyone who was visibly pregnant to make the trip to Washington, DC: "If you are expecting a baby between early June and mid-September, or can recruit someone who is, please send your name and address and expected date of birth to WAND." The letter explained the underlying rationale: "It is difficult to imagine ignoring the moral authority of a contingent of visibly pregnant women."[67]

Much as they had at Three Mile Island, these appeals to women stood in complex relation to feminism. On the one hand, they illustrated women's empowerment vis-à-vis issues like the arms race that had once been construed as the exclusive domain of male leaders and policymakers. But on the other hand, they undermined the feminist plea that women not be reduced to their identities as mothers. Meanwhile, Caldicott's call for a contingent of visibly pregnant women again evoked the unborn in ways that suggested an affinity between the nuclear issue and the abortion war. Women's centrality within the freeze also converged with their growing visibility within the professional middle classes. A membership poll of the American Association of University Women (AAUW) conducted in 1983 found that its members, almost half registered Republicans, ranked nuclear war higher than the Equal Rights Amendment and educational opportunity as a pressing women's issue.[68] But above all, the appeal to motherhood worked to solidify the movement's nonpartisan, mid-American character. Mother's Day rallies and vigils for the freeze were held in traditionally conservative parts of the country, like Little Rock, Arkansas, Helena, Montana, and Albuquerque, New Mexico, and leaders were encouraged that the

WHAT DO YOU FEEL ABOUT THE UNTHINKABLE?

Nuclear war is a terrifying prospect.

In fact, most people try not to think about it. Or even to feel.

But ignoring this nightmare won't make it go away. It's time we faced our fears about the future and started doing something about them.

We invite you to join other families with the courage to think about the unthinkable and discover new avenues toward peace.

To explore not only your fears but your more positive feelings, your hopes and dreams for yourself and those you love.

There's a community gathering to help you do just that. It's called "The Day Before."

A time to consider what's ultimately important, to talk, to feel, to share with one another. Only then will we be free to act, to really make a difference, to reaffirm life and all we hold dear.

Everyone is welcome — including children. We invite you to come.

Because we all know the day after will be too late.

The day before is here. And now.

"The Day After" is an ABC TV Movie. It is a graphic and highly realistic story about the unthinkable — nuclear war. Americans who have been passive observers of the arms race witness missiles leaving their silos in Kansas. This may be the last thing they ever see...

The Day Before

P.O. Box 8493, Emeryville, California 94662   (415) 644-3391

INSERT LOCAL INFORMATION HERE

Public Media Center

FIGURE 4.3. What Do You Feel About the Unthinkable? Courtesy of the State Historical Society of Missouri.

participation of mothers at these events "generated considerable interest" in the local press. "Someone once criticized the freeze as a mom-and-apple pie issue," observed Vermont-based organizer David McAuley. And "that's exactly what it is," he proclaimed proudly.[69]

Along with women, religious leaders helped to translate the atomic imaginary into the ecological one via the figure of the unborn. As we have seen, many local clergy had facilitated the transformation of Christian residents into activists at Three Mile Island, and a similar dynamic pervaded freeze activism. Freeze leaders cast disarmament as a spiritual as much as a geopolitical imperative. Randy Kehler's turn to freeze activism had been accompanied by what he called a "profound spiritual awakening."[70] Not surprisingly, the original *Call to Halt the Arms Race* was endorsed by pacifist religious organizations like the American Friends Service Committee, Clergy and Laity Concerned, and the Fellowship of Reconciliation. But by the end of 1981, several mainline church organizations had endorsed it as well. These included the Presbyterian Church USA, the United Methodist Church, the American Baptist Church, the National Council of Churches of Christ, the Episcopal House of Bishops, and the Lutheran Church. Local parishes throughout the country became pipelines through which organizers met with congregants and distributed profreeze literature.[71]

But it was the Roman Catholic Church that provided the movement with its most influential backing. The international Catholic peace group Pax Christi distributed copies of the call to its members for Lent, several Catholic orders and nuns' associations endorsed it, and one bishop even advised members of his diocese not to seek employment in the nuclear industry. The decisive movement came in May 1983, when the country's Roman Catholic bishops ratified by an overwhelming margin a pastoral letter on war and the nuclear arms race, *The Challenge of Peace: God's Promise and Our Response.*[72] While the bishops insisted that they were not formally endorsing any specific course of action, the letter described the arms race as "one of the greatest curses" on humanity. It took direct aim at the concept of a limited nuclear war, and it expressed support for a bilateral verifiable agreement to halt (not curb, a term that had appeared in earlier drafts) the testing, production, and deployment of new nuclear weapons systems. The ratification of the letter constituted a watershed for the Catholic Church. "Many of the 50 million Catholics in the United States," wrote the *New York Times*, "consider the bishops' action to be the boldest and most decisive step on social issues in the history of the American hierarchy."[73] Over a million copies were distributed and studied at churches throughout the United States and the world. At forty-five thousand words, the letter was wide-ranging. It elaborated the Church's position on war, the policy of deterrence, the arms race and disarmament, nonviolence, and how to best promote peace.

Crucially, the statement also tethered the nuclear arms race to the practice of abortion by describing both as mutually reinforcing malevolent forces that threatened innocent lives and diminished their worth. The secular culture's tolerance of abortion had dulled its collective sense of horror toward the prospect of nuclear war, the letter maintained. "In a society where the innocent unborn are killed wantonly," the bishops asked, "how can we expect people to feel righteous revulsion at the act or threat of killing noncombatants in war?" The unintended loss of innocent human lives during conventional war, while tragic, could "conceivably be proportionate to the values defended." But nuclear warfare was different because its weaponry was designed precisely to "kill millions of defenseless human beings." There was no justification for a "direct attack on human life, in or out of warfare," and abortion was just such an attack.

Abortion thus emerged in the letter not simply as an analog to nuclear war, but as a gateway to it. According to one passage, "We must ask how long a nation willing to extend a constitutional guarantee to the 'right' to kill defenseless human beings by abortion is likely to refrain from adopting strategic warfare policies designed to kill millions of defenseless human beings, if adopting them should come to seem 'expedient.'" The pastoral letter thus provided the bishops with an opportunity not only to weigh in on the escalating arms race, but also to formulate what they called a "consistent ethic of life" that traversed genetics, abortion, capital punishment, modern warfare, and euthanasia. "Some see clearly the application of the principle to abortion, but contend the bishops overstepped their bounds when they applied it to choices of national security," explained Cardinal Joseph L. Bernardin (who had chaired the committee that wrote the letter) at a speech at Fordham University. "Others understand the power of the principle in the strategic debate, but find its application to abortion a violation of the realm of private choice. I contend the viability of the principle depends upon the consistency of its application."[74] In its attempt to articulate a consistent principle, the pastoral letter again placed the figure of the unborn at the center of the nuclear threat. The practice of abortion, it contended, had inured the nation to the mass killing of innocent people.

The seemingly disparate issues of disarmament and abortion thus converged around the unborn, and the unborn was the cord that tethered the earlier atomic age to the emergent ecological one. In the 1950s, test ban advocates had appealed to the unborn in order to condemn contamination without representation. At Three Mile Island, residents evoked the same figure to sound the alarm over future harm. The unborn surfaced again within disarmament activism, this time as a symbol of a systemic degradation of human life that tied the practice of abortion to nuclear proliferation. Thus within disarmament activism, one could see how ecological symbols and images—the threatened fetus, the irradiated body—were circulating throughout the political field of the 1980s, creating deeply ambiguous social movements that could be pulled in any number of directions but that would gravitate rightward over the course of the decade.

This ambiguity shaped disarmament activism. As we have seen, from the beginning, this activism had woven together discrete and even contradictory elements. It appealed to centrism but was driven by a sense of urgency rather than moderation. It enlisted professionals to steel itself against charges of radicalism. It drew women into its orbit but often in their exclusive capacities as mothers. It identified itself as a spiritual, global movement and singled out the church as one of its vital epicenters. By the mid-1980s, freeze activists had adopted another tactic: the reclamation of a patriotic ideal that would establish that they were motivated by a deep love of country. After voting in their town halls and parishes to endorse the call, citizens would stand up and sing "God Bless America." One strategist urged freeze groups to use the American flag and anthem at public events, insisting that doing so was at once a moral and political imperative.[75] Activists worked hard to "protect this beautiful country from devastation and to save the lives of tens of millions of our fellow Americans," he maintained, "By all moral right, we should consider ourselves to be at least as sincere patriots as our opponents," going on to suggest campaign slogans like "Love America—Let Us Live," "Nuclear Freeze: Save American Lives," and "Keep America Beautiful: Prevent Nuclear Holocaust."[76] These appeals to patriotism signaled the rise of a biotic, body-centered nationalism that placed a premium on American lives over others. At the same time, they reflected the movement's desire to win the political center and disaffiliate from the "hippies and the flag-burning that were so prominent in the peace movement of that day."[77]

This attempt at disaffiliation effaced the complex role that patriotism had played in the earlier antiwar movement. Indeed, some opponents of the war had claimed the mantle of patriotism, insisting that they were truer patriots than the war's defenders and that opposition to war constituted the highest form of patriotism. But now, within disarmament activism, patriotism became bound up not with the issue of war, but rather with reproduction. "Center the issue" of children, advised Educators for Social Responsibility in a brochure. "The health and survival of children is a mainstream issue. It is a patriotic issue. Let's carry the flag and stand on the parade ground as we teach others about the ways that nuclear weapons subvert our political ideals and undermine the rights of human beings everywhere."[78] After all, what could be more patriotic than wanting to save the lives of the nation's children?

In its embrace of patriotism, freeze activism tracked a political realignment as the country gravitated rightward, a center-right hegemony consolidated, and the left became marginalized. The freeze's move toward the center was at least in part a tactical response to critics. For no matter how hard disarmament activists worked to establish their patriotic bona fides, there were always groups, such as Young Americans for Freedom (YAF), the Moral Majority, and the American Security Council, that attacked them from the right. Some conservatives, for example, accused freeze activists of being tools of the Kremlin. The call for nuclear disarmament was a deceptive cover, claimed the Alliance to Halt the Advance of Marxism in the Americas. "Don't march for this phony 'peace' plan," warned one of its flyers. "This plan was designed in Moscow to help the enemy bury us."[79] In a letter to Moral Majority members, Jerry Falwell observed that "Here in America the 'freeze-niks' are hysterically singing Russia's favorite song: a unilateral nuclear freeze—and the Russians are loving it!"[80] Critics like Falwell contended that because American strength had declined precipitously over the previous decade, a freeze would permanently lock a Soviet military advantage in place. The movement's attempts to distance itself from the taint of the 1960s left these critics wholly unconvinced. As the American Security Council portrayed it, the movement was led by a "small contingent of radical leftists and Marxist leaning 60s leftovers ... whose whole lives have been devoted to bringing about the eventual end of the capitalistic system in America."[81]

This charge overlooked the cleavages between disarmament activism and leftist opposition to US militarism. For their part, leftist critics recognized the nationalist tendencies within disarmament activism, critiqued those tendencies on universalist and cosmopolitan grounds, and urged the movement to expand its vision. The very quality that made the freeze so compelling as a recruiting tool—namely, its focus on a narrow, specific goal—could also be construed as a liability, for it precluded the development of a more thoroughgoing critique of US militarism. For some longtime pacifists and social justice advocates, the voicing of collective concern about nuclear war ran an inch deep and a mile wide. As one peace activist dismissively wrote in a letter to the national office, the freeze movement was made up of "philosophically, politically, and socially disparate people whose only bond is their anxiety about being incinerated."[82] Mark Niedergang, who worked full-time for the campaign in the early 1980s, urged the movement to go beyond what he called "apoco-porn" and engage more directly with policy questions. If it failed to do so, he warned, it could set the stage for a scenario in which nuclear weapons were traded for "an unnecessary and expensive increase in conventional military forces."[83]

For critics on the left, the movement's preoccupation with a nuclear attack *in the future* was effacing forms of violence being unleashed by US conventional weapons *in the present*. In December 1981, Beverly Woodward, a Fellowship of Reconciliation member and a trainer in nonviolent action, wrote to Freeze director Randy Kehler in order to make this point. "The military itself may decide to 'save' the war system by deemphasizing nuclear weapons and moving to other horribles," she speculated. "And as you know, even if we get rid of all nuclear weapons (an achievement that would go considerably beyond the freeze), the Third World would not perceive itself to be a great deal better off."[84] Along with her letter, she included a copy of a correspondence with Noam Chomsky, who elaborated on her argument. The war system could cause "horrendous suffering and damage even without nuclear weapons," Chomsky observed, and he questioned whether the freeze campaign was deepening people's understanding of "how we got where we are." "An emphasis on the disastrous consequences of nuclear war is reasonable, but not the main point in my view," Chomsky wrote. "The point that should be constantly pressed, I believe, is that the cold war system has been highly functional for the superpowers as a device for legitimizing and mobilizing popular support for their respective programs of aggression, terror, and operation—in pretended defense against the superpower enemy. For the peasants of Guatemala, or the people of Afghanistan or Timor, the effects of nuclear bombardment are a secondary matter, or plainly irrelevant, since they are already suffering something similar. So called 'conventional' weapons are, in my view, possibly even more dangerous than strategic weapons, for which the motivation is largely either propaganda or military Keynesianism, or supporting the internal power of military-bureaucratic-industrial elites; the 'conventional' weapons, in contrast, are used."[85]

For critics like Chomsky, the freeze movement's exclusive focus on nuclear weapons over conventional ones constituted at once a temporal and a spatial misstep. Its temporal misstep was that it accorded priority to a theoretical future scenario (a nuclear war) in ways that occluded suffering in the present (much of it perpetrated by the US military). Its spatial misstep was that it relocated violence away from actual theaters of military conflict (Afghanistan, Guatemala) and grafted it onto the domestic space of the United States, if only in people's worst nightmares. Both moves implicitly valued American lives over others; Afghans and Guatemalans, to borrow from Judith Butler, were thus "un-mourned."[86] The freeze's temporal emphasis on futurity posed yet another problem. It made it difficult for the campaign to move beyond its overwhelmingly white, middle-class base of support within the United States. Patricia Williams, an African American hired by the campaign to work on minority outreach, observed that "few black leaders are inclined to put aside what they call 'immediate survival issues' in order to accommodate themselves to the overwhelmingly white antinuclear movement."[87] The freeze's strategy of using such a tight, single-issue focus to attract conservative and Republican constituencies, she speculated, had come at the "expense of bringing in the masses of poor, black, and other minorities who are already on our side."[88]

Thus even as freeze activists condemned the Second Cold War, they unwittingly aligned themselves with the new nationalism of the 1980s by invoking patriotism and distancing themselves from the antiwar left. They did this to deflect redbaiting, but in the process, they disowned their own debt to what had come before. That debt was not hard to see. Randall Forsberg's original call to halt the nuclear arms race built on the prior work of organizations like Mobilization for Survival (founded by antiwar activists who in the late 1970s turned to the nuclear threat), as well as groups like the American Friends Service Committee and the Fellowship of Reconciliation that had actively opposed the Vietnam War. Randy Kehler, who headed the freeze campaign in the early 1980s, had himself cut his political teeth on antiwar activism. He spent twenty-two months in prison for defying the draft in 1969. The freeze strategy of using a simple demand that cut through the mystique of military jargon took its inspiration from an earlier antiwar movement that had indicted a cult of foreign policy experts whose authority had gone unquestioned for far too long, with devastating results.[89] Yet freeze strategists sometimes suppressed this shared history. A set of outreach guidelines titled *Depolarizing Disarmament Work* cautioned against labeling people as "hawks" or "doves" and called for close attention to language when talking with potential recruits. "The words right-wing, hawk, dove, conservative, radical, or left-wing all tend to peg people in a certain position from which it becomes difficult to move. Once people feel that the alternatives are staying 'hawkish' or turning into a 'dove' they may decide it is safer to stay where they are." The guidelines went on to urge activists to think twice before bringing up *any* connection between the fight for disarmament and the earlier movement against the war:

Disarmament is an issue that can have appeal beyond right or left wing: it is an issue of human security which cuts across ideologies. In this respect, another area of caution is the Vietnam connection. By assuming that your audience must be convinced that U.S. participation in the Vietnam War was wrong in order for them to now support disarmament, you may be hurting their potential for change in both areas. Even though you may believe, as I do, that it was wrong, there are a lot of people with psychological wounds from the Vietnam War for whom the worst possible thing may be to attack them on that issue to begin with. If you agree, you may even want to avoid using the example of "How the peace movement helped to end the Vietnam War" as an example of effective action. What if your audience does feel open to reducing armaments now, but still is not sure about the Vietnam experience? Just think twice before you bring it up.[90]

Organizers felt that this strategy was especially crucial in conservative bastions of the country. In January 1983, a freeze field worker in Kearney, Nebraska, reported to the national office that "Nebraska is conservative and does not like lots of noise, conflict, polarization, and banner-waving." Instead, campaigners had successfully used local churches and service clubs to quietly educate people about the freeze. Through hard work, they had also won over Kearney's local media. As one activist reported back to the national office, "We avoided the scruffy, protest image of the 60s."[91] At a moment when the culture wars were creating new fractures and fault lines within the body politic, freeze activists deployed a conscious strategy of *depolarization* when it came to the question of disarmament. This strategy reflected the very real sense of urgency that animated their work, but it effaced the movement's own political debts. Meanwhile, a steady but protean preoccupation with reproduction opened the door to the ecological age.

REPRODUCTION, NUCLEAR WINTER, AND THE EXTINCTION THREAT

In the early 1980s, the revival of the nuclear war threat generated its own set of questions about the fate of reproduction. Vivid descriptions of the immediate and short-term radiological effects of a nuclear attack often overwhelmed any consideration of its latent, slower-moving effects on the gene pool. Yet thought experiments about nuclear war did speculate about the genetic legacy that such a war might leave behind, thus harkening back to the fears voiced at Three Mile Island. Imagining the decades that would follow even a limited attack, Jonathan Schell predicted that survivors would face not only a contaminated and degraded environment, but contaminated "flesh, bones, and genetic endowment" as well. "The generations that would be trying to rebuild a human life," he wrote, "would be sick and possibly deformed."[92] In addition to unleashing a fatal cancer epidemic, doctors warned, a nuclear war would leave behind high rates of sterility and genetic damage.[93] Unlike a conventional war that has a beginning, middle, and end, a nuclear one would redound indefinitely. In a brochure titled *What About the Children?*, Parents and Teachers for Social Responsibility declared that "we have set the stage to annihilate the next generation and perhaps all generations thereafter."[94] Drawing again on Hiroshima and Nagasaki, doctors speculated that pregnant women would suffer spontaneous miscarriages and give birth to babies with physical and mental defects during the postattack period. In light of that, they wondered whether abortions should be provided en masse in the wake of a nuclear attack. Members of PSR elaborated on this idea. Since there was an accepted place for therapeutic abortion after rubella exposure in the first trimester, there should also be a place for mass abortion in the postattack period.[95]

Much as it had been at Three Mile Island, the unborn was evoked in a dual sense throughout these accounts—as both a living fetus vulnerable to radiological danger and a shadowy, futuristic figure that was doomed before it had even been conceived. In fictional depictions of nuclear war, newborns and infants got sick first. "Doctor, my baby wouldn't take my milk this morning," a new mother tells a physician in *Testament* the day after a nuclear detonation levels nearby San Francisco. "She threw it up, maybe that's nothing. Maybe she'll be fine in the morning. How do I know? Is there something I can do?"[96] The dialogue was consistent with the warnings of doctors, who predicted that after a nuclear attack, babies and infants would be the first to die.[97] Thus even as radiation's symptomatology underwent revision as weapons supplanted power plants in the nuclear imaginary, the front line of victims remained the fetus, the unborn, the newborn, the infant.

Reproduction loomed large over the nuclear war threat in another way. This was because the debate about civil defense was implicitly about *social reproduction*. With roots in both Marxist and feminist theory, the term *social reproduction* refers to all of the activities and relationships that are required for people's survival, both from one day to the next and across successive generations. If biological reproduction encompasses conception, gestation, pregnancy, and birth, social reproduction encompasses all of the daily practices that Marx saw as vital to the maintenance of any system of economic production. These included the purchasing of household goods, food preparation and service, the laundering and mending of clothes, the maintenance of the home, the socialization of children, and the provision of emotional and physical care to the young, the sick, and the elderly.[98] Of course, when policymakers within the Reagan Administration spoke of survival and recovery from a limited nuclear war, they did not use the language of social reproduction. Yet this was precisely what they were talking about. Their championing of civil defense hinged on the premise that a postattack social world could be made to resemble what had come before. If a strong civil defense program were in place at the time of an attack, they predicted, people could subsequently secure food, water, shelter, and medical care, electricity could be restored quickly, and infrastructure could be rebuilt. Disarmament activists, in contrast, predicted that even a limited nuclear war would make it impossible to reproduce the social conditions that were a prerequisite for life to go on. The true meaning of survival, they contended, was social, not biological. For PSR's Jack Geiger, the issue was not "the biological possibility of the survival of the last humans," but "the possibility of the survival of organized human social existence."[99] Jonathan Schell cautioned against imagining that the postattack period would in any way mimic the aftermath of a natural disaster in which rescuers and unaffected survivors would provide food, clothes, and medical care to the injured, who would then be able to make their way to safe communities. Instead, the detonation of a nuclear weapon would "attack the support system of life at every level"; there would be no untouched place. It would kill both directly and indirectly—"by breaking down the man-made and the natural systems on which individual lives collectively depend." "Human beings," Schell observed, "require constant provision and care, supplied by both their societies and by the natural environment, and if these are suddenly removed people will die just as surely as if they had been struck by a bullet." It was no coincidence that the plotlines of *The Day After* and *Testament* chart the gradual realization on the part of a doctor and a mother—two pillars of social reproduction—that, in the aftermath of an attack, there is nothing they can do to care for their patients and children.

The ultimate message of *The Day After* was that in the event of a nuclear war, there would be no postattack recovery as FEMA conceived of it. When critics on the right complained that the film implicitly undermined the strategy of deterrence, Brendon Stoddard of ABC Motion Pictures countered that *The Day After* contained no political content at all: "The movie simply says that nuclear war is horrible. That is all it says. That is a very safe statement."[100] But both the accusation and Stoddard's defense missed the point. The political message of *The Day After* was not that deterrence would necessarily fail, but that should a nuclear war come to pass, civil defense would *definitely* fail. The film paints an unreservedly grim picture of physical and social disintegration after the attack. There is no electricity or telephone service, roads and buildings have been destroyed, food and water have been contaminated, the soil in the ground has been poisoned, and livestock lie dead in the fields. Survivors on the outskirts of Kansas City wander in a daze in search of food, shelter, and medical help. As it becomes clear that no such help is coming, violence breaks out. There are food riots, looting, and firing squads. The lone allusion to civil defense planning is in a scene in which representatives from the National Emergency Reconstruction Administration (modeled on the Office of Defense Resources, which would supplant FEMA after a nuclear war) advise a group of farmers on how to decontaminate their fields by removing several inches of top soil and only planting UV-resistant crops. One of the farmers questions the directive. "How do you know what safe is?" he asks. "Where did you get all of this information? This good advice? Out of some government pamphlet?" One of the final scenes of the film shows survivors in Lawrence huddling around a single salvaged short-wave radio, listening to the president as he assures them that the government is prepared to "make every effort to coordinate relief and recovery programs at the state and local levels." But the president's message is steadily belied by a montage of bleak images: fields full of rotting corpses, the faces of stunned survivors, and a hospital hall packed with dying burn victims. While the creators of *The Day After* deliberately shrouded the war's causes in ambiguity, they were considerably more forthcoming about its aftermath. Civil defense would be a complete failure, and any official claims to the contrary could not be trusted. "Anyone who advocates limited survivable nuclear war is not going to be happy with this movie," Democratic representative Edwin Markey surmised.[101]

Running alongside these predictions about the collapse of social reproduction was an even more totalizing scenario about species reproduction: a nuclear war could constitute an extinction-level event. This view found expression in the theory of a nuclear winter (NW), which postulated that in a nuclear war, multiple detonations and fires would release large amounts of dust, soot, and particulate matter into the stratosphere and smoke into the troposphere, blocking sunlight from reaching the earth. Under these conditions, a deep freeze would settle over the northern hemisphere, soot would block out the sun, noon would look like midnight, average temperatures would drop precipitously, water supplies would freeze, and the subfreezing weather—which could last for months—would lead to catastrophic crop failure. NW research brought together scientists from several disciplines, but the theory's origins resided in the field of areology, the study of Mars. In 1971, Mariner 9 orbited Mars and recorded images of a global dust storm that was absorbing sunlight and preventing it from reaching the planet's surface. The discovery prompted scientists to ask if a nuclear war could produce a similar effect on earth. Since they could not test the hypothesis through real-world experimentation, scientists relied on computer simulations in order to play out various scenarios. While they debated certain elements of NW theory, there was an emerging consensus that, in addition to producing immediate megadeath, a nuclear war would have long-term planetary environmental consequences. By 1983, the theory of nuclear winter was circulating within both scientific circles and the broader culture. A conference on the topic was held in Cambridge, Massachusetts, in April of that year, articles on it appeared in journals like *Science*, *Nature*, and the *Bulletin of Atomic Scientists*, and in October 1983 astrophysicist Carl Sagan published an article in *Parade* magazine that explained the theory to a lay audience.[102] Along with the discovery in the late 1970s that chlorofluorocarbons were eroding the ozone layer, the theory of nuclear winter anticipated subsequent discussions of anthropogenic climate change in its claim that human activity (in this case, nuclear detonations rather than carbon emissions) could radically alter the earth's climate, with devastating consequences.[103]

At the heart of NW theory was a core insight of modern ecology. As Barry Commoner famously put it, everything was connected to everything else. If the northern hemisphere were suddenly shrouded in darkness and cold, its biological support system would collapse. Without light, the process of photosynthesis would fail, killing off green plants. All crops would be destroyed, herbivores would starve (thus depriving carnivores of food), and plankton would disappear, fatally derailing the entire marine food chain. In other words, the entire biological foundation on which human beings relied for their survival would be shattered, leading to mass starvation. "The delicate ecological relations that bind together organisms on Earth in a fabric of mutual dependency would be torn, perhaps irreparably," predicted Carl Sagan. "There is little question that our global civilization would be destroyed," he continued. "The human population would be reduced to prehistoric levels, or less. Life for any survivors would be extremely hard. And there seems to be a real possibility of the extinction of the human species."[104] Among the most frightening dimensions of the NW scenario was that scientists could not predict how the multiple assaults of a nuclear winter—darkness, freezing temperatures, ionizing radiation, toxic air pollution—would synergistically amplify one another. University of California physicist John Harte explained that synergies worked either for or against human survival and could shift gears.[105] Analogizing the human relationship to the ecosystem to an intensive care patient's dependency on IV-bottles and life-supporting medical equipment, Harte likened the waging of nuclear war to "throwing a stick of dynamite into an intensive care ward, rupturing the vital links that ensure survival."[106] Anyone who spoke of winning or even surviving a nuclear war was "gambling, ignorantly and arrogantly, with the chain of life itself, with the whole intricate web from phytoplankton to man," H. Jack Geiger told the International Physicians for the Prevention of Nuclear War in 1984 in a speech on nuclear winter.[107] While critics of civil defense predicted that a nuclear war would fatally derail social reproduction, nuclear winter theorists contended that species reproduction itself hung in the balance.

These predictions suggested that nuclear war would shatter national boundaries. Even with its transnational dimensions, the freeze movement in the United States relied on a nation-statist framework when it forecasted the effects of a nuclear war on American towns and cities. But NW theory cast nuclear war as a *planetary* emergency. While NW scenarios were often based in the northern hemisphere, scientists pointed out that the global south would experience effects that, while less severe, would be devastating. Sagan predicted that a cloud of fine particles would travel across the equator, bringing the cold and dark with it.[108] Anne Ehrlich painted a grotesque picture of postwar survival in the southern hemisphere, where small bands of people "might persist for several generations in a strange, inhospitable environment . . . their adaptive capacities sapped by inbreeding and a burden of genetic defects from the postwar exposure to ionizing radiation and increased ultraviolet B—a classic recipe for extinction."[109] Three Mile Island residents had challenged the notion that evacuation could protect residents from the radiation threat in the event of an accident, and now NW theory shattered any remaining illusion that one could outrun a nuclear war by fleeing south. "Where does one go from Kansas City?" a fellow doctor asks Russ Oakes in *The Day After* as the geopolitical situation deteriorates, "The Yukon? Tahiti? We are not talking about Hiroshima anymore." The vision of a nuclear winter, in other words, was a distinctly *global* vision that punctured an intuitive model of disaster that assumed that there was always an outside that could be relied upon for aid.[110] NW theory made clear that in the event of a nuclear war there would be no such outside. It thus constituted the ominous underbelly of Buckminster Fuller's "spaceship earth" and the Apollo's famous "blue marble" satellite photograph of the earth from space. And it contained within it the same environmentalist caveat. "The message of nuclear winter . . . is that we are one human family, living in one indivisible home, our planet earth."[111]

FIGURE 4.4. "The Earth Is Enveloped." Copyright held by Council for a Livable World Education Fund. Courtesy of State Historical Society of Missouri.

These words, delivered by H. Jack Geiger in Helsinki in 1984, signaled the emergence of a planetary consciousness as the atomic age gave way to the ecological one.

Much as it had at Three Mile Island and throughout freeze activism, reproduction loomed over NW theory. That theory speculated about a scenario in which the ecosystems required for species reproduction could suddenly collapse. This vision of collapse signaled a paradigm shift in the history of the concept of extinction. That concept first emerged in revolutionary France, when naturalist Georges Cuvier studied mastodon bones and other large mammalian fossils and concluded that they came from what he called "espèces perdues," or "lost species." Thomas Jefferson famously rejected the idea, stating that "such is the economy of nature that no instance can be produced of her having permitted any one race of her animals to become extinct; of her having formed any link in her great work as to be broken." Over the nineteenth century, the concept of extinction took hold, but questions remained about its causes and its character. Could extinctions happen quickly enough to be observed by humans? Or did they occur very slowly over long expanses of time? Was extinction a result of Darwinian evolution—that is, had Cuvier's "lost species" been transformed through a gradual process of natural selection? Or were extinctions the result of a singular catastrophic event? Based on his review of the fossil record, Cuvier went with the latter theory. "Life on earth," he wrote, "has often been disturbed by terrible events. Living organisms without number have been the victims of these catastrophes."[112] In 1980, as Cold War relations approached a new nadir, the extinction debate among scientists was thrust into the public when Luis and Walter Alvarez, a father-son physicist-geologist team, published an article in *Science* titled "Extraterrestrial Cause for the Cretaceous-Tertiary Extinction."[113] The piece postulated a new and dramatic theory to explain the extinction of the dinosaurs sixty-five million years earlier: a large asteroid had collided with the earth, sending massive quantities of particulates into the air, blocking sunlight, suppressing photosynthesis, and fatally breaking the food chain. This hypothesis, along with advances in areology, provided the inspiration for NW theory. Carl Sagan and other astrophysicists began to ask if nuclear detonations could cause similar effects, and in the spring of 1982, after learning of the Alvarez theory, the National Academy of Sciences decided to study the long-term consequences of nuclear war, and specifically the effects of dust. The asteroid theory vindicated Cuvier's original hunch that species extinctions could occur with remarkable rapidity. The fate of the dinosaurs had irrevocably changed course on what science writer Elizabeth Kolbert—riffing on the title of a famous children's book—has called one "terrible, horrible, no good, very bad day." NW theory grafted the Alvarez hypothesis onto a nuclear future, but with one crucial difference. The extinction-level event would not emanate from some extraterrestrial force, but would come from right here on earth. In the event of a nuclear winter, humans would simultaneously be the asteroid and the dinosaur.

An extinction-level event would revise the prior rules of the evolutionary game by upending the species hierarchies that had been in place before the catastrophe. In the aftermath of a nuclear war, mammals—including humans—would be the most vulnerable to death from radiation exposure, while insects would be the most likely to endure. Biologists pointed out that those species with short life cycles and high reproductive potential would be quicker to recover from radiation's damaging effects.[114] These species included pests, fungi, bacteria, and viruses. Jonathan Schell famously labeled a postnuclear landscape a "republic of insects and grass," and PSR imagined a world overrun with pests: "mosquitos would multiply rapidly after an attack . . . the fly population would explode. Most domestic animals and wild creatures would be killed. Trillions of flies would breed in dead bodies."[115] In *The Day After*, Russ Oakes spies a cockroach scurrying across the hospital floor, which he regards with envy rather than repulsion. "Impervious to radiation. You are looking at man's legacy. The only guaranteed survivor of a nuclear war." This insight was at the heart of the concept of extinction. If the ecological context changed, species hierarchies of strength and dominance could be rearranged. Charles Darwin grasped as much in *The Origins of the Species*, recognizing that humans, like all other species, were not immune to environmental contingency. "Looking to the future," he wrote, "we can predict that the groups of organic beings which are now large and triumphant, and which are least broken up, that is, which as yet have suffered least extinction, will for a long period continue to increase. But which groups will ultimately prevail, no man can predict; for we well know that many groups, formerly most extensively developed, have now become extinct."[116] At Three Mile Island, animals functioned primarily as augurs for humans. Throughout forecasts of a nuclear attack, however, they were both fellow victims (in the case of mammals) and victors (in the case of insects) in the postwar evolutionary contest for species survival.

The fear of extinction built upon but also transcended the fear of death. Death always occurred in "a biological and social world that survives," explained Jonathan Schell.[117] Robert Jay Lifton described an "endless biological chain of being" that linked individuals to those who had come before and those who would come after, making a single life a link in a larger chain.[118] The horror of nuclear war was that it threatened to break the chain, not only by killing everyone on earth, but also by voiding all future generations.[119] To make the point, Schell posed two different global catastrophic scenarios. In the first, most people were killed in a nuclear confrontation, but there were enough survivors to repopulate the earth. In the second, a substance was released into the environment that sterilized all human beings, gradually emptying the world of all people. A full-scale nuclear war would do both things at once. "In extinction by nuclear arms," Schell wrote, "the death of the species and the death of all people in the world would happen together."[120] An individual death extinguished life, but extinction "cut off birth." "We have always been able to send people to their death," Schell wrote, "but only now it has become possible to prevent all birth and so doom all future human beings to uncreation."[121]

Predictions of species extinction again placed the unborn at the center of the nuclear threat, and nowhere more so than in Schell's award-winning *The Fate of the Earth*. Nuclear war, in Schell's words, would stop "future generations from entering into life" by canceling out "the numberless multitude of unconceived people."[122] For Schell, this made the term *disaster* a misnomer. "In extinction," he explained, "there is no disaster, no falling buildings, no killed or injured people, no shattered lives, no mourning survivors. All of that is dissolved in extinction, along with everything else that goes on in life." Extinction left only "the ghostlike cancelled future generations, who, metaphorically speaking, have been waiting through all past time to enter into life but have now been turned back by us."[123] Imagining extinction required conjuring something that existed outside linear time: one had to "gaze past everything human to a dead time that falls outside the human tenses of past, present, and future."[124] For Schell, extinction was the biosocial analog to totalitarianism, but while totalitarianism sought to destroy memory, extinction voided the future.[125] This placed a terrible burden on the living: they had to remember something that had not yet happened on behalf of those who might never be born. Extinction was the collective murder of unborn victims, obliging the living not only to never forget, but to *never allow*.

Here the rituals of marriage and mating enter the picture. When films like *The Day After* paid so much attention to heterosexual love, marriage, romance, and courtship, critics found these plot elements cloying and sentimental—distractions from the "real story" of nuclear war. But the extinction threat made clear that because they were so tightly bound up with reproduction, these elements *were* the real story. Thus Jonathan Schell only ostensibly veers off course in *The Fate of the Earth* when he champions the institution of marriage in profoundly traditional terms. As the conduit for bringing children into the world, Schell contended, it was this institution above all others that enshrined the "biological continuity of the species." When a man and a woman made their marital vows, they showed the world that they were "fit for receiving what the Bible calls 'the grace of life.'" Those who bore witness to the exchange were announcing their own stake in life's continuity. Thus for Schell, marriage was not only a personal act but a collective one as well. "In a world that is perpetually being overturned and plowed under by birth and death," Schell wrote, "marriage—which for this reason is rightly called an 'institution'—lays the foundation for the stability of the human world that is built to house all the generations." Marriage established "a map of hereditary lines across the unmarked territory of generational succession, shaping the rudiments of a common world out of biological reproduction."[126] The peril of extinction threatened to undo this. At the end of *The Day After*, Russ Oakes tells a traumatized overdue pregnant woman that by refusing to go into labor, she is "holding back hope." "Hope for what?" she asks him angrily. "What do you think is going to happen out there?" In *Testament*, the pubescent daughter asks her mother what it is like to make love. The mother speaks to her of feelings of closeness, longing, desire, and intimacy, to which the daughter—who is already exhibiting symptoms of radiation poisoning—whispers, "not for me." One critic dismissed *Testament* as a "post-nuclear feminist weepie."[127] But he mistakes as subterfuge what is the heart of the nuclear threat: the end of reproduction.

Since the publication of *Silent Spring* in 1962, the ecological imaginary had swung back and forth between images of reproduction-gone-awry and reproduction-run-amuck. While Rachel Carson focused on toxic threats *to* reproduction, later works like Paul Ehrlich's *The Population Bomb* (1968) and *Soylent Green* (1973) focused on the threat posed *by* reproduction in an overpopulated world of rapidly depleting resources. With the accident at Three Mile Island, the pendulum swung back again to the specter of imperiled reproduction. The culture of dissociation shattered, and as it did, the community's fears came to center on the fate of the unborn. The Second Cold War of the 1980s routed those fears back to weaponry and located extinction—overpopulation's inverted twin—at the center of a vision of planetary catastrophe. Disarmament activists raised the alarm over the extinction threat posed by the revival of the nuclear arms race. As we have seen, along the way, they helped to consolidate an ecologically inflected, reproduction-centered nationalism that consigned left universalism to the margins of US political culture. Meanwhile, the nuclear power issue did not go away.

NUCLEAR POWER IN THE SHADOWS

As images of nuclear annihilation circulated throughout the public sphere in the 1980s, the US nuclear power industry lay dormant and quiet. After the Three Mile Island accident, the NRC stopped licensing new plants. Meanwhile, fossil fuel costs—the object of so much consternation during the long energy crisis of the 1970s—declined. In an era of newly cheap oil and natural gas, nuclear power no longer appeared worth the investment. Its high capital costs, its poor operating performance, its regulatory requirements, and its unresolved safety questions led the Office of Technology Assessment to forecast a bleak outlook for the technology and to predict that, beyond the reactors already under construction, there would be no future nuclear expansion in the United States.[128] Investors viewed nuclear power as a brittle industry in which enormous capital investments could be voided literally overnight by one bad accident. In 1985, *Forbes* ranked the failure of the US nuclear power program as "the largest managerial disaster in business history, a disaster on a monumental scale."[129] To be sure, nuclear power did not disappear. By the mid-1980s, there remained 102 operating nuclear power plants in the United States, providing approximately 20 percent of the country's electricity. But within the ecological imaginary, the icon of the reactor cooling towers that had dominated antinuclear activism in the 1970s was displaced by the mushroom cloud, now multiplied a thousandfold. The heightened attention to nuclear war in the 1980s upended one presumption of the early years of the Cold War: that the domestic space of the nation could somehow remain insulated from radiological violence. But it also hardened the distinction between weaponry and reactors on which the culture of dissociation had long relied.

Despite the challenges besetting the nuclear industry, its public relations plowed ahead. In 1983, the US Committee for Energy Awareness (which would later be folded into the Nuclear Energy Institute [NEI], the industry's main lobbying group) launched a thirty-million-dollar campaign funded by utility companies and nuclear power plant vendors called "Nuclear Power: Time for a Comeback."[130] The campaign strategy relied on the same logic that had structured nuclear PR during the industry's high tide of the late 1950s and 1960s. The industry would need to rely on experts and specialists to foster what it called a rational dialogue with a public that it saw as misinformed.[131] It would also need to highlight the naturalness of radiation. At the same moment that popular culture was graphically depicting acute radiation poisoning, Illinois's Argonne National Laboratory proposed a nuclear power exhibit that included a montage showing how radiation coursed through both the "natural world" and the world of "man-made objects." Images of the sun, X-ray machines, a granite wall, the ground, food, water, a television set, a gas pilot light, and a smoke detector would convey radiation's ubiquity and harmlessness.[132] The proposal returned to and updated the message that the industry had honed decades earlier: only nuclear power could guarantee the reproduction of middle-class domestic consumption. Now the message acknowledged new social realities, like the fact that more women were working for wages outside the home. The exhibit proposal imagined a "cutaway of a modern home." Each room would contain "a family vignette—father and son, mother and daughter—but a modern one, in terms of clothes, hairdos, and expressions; it should not look like Norman Rockwell, but a 1980s two career family." This was the home "made possible by electric power—controlling the extremes of climate and bringing the world into the living room through communications."[133] The affinity between nuclear power and the middle-class home had emerged out of the industry's earlier public relations efforts, which implied that nuclear power could provide an endless supply of electricity that was cheap, safe, reliable, efficient, and clean. The accident at Three Mile Island had momentarily ruptured that fantasy. But by the

mid-1980s, PR experts were reviving and refurbishing it in order to rehabilitate an industry that had lost public and investor confidence.

These publicity efforts were again derailed in April 1986, when an accident occurred at Unit Four of the Chernobyl nuclear reactor in Ukraine.
This crisis was far more deadly than the one at Three Mile Island, ranking
a seven on the International Nuclear Event Scale (the TMI accident had
ranked a level five). Two explosions and a fire at the unit produced a radioactive cloud that ascended and traveled across Belarus, Ukraine, Russia,
and Western Europe, exposing tens of thousands of people to radioactive
iodine that would soon lead to an outbreak of thyroid cancer among both
children and adults in the region surrounding the plant. Soviet medical officials diagnosed 134 people with acute radiation sickness and set the official
death toll at thirty-one workers. Both the accident itself and the subsequent
cleanup exposed over six hundred thousand workers, soldiers, firemen,
men, women, and children to radiation. The explosions alone had released
one hundred times the radioactivity unleashed at Hiroshima, contaminat-
ing large areas of northern Ukraine, southern Belarus, and western Russia.
As word of the release spread, public officials recommended restrictions and
bans on fruit, vegetables, fresh meat, fish, and milk from Eastern Europe in
Italy, West Germany, Austria, Sweden, and Britain, often singling out pregnant women and children for special warning. The specter of a large cloud of
plutonium, iodine-131, strontium-90, and cesium-137 traversing the northern hemisphere evoked images of nuclear winter, and pointed to the impos-
sibility of containing radiological danger within national borders.

Much as they had at Three Mile Island, parents expressed concern that
their children had been exposed to low-dose radiation in the immediate
days after the accident (Mikhail Gorbachev had waited over two weeks before publicly acknowledging the radiation releases). Anecdotal reports of
postaccident declines in fertility and elevated rates of abortion circulated
widely in the years that followed, and medical workers reported a degradation of health, especially among the Byelorussian population, including
epidemics of thyroid cancer, birth defects, immune disorders, anemia, and
chronic respiratory and digestive illnesses. As one health worker put it
two decades later, "In hospitals and villages throughout Belarus, I've met
women who are afraid to bear children or to breastfeed and countless families who struggle not only with poverty but with alcohol addiction, chronic
health problems, confusion about how to protect their health and despair

for their children's future."[134] Like the Three Mile Island accident, the Chernobyl disaster propelled the surrounding population into a state of uncertainty vis-à-vis its reproductive fate.

For the US nuclear industry, the Chernobyl accident appeared to be another public relations disaster. Polling indicated that public support for nuclear power plummeted immediately after Chernobyl, capturing how an accident anywhere could derail national planning for nuclear power.[135] As NRC member James K. Asseltine observed at the time, Chernobyl demonstrated that nuclear safety "is a truly global issue." "In a very real sense," he concluded, "we are all hostage to each other's performance."[136] But within the context of the Second Cold War, the US nuclear industry was able to go on the offensive, attributing the disaster to the obsolete design of the Chernobyl reactor, which had not been used in the United States for over three decades. As physicist Hans Bethe wrote in an editorial in the *New York Times*, "A Chernobyl accident cannot happen here. The design of a Chernobyl-type reactor is completely different from any reactor in the West; it would never have been licensed in any Western country."[137] The Union of Concerned Scientist's Robert Pollard rejected the logic, countering that "differences in design between US and Soviet plans mean that the accident could not happen in precisely the same way here. What they do not tell the public is that an accident with as large a release as Chernobyl or worse, could happen."[138] But during an era when Reagan had denounced the Soviet Union as an "evil empire," the reactor's failed design emerged as a symbol not simply of a retrograde Soviet technology, but of the moral bankruptcy, arrogance, and dissemblance that purportedly corrupted the entire Soviet political and cultural system. A decade later, a *New York Times* editorial would describe the disaster as "a manifestation of the political, moral, and technological rot that was metastasizing in the Soviet system and would soon kill it."[139]

Thus rather than raising broader questions about nuclear power safety, the accident fostered a tendency within US policy circles to contrast the opacity of the Soviet political system to the transparency of the American one. In a letter to Soviet officials written in 1986, Representative Edwin Markey recalled that at the time of the Three Mile Island accident, the world's citizens knew what was happening "through the open release of information as the accident developed."[140] Markey's recollection was faulty, disregarding the considerable difficulties that had attended the acquisition of basic information at Three Mile Island and overlooking what the two accidents had in common. Both had placed an unknowing population in the path of radiological threat. Yet the US nuclear industry reworked the Chernobyl accident into a Cold War parable that indicted the Soviet system and endorsed its own safety standards.

Meanwhile, the promotion of nuclear power as a *clean* energy source took center stage as the climate change threat came into view. The hypothesis that emissions of greenhouse gases could alter the climate first took shape in the nineteenth century, and atmospheric scientists had debated what they called the "greenhouse effect" throughout the 1960s and 1970s. But the year 1988 marked a turning point in public awareness. In June, amid a catastrophic drought and heat wave throughout the Great Plains and the Midwest, James Hansen, the director of NASA's Goddard Institute for Space Studies, appeared before Congress and warned of a real and discerning warming trend. The same month, the World Conference on the Changing Atmosphere gathered in Toronto, Canada, where for the first time they discussed carbon emission reductions. The United Nations Intergovernmental Panel on Climate Change (IPCC), the leading international body for the assessment of climate change, was established that December. In a play on its annual "person of the year" issue, *Time* magazine's cover for January 2, 1989, was titled "Planet of the Year: Endangered Earth." The following September, the first book-length treatment of climate change, Bill McKibben's *The End of Nature*, was serialized in the *New Yorker*, and by the end of 1989, one poll found that nearly 80 percent of Americans had heard of the greenhouse effect.[141] As the Cold War wound down, the threat of megadeath in a nuclear war did not disappear, but it was slowly eclipsed by the threat of incremental species extinction on a feverishly overheating Earth.

Heightened attention to the dangers of rising carbon emissions created what one booster described as a window of opportunity for the nuclear industry.[142] While its public relations teams continued to stress both the ubiquity and the safety of radiation, they now emphasized what nuclear power plants did *not* emit into the atmosphere: carbon dioxide, sulfur dioxide, and nitrogen oxide. One NEI strategic report was typical in its portrait of nuclear energy as "the largest source of emission free electricity, avoiding annually discharges of 150 million metric tons of carbon, 4.8 million metric tons of sulfur dioxide, and 2.5 million metric tons of nitrogen oxide."[143] By the early 1990s, advertisements appeared in nationally syndicated newspapers and magazines championing the industry as a nonpolluter, often accompanied by captions like "Every Day Is Earth Day with Nuclear Energy." Nuclear critics cited the move as a damning example of corporate green washing, a tactic that came to the fore in the mid-1980s.[144] Of course this branding of nuclear power as clean and natural was not new; it harked back to the earliest utopian ambitions for civilian atomic power. But what critics got right was that this strategy dodged long-standing and unresolved questions about radiological contamination. In 1991, as the nuclear industry was tactically repositioning itself as a green technology, the Environmental Protection Agency reported that there were over 45,300 sites of radiation contamination in all fifty states, ranging "from severely contaminated nuclear weapons production sites to small sealed sources used for research, manufacturing, and medicine, to oil and gas wells, to nuclear weapons accidents." With the lone exception of the handling of uranium mill tailings, there were no federal standards in place for cleaning up the contamination, which the EPA warned was impossible to fully quantify, observing that a "truly accurate inventory of radiological contamination in the United States does not exist."[145] Appearing before Congress in 1990, *Nuclear Monitor* founder Michael Mariotte imagined that history would one day regard "the use of commercial nuclear power as the irrational equivalent of a declaration of war by governments upon their own people—a slow nuclear war that is beginning to show casualties comparable to those of shooting wars."[146] Yet industry spokesmen heralded nuclear power as a nonpolluter that, by virtue of its existence, had kept oil in the ground and carbon dioxide, sulfur dioxide, and nitrous oxide out of the air.

By the end of the 1980s, the culture of dissociation had been sutured back together again. The Three Mile accident quietly receded into memory and would later be recalled only as a juncture in the history of commercial nuclear power. But it had been much more. At Three Mile Island, the atomic age came apart and reassembled itself into the ecological one. The cord running between these two ages was the unborn, a figure that first appeared at Hiroshima and Nagasaki in 1945. The accident illuminated how this figure was shaping the political transformation of the late 1970s. As the country hovered between left and right, conservatives consolidated their power by knitting ecological images into a biotic nationalism. This nationalism accorded a crucial role to women as guardians of reproduction at the precise moment that civic nationalism was championing women's liberal rights and freedoms in the age of feminism. This body-centered nationalism first found expression at Three Mile Island, where residents perceived themselves as patriots-turned-activists. And it appeared again within disarmament activism, as freeze organizers strategically positioned themselves as activists-turned-patriots. The new politics of the ecological age was deeply indebted to the protest cultures of the 1960s, yet time and again that debt was disavowed. Within a mutated political landscape, the social and cultural revolutions of the late 1960s would remain—not unlike radiation—everywhere and nowhere at all.

During the long 1970s, the economic structure, political culture, and social organization of the United States underwent profound transformation. The nation shifted from a state-centered industrial society to a finance-centered globalized economy, one increasingly dependent on services, information, and what economists call rent. Trade restrictions were lifted, capital began moving with greater ease across national borders, and banks emerged as controllers of world liquidity. As the political economy "fled toward the global," the state replaced managed Keynesianism with monetarism, embraced a neoliberal faith in the market, and shed much of its earlier regulatory functions, thus reducing its role to that of crisis manager.[1] The country evolved from a hierarchical, white, and male-dominated system of status to a multicultural, multiracial, antinomian democracy. With the benefit of hindsight, we can see that the successive crises that shook US society in the 1970s—the Vietnam War, the energy crisis, economic recession—were part of this global restructuring. But at the time, these crises were interpreted in profoundly nationalist terms, as symptomatic of a loss of American power and stature. Amid pervasive fears of national decline, an organic, biological sense of the nation reasserted itself, even as civic nationalism flourished. *Radiation Nation* has used the story of Three Mile Island to show how ecology gave shape to a biotic nationalism in the 1970s that both imagined the nation as a wounded body and presented sickened bodies as evidence of betrayal.

It was ecology's preoccupation with reproduction and generational continuity that made it such a rich resource for biotic nationalism. That preoccupation began with the threat of global self-destruction introduced in 1945, a year that "changed everything," to borrow a phrase from Naomi Klein.[2] The dropping of atomic bombs on two Japanese cities, combined with routine weapons testing, introduced a new constellation of fears surrounding reproductive futurity. The atomic age ushered in a core revelation of the Anthropocene: human activity could lead to species extinction. The extinction threat, in turn, became embodied in the figure of the unborn. This figure armed contemporary environmental politics with a powerful corrective to petrocapitalist logics of resource extraction and short-term profit maximization. Harms to air, water, and land can play out across long time horizons and rebound into an indeterminate future. To be sure, there is also a spatial dimension to the maldistribution of environmental harms: they often target poor communities and people of color.[3] But the figure of the unborn introduced *temporal* considerations. Burdens and injuries can be maldistributed not only across space but also across time, that is, across generations. The unborn embodied questions about intergenerational care and injury that are at the center of modern social thought.

This ecological attention to the unborn appears most recently in Klein's book *This Changes Everything: Capitalism vs. the Climate*, published in 2014. During the years that she researched petrocapitalism's planetary impacts, Klein also struggled to conceive a child, and the two became parts of a whole for her. From the oil-infested Gulf Coast marshes to Louisiana's "Cancer Alley," from the fracked landscape of rural Colorado to the acidified waters of the Pacific Northwest, Klein encountered species who were "bashing up against their own infertility walls, finding it harder and harder to successfully reproduce and harder still to protect their young." In Mossville, Louisiana, a predominantly African American town ringed by fourteen chemical plants and refineries, she found a "woman's womb of chemicals." After the BP oil spill, Klein traveled through the bayous of the Mississippi River Delta, where the zooplankton that should grow into adult shrimp, oysters, crabs, and finfish were failing to thrive. She labeled the scene an aquatic miscarriage. In Louisiana she surveyed the oil-soaked surface of Redfish Bay and imagined herself "suspended . . . in amniotic fluid, immersed in a massive multi-species miscarriage." What struck Klein was how imperceptibly this destruction unfolded: "no corpses, just an absence." Five decades after Rachel Carson described the "shadow of sterility" left behind by DDT, Klein saw petrocapitalism depriving "life-forms of their most essential survival tool: the ability to create new life and carry on their genetic lines." The spark of life was "being extinguished, snuffed out in its earliest, most fragile days: in the egg, in the embryo, in the nest, in the den."[4]

Until the 1970s, it was Cold War dissenters who made this move of connecting fertility crisis to ecological crisis; Women Strike for Peace and *Silent Spring* are two examples. The link did not appear within dominant discourses of US nationalism, which remained triumphalist and optimistic during the postwar years. This was because in addition to marking a rupture within the history of the Anthropocene, the year 1945 constituted a geopolitical turning point for the United States, which fully consolidated itself as a global (as opposed to continental) power. The years between 1945 and 1973 were the age of an American imperium, what Henry Luce called "the American Century," characterized by unipolar dominance, unprecedented military, political, and economic power, and a moral authority that had emerged out of the fight against fascism. This age came to a precipitous close in the early 1970s, when amid war and recession, many policymakers and citizens alike perceived a nation in the throes of decline. Most devastating was the military defeat in Vietnam. Others saw the shuttering of factories and the relocation of manufacturing jobs overseas as evidence that the economy was faltering. Still others saw the emergence of movements for racial, sexual, and cultural liberation as a troubling sign that older institutions, especially the traditional family, were coming apart. At Three Mile Island, these fears of national decline collided with fears of radiological disaster and a collapse of trust in the state. As this happened, the atomic-cum-ecological construction of the unborn as an object of vulnerability in need of protection, earlier aligned with Cold War dissent, became incorporated into a conservative nationalism that leveled three charges: the nation had been weakened, the official story could not be believed, and patriots had been betrayed.

This conservative nationalism accorded a crucial role to the human body. The insight that the body could be a site of political contestation had its origins in the social upheavals of the 1960s. The black freedom movement demanded more than formal equality under the law; it called for both a fuller accounting of racism's depredations and new forms of liberation. As they fought to expose epidemics of police brutality and mass imprisonment within black communities, activists singled out the black body as a locus of extraordinary political violence. Simultaneously, Afrocentric reclamations of black culture and identity imagined the black body as a site of emancipation and recovery.[5] With the rise of women's and gay liberation in the late 1960s, the human body—its inviolabilities, its capacities, and its pleasures—assumed an even more prominent role within the political field as activists demanded sexual freedom and autonomy. Meanwhile, the black and women's health movements insisted that sickness itself could be deeply embedded in structures of inequality. This heightened attention to the body deepened the liberal tradition of individual rights by pushing it beyond an earlier emphasis on reason and rationality.

By the 1970s, conservatives were developing a body politics of their own. This politics went beyond efforts to regulate the bodies of others, whether through a criminal justice system that meted out violence against black and brown bodies or through laws that sought to control the bodies of women and gay people. Unlike the social movements of the 1960s, which were animated by universalist ideals, conservative activists were driven by the sense that *their* bodies and the bodies of the people they loved—the patriot, the veteran, the radiation victim, the loyal American—had been injured and betrayed by the government. This was patriotic body politics. In the 1970s, as the nation hovered between left and right, the symbol of the suffering body migrated across the political landscape and ultimately tipped the balance rightward.

At first, patriotic body politics centered on the martial masculine body: the POW and the MIA, the wounded soldier, the disabled and atomic veteran. But at Three Mile Island, those bodies were displaced by the bodies of women, children, and the unborn. The crisis thus captured women's dualistic role within the political realignment of the decade. On the one hand, women's liberation exemplified a civic nationalist vision that cited gender and sexual freedom as evidence of the nation's redemptive capacities for democratization. The push for women's political, economic, and social equality appeared to hold out the promise of a country that could become more meritocratic precisely through decoupling women from their role in reproduction, laying waste once and for all to the retrograde claim that biology was destiny, and incorporating women into a late-capitalist, postindustrial market society no longer organized around the male breadwinner ideal. Yet on the other hand, the core insight of the atomic-cum-ecological age—that the future of *all* reproduction hung in the balance—meant that women would also play an outsized role within an alternative biotic nationalism. The Three Mile Island story makes this clear. After the accident, women positioned themselves as the guardians of reproduction rather than the victims of its patriarchal imperatives. In the process, they crafted a homegrown conservative ecological politics that reflected the influence of feminists who had fought against sexist exclusion in the public sphere and had seen the body as a locus of political struggle. Yet while feminism strove to protect women from the reproduction mandate, the women at Three Mile Island fought to protect reproduction itself from a damaged reactor, a rapacious utility company, and a negligent regulatory commission. If the civic nationalism of the 1970s relied on moving women away from reproduction, biotic nationalism propelled them toward it.

This biotic nationalism was not wholly new, of course. Rather, it drew on an earlier ethnonationalist tradition that saw the nation as an organic, bounded entity that possessed a lifecycle and an inner life. Throughout US history, ethnonationalism has exploded to the surface at moments of perceived community peril: when Puritan villagers felt threatened by heathen "natives"; during and after the Civil War, when white, Anglo-Saxon Southerners fought to defend slavery; when nativists have attempted to exclude immigrants from citizenship; and throughout the Cold War, when governmental institutions and media outlets were gripped by anti-Communist paranoia. This sense of ethnic community peril resurfaced in the 1970s as de jure segregation toppled. In cities like Atlanta, Boston, Richmond, and Charlotte, white citizens swung back against court-mandated busing, taxation, and integration, portraying themselves as victims of hostile external forces, including the courts, the liberal welfare state, and newly empowered minority groups.[6] The atomic threat at Three Mile Island supplied this vision of peril with something new: the symbol of an irradiated body betrayed by its own government. Biotic nationalism thus introduced an ecological dimension into this earlier ethnonationalist strain and hitched it to the fear of national decline. The result was the rise of an aggrieved nationalism in the 1970s, predicated on the claim that the nation had sustained wounds that threatened not just its power and authority but its very identity. These were wounds that had come from within. The political triumph of Ronald Reagan in 1980 can be explained, at least in part, by his shrewd ability to redirect this blame and fear outward during the Second Cold War.

But the Reagan Revolution could never fully resolve the political contradictions of the 1970s. This was because Reagan-era conservatism was never simply a reaction to the left, so much as a relation of selective and often deft incorporation. After all, Three Mile Island residents could never have done what they did without drawing on what had come before: a political left that questioned authority during the Vietnam War, women's and black health activists who insisted that illness was a political issue, and an ecology movement that sounded the alarm over environmental degradation. When they repurposed core insights from these movements, local activists at Three Mile Island demonstrated how concepts and insights were not only circulating widely by the late 1970s, but also shape-shifting along the way. Ecology supplied the field in which these concepts migrated, scrambling any simple political dichotomy between left and right.

This story of incorporation helps make sense of more recent moments when an ecological orientation has defied easy political categorization. The nature film *March of the Penguins*, released in 2005, took a classical leftist trope—the responsibility of the community for its most vulnerable members—and converted it into a seemingly apolitical morality tale. The film became a cult favorite among the Christian Right. Fears of childhood vaccination bring together clean-living new-agers and right-leaning libertarians, while feminists, fundamentalists, hippies, yuppies, physicians, and neoliberal politicians all unite in promoting breastfeeding.[7] Republican property-owners and climate justice activists have forged an alliance against hydraulic fracturing and the Keystone XL Pipeline. These are not messy, inchoate moments of exception. Rather, ecological preoccupations with the vulnerability of species reproduction and bodily contamination traverse the contemporary political landscape, even as legislative and policy fights over climate change and energy strategy remain sharply divided along partisan lines. If the culture wars suggest polarity, the ecological age has been characterized by a transpartisan culture of suspicion that often indicts the state, creating bedfellows that only appear strange.

Meanwhile, the state's role under neoliberalism has pivoted from that of regulator to crisis manager. At the very moment that multiple ecological threats demanded a *more* aggressive regulatory regime, neoliberalism moved in the opposite direction. The dismantlement of the state as a regulatory body has gone hand in hand with its consolidation as an agent of emotional control and quasi-therapeutic manipulation. The roots of this lie in the Cold War culture of dissociation. Consolidating their authority at a time when psychiatry wielded great influence in the United States, civil defense planners cited extreme emotions within the population, like panic and hysteria, as national security risks. Indeed, panic prevention was a—if not *the*—primary goal of civil defense drills. Sociologist Jackie Orr describes this as the emergence of psychopower, which "works by multiplying the possible surfaces of contact between psychic processes and their regulation and by legitimating power itself as a kind of therapeutic activity."[8] Psychopower was exercised at Three Mile Island, where Richard Thornburg sought to reassert his command over the crisis by claiming to have contained a public panic. That claim displaced the actual radiological threat with the conjured threat of an out-of-control, emotionally overwrought population. First operationalized within Cold War civil defense, psychopower has lived on in the post–Cold War era. It can be seen in both an unending war on terror and a neoliberal war on the regulation of petrocapitalist corporations and invasive private industries.[9] What has taken shape is a palliative, therapeutic mode of governance, one that we can expect to see more of moving forward, as the state appears inadequate to the task of enforcing the global structures required to combat the threat posed by rising carbon emissions.[10]

The political settlement that followed the upheavals of the 1970s—the consolidation of the neoliberal state, the rise of a global capitalist class with little sense of national obligation, a meritocratic as opposed to egalitarian cultural politics, a wounded sense of national identity, and a succession of epidemiological and ecological crises—has left the United States ill prepared to deal with the challenge posed by anthropogenic climate change and the question of nuclear power's role in the transition away from fossil fuels. Between 2000 and 2010, policymakers heralded a coming nuclear renaissance, predicting that nuclear power would be an essential component of the nation's future energy mix. The Energy Act of 2005, passed amid rising oil prices and grim forecasts about climate change, included a range of financial incentives to encourage the private sector to build new reactors, and by early 2009, license applications for twenty-six new reactors had been filed with the NRC.[11] Both John McCain and Barack Obama endorsed the expansion of nuclear power during their 2008 presidential campaigns, and in 2010, President Obama announced an $8 billion loan guarantee for the construction of a nuclear power plant in Georgia, the first new reactor to be built in close to three decades. Carol Browner of the White House Office of Energy and Climate Change Policy said that the Georgia reactors were "just the first of what we hope will be many new nuclear projects."[12]

Yet as of this writing, the vaunted nuclear renaissance has yet to materialize. While five new reactors are under construction, thirty-three aging reactors have been decommissioned.[13] Three Mile Island is scheduled to close in 2019. What happened? Energy analysts cite several hindrances, including a lack of production capacity, high capital costs, and still-unresolved questions about nuclear waste disposal and reactor safety, questions brought into terrifying relief by the Fukushima-Daiichi accident in 2011.[14] But the most powerful deterrent has been the recent boom in shale oil and natural gas, as the fossil fuel industry develops more invasive methods of resource extraction. From the bitumen (heavy crude oil) of the Alberta tar sands and deep-water oil drilling in the Gulf of Mexico to hydraulic fracturing (fracking) in Pennsylvania, Wyoming, the Dakotas, and Colorado and mountaintop removal in Appalachia, the goal is to penetrate ever more deeply beneath the earth's surface in willful defiance of earlier predictions that the oil supply is peaking and that petrocapitalism is on borrowed time. In this light, the command "drill, baby, drill" can be read as a manic defense. The cumulative result is what Naomi Klein has described as an "upping of the ante" as the industry moves from conventional fossil fuel sources to ever more dangerous, dirty versions, ushering in what Stephanie LeMenager has described as the age of "tough oil."[15]

At the time of this writing, then, investors appear more interested in shale oil and natural gas, while some of the most outspoken proponents of nuclear power are environmentalists, some of whom cut their political teeth on antinuclear organizing in the 1970s but who have since become convinced that nuclear power will be essential in the coming battle against catastrophic climate change. These include *Whole Earth Catalogue* founder Stewart Brand, environmental writers Mark Lynas, Michael Shellenberger and Gwyneth Cravens, and figures like climatologist James Hansen and futurist James Lovelock, who in the 1960s advanced the Gaia hypothesis, which sees the earth as a self-regulating, homeostatic system. The feature-length documentary film *Pandora's Promise*, released in 2013, stakes out this pronuclear, environmentalist position. In the film, one environmentalist after another describes how through the careful acquisition of knowledge, an early opposition to nuclear power gradually gave way to a conviction that the direness of the climate change threat meant that nothing—including nuclear energy—should be taken off the table. The power of the film resides in observing thoughtful people as they puzzle through a problem and arrive at different place from where they began. Simply put, there is something fascinating about watching a smart person change his or her mind.

And yet the film's "greening" of nuclear power is not new. It harks back to nuclear power's early Cold War origins, both when it speculates that a new generation of reactors can transform the quality of life in the global South and when it aligns radiation with both nature and healing. One scene shows an older man at a beach in Brazil that has naturally high radiation levels that help him with his body pains. And the film's basic premise is that public irrationality is the single largest obstacle to any nuclear revival. The film opens with shots of environmental writer Mark Lynas watching television news coverage of the Fukushima Daiichi disaster and telling himself to mobilize his internal resources to stave off panic—an injunction to viewers to "keep their heads." And if there are any villains, it is those activists who remain wedded to a paranoid antinuclear position. They are steadily ridiculed throughout the film.[16]

This turn to nuclear power as a remedy for runaway climate change is laden with irony. For one thing, the nuclear industry, like everything else, will be subjected to new pressures as a result of harsher climactic conditions. Reactors require large amounts of water for cooling, made ever more challenging in an age of megadroughts and water scarcity. And extreme heat places strain on reactors. During the European heat wave of 2003, nuclear plants throughout the continent were shut down, and France lost roughly a reactor year of power generation.[17] But the deeper historical irony is that it was the advent of atomic power that anticipated the core contradiction of contemporary petrocapitalism, namely, that the energy regimes we rely on to reproduce certain modes of living in the short term can set in motion processes that threaten to radically transform those same modes over the long term. The rise of civilian nuclear power in the 1950s facilitated the birth of a high-energy society, but unresolved questions about radiological safety raised the possibility that a planetary and somatic price might be paid down the generational line. And the figure of the irradiated body that first surfaced during the radiation scare anticipated our own chemical embodiment in the twenty-first century. Every person who has lived in the United States since 1951 has been exposed not only to radioactive fallout, but to a host of synthetic and petroindustrial chemicals, the vast majority of which have never been tested by the EPA. Styrene, ethyl phenol, toluene, polychlorinated biphenyls, mercury, and phthalates: these are all commonly found in human fat, blood, semen, urine, placental tissue, amniotic fluid, and breast milk. As historian Michelle Murphy puts it, "In the twenty first century, humans are chemically transformed beings."[18] While the fear of nuclear catastrophe has been largely—though not entirely—supplanted by the fear of runaway climate change, it was the atomic age that prefigured petrocapitalism's contemporary status as an unregulated experiment on both a geoplanetary and a bodily scale. When viewed through the lens of the commingled histories of the atomic age and the ecological age, the turn to nuclear power as a remedy for catastrophic climate change looks less like a viable solution and more like a Faustian choice between one form of intergenerational poison and another.

Technological fixes are no substitute for politics. So what kind of politics will this vast geoplanetary experiment require in the twenty-first century? Three Mile Island provides a cautionary tale. Righteous anger over the contamination of landscapes and bodies will not be enough; there is no pristine community or chemically pure body to return to. The oceanographers and earth scientists who first monitored radioactive fallout in the late 1940s discovered that there is no baseline to fall back on. If the only goal is the removal of a contamination threat from any single community, the threat will simply be outsourced somewhere else, where environmental hazards often join class and race as indices of vulnerability. And while modern environmentalism's turn to temporal questions is profound, it also will not be enough. There are multiple forms of violence bearing down on the most vulnerable populations in the here and now. For many communities both within the United States and throughout the globe, the extinction threat is neither new nor theoretical. The emergency that environmentalists project onto the future is already well underway for many, not just because of polluted air and toxic water, but also because of all that is knitted together with them: militarization and neoimperialism, racism and the carceral state, neoliberal labor regimes, and the ever-widening chasm between the one percent and the rest. Nor can it be assumed that the charge of intergenerational harm is always or necessarily aligned with social justice. One need only look at the advocates of economic austerity, who claim that belts must be tightened to protect future generations, to see that this charge cuts both ways. How can we sound the alarm over future harm while attending to the systemic violence bearing down on precarious lives in the present? Finding the answer will entail a collective repossession of the debt that was at once mined and repudiated at Three Mile Island: that of an ethically oriented, historically grounded, democratic socialist left.

In 1976, when I was six years old, Stevie Wonder sang that his devotion to his beloved would always be there, just as surely as "the rosebuds know to bloom in early May" and "the seasons know exactly when to change." Four decades on, I have to ask: Do the rosebuds still know when to bloom? Do the seasons still know when to change? I wonder what future winters and springs will bring, and whether they will resemble those that came before, or whether they will take new forms that I do not recognize. Writer Andrew Solomon once observed that there is "no such thing as reproduction," by which he means that parents cannot replicate themselves in their offspring.[19] This has always been true. But the ecological age is marked above all by a new awareness that reproduction's predictive logic—its circles and cycles, its recurrences and repetitions, its rhythms and rhymes, its eternal returns— no longer applies to our world.

NOTES

ABBREVIATIONS

In additions to the abbreviations used in the text, the following abbreviations are used in the notes.

DCASC   Dickinson College Archive and Special Collections
DT   Dick Thornburgh Papers
JCPL   Jimmy Carter Presidential Library
LMOHI   Lonna Malmsheimer Oral History Interviews
NAII   National Archives II
SCPC   Swarthmore College Peace Collection
SHSM   State Historical Society of Missouri
TMIA   Three Mile Island Alert Papers
TMIC   Three Mile Island Collection
UPSC   University of Pittsburgh Special Collections

PREFACE

1. Anatol Lieven, *America Right or Wrong: An Anatomy of American Nationalism* (New York: Oxford University Press, 2004), 1.

INTRODUCTION

1. Throughout this book, I use the terms *accident, crisis, partial meltdown,* or *near-meltdown* interchangeably to describe what occurred inside the Three Mile Island

reactor in the spring of 1979. I have carefully considered my choice of terminology, having discovered in the course of my research that such choices mattered a great deal at the time: utility company spokespeople at first described what happened at the plant as an "incident," while antinuclear activists would later describe it as a "catastrophe," terms that advanced two divergent interpretations of what had occurred and indexed the considerable contestation surrounding the events in question. My choice to go with the seemingly neutral term *accident* invariably runs certain risks—either of minimizing the seriousness of what happened inside the containment building or of tacitly endorsing the industry's own claim that accidents are rare aberrations that affirm the safety, reliability, and predictability of reactors during ostensibly normal operations. However, in the pages that follow, I attempt to use the term *accident* in the sense classically elaborated by Charles Perrow, who contends that within highly complex technological systems like nuclear power, accidents are not the exception, but rather the rule. See Charles Perrow, *Normal Accidents: Living with High Risk Technologies* (New York: Basic, 1984).

2. The authoritative study of the accident, one that provides a blow-by-blow account, is J. Samuel Walker, *Three Mile Island: A Nuclear Crisis in Historical Perspective* (Berkeley: University of California Press, 2004). While exhaustive in both its detailing of the accident and its explanation of its impact on commercial nuclear energy, the book does not explore the broader cultural and political implications of the partial meltdown. My analysis also relies heavily on the official report of the Kemeny Commission. See John Kemeny, *Accident at Three Mile Island: The Need for Change, the Legacy of TMI* (Oxford: Pergamon, 1979).

3. On the place of the bombings in the history of oceanography, earth sciences, and modern environmentalism, see Jacob Hamblin, *Oceanographers and the Cold War: Disciples of Marine Science* (Seattle: University of Washington Press, 2005); Hamblin, *Poison in the Well: Radioactive Waste in the Oceans at the Dawn of the Nuclear Age* (New Brunswick, NJ: Rutgers University Press, 2009); and Hamblin, *Arming Mother Nature: The Birth of Catastrophic Environmentalism* (New York: Oxford University Press, 2013); and Joseph Masco, "Bad Weather: On Planetary Crisis," *Social Studies of Science* 40, no. 1 (February 2010): 7–40. The debate over how to best periodize the Anthropocene is extensive and evolving quickly. Atmospheric chemist Paul Crutzen first popularized the term in 2002. See Paul Crutzen, "Geology of Mankind," *Nature* 415 (January 3, 2002): 415, 23. For a useful recent overview of the debate, see Simon L. Lewis and Mark Maslin, "Defining the Anthropocene," *Nature* 519 (March 12, 2015): 171–180; and a subsequent response, Dana Luciano, "The Inhuman Anthropocene," *Avidly: The Los Angeles Review of Books* (March 22, 2015), http://avidly.lareviewofbooks.org/2015/03/22/the-inhuman-anthropocene/. On how the concept of the Anthropocene undermines the distinction between human and natural histories, see Dipesh Chakrabarty, "The Climate of History: Four Theses," *Critical Inquiry* 35, no. 2 (Winter 2009): 197–222. Jedediah Purdy situates the contemporary debate about the Anthropocene within a longer history of the American environmental imagination. See Jedediah Purdy, *After Nature: A Politics for the Anthropocene* (Cambridge: Harvard University Press, 2015). Roy Scranton offers up a grimmer view of our current predicament in *Learning to Die in the Anthropocene* (San Francisco: City Lights, 2015). Recently, scholars have taken aim at the Anthropocene for its universalist presumptions and in particular its totalizing claim that humanity writ large is to blame for the climate crisis. In this vein, Jason Moore proposes the alternative term *capitalocene* in *Capitalism*

in the Web of Life: Ecology and the Accumulation of Capital (London: Verso, 2015). See also Andreas Malm, "The Geology of Mankind? A Critique of the Anthropocene Narrative," *Anthropocene Review* 1, no. 1 (April 1, 2014): 62–69; and Malm, "The Anthropocene Myth," *Jacobinmag.com*, March 30, 2015, www.jacobinmag.com/2015/03/anthropocene-capitalism-climate-change/. Donna Haraway proposes the "Chthulucene" in lieu of the Anthropocene as a way to designate an epoch shaped by human and nonhuman interaction. See Donna Haraway, *Staying with the Trouble: Making Kin in the Chthulucene* (Durham: Duke University Press, 2016).

4. Bill McKibben, *Eaarth: Making a Life on a Tough New Planet* (New York: St. Martin's, 2011).

5. On the debate over radioactive fallout in the 1950s, see Paul Boyer, *By the Bomb's Early Light: American Thought and Culture at the Dawn of the Atomic Age* (Chapel Hill: University of North Carolina Press, 1994); Boyer, *Fallout: A Historian Reflects on America's Half-Century Encounter with Nuclear Weapons* (Columbus: Ohio State University Press, 1998); and Boyer, "From Activism to Apathy: The American People and Nuclear Weapons, 1963–1980," *Journal of American History* 70, no. 4 (March 1984): 821–844; Robert A. Divine, *Blowing on the Wind: The Nuclear Test Ban Debate, 1954–1960* (New York: Oxford University Press, 1978); Milton Katz, *Ban the Bomb: A History of SANE, 1957–1985* (Westport, CT: Greenwood Press, 1986); and Joseph Masco, *Nuclear Borderlands: The Manhattan Project in Post-Cold War New Mexico* (Princeton: Princeton University Press, 2006), 43–98. On *Silent Spring*, see K. Hamilton Lytle, *The Gentle Subversive: Rachel Carson, Silent Spring, and the Rise of the Environmental Movement* (New York: Oxford University Press, 2007); and Thomas Dunlap, *DDT, Silent Spring, and the Rise of Environmentalism* (Seattle: University of Washington Press, 2008). On the Santa Barbara oil spill, see Robert Easton, *Black Tide: The Santa Barbara Oil Spill and Its Consequences* (New York: Delacorte, 1972). On Love Canal, see Elizabeth Blum, *Love Canal Revisited: Race, Class, and Gender in Environmental Activism* (Lawrence: University Press of Kansas, 2008); Lois Marie Gibbs, *Love Canal and the Birth of the Environmental Health Movement* (Washington, DC: Island, 2010); and Richard Newman, *Love Canal: A Toxic History from Colonial Times to the Present* (New York: Oxford University Press, 2015). On the history of US environmentalism since 1945 more broadly, see Steven Stoll, *US Environmentalism Since 1945: A Brief History with Documents* (New York: Bedford St. Martin's, 2007); Robert Gottlieb, *Forcing the Spring: The Transformation of the American Environmental Movement* (Washington, DC: Island, 2005); Adam Rome, *The Bulldozer in the Countryside: Suburban Sprawl and the Rise of American Environmentalism* (New York: Cambridge University Press, 2001); and Rome, *The Genius of Earth Day: How a 1970 Teach In Unexpectedly Made the First Green Generation* (New York: Hill and Wang, 2014).

6. Rachel Carson, *Silent Spring* (New York: Houghton Mifflin, 1962), 6.

7. I borrow the concept of a "weirded world" from Heather Houser, *Ecosickness in Contemporary US Fiction: Environment and Affect* (New York: Columbia University Press, 2014), 118.

8. See Rob Nixon, *Slow Violence and the Environmentalism of the Poor* (Cambridge: Harvard University Press, 2011).

9. See Don DeLillo, *White Noise* (New York: Penguin, 1986).

10. I borrow the term *reproductive futurity* from queer theorist Lee Edelman, who uses it to describe a political field in which the pursuit of socials good is always

rationalized in terms of the safeguarding of the future, which is symbolized by the child. I use the term here to refer to the future of healthy reproduction more broadly. But my argument throughout is influenced by Edelman's insight about the how the future is emblematized by the child in much contemporary political discourse. See Lee Edelman, *No Future: Queer Theory and the Death Drive* (Durham: Duke University Press, 2004).

11. See Carson, *The Silent Spring*; and Paul Ehrlich, *The Population Bomb* (San Francisco: Sierra-Ballantine, 1971).

12. See Sara Dubow, *Ourselves Unborn: A History of the Fetus in Modern America* (New York: Oxford University Press, 2010).

13. Throughout this book, I use the term *imaginary* not in the Lacanian sense, but rather to refer to how social life is collectively imagined by a group of people at a particular historical moment. Here, I am drawing inspiration from Charles Taylor's concept of a social imaginary. Dilip Parameshwar Gaonkar describes this concept thus: "Within the folds of a social imaginary, we see ourselves as agents who traverse a social space and inhabit a temporal horizon, entertain certain beliefs and norms, engage in and make sense of our practices in terms of purpose, timing, and appropriateness, and exist among other agents. The social imaginary is something more than an immediate practical understanding of how to do particular things—such as how to buy a newspaper, ride a subway, order a drink, wire money, make small talk, or submit a petition. It involves a form of understanding that has a wider grasp of our history and social existence. . . . It gives us a sense of who we are, how we fit together, how we got where we are, and what we might expect from each other in carrying out collective practices that are constitutive of our way of life." Dilip Parameshwar Gaonkar, "Toward New Imaginaries: An Introduction," *Public Culture* 14, no. 1 (Winter 2002): 10. See also Charles Taylor, *Modern Social Imaginaries* (Durham: Duke University Press, 2003).

14. Here, I draw a distinction between an ecological consciousness with ties to the counterculture and environmental reform, which was a well-known bipartisan project of the 1970s.

15. On the body as a locus of sexual pleasure within the women's movement, see Alice Echols, *Daring to Be Bad: Radical Feminism in America, 1967–1975* (Minneapolis: University of Minnesota Press, 1989); Jane Gerhard, *Desiring Revolution: Second Wave Feminism and the Rewriting of American Sexual Thought, 1920–1982* (New York: Columbia University Press, 2001); and Kathy Peiss and Christina Simmons, eds., *Passion and Power: Sexuality in History* (Philadelphia: Temple University Press, 1989). On the history of the women's health movement, see Kathy Davis, *The Making of Our Bodies, Ourselves: How Feminism Travels Across Borders* (Durham: Duke University Press, 2007); Wendy Kline, *Bodies of Knowledge: Sexuality, Reproduction, and Women's Health in the Second Wave* (Chicago: University of Chicago Press, 2012); Sandra Morgen, *Into Our Own Hands: The Women's Health Movement in the United States, 1969–1990* (New Brunswick, NJ: Rutgers University Press, 2002); and Jennifer Nelson, *More Than Medicine: A History of the Feminist Women's Health Movement* (New York: New York University Press, 2015). On the centrality of medical discrimination within the black power movement, see Alondra Nelson, *Body and Soul: The Black Panther Party and the Fight Against Medical Discrimination* (Minneapolis: University of Minnesota Press, 2011). On the politicization of science and health throughout the AIDS

crisis, see Steven Epstein, *Impure Science: AIDS, Activism, and the Politics of Knowledge* (Berkeley: University of California Press, 1996); and Debra Gould, *Moving Politics: Emotion and ACT-UP's Fight Against AIDS* (Chicago: University of Chicago Press, 2009). Books that explore grassroots health movements and popular epidemiology include Jason Corburn, *Street Science: Community Knowledge and Environmental Health Justice* (Cambridge: MIT Press, 2005); and Steve Kroll Smith, Phil Brown, and Valerie J. Gunter, eds., *Illness and the Environment: A Reader in Contested Medicine* (New York: New York University Press, 2000).

16. For a more extended discussion of patriotic body politics, see Natasha Zaretsky, "Radiation Suffering and Patriotic Body Politics," *Journal of Social History* 48, no. 3 (Spring 2015): 487–510.

17. See Michael J. Allen, *Until the Last Man Comes Home: POWs, MIAs, and the Unending Vietnam War* (Chapel Hill: University of North Carolina Press, 2011).

18. See John Kinder, *Paying with Their Bodies: American War and the Problem of the Disabled Veteran* (Chicago: University of Chicago Press, 2015).

19. This shift in blame is indexed in the famous *Rambo* films of the 1980s. See Susan Jeffords, *Hard Bodies: Hollywood Masculinity in the Reagan Era* (New Brunswick, NJ: Rutgers University Press, 1993). Other cultural studies works that take up this figure include David Savran, *Taking It Like a Man: White Masculinity, Masochism, and Contemporary American Culture* (Princeton: Princeton University Press, 1998); Peter Lehman, ed., *Masculinity: Bodies, Movies, Culture* (New York: Routledge, 2001); Kaja Silverman, *Male Subjectivity at the Margins* (New York: Routledge, 1992); and Sarah Hagelin, *Reel Vulnerability: Power, Pain, and Gender in Contemporary American Film and Television* (New Brunswick, NJ: Rutgers University Press, 2013).

20. See Amy Swerdlow, *Women Strike for Peace: Traditional Motherhood and Radical Politics in the 1960s* (Chicago: University of Chicago Press, 1993).

21. On the history of women's reproduction and reproductive politics, see the classic book by Linda Gordon, *Woman's Body, Woman's Right: Birth Control in America*, rev. ed. (New York: Penguin, 1990). See also Johanna Shoen, *Choice and Coercion: Birth Control, Sterilization, and Abortion in Public Health and Welfare* (Chapel Hill: University of North Carolina Press, 2005); Rickie Solinger, *Pregnancy and Power: A Short History of Reproductive Politics in America* (New York: New York University Press, 2007); and Solinger, *Reproductive Politics: What Everyone Needs to Know* (New York: Oxford University Press, 2013). While white, middle-class feminists focused on the securing of abortion rights, feminists of color sometimes advanced a countervailing politics of reproductive rights that aimed to expose the history of state-sponsored forced sterilization campaigns directed against African American, Latina, and Native American women. On this history and the feminist response to it, see Jennifer Nelson, *Women of Color and the Reproductive Rights Movement* (New York: New York University Press, 2003); and Laura Briggs, *Reproducing Empire: Race, Sex, Science, and US Imperialism in Puerto Rico* (Berkeley: University of California Press, 2002); and Briggs, *Somebody's Children: The Politics of Transracial and Transnational Adoption* (Durham: Duke University Press, 2012).

22. See, for example, Jefferson Cowie, *Stayin' Alive: The 1970s and the Last Days of the Working Class* (New York: New Press, 2012); Andrew Hartman, *A War for the Soul of America: A History of the Culture Wars* (Chicago: University of Chicago Press, 2015); Matthew Lassiter, *The Silent Majority: Suburban Politics in the Sunbelt South* (Princeton: Princeton University Press, 2012); Rick Perlstein, *Nixonland: The Rise of*

a President and the Fracturing of America (New York: Scribner, 2009); Bruce J. Schulman, *The Seventies: The Great Shift in American Culture, Society, and Politics* (New York: Da Capo, 2002); Robert Self, *All in the Family: The Realignment of American Democracy Since the 1970s* (New York: Hill and Wang, 2012); and Natasha Zaretsky, *No Direction Home: The American Family and the Fear of National Decline, 1968–1980* (Chapel Hill: University of North Carolina Press, 2007).

23. For an influential example of the former, see Bruce J. Schulman and Julian Zelizer, eds., *Rightward Bound: Making America Conservative in the 1970s* (Cambridge: Harvard University Press, 2008). Examples of the later include Dan Berger, *The Hidden 1970s: Histories of Radicalism* (New Brunswick, NJ: Rutgers University Press, 2010); and Michael Foley, *Front Porch Politics: The Forgotten Heyday of American Activism in the 1970s and 1980s* (New York: Hill and Wang, 2013).

24. My argument here is indebted to Jeremy Varon, who encouraged me to provide clarification on this crucial point.

25. Lisa McGirr, *Suburban Warriors: The Origins of the New American Right* (Princeton: Princeton University Press, 2002); Kevin Kruse, *White Flight: Atlanta and the Making of Modern Conservatism* (Princeton: Princeton University Press, 2005); and Elizabeth Shermer, *Sunbelt Capitalism: Phoenix and the Transformation of American Politics* (Philadelphia: University of Pennsylvania Press, 2013). Other monographs that trace a political transformation in one locale or region include Lassiter, *The Silent Majority*; and Robert Self, *American Babylon: Race and the Struggle for Postwar Oakland* (Princeton: Princeton University Press, 2005).

26. See, for example, Eric Foner, *The Story of American Freedom* (New York: Norton, 1999).

27. My account of two competing strains of nationalism takes its cues from the well-known contrast between civic nationalism and ethnonationalism in US political culture. See, for example, Gary Gerstle, *American Crucible: Race and Nation in the Twentieth Century* (Princeton: Princeton University Press, 2002). See also Rogers M. Smith, *Civic Ideals: Conflicting Visions of Citizenship in U.S. History* (New Haven: Yale University Press, 1999); and Anatol Lieven, *America Right or Wrong* (New York: Oxford University Press, 2004).

1. THE CULTURE OF DISSOCIATION AND THE RISE OF THE UNBORN

1. Quoted in William Graebner, *The Age of Doubt: American Thought and Culture in the 1940s* (New York: Twayne, 1991), 20.

2. Later, he reportedly told Teller, "You have done just that." Quoted in Shiloh R. Krupar, *Hot Spotter's Report: Military Fables of Toxic Waste* (Minneapolis: University of Minnesota Press, 2013), 160.

3. On cancer epidemics as slow motion disasters, see Kate Brown, *Plutopia: Nuclear Families, Atomic Cities, and the Great Soviet and American Plutonium Disasters* (New York: Oxford University Press, 2013).

4. On the role of extreme emotion in modern mass politics, see Daniel Bell, ed., *The Radical Right: The New American Right* (New York: Doubleday, 1963); Richard Hofstadter, *The Age of Reform: From Bryan to FDR* (New York: Random House, 1955);

and Michael Rogin, *The Intellectuals and McCarthy: The Radical Specter* (Cambridge: MIT Press, 1967). On civil defense as a form of emotional management, see Jackie Orr, *Panic Diaries: A Genealogy of Panic Disorders* (Durham: Duke University Press, 2006).

5. On the history of the Manhattan Project, see Howard Ball, *Justice Downwind: America's Atomic Testing Program in the 1950's* (Oxford: Oxford University Press, 1986); James Delgado, *Nuclear Dawn: The Atomic Bomb from the Manhattan Project to the Cold War* (Oxford: Osprey, 2009); Joseph Masco, *Nuclear Borderlands: The Manhattan Project in Post-Cold War New Mexico* (Princeton: Princeton University Press, 2006); and Michael Sherry, *In the Shadow of War: The United States Since the 1930s* (New Haven: Yale University Press, 1997). On the ways in which atomic power transformed the institution of the presidency, see Garry Wills, *Bomb Power: The Modern Presidency and the National Security State* (New York: Penguin, 2011).

6. "Atoms for Peace," address by Dwight D. Eisenhower to the 470th plenary meeting of the United Nations General Assembly, December 8, 1953. Reprinted in *Public Papers of the Presidents of the United States, Dwight D. Eisenhower: Containing the public Messages, Speeches, and Statements of the President, January 20, 1953 to January 20, 1961* (Washington, DC: US Government Printing Office, 1958–1961), 813–822.

7. See Helen Caldicott, *Nuclear Power Is Not the Answer* (New York: New Press, 2006).

8. David Lilienthal, "Whatever Happened to the Peaceful Atom?," *Harper's Magazine* 227, no. 10 (October 1963): 42–43.

9. Sherry, *In the Shadow of War*, 134–135, 143, 183, 195–196, 221, 224, 335, 381.

10. William James, "On a Certain Blindness in Human Beings," in *Talks to Teachers on Psychology and to Students on Some of Life's Ideals* (New York: Holt, 1915). Quoted in Louis Menand, *The Metaphysical Club* (New York: Farrar, Straus and Giroux, 2001), 372.

11. John Dower, *Cultures of War: Pearl Harbor/Hiroshima/9-11/Iraq* (New York: Norton, 2011), 259.

12. Ibid., 260.

13. Ibid., 261, 264.

14. Lilienthal, "Whatever Happened to the Peaceful Atom?," 42–43.

15. See, for example, Glenn Seaborg, "Need We Fear Our Nuclear Future?," *Bulletin of Atomic Scientists* 24, no. 1 (January 1, 1968): 36–42; Paula Fozzy, "Atomic Energy: New Peaceful Uses," *Bulletin of the Atomic Scientists* 18, no. 1 (January 1, 1962): 42–44; "Atoms for Peace: the Dream, the Reality," *New York Times Magazine*, August 1, 1965. The utopian aspirations for civilian nuclear energy during this period are examined in Spencer R. Weart, *Nuclear Fear: A History of Images* (1989; Cambridge: Harvard University Press, 2012), 171–174. See also Michael L. Smith, "'Planetary Engineering': The Strange Career of Progress in Nuclear American," in *Possible Dreams: Enthusiasm for Technology in America*, ed. John L. Wright (Dearborn, MI: Henry Ford Museum and Greenfield Village, 1992), 111–123.

16. Steven Spencer, "The Atom Is Going to Work," *Saturday Evening Post* 231, no. 32 (February 7, 1959): 29, 110.

17. Luis Campos, *Radium and the Secret of Life* (Chicago: University of Chicago Press, 2015), 12.

18. On the entwined histories of radiation and radium, see Lawrence Badash, "Radium, Radioactivity, and the Popularity of Scientific Discovery," *Proceedings of the*

American Philosophical Society 122 (1978): 145–154; Luis Campos, "The Birth of Living Radium," *Representations* 97 (Winter 2007): 1–27; Marjorie Malley, *Radioactivity: A History of a Mysterious Science* (New York: Oxford University Press, 2011); Carolyn de La Pena, *The Body Electric: How Strange Machines Built the Modern American* (New York: New York University Press, 2005), 173–174; and J. Samuel Walker, *Permissible Dose: A History of Radiation Protection in the Twentieth Century* (Berkeley: University of California Press, 2000). On the radiological safety program developed during the Manhattan Project, see Barton Hacker, *The Dragon's Tail: Radiation Safety in the Manhattan Project, 1942–1946* (Berkeley: University of California Press, 1987). On radiation's effects on survivors at Hiroshima and Nagasaki, see Susan Lindee, *Suffering Made Real: American Science and the Survivors at Hiroshima* (Chicago: University of Chicago Press, 1997). See also Catherine Caufield, *Multiple Exposures: Chronicles of the Radiation Age* (Chicago: University of Chicago Press, 1990).

19. Weart, *Nuclear Fear*, 164.

20. Quoted in ibid., 158–159.

21. Spencer, "The Atom Is Going to Work."

22. See Gabrielle Hecht, *Being Nuclear: Africans and the Global Uranium Trade* (Cambridge: MIT Press, 2012), 3; Penny von Eschen, "Duke Ellington Plays Baghdad: Rethinking Hard and Soft Power from the Outside In," in *Contested Democracy: Freedom, Race, and Power in American History*, ed. Manisha Sinha and Penny Von Eschen (New York: Columbia University Press, 2007), 279–300.

23. "Mental Health Aspects of the Peaceful Uses of Atomic Energy: Report of a Study Group," No. 151, World Health Organization, Technical Paper, Geneva, 1958, 4–5.

24. See Weart, *Nuclear Fear*, 173.

25. On the origins of the Price-Anderson Act, see Christian Joppke, *Mobilizing Against Nuclear Energy: A Comparison of the United States and Germany* (Berkeley: University of California Press, 1993), 25, 222.

26. Ibid., 25.

27. See Weart, *Nuclear Fear*, 168–169.

28. John Cockcroft, "Peaceful Uses of Atomic Energy: The Second International Conference," *Bulletin of the Atomic Scientists* 15, no. 1 (January 1, 1959): 18.

29. On the "domestication" of the atom and attempts to explain the atom to popular audiences, see Carroll Pursell, *Technology in Postwar America* (New York: Columbia University Press, 2007), 59–77; Joshua Silverman, "Nuclear Technology," in *A Companion to American Technology*, ed. Carroll Pursell (Malden, MA: Blackwell, 2005), 305; and Michael L. Smith, "Advertising the Atom," in *Government and Environmental Politics: Essays on Historical Development Since World War Two*, ed. Michael J. Lacey (Baltimore: Johns Hopkins University Press, 1991).

30. Reddy Kilowatt Coloring Book, Record Group 220 (hereafter referred to as RG 220), Central Files, Box 79, File 61900641B, Papers of the President's Commission on the Accident at Three Mile Island, National Archives II, University of Maryland, College Park (hereafter referred to as NA II).

31. For examples, see *You Can Understand the Atom* (Washington, DC: Atomic Energy Commission, 1951); and Selig Hecht, *Explaining the Atom* (New York: Viking, 1947). The AEC relied on a range of mediums for popularizing the atom: Atomic Energy Clubs, comic books, animated color film series, and newsreels. See Weart, *Nuclear Fears*, 170.

32. On the historic role of cheap energy in successive waves of capital accumulation, see Jason W. Moore, *Capitalism in the Web of Life: Ecology and the Accumulation of Capital* (London: Verso, 2015).

33. Outline of Master Plan for Public Education and Public Relations, 1975, Metropolitan Edison, RG 220, Central Files, Box 80, Folder: Speech Copy Outlines, Papers of the President's Commission on the Accident at Three Mile Island, NA II.

34. Weart, *Nuclear Fears*, 177.

35. One-Minute Radio Script, Metropolitan Edison, RG 220, Central Files, Box 80, Folder: Radio Commercials, 1966–3/27/79, Papers of the President's Commission on the Accident at Three Mile Island, NA II.

36. Quotation comes from a spokesperson for New England Power Company (NEPCO) and was reprinted in Jerry Elmer, "Power Plants and Weapons: The Nuclear Connection," SANE, Inc. Records, Series G, Box 137, Folder 1, Swarthmore College Peace Collection (hereafter referred to as SCPC).

37. Ibid.

38. See, for example, Brochure on Observation Center, RG 220, Central Files, Box 79, Folder 61900641B, Papers of the President's Commission on the Accident at Three Mile Island, NA II.

39. Glenn Seaborg, "Our Nuclear Future," *Bulletin of Atomic Scientists* 26, no. 6 (June 1, 1970): 7–14.

40. Met-Ed Brochure, RG 220, Central Files, Box 80, Folder: Nuclear Brochures, Information produced by Met-Ed, 6191068, Papers of the President's Commission on the Accident at Three Mile Island, NA II.

41. Nuclear Power Brochure, RG 220, Central Files, Box 79, Folder 61900641B, Papers of the President's Commission on the Accident at Three Mile Island, NA II.

42. One Minute Radio Script for Metropolitan Edison, RG 220, Central Files, Box 80, Folder: Radio Commercials, 1966–3/27/79, Papers of the President's Commission on the Accident at Three Mile Island, NA II.

43. On the history of atomic weapons testing, see Robert A. Divine, *Blowing on the Wind: The Nuclear Test Ban Debate, 1954–1960* (New York: Oxford University Press, 1978); and Masco, *Nuclear Borderlands*, 43–98.

44. Masco, *Nuclear Borderlands*, 60.

45. Although the earliest postwar tests were conducted in the Pacific, President Truman approved the Nevada site in December 1950 ostensibly in response to China's invasion of Korea two months earlier. That invasion supposedly convinced him of the need for a secure test site within the territorial boundaries of the United States.

46. Weart, *Nuclear Fears*, 187.

47. On this dilemma, see Jacob Hamblin, *Arming Mother Nature: The Birth of Catastrophic Environmentalism* (New York: Oxford University Press, 2013), 85–107.

48. United States Congress, Hearings Before the Special Subcommittee on Radiation of the Joint House and Senate Committee on Atomic Energy, "Fallout from Nuclear Weapons Tests," 86th Cong., 1st sess., June 1959.

49. See, for other examples, "Atomic Fallout—How Bad? The Facts and the Intrigue," *Newsweek*, April 6, 1959, 36–38; "These Precious Days," *New Yorker*, May 16, 1959, 180; and "The Silent Killer," *Saturday Evening Post*, August 29, 1959, 25. The edition of *Scientific American* from September 1959 was devoted to the theme of ionizing radiation.

50. Kai Erikson, *A New Species of Trouble: The Human Experience of Modern Disasters* (New York: Norton, 1995), 144. On the significance of radiation's invisibility, see Barbara Adam, *Timescapes of Modernity: The Environment and Invisible Hazards* (London: Routledge, 1998), 193–211. For a classic anthropological study on the broader theme of contamination, see Mary Douglas, *Purity and Danger: An Analysis of Concepts of Pollution and Taboo* (New York: Taylor, 2002).

51. On the question of whether there is such a thing as a safe threshold of radiation, see Walker, *Permissible Dose*. See also Divine, *Blowing on the Wind*, 134, 225.

52. "Radiation Report," *New York Times*, May 9, 1960.

53. Jacob Hamblin, "A Dispassionate and Objective Effort: Negotiating the First Study on the Biological Effects of Atomic Radiation," *Journal of the History of Biology* 40, no. 1 (Spring 2007): 147–177.

54. Weart, *Nuclear Fears*, 185; "Increased Radiation Found in East; Laid to Atom Tests, Held Harmless," *New York Times*, February 3, 1951; "AEC Calls Rate of Fall-Out Safe," *New York Times*, April 5, 1958; "AEC Denies Peril: Radiation Level in US Held High," *New York Times*, April 7, 1958; "Radiation Report: Expert Panels See No Major Rise in Perils of Radioactivity," *New York Times*, May 8, 1960.

55. "Science in Review: UN Report on Fall-Out Reveals Agreement on Radiation's Deleterious Effects," *New York Times*, August 17, 1958; Divine, *Blowing on the Wind*, 32; Ralph Lapp, "Civil Defense Faces New Peril," *Bulletin of Atomic Scientists* 10, no. 9 (November 1954): 349–351.

56. "Radiation Limit for Public Reached in 15-Nation Agreement," *New York Times*, November 2, 1959.

57. Walter Cannon, *The Wisdom of the Body* (New York: Norton, 1932).

58. Linda Nash, "Purity and Danger: Historical Reflections on Environmental Regulations," *Environmental History* 13, no. 4 (October 2008): 651–658.

59. Sarah Vogel, "From 'The Dose Makes the Poison' to 'The Timing Makes the Dose': Conceptualizing Risk in the Synthetic Age," *Environmental History* 13, no. 4 (October 2008): 667–673; and Vogel, "The Politics of Plastics: The Making and Unmaking of Bisphenol A 'Safety,'" *American Journal of Public Health* 99, no. S3 (September 3, 2009): 559–566.

60. Finis Dunaway discusses the "ecological body," and in particular its deployment in visual representations of environmental risk in Dunaway, *Seeing Green: The Use and Abuse of Environmental Images* (Chicago: University of Chicago Press, 2015). See also Stacey Alaimo, *Bodily Natures: Science, Environment and the Material Self* (Bloomington: Indiana University Press, 2010); and Heather Houser, *Ecosickness in Contemporary US Fiction: Environment and Affect* (New York: Columbia University Press, 2014).

61. On this association, again see Houser, *Ecosickness*.

62. On milk, see Kendra Smith-Howard, *Pure and Modern Milk: An Environmental History Since 1900* (New York: Oxford University Press, 2013); and Greta Gaard, "Toward a Feminist Postcolonial Milk Studies," *American Quarterly* 65, no. 3 (September 2013): 595–619.

63. "SR 90 in Milk: St. Louis Concerned Over a High Radioactivity Count," *New York Times*, July 31, 1960; and "A Radiation Rise in Milk Detected," *New York Times*, October 13, 1961. The concern surrounding Strontium-90 is discussed at length in Divine, *Blowing on the Wind*.

64. The scene is described in Robert Peter Gale and Eric Lax, *Radiation: What It Is, and What You Need to Know* (New York: Vintage, 2013), 113.

65. On the symbolic significance of the child in the fallout debate, see Finis Dunaway, *Seeing Green*; and Margaret Peacock, *Innocent Weapons: The Soviet and American Politics of Childhood in the Cold War* (Chapel Hill: University of North Carolina Press, 2014).

66. "A-Bomb Tests: Cold War Fears Stifled Doubts," *New York Times*, May 13, 1979.

67. On children's vulnerability to radiation exposure, see Divine, *Blowing on the Wind*, 274. In 1962, the AEC Fallout Studies Branch released the Knapp report, which showed that children in communities downwind from testing sites had received hundreds of roentgens of Iodine-131. At the time, the Federal Radiation Council recommended that infants be limited to doses of half a roentgen a year in peacetime. In August 1963, Dr. Eric Reiss, an associate professor of medicine at Washington University School of Medicine, told a congressional panel that several thousand children in Nevada and Utah had probably received hazardous doses of fallout and predicted ten to twelve cases of thyroid cancer as a result. The following October, the AEC acknowledged that a few children in Utah might have received radiation doses exceeding permissible peacetime levels. Also worrying government officials was an inquiry into leukemia deaths that expanded in 1963 into a study of thyroid nodules in children. In an internal memorandum written in 1962, government experts had termed the discovery "genuinely disturbing." In 1969, a separate study of thyroid surgery in Utah revealed a fourfold increase in thyroid cancer in the state, primarily among people between the ages of twenty and twenty-nine. These studies are discussed at length in SANE, Inc. Records, DG 58, Series G, Box 140, Folder: Low Level Radiation Materials, 1978–1980, SCPC.

68. On the Edward Murrow episode, see Weart, *Nuclear Fears*, 206; "Our Irradiated Children," *New Republic* 136, no. 24 (June 17, 1957): 9–12; and "Radioactivity Is Poisoning Your Children," *McCall's*, January 1957, cover.

69. "Nuclear Fallout Danger Stirs Widespread Fears," *New York Times*, October 15, 1961.

70. Dower, *Cultures of War*, 282. Postbomb images of mothers and children also figure prominently in John Hersey, *Hiroshima* (New York: Knopf, 1946); and Robert Jay Lifton, *Death in Life: Survivors of Hiroshima* (Chapel Hill: University of North Carolina Press, 1991). See also Lisa Yoneyama, *Hiroshima Traces: Time, Space, and the Dialectics of Memory* (Berkeley: University of California Press, 1999).

71. See Siddhartha Mukherjee, *The Emperor of All Maladies: A Biography of Cancer* (New York: Scribner, 2011). Other books that look at the cultural significance of cancer include James Patterson, *The Dread Disease: Cancer and American Culture* (Cambridge: Harvard University Press, 1989); Susan Sontag, *Illness as Metaphor* (New York: McGraw-Hill, 1977); and Robert Proctor, *Cancer Wars: How Politics Shapes What We Know and Don't Know About Cancer* (New York: Basic, 1995).

72. Quoted in "Science Notes," *New York Times*, September 11, 1960. A UN report from 1962 confirmed that the developing embryo was more susceptible to radiological injury than children and adults, even at low doses.

73. See Divine, *Blowing on the Wind*, 33.

74. Quoted in "Scientists Term Radiation a Peril to Future of Man," *New York Times*, June 13, 1956.

75. Quoted in "Science in Review: UN Report on Fall-Out Reveals Agreement on Radiation's Deleterious Effects," *New York Times*, August 17, 1958.

76. Linus Pauling, "Genetic and Scientific Effects of Carbon-14," *Science* 128 (November 14, 1958). Pauling is discussed at length in Divine, *Blowing on the Wind*. See also Barbara Marinacci and Ramesh Krishnamurthy, eds., *Linus Pauling on Peace: A Scientist Speaks Out on Humanism and World Survival* (Los Altos: Rising Star, 1998).

77. "Text of Genetics Committee Report Concerning Effects of Radioactivity on Heredity," *New York Times*, June 13, 1956.

78. Quoted in Divine, *Blowing on the Wind*, 54.

79. On the postwar history of genetics research, see Soraya de Chadarevian, "Mice and the Reactor: The Genetics Experiment in 1950s Britain," *Journal of the History of Biology* 39 (2006): 707–735; and Peter Harper, *A Short History of Medical Genetics* (New York: Oxford University Press, 2007).

80. My discussion in this paragraph is indebted to Sara Dubow, *Ourselves Unborn: A History of the Fetus in Modern America* (New York: Oxford University Press, 2010).

81. The radiation scare anticipated subsequent revelations about the impact of rubella, DES, and thalidomide on fetal development. On rubella, see Leslie Reagan, *Dangerous Pregnancies: Mothers, Disabilities, and Abortion in Modern America* (Berkeley: University of California Press, 2012). On DES, see Nancy Langston, *Toxic Bodies: Hormone Disrupters and the Legacy of DES* (New Haven: Yale University Press, 2011). On the history of thalidomide, see Andrea Tone, *The Age of Anxiety: A History of America's Turbulent Affair with Tranquilizers* (New York: Basic, 2011), 147–151.

82. On the Hibakusha, see Robert Jay Lifton, *Death in Life: Survivors of Hiroshima* (Chapel Hill: University of North Carolina Press, 1991); and Lisa Yoneyama, *Hiroshima Traces: Time, Space, and the Dialectics of Memory* (Berkeley: University of California Press, 1999).

83. Dubow writes that "atomic sciences and the science of embryology became at least loosely linked in the public imagination." Dubow, *Ourselves Unborn*, 52.

84. On Women's Strike for Peace and the larger theme of maternalism in women's pacifist organizing in the 1950s and 1960s, see Amy Swerdlow, *Women Strike for Peace: Traditional Motherhood and Radical Politics in the 1960s* (Chicago: University of Chicago Press, 1993); Harriet Hyman Alonso, *Peace as a Women's Issue: A History of the U.S. Movement for World Peace and Women's Rights* (Syracuse: Syracuse University Press, 1993); and Harriet Hyman Alonso, "Mayhem and Moderation: Women Peace Activists During the McCarthy Era," in *Not June Cleaver: Women and Gender in Postwar America, 1945–1960*, ed. Josanne Meyerowitz (Philadelphia: Temple University Press, 1994), 128–150. The definitive history of SANE is Milton Katz, *Ban the Bomb: A History of SANE, 1957–1985* (Westport, CT: Greenwood Press, 1986).

85. Quoted in Divine, *Blowing on the Wind*, 59.

86. Albert Schweitzer, *The Rights of the Unborn and the Peril Today: Statement with Reference to the Present Nuclear Crisis in the World* (Chicago: Albert Schweitzer Education Foundation, 1958).

87. "Facts of Life in the Age of the Hydrogen Bomb: Q and A for Americans," 10, SANE, Inc. Records, DG 058, Series A, Box 15, Folder 1: Advertisement, March 24, 1958, "No Contamination Without . . .," SCPC.

88. "The World's Peoples Have a Right to Demand No Contamination Without Representation: Questions and Answers for Americans About Hydrogen Bombs," February 27, 1968, 58, SANE, Inc. Records, DG 058, Series A, Box 15, Folder 1: Advertisement, March 24, 1958, SCPC.

89. Quoted in Divine, *Blowing on the Wind*, 139.

90. Schweitzer, *The Perils of the Unborn*.

91. Ibid.

92. Excerpt from a Speech Given by Krishna Menon to the UN General Assembly, October 16, 1957, SANE, Inc. Records, DG 58, Series A, Box 14, Folder 8: Advertisement, November 15, 1957, "We are facing a danger . . .," SCPC.

93. Divine, *Blowing on the Wind*, 204.

94. Letter from Lewis Mumford to Clarence Pickett and Norman Cousins, July 15, 1959, SANE Inc., Records, DG 58, Series A, Box 16, Folder 1: Advertisement, August 13, 1959, "Humanity Has a Common Will . . .," SCPC.

95. Ibid.

96. SANE, Inc. Records, DG 58, Series A, Box 14, Folder 7: "Scientists for SANE," SCPC.

97. Ernest Sternglass, "Infant Mortality and Nuclear Tests," *Bulletin of the Atomic Scientists* 25, no. 4 (April 1969): 18–20; Sternglass, "Can Infants Survive?," *Bulletin of the Atomic Scientists* 25, no. 6 (June 1969): 26–27; Sternglass, "The Death of All Children: A Footnote in the ABM Controversy," *Esquire* 72 (September 1969): 1a–1d. For secondary discussions, see Brian Balogh, *Chain Reaction: Expert Debate and Public Participation in American Commercial Nuclear Power, 1945–1975* (Cambridge: Cambridge University Press, 1991), 265–285, Philip Boffey, "Ernest Sternglass: Controversial Prophet of Doom," *Science* 166 (October 10, 1969): 195–200; Joppke, *Mobilizing Against Nuclear Energy*, 27–28; and Walker, *Permissible Dose*, 36–44.

98. Quoted in Joppke, *Mobilizing Against Nuclear Energy*, 28.

99. The decision no doubt contributed to the two scientists' eventual alliance with the antinuclear movement. Tamplin would join the Natural Resources Defense Council, and John Gofman later founded the Committee for Nuclear Responsibility.

100. Mancuso charged the Energy Research and Development Administration (which had assumed the AEC's nonregulatory duties in 1974) with retaliation and with muzzling him because it did not like his conclusions. Thomas Mancuso, Alice Stewart, and George Kneale, "Radiation Exposures of Hanford Workers Dying from Cancer and Other Causes," *Health Physics* 33 (November 1977): 369–385. For a discussion of the controversy, see Walker, *Permissible Dose*, 94–95; "The Government's Quiet War on Scientists Who Know Too Much," *Rolling Stone*, March 23, 1978, 42–44.

101. On the resignations, see Thomas Wellock, *Critical Masses: Opposition to Nuclear Power in California, 1958–1978* (Madison: University of Wisconsin Press, 1998), 147–148; and "News from Environmental Coalition on Nuclear Power," February 1976, RG 220, Central Files, Box 81, Folder: Anti-Nuclear Information, NA II.

102. On the public advocacy and direct action wings of the antinuclear movement in the United States, see Joppke, *Mobilizing Against Nuclear Energy*, 51–90.

103. On the ways in which these traditions of political radicalism endured into the 1970s and 1980s, see Dan Berger, *The Hidden 1970s: Histories of Radicalism* (New Brunswick, NJ: Rutgers University Press, 2010); and Michael Foley, *Front Porch*

Politics: The Forgotten Heyday of American Activism in the 1970s and 1980s (New York: Hill and Wang, 2013).

104. Historical work on the antinuclear movement has focused largely on local battles over plant-sitings, and with good reason. The stories of grassroots fights against nuclear power at places like Seabrook Station, New Hampshire, and Diablo Canyon, California, provide deeply moving accounts of nonviolent direct action in the 1970s and the 1980s. Case studies of local battles over plant sitings include Henry Bedford, *Seabrook Station: Citizen Politics and Nuclear Power* (Amherst: University of Massachusetts Press, 1990); Barbara Epstein, *Political Protest and Cultural Revolution: Non-Violent Direct Action in the 1970s and 1980s* (Berkeley: University of California Press, 1991); and Wellock, *Critical Masses*. Christian Joppke's *Mobilizing Against Nuclear Energy* offers an illuminating comparative analysis of the antinuclear movement in the United States and West Germany. In this vein, also see Dorothy Nelkin and Michael Pollak, *The Atom Besieged: Anti-Nuclear Movements in France and Germany* (Cambridge: MIT Press, 1982). For a more critical reading of the movement's localism, see Ursula Heise, *Sense of Place and Sense of Planet: The Environmental Imagination of the Global* (New York: Oxford University Press, 2008).

105. Kristin Iverson, *Full Body Burden: Growing Up in the Shadow of Rocky Flats* (New York: Crown, 2012).

106. Timothy Pachirat, *Every Twelve Seconds: Industrial Slaughter and the Politics of Sight* (New Haven: Yale University Press, 2011).

107. Pamphlet: Radiation: The Human Cost, SANE, Inc. Records, Series G, Box 139, Folder: Low Level Radiation Pamphlet, 1979, SCPC.

108. See, for example, Richard Curtis and Elizabeth Hogan, *Perils of the Peaceful Atom: The Myth of Safe Nuclear Plants* (New York: Doubleday, 1969); "Did You Give Permission for Nuclear Power Plants? 14 Reasons for Paying Attention," Limerick Ecology Action, RG 220, Central Files, RG 220, Central Files, Box 79, File 61900641B, Box 81, Folder: Anti-Nuke Info, Papers of the President's Commission on the Accident at Three Mile Island, NA II; "The Nuclear Menace," Shad and Clamshell Alliance Papers, unprocessed, SCPC; Leaflet for August 5–9 Days of Action, Shad and Clamshell Alliance Papers, unprocessed, SCPC; and Fundraising Letter from SANE, April 25, 1979, SANE, Inc. Records, DG 58, Series G, Box 96, Folder: Fundraising, Direct mail, Third Renewal, Three Mile Island, SCPC.

109. Examples of this line of argument can be seen in "Did You Give Permission for Nuclear Power Plants? 14 Reasons for Paying Attention," RG 220, Central Files, Box 81, Folder: Limerick Ecology Action, Anti-Nuke Info, Papers of the President's Commission on the Accident on the Accident at Three Mile Island, NA II; "What Are the Dangers of Nuclear Power?," Shad and Clamshell Alliance Papers, unprocessed, SCPC; Resolution Proposed by the 1979 National NOW Conference by NOW-New Jersey, SANE, Inc. Records, Series G, Box 139, Folder: Low Level Radiation Pamphlet, 1979, SCPC; Statement adopted by the National Board of SANE at its meeting on June 2, 1979, SANE, Inc. Records, Series G, Box 139, Folder: Low Level Radiation Pamphlet, 1979, SCPC; Clamshell Alliance Declaration of Nuclear Resistance, Clamshell Alliance and Shad Alliance Documents, unprocessed, SCPC.

110. Illustration of Ionizing Radiation in the Female Body, Clamshell Alliance and Shad Alliance Documents, unprocessed, SCPC. Also located at SANE, Inc. Records, DG 58, Series G, Box 140, Folder: Low Level Radiation Materials, 1978–1980, SCPC.

111. Kristin Iverson writes, "In the geography of the land and the geography of the body, some things are seen and some are unseen." Iverson, *Full Body Burden*, 338.

112. Ernst Kantorowicz, *The King's Two Bodies: A Study in Medieval Political Theology* (Princeton: Princeton University Press, 1958); Antoine de Baecque, *The Body Politic: Corporeal Metaphor in Revolutionary France, 1770–1880* (Stanford: Stanford University Press, 1997); and Jonathan Gil Harris, *Foreign Bodies and the Body Politic: Discourses of Social Pathology in Early Modern England* (Cambridge: Cambridge University Press, 2006).

113. On the NTS in particular and the American West as a site of nuclear toxicity more broadly, see Valerie Kuletz, *The Tainted Desert: Environmental Ruin in the American West* (New York: Routledge, 1998); and Kuletz, "Invisible Spaces, Violent Places: Cold War Nuclear and Militarized Landscapes," in *Violent Environments*, ed. Nancy Lee Peluso and Michael Watts (Ithaca: Cornell University Press, 2001), 237–260. See also John Beck, *Dirty Wars: Landscape, Power, and Waste in Western American Literature* (Lincoln: University of Nebraska Press, 2009); Kevin Ferlund, ed., *The Cold War American West* (Albuquerque: University of New Mexico Press, 1998); Tom Vanderbilt, *Survival City: Adventures Among the Ruins of Atomic America* (Princeton: Princeton Architectural Press, 2002); and Peter C. van Wyck, *Signs of Danger: Waste, Trauma, and Nuclear Threat* (Minneapolis: University of Minnesota Press, 2005). On the history of the plutonium industry in Hanford, see Hill Williams, *Made in Hanford: The Bomb That Changed the World* (Pullman: Washington State University, 2011); Brown, *Plutopia*; and William J. Kinsella and Jay Mullen, "Becoming Hanford Downwinders: Producing Community and Challenging Discursive Containment," in *Nuclear Legacies: Communication, Controversy, and the US Nuclear Weapons Complex*, ed. Bryan C. Taylor et al. (Lanham, MD: Lexington, 2007). On Rocky Flats, see Len Ackland, *Making a Real Killing: Rocky Flats and the Nuclear West* (Albuquerque: University of New Mexico Press, 1999); Iverson, *Full Body Burden*; and Krupar, *Hot Spotter's Report*. On atomic veterans, see Eileen Welsome, *The Plutonium Files: America's Secret Medical Experiments in the Cold War* (New York: Dial, 1999). The NTS, Rocky Flats, and Hanford are all analyzed as sites of Cold War commemoration in Jon Weiner, *How We Forgot the Cold War: A Historical Journey Across America* (Berkeley: University of California, 2012).

114. For a more extensive discussion of this politics and its relation to radiation activism, see Natasha Zaretsky, "Radiation Suffering and Patriotic Body Politics," *Journal of Social History* 48, no. 3 (Spring 2015): 487–510.

115. US Congress, Joint Hearings, Subcommittee on Oversight and Investigations of House Committee on Interstate and Foreign Commerce, and Health and Scientific Research Subcommittee of the Senate Labor and Human Resources Committee and Committee on the Judiciary, *Health Effects of Low-Level Radiation, Volume 1*, 96th Cong., 1st sess., April 19, 1979, 8.

116. These studies are discussed at length in the SANE, Inc. Records, DG 58, Series G, Box 140, Files of SANE Publications Directors, 1978–1985, Folder: Low Level Radiation: Reference Material, 1978–1980, SCPC. On children's particular vulnerability to radiation exposure, see Divine, *Blowing on the Wind*, 274.

117. See Ball, *Justice Downwind*; "Citizens Hearings for Radiation Victims," 1980, SANE, Inc. Records, Series G, Box 137, Folder 5, SCPC; Folder: Radiation Victims, 1980–3, SANE, Inc. Records, Series G, Box 137, SCPC; US Congress, House of Representatives,

Hearing Before the Subcommittee on Natural Resources and Environment of the Committee on Science and Technology, *Research on Health Effects of Nonionizing Radiation*, 96th Congress, 1st sess., July 12, 1979; and US Congress, Joint Hearing, *Health Effects of Low-Level Radiation: Volume 1.*

118. See Ball, *Justice Downwind*, 45. After 1970, the public sphere became filled with still more information. Some radiation-induced leukemias appeared soon after exposure, while other cancers could lie dormant for decades. Starkly put, by the mid-1970s more downwinders had fallen ill and died, and as a result, their survivors had accrued a larger and more damning body of evidence against the AEC. In addition, the Utah Cancer Registry only started compiling cancer mortality information in the late 1960s. Its official findings, first published in 1972 and 1975, confirmed what downwinders already suspected: acute leukemia and cancer rates had increased significantly in those counties closest to the NTS. An article published in 1979 in the *New England Journal of Medicine* buttressed the registry data. It found that rates of pediatric leukemia had risen sharply in southern Utah between 1951 and 1958.

119. Hannah Arendt, "Lying in Politics: Reflections on the Pentagon Papers," in *Crises of the Republic* (New York: Harcourt Brace Jovanovich, 1972).

120. "A Flinty Grandmother Battles for the Victims of Utah's Nuclear Tragedy," *People* 12, no. 14 (October 1, 1979): 26–28.

121. On accidental activists, see Foley, *Front Porch Politics*. In the late 1970s and early 1980s, radiation activists founded several organizations based in the US Southwest, including Citizens Call, started in 1978 by a Utah woman whose brother had died at the age of twenty-seven from pancreatic cancer; Downwinders, a Salt Lake City group formed in 1980 by a southern Utah native and cancer survivor; and the NTS Radiation Victims Association, which was launched on behalf of military personnel who had worked at the site and subsequently fallen ill. Activists founded organizations for members of the US military and their families, such as the Committee for US Veterans of Hiroshima and Nagasaki, the National Association of Atomic Veterans, and Atomic Widows, an organization that assisted the wives of deceased veterans who were convinced that their husbands' deaths had been caused by radiation exposure sustained during their service. There were also organizations like the National Committee for Radiation Victims and the National Association of Radiation Survivors that created a national network by bringing hundreds of radiation victims together under a shared umbrella. These groups engaged in work along several different axes.

122. Transcript of testimony of O. T. Weeks presented before the Citizens' Commission Panel, National Citizens' Hearings for Radiation Victims, Washington, DC, April 11–14, 1980, SANE, Inc. Records, Series G, Box 137, Files of E. Glennon, Folder: Radiation Victims, 1980–3, SCPC. Howard Ball discusses several of these organizations in *Justice Downwind*.

123. On the concept of the nuclear sublime, see Frances Ferguson, "The Nuclear Sublime," *Diacritics* 14, no. 2 (Summer 1984): 4–10; Joseph Masco, "Nuclear Technoaesthetics: Sensory Politics from Trinity to the Virtual Bomb in Los Alamos," *American Ethnologist* 31, no. 3 (2004): 349–373; Masco, *The Nuclear Borderlands*, 55–68; Hugh Gusterson, "(Anti)nuclear Pilgrims," *Anthropologiska Studier* 62–63:61–66; and Gusterson, "Nuclear Tourism," *Journal for Cultural Research* 8, no. 1 (2004): 23–31. For a critique of the concept, see David Nye, *American Technological Sublime* (Cambridge: MIT Press, 1994).

124. "The Atomic Age: A Trail of Victims," 3, SANE, Inc. Records, Series G, Box 139, Folder: Citizens Hearings for Radiation Victims, 1980, SCPC.

125. "The Forgotten Nevada Test Site Workers," *Las Vegas Sun*, August 22, 1980. Found in SANE, Inc. Records, Series G, Box 137, Folder 5: Citizens' Hearings for Radiation Victims, 1980, SCPC.

126. Testimony of Robert Jay Lifton, Transcript of Testimony Presented Before the Citizens' Commission Panel, April 12, 1980, SANE, Inc. Records, Series G, Box 137, Folder: Radiation Victims, 1980–3, SCPC.

127. On this dual conception of witnessing, see Kelly Oliver, *Witnessing: Beyond Recognition* (Minneapolis: University of Minnesota Press, 2001).

128. On the women's health movement of the 1970s, see Wendy Kline, *Bodies of Knowledge: Sexuality, Reproduction, and Women's Health in the Second Wave* (Chicago: University of Chicago Press, 2012); Jennifer Nelson, *Women of Color and the Reproductive Rights Movement* (New York: New York University Press, 2003); and Jennifer Nelson, *More Than Medicine: A History of the Feminist Women's Health Movement* (New York: New York University Press, 2015). For an incisive look at the centrality of the politics of health to the Black Panther Party, see Alondra Nelson, *Body and Soul: The Black Panther Party and the Fight Against Medical Discrimination* (Minneapolis: University of Minnesota Press, 2011). On race and medical discrimination, see also Rebecca Skloot, *The Immortal Life of Henrietta Lacks* (New York: Broadway, 2011).

129. Report on National Citizens Hearings for Radiation Victims, April 11–14, 1980, SANE World, Periodicals Collection, *SANE World* (September 1979), January 1965–October 1986, SCPC.

130. *National Association of Radiation Survivors Newsletter*, Winter 1985, SANE, Inc. Records, DG 58, Series G, Box 96, Folder: Fundraising, Direct Mail, Third Renewal, Three Mile Island, SCPC.

131. Transcript of testimony of Dr. Henry Vyner, psychiatrist and member of Physicians for Social Responsibility, Citizens' Commission Panel, National Citizens' Hearings for Radiation Victims, Washington, DC, April 11–14, 1980, SANE, Inc. Records, Series G, Box 137, Files of E. Glennon, Folder: Radiation Victims, 1980–3, SCPC.

132. Downwinders often quoted AEC Chairman Thomas Murray, who in 1955 declared, "we must not let anything interfere with this series of tests, nothing." For example, see Terry Tempest Williams, *Refuge: An Unnatural History of Family and Place* (New York: Vintage, 1991), 284.

2. THE ACCIDENT AND THE POLITICAL TRANSFORMATION OF THE 1970s

1. For studies that show how disasters expose social fraying, see Kai Erikson, *A New Species of Trouble: Explorations in Disaster, Trauma, and Community* (New York: Norton, 1994); and Eric Klinenberg, *Heatwave: A Social Autopsy of Disaster in Chicago* (Chicago: University of Chicago Press, 2002). For a study that foregrounds disaster's communitarian dimensions, see Rebecca Solnit, *A Paradise Built in Hell: The Extraordinary Communities That Arise in Disaster* (New York: Viking, 2009).

2. Thomas Borstelmann, *The 1970s: A New Global History from Civil Rights to Economic Inequality* (Princeton: Princeton University Press, 2013); Cowie, *Stayin' Alive*;

Meg Jacobs, *Panic at the Pump: The Energy Crisis and the Transformation of American Politics in the 1970s* (New York: Hill and Wang 2016); Daniel Rodgers, *Age of Fracture* (Cambridge: Harvard University Press, 2011); Robert Self, *All in the Family: the Realignment of American Democracy Since the 1970s* (New York: Hill and Wang, 2012).

3. On the significance of the pregnant woman as a symbol of environmental risk, see Finis Dunaway, "Gas Masks, Pogo, and the Ecological Indian: Earth Day and the Visual Politics of American Environmentalism," *American Quarterly* 60, no. 1 (March 2008): 67–99; and Dunaway, *Seeing Green: The Use and Abuse of Environmental Images* (Chicago: University of Chicago Press, 2015).

4. For examples, see letters to the Kemeny Commission from Nikki Naumann and Mary M. Wertman, RG 220, Central Files, Box 307, unnamed folder, Papers of the President's Commission on the Accident at Three Mile Island, NA II.

5. J. Samuel Walker, *Three Mile Island: A Nuclear Crisis in Historical Perspective* (Berkeley: University of California Press, 2004); and John Kemeny, *Accident at Three Mile Island: The Need for Change, the Legacy of TMI* (Oxford: Pergamon, 1979).

6. Spencer R. Weart, *Nuclear Fear: A History of Images* (1989; Cambridge: Harvard University Press, 2012), 299.

7. "What Is Radiation?," RG 220, Central Files, Box 80, Folder 6190068: Nuclear Brochures, Information Produced by Met-Ed, Papers of the President's Commission on the Accident at Three Mile Island, NA II; "The Social and Economic Effects of the Accident at TMI," Study Prepared for the Nuclear Regulatory Commission by Mountain West and Social Impact Research, Series XI: Governor of Pennsylvania, 1979–1987, Subseries 7: Three Mile Island, Box 197, Folder 1, Dick Thornburgh Papers (hereafter referred to as DT Papers), University of Pittsburgh Special Collections (hereafter referred to as UPSC).

8. On the Rasmussen Report, see Weart, *Nuclear Fear*, 335.

9. Quoted in Lee Clarke, *Worst Cases: Terror and Catastrophe in the Popular Imagination* (Chicago: University of Chicago Press, 2005), 43.

10. Select Committee's Report of the Hearings Concerning TMI, Statement by Mayor Robert Reid, Goldsboro Fire Hall, Public Meeting, June 6, 1979, Series XI: Governor of Pennsylvania, 1979–1987, Subseries 7: Three Mile Island, Box 199, Folder 13, DT Papers, UPSC.

11. On the survey data and the two groups, see "The Social and Economic Effects of the Accident at TMI," Study Prepared for the Nuclear Regulatory Commission by Mountain West and Social Impact Research, Series XI: Governor of Pennsylvania, 1979–1987, Subseries 7: Three Mile Island, Box 197, Folder 1, DT Papers, UPSC.

12. On TMIA, see Susan Stranahan, *Susquehanna, River of Dreams* (Baltimore: Johns Hopkins University Press, 1995), 207–208.

13. "Three Years Later, Middletown Remembers," *Harrisburg Evening News*, April 2, 1982.

14. On the decline of steel and the transformation of the industrial rustbelt, see Judith Stein, *Running Steel, Running America: Race, Economic Decline, and the Decline of Liberalism* (Chapel Hill: University of North Carolina Press, 1998); and Stein, *Pivotal Decade: How the United States Traded Factories for Finance in the Seventies* (New Haven: Yale University Press, 2010).

15. Dauphin County, where TMI was located, was almost 85 percent white; the African Americans who lived in Dauphin County were centered in Harrisburg. The

other counties surrounding the plant had larger white majorities. See US Census of Population and Housing: 1980 Census Tracts, Harrisburg-Hickory. For an excellent compilation of census demographic data on Pennsylvania's counties, see Renee Lamis, *The Realignment of Pennsylvania Politics Since 1960: Two Party Competition in a Battleground State* (University Park: Pennsylvania State University Press, 2009), appendix D, 354–360. Of the approximately 35,500 people who lived within five miles of the plant, 97 percent were white and 83 percent were native Pennsylvanians. See TMI Population Registry, Jane Lee Papers, Box 1, Folder 23, Three Mile Island Collection (hereafter referred to TMIC), Dickinson College Archives and Special Collections (hereafter referred to as DCASC).

16. Paul Beers, *City Contented, City Discontented: A History of Modern Harrisburg* (Harrisburg, PA: Midtown Scholar, 2011), 259.

17. Robert Del Tredici, *The People of Three Mile Island* (San Francisco: Sierra Club, 1980), 64.

18. Association of Religious Data Archives, www.thearda.com/mapsReports /reports/counties/42043_1980.asp.

19. On both the political economy and the political culture of the Susquehanna Valley, see Walker, *Three Mile Island*; Susan Stranahan, *Susquehanna, River of Dreams* (Baltimore: Johns Hopkins University Press, 1995); "The Social and Economic Effects of the Accident at TMI," Study Prepared for the NRC by Mountain West and Social Impact Research, Series XI: Governor of Pennsylvania, 1979–1987, Subseries 7: Three Mile Island, Box 197, Folder 1, DT Papers, UPSC. The quotation comes from "Innocence Lost," *Pennsylvania Illustrated*, August 1979, 30, Series XI: Governor of Pennsylvania, 1979–1987, Subseries 7: Three Mile Island, Box 200, Folder 1, DT Papers, UPSC.

20. Charles Perrow, *Normal Accidents: Living with High Risk Technologies* (New York: Basic, 1984).

21. On the experience of the control room operators, see Kemeny, *Accident at Three Mile Island*, 11, 92–93. Scholars of technological disasters have argued that redundant systems—designed to eliminate risk—often generate new and unanticipated risks of their own. Sociologist Lee Clarke writes that "safety devices can bring systems down, adding more guards can increase opportunities for failure, having extra people can diffuse responsibility, heaping on redundant devices can increase production pressure." Clarke, *Worst Cases*, 181.

22. Deposition of Edward Frederick, RG 220, Central Files, Box 11, Folder: Deposition of Edward Frederick, Papers of the President's Commission on the Accident at Three Mile Island, NA II, 271, 276.

23. See Del Tredici, *The People of Three Mile Island*, 10–11. On emergency procedures and the protocol for contacting different agencies, see page 3A of Statement of Oran Henderson, Transcript, News Conference, March 28, 1979, 10:55 AM, Series XI: Governor of Pennsylvania, 1979–1987, Subseries 7: Three Mile Island, Box 194, Folder 1, DT Papers, UPSC.

24. Transcript, News Conference, March 28, 1979, 10:55 AM, Series XI: Governor of Pennsylvania, 1979–1987, Subseries 7: Three Mile Island, Box 194, Folder 1, DT Papers, UPSC.

25. Ibid., 4–5.

26. Walker, *Three Mile Island*, 80–84.

27. Statement by William Scranton in transcript of press conference, March 28, 1979, 4:30 PM, Series XI: Governor of Pennsylvania, 1979–1987, Subseries 7: Three Mile Island, Box 194, Folder 1, DT Papers, UPSC.

28. Press conference transcript, March 28, 1979, 10:30 PM, 8, Series XI: Governor of Pennsylvania, 1979–1987, Subseries 7: Three Mile Island, Box 194, Folder 1, DT Papers, UPSC. Gallina's statement refuted information already coming into the NRC. On the discrepancies between Gallina's statements and those coming out of NRC headquarters, see Walker, *Three Mile Island*, 99. "Cold shutdown" refers to when the temperature of the core's water goes below the boiling point.

29. Walker, *Three Mile Island*, 105.

30. Ibid., 106.

31. In fact, the plant's wastewater was routinely discharged into the river, but Met-Ed had halted the discharge when the accident occurred. By Thursday, the water tanks on the island were close to overflowing with four hundred thousand gallons of water, now contaminated with the radioactive gas xenon.

32. Ibid., 115–118.

33. Ibid., 84: The reading was of twelve hundred millirems per hour. Walker writes: "The permissible dose for individual members of the general population was one tenth of the occupational level, or .5 rem per year. This was usually expressed as 500 millirems—a millirem is one-thousandth of a rem. The average allowable exposure for large population groups, such as the population around TMI, was one-thirtieth of the occupational level, or 170 millirems per year. The NRC further required that nuclear plants restrict their emissions during normal operation so that a person who stood on the boundary of a plant twenty four hours a day, 365 days a year, would not be exposed to more than about 5 millirems per year."

34. "Commissioners Deplored a Lack of Information," *New York Times*, April 13, 1979. See also Walker, *Three Mile Island*, 119–150.

35. US Congress, *Joint Hearings Before the Subcommittee on Nuclear Regulation of the Senate Committee on Environmental and Public Works, and the Subcommittee on Energy and the Environment of the House Committee on Interior and Insular Affairs*, Testimony of John Kemeny, Report of the President' Commission on the Three Mile Island Accident, 96th Congress, 1st sess., October 31, 1979, 16.

36. Walker, *Three Mile Island*, 150.

37. Quoted in Eli Zaretsky, *Why America Needs a Left: A Historical Argument* (London: Polity, 2012), 128.

38. Quoted in Christopher Hayes, *Twilight of the Elites: America After Meritocracy* (New York: Broadway, 2012), 119; Letters to the Editor, *New York Times*, October 4, 1973.

39. Both of these quotations come from Public Information Task Force Interview of Reporters, Interviews with Roger Witherspoon and Curtis Wilkie, RG 220, Central Files, Box 472, unnamed folders, Papers of the President's Commission on the Accident at Three Mile Island, NA II.

40. Letter from Carlton Walls to Health Resources Planning and Development, RG 220, Central Files, Box 307, unfiled, Papers of the President's Commission on the Accident at Three Mile Island, NA II.

41. "Watergate cover-up feeling" comes from undated letter from Thomas Busch to health resource planning and development, RG 220, Central Files, Box 307, unfiled,

Papers of the President's Commission on the Accident at Three Mile Island, NA II. Song comes from Gary Punch, "TMI Fallout: Trust in Officials Collapse," *Pittsburgh Post-Gazette*, April 19, 1979.

42. Deposition of Walter Creitz, 100–2, RG 220, Central Files, Box 6, Folder: Deposition of Walter Creitz, Papers of the President's Commission on the Accident at Three Mile Island, NA II.

43. Interview with Walter Creitz, 21, RG 220, Central Files, Box 467, Folder: Interview with Walter Creitz, Papers of the President's Commission on the Accident at Three Mile Island, NA II.

44. Union of Concerned Scientists, *Press Backgrounder: The TMI Accident Fifth Anniversary: Industry Hasn't Learned from Its Mistakes*, March 2, 1984, 12, Series XI: Governor of Pennsylvania, 1979–1987, Subseries 13: Office of General Counsel, Box 352, Folder 12, DT Papers, UPSC.

45. See Walker, *Three Mile Island*.

46. Transcript, press conference, March 30, 1979, 10 PM, Part 2, 1A, Series XI: Governor of Pennsylvania, 1979–1987, Subseries 7: Three Mile Island, Box 194, Folder 3, DT Papers, UPSC.

47. "Report by the Democratic Members of the TMI Committee," Pennsylvania House of Representatives, 48, Series XI: Governor of Pennsylvania, 1979–1987, Subseries 12: Press Secretary, Box 334, Folder 11, DT Papers, UPSC.

48. Kemeny, *Accident at Three Mile Island*, 53.

49. US Congress, Joint Hearings, Subcommittee on Nuclear Regulation of the Senate Committee on Environment and Public Works and the Subcommittee on Energy and the Environment of the House Committee on Interior and Insular Affairs, *Report of the Presidential Commission on the Three Mile Island Accident*, Congress, 96th Cong., 1st sess., October 31, 1979, 20.

50. Transcript of Proceedings, Commission, 47, Series XI: Governor of Pennsylvania, 1979–1987, Subseries 7: Three Mile Island, Box 198, Folder 3, DT Papers, UPSC.

51. US Congress, House of Representatives, Committee on Science and Technology, *Hearings Before the Subcommittee on Natural Resources and the Environment*, Prepared Statement by Richard Thornburgh, 96th Cong., 1st sess., June 2, 1979, 49–50 (Washington, DC: US Government Printing Office, 1980).

52. Deposition of Richard Thornburgh, 25, RG 220, Central Files, Box 30, Folder: Deposition of Richard Thornburgh, Papers of the President's Commission on the Accident at Three Mile Island, NA II.

53. Transcript of statement by William Scranton, "Incident at TMI," press conference held on March 28, 1979, 4:30 PM, Part 1, 3, Series XI: Governor of Pennsylvania, 1979–1987, Subseries 7: Three Mile Island, Box 194, Folder 1, DT Papers, UPSC.

54. Press Conference, March 31, 1979, 11 PM, Part 1, 8, Series XI: Governor of Pennsylvania, 1979–1987, Subseries 7: Three Mile Island, Box 194, Folder 7, DT Papers, UPSC.

55. "TMI and the Politics of Public Health," Gordon MacLeod, Lecture Prepared for Physicians for Social Responsibility, November 22, 1980, Beverly Hess Papers, Box 5, Folder 6, TMIC, DCASC. See also Gordon MacLeod, "Some Public Health Lessons from Three Mile Island: A Case Study in Chaos," *Ambio* 10, no. 1 (1981): 18–23.

56. See Walker, *Three Mile Island*, 228.

57. Quotation is from interview with Bryce Nelson, reporter from the *Los Angeles Times*, Public Information Task Force, Interview with Reporters, RG 220, Central

Files, Box 472, unnamed folder, Papers of the President's Commission on the Accident at Three Mile Island, NA II.

58. Transcript of Kemeny Commission Interview with Karl Abraham, 73, RG 220, Central Files, Box 466, unnamed folder, Papers of the President's Commission on the Accident at Three Mile Island, NA II.

59. Interview with Roger Witherspoon, reporter for *Atlanta Constitution*, Public Information Task Force Interview of Reporters, 3, RG 220, Central Files, Box 472, unnamed folder, Papers of the President's Commission on the Accident at Three Mile Island, NA II.

60. "Townfolks Shrug Off Radioactivity," *Los Angeles Times*, March 30, 1979.

61. See, for example, Interview with Business Employee and Spouse, August 20, 1979, and Interview with College Administrator #4, June 7, 1979, Lonna Malmsheimer Oral History Interviews (hereafter referred to as LMOHI), TMIC, DCASC. Resource Center of threemileisland.org, www.threemileisland.org/resource/index.php?aid=00024.

62. "Establishing a Viable Public Information Center," Series XI: Governor of Pennsylvania, 1979–1987, Subseries 7: Three Mile Island, Box 194, Folder 20, DT Papers, UPSC. On the difference between technological and natural disaster in this regard, see Susan Cutter, *Living with Risk: the Geography of Technological Hazards* (New York: Wiley, 1995).

63. Interview with Curtus Wilkie, Public Information Task Force Interview of Reporters, RG 220, Central Files, Box 472, unnamed folder, Papers of the President's Commission on the Accident at Three Mile Island, NA II.

64. On these measures, see *Washington Post Special Report*, Series XI: Governor of Pennsylvania, 1979–1987, Subseries 7: Three Mile Island, Box 200, Folder 1, DT Papers, UPSC; Box 194, Folder 1, DT Papers, UPSC; and Box 194, Folder 16, DT Papers, UPSC. See also "Population Dose and Health Impact of the Accident at the TMI Nuclear Station," Series XI: Governor of Pennsylvania, 1979–1987, Subseries 7: Three Mile Island, Box 194, Folder 19, DT Papers, UPSC.

65. Public Information Task Force Interviews of Reporters, 2, RG 220, Central Files, Box 472, unnamed folder, Papers of the President's Commission on the Accident at Three Mile Island, NA II.

66. Interview with John Baer, Public Information Task Force Interviews of Reporters, RG 220, Central Files, Box 472, unnamed folder, Papers of the President's Commission on the Accident at Three Mile Island, NA II.

67. On safety protocols at the plant, see Deposition of Joseph Deman, RG 220, Central Files, Box 6, Folder: Deposition of Joseph Deman, Papers of the President's Commission on the Accident at Three Mile Island, NA II.

68. "Radiation Overdose: All in a Day's Work," *New York Times*, April 4, 1979.

69. Ibid.

70. "Townfolks Shrug Off Radioactivity."

71. Adriana Petryna, *Life Exposed: Biological Citizens After Chernobyl* (Princeton: Princeton University Press, 2003). In this book, Petryna looks at how biological health became a realm of entitlement within Ukrainian state formation after the dissolution of the Soviet Union. Here, I am using the category of biological citizenship more broadly.

72. I use the formulation atomic-cum-ecological age to suggest that the ecological age emerged out of the atomic one, but also that there are significant continuities between the two epochs.

73. US Congress, Senate, *Hearings Before the Subcommittee on Energy, Nuclear Proliferation, and Federal Services of the Committee on Governmental Affairs*, 96th Cong., 1st sess., 1979.

74. Interview with Tate, Public Information Task Force Interviews of Reporters, 2, RG 220, Central Files, Box 472, unnamed folder, Papers of the President's Commission on the Accident at Three Mile Island, NA II.

75. Letter from Thomas Busch to health resource planning and development, RG 220, Central Files, Box 307, unfiled, Papers of the President's Commission on the Accident at Three Mile Island, NA II.

76. Interview with Business Employee and Spouse, August 20, 1979, LMOHI, TMIC, DCASC. Accessed at Resource Center of threemileisland.org, www.three-mileisland.org/resource/item_detail.php? item_id=00000220.

77. Scranton quoted in Walker, *Three Mile Island*, 81. See also Richard Thornburgh Deposition, RG 220, Central Files, Box 30, Folder: Richard Thornburgh Deposition, Papers of the President's Commission on the Accident at Three Mile Island, NA II.

78. There were six counties that fell within the ten-mile radius alone. They were York County, Lancaster County, Lebanon County, Dauphin County, Perry County, and Cumberland County.

79. The Nuclear Regulatory Commission recommended a 2.2-mile evacuation plan. The state had a plan for a five-mile evacuation. On Middletown, see interview with Robert Reid in Del Tredici, *The People of Three Mile Island*, 17. Those plans in place were often short on detail. The emergency-planning document for Dauphin County, where TMI was located, offers an example. The document included lists of possible suppliers (such as bus companies and ambulance services) that could be utilized in the event of an emergency. It also included phone listings for people and agencies to be contacted if an accident occurred at the plant. But missing from the document was any recommended evacuation routes or provision for mass care centers beyond the five-mile ring. "The Social and Economic Effects of the Accident at TMI," Series XI: Governor of Pennsylvania, 1979–1987, Subseries 7: Three Mile Island, Box 197, Folder 1, DT Papers, UPSC.

80. Kemeny, *Accident at Three Mile Island*, 15.

81. Interview with Brian McKay in Del Tredici, *The People of Three Mile Island*, 112.

82. "TMI and the Politics of Public Health," Gordon MacLeod, Lecture Prepared for Physicians for Social Responsibility, November 22, 1980, Beverly Hess Papers, Box 5, Folder 6, TMIC, DCASC.

83. Interview with College Administrator #8, LMOHI, TMIC, DCASC. Resource Center of threemileisland.org, www.threemileisland.org/resource/item_detail.php ?item_id=00000222.

84. Deposition of Harold Denton, 133, RG 220, Central Files, Box 6, Folder: Deposition of Harold Denton, Papers of the President's Commission on the Accident at Three Mile Island, NA II.

85. On the concept of defense-in-depth, see Walker, *Three Mile Island*, 52–54.

86. See, for example, Letter from John and Patricia Longnecker to the Kemeny Commission, RG 220, Central Files, Box 8, unnamed folder, Papers of the President's Commission on the Accident at Three Mile Island, NA II; Letter from Judith Johnsrud and Chauncey Kepford, The Environmental Coalition, September 20, 1979, Select Committee's Report of the Hearings Concerning TMI, Series XI: Governor of

Pennsylvania, 1979–1987, Subseries 7: Three Mile Island, Box 199, Folder 13, DT Papers, UPSC. The difficulties in coordinating an evacuation in response to a nuclear accident reflected the roots of emergency planning in the Cold War. The Civil Defense Act had emphasized nuclear attack rather than reactor events, and evacuations were not considered a realistic response.

87. Richard Thornburgh statement before the US Senate Subcommittee on Nuclear Regulation, April 23, 1979, Series XI: Governor of Pennsylvania, 1979–1987, Subseries 7: Three Mile Island, Box 195, Folder 6, DT Papers, UPSC. My italics.

88. See Richard Thornburgh Deposition, RG 220, Central Files, Box 30, Folder: Richard Thornburgh Deposition, Papers of the President's Commission on the Accident at Three Mile Island, NA II; and Kemeny, *Accident at Three Mile Island*, 120.

89. "The Social and Economic Effects of the Accident At TMI: Findings to Date," Prepared by the Nuclear Regulatory Commission, 59–60, Series XI: Governor of Pennsylvania, 1979–1987, Subseries 7: Three Mile Island, Box 197, Folder 1, DT Papers, UPSC.

90. Transcript of Proceedings, Commission, 25–6, Box 198, Folder 3, DT Papers, UPSC.

91. See Jackie Orr, *Panic Diaries: A Genealogy of Panic Disorders* (Durham: Duke University Press, 2006); and Philip Wylie, "Panic, Psychology, and the Bomb," *Bulletin of Atomic Scientists* 10, no. 2 (February 1954): 37–40.

92. See Joanna Bourke, *Fear: A Cultural History* (Berkeley: Counterpoint, 2007), 269.

93. Colonel Oran Henderson testimony to House Armed Services Committee, 6, Series XI: Governor of Pennsylvania, 1979–1987, Subseries 7: Three Mile Island, Box 195, Folder 1, DT Papers, UPSC.

94. On the panic myth, see Enrico Quarantelli, "Conventional Beliefs and Counterintuitive Realities," *Social Research* 75, no. 3 (Fall 2008): 873–904. See also Solnit, *A Paradise Built in Hell*; and Clarke, *Worst Cases*.

95. Lee Clarke quoted in Solnit, *A Paradise Built in Hell*, 131. See also Clarke, *Worst Cases*. In this way, the TMI story provides an illustrative example of the ways that panic myths, in Clarke's words, work to "reinforce particular institutional interests."

96. Quoted in Walker, *Three Mile Island*, 137.

97. Ibid., 107.

98. *Washington Post Special Report*, Series XI: Governor of Pennsylvania, 1979–1987, Subseries 7: Three Mile Island, Box 200, Folder 1, DT Papers, UPSC. News stories detailing the evacuation often mobilized a gendered logic by implying that local women were more fearful and local men more stoic in the face of the accident. Indeed, even a new term—*nuclear macho*—was coined to describe male residents who were staying put. On nuclear macho, see Peter M. Sandman and Mary Paden, "At Three Mile Island," *Columbia Journalism Review* (July/August 1979): 43–58. See also "Three Years Later, Middletown Remembers," *Harrisburg Evening News*, April 2, 1982.

99. "A Young Mother's Story: Three Mile Island Happened to Us," *Redbook*, April 1980, and "The Social and Economic Effects of the Accident at TMI: Findings to Date," prepared for the US Nuclear Regulatory Commission, Series XI: Governor of Pennsylvania, 1979–1987, Subseries 7: Three Mile Island, Box 197, Folder 1, DT Papers, UPSC.

100. See Dunaway, "Gas Masks, Pogo, and the Ecological Indian."

101. See Cowie, *Stayin' Alive*.

102. Borstellman, *The 1970s: A New Global History*, 15.

103. Quoted in Greg Adamson, *We All Live on Three Mile Island Now: The Case Against Nuclear Power* (Sydney: Pathfinder, 1981), 107.

104. Ibid., 108.

105. These included the United Mine Workers, the International Association of Machinists and Aerospace Workers, International Chemical Workers Union, Graphic Arts International Union, United Auto Workers, International Longshoremen's and Warehousemen's Union, United Furniture Workers of America, International Woodworkers of America, and the National Education Association.

106. For several illustrative examples, see *Washington Post Special Report*, Series XI: Governor of Pennsylvania, 1979–1987, Subseries 7: Three Mile Island, Box 200, Folder 1, DT Papers, UPSC.

107. Quoted in Walker, *Three Mile Island*, 156.

108. The data on evacuation is varied. According to both the NRC and the Pennsylvania Department of Health, 60 percent of people living within the five-mile ring left (approximately twenty-one thousand people), 44 percent of people within the five- to ten-mile ring (approximately fifty-six thousand people), and 32 percent of people within the ten- to fifteen-mile ring (approximately sixty-seven thousand people). See "The Social and Economic Effects of the Accident at TMI."

109. Televised address of Richard Thornburgh, April 6, 1979, Series XI: Governor of Pennsylvania, 1979–1987, Subseries 7: Three Mile Island, Box 194, Folder 10, DT Papers, UPSC.

110. "Neighbors Find TMI A Strain," *Philadelphia Inquirer*, December 8, 1982; "TMI Still Frightens Neighbors," *Pittsburgh Press*, March 28, 1982; "Fears Caused by Three Mile Island Endure," *New York Times*, November 11, 1982.

111. "TMI: Anxiety, Apathy Live Side by Side at Middletown," *Pittsburgh Press*, March 25, 1984.

112. Quoted in Edward J. Walsh, *Democracy in the Shadows: Citizen Mobilization in the Wake of the Accident at Three Mile Island* (New York: Greenwood, 1988), 39.

113. Ibid., 47.

114. Quoted in Walker, *Three Mile Island*, 205. On the findings of radiation monitoring, see Walker, *Three Mile Island*, 204–208; Press release of the Nuclear Regulatory Commission, April 20, 1979, Series XI: Governor of Pennsylvania, 1979–1987, Subseries 7: Three Mile Island, Box 194, Folder 1, DT Papers, UPSC; White House press release, April 6, 1979, Box 194, Folder 1, DT Papers, UPSC; press release, Governor Thornburgh's office, April 3, 1979, 9:30 PM, Series XI: Governor of Pennsylvania, 1979–1987, Subseries 7: Three Mile Island, Box 194, Folder 7, DT Papers, UPSC; "Social and Economic Effects of the TMI Accident"; "Summary of TMI Nuclear Accident," Bureau of Food and Chemistry, Pennsylvania Department of Agriculture, Series XI: Governor of Pennsylvania, 1979–1987, Subseries 7: Three Mile Island, Box 194, Folder 16, DT Papers, UPSC; "Population Dose and Health Impact of the Accident at TMI Nuclear Station," Series XI: Governor of Pennsylvania, 1979–1987, Subseries 7: Three Mile Island, Box 194, Folder 19, DT Papers, UPSC.

115. Walker, *Three Mile Island*, 207.

116. Ibid., 84.

117. Ibid., 207.

118. Evelyn Bromet et al., "Three Mile Island: Mental Health Findings," the Department of Health and Human Services, the National Institute of Mental Health and the Disaster Assistance and Emergency Mental Health Section, October 1980, Series XI: Governor of Pennsylvania, 1979–1987, Subseries 8: Office of Policy Development, Three Mile Island, Box 218, Folder 12, DT Papers, UPSC.

119. Interview with College Administrator #5, July 10, 1979, LMOHI, TMIC, DCASC. Resource Center of threemileisland.org, www.threemileisland.org/resource /item_detail.php?item_id=00000187.

120. Transcript, National Nuclear Debate, the Pennsylvania State University Capitol Complex, DT Papers, Series XI: Governor of Pennsylvania, 1979–1987, Subseries 7: Three Mile Island, Box 197, Folder 5, UPSC. My italics.

121. See *Washington Post Special Report*, Series XI: Governor of Pennsylvania, 1979–1987, Subseries 7: Three Mile Island, Box 200, Folder 1, DT Papers, UPSC.

122. CBS morning news transcript, March 30, 1979, Series XI: Governor of Pennsylvania, 1979–1987, Subseries 7: Three Mile Island, Box 194, Folder 3, DT Papers, UPSC.

123. See, for example, *Health Effects of Low-Level Radiation: Volume I*, Joint Hearing, House Committee on Interstate and Foreign Commerce, Senate Committee on Labor and Human Resources, Senate Committee on the Judiciary, April 19, 1979 (Washington, DC: US Government Printing Office, 1979), 243.

124. "Radioactive Ignorance," reprinted by permission, *Washington Post*, 1979, in "Radiation in Medicine and Industry," Series XI: Governor of Pennsylvania, 1979–1987, Subseries 7: Three Mile Island, Box 197, Folder 2, DT Papers, UPSC.

125. Three Mile Island Revisited, October 1982, Interview by Aileen Smith and Mitsuru Katagiri of Becky Mease, Beverly Hess Papers, Box 5, Folder 6, TMIC, DCASC.

126. Transcript, National Nuclear Debate, the Pennsylvania State University Capitol Complex, DT Papers, Box 197, Folder 5, UPSC. See also Mary Meredith, "TMI Coalition: Prospectus for a Three Mile Island Legal Fund and a Public Interest Resource Center," February 29, 1980, Beverly Hess Papers, Box 2, Folder 1, TMIC, DCASC.

127. Letter from C. Pfeffer to President Carter, York Haven, PA, received July 18, 1979, Records of the Office of the Staff Secretary, Box 38, Folder: Nuclear Issues and TMI, Jimmy Carter Presidential Library (hereafter referred to as JCPL).

128. Quoted in Walsh, *Democracy in the Shadows*, 55.

129. Public Hearing, Personal Health Effects of the Three Mile Island Accident, Penn State Capitol Campus, Middletown, PA, RG 220, Central Files, May 22, 1979, Box 9, unnamed folder, Papers of the President's Commission on the Accident at Three Mile Island, NA II.

130. "Pennsylvania's Governor Says Area Is Now Safe for Pregnant Women," *New York Times*, April 10, 1979; on Three Mile Island Action Alert, see public hearing statement of Michael Klinger, May 24, 1979, RG 220, Central Files, Box 307, unnamed folder, Papers of the President's Commission on the Accident at Three Mile Island, NA II. See also Interview with Physician #1, October 4, 1979, LMOHI, TMIC, DCASC. Resource Center of threemileisland.org, www.threemileisland.org/resource/item_detail .php?item_id=00000177.

131. Interview with Obstetrician-Gynecologist, September 25, 1979, LMOHI, TMIC, DCASC. Resource Center of threemileisland.org, www.threemileisland.org /resource/item_detail.php?item_id=00000125.

132. Press Release from American College of Obstetrics and Gynecologist, April 13, 1979, RG 220, Central Files, Box 7, unnamed folder, Papers of the President's Commission on the Accident at Three Mile Island, NA II.

133. Interview with College Administrator #10, May 6, 1979, LMOHI, TMIC, DCASC. Resource Center of threemileisland.org, www.threemileisland.org/resource /item_detail.php?item_id=00000278.

134. Department of Health News Release, "Health Department Discounts TMI as Connected to Infant Deaths," May 19, 1980, Series XI: Governor of Pennsylvania, 1979–1987, Subseries 7: Three Mile Island, Box 194, Folder 21, DT Papers, UPSC.

135. Testimony of Ms. Dominoski, Public Hearing, Health Resource Planning and Development, May 24, 1979, RG 220, Central Files, Box 307, unnamed folder, Papers of the President's Commission on the Accident at Three Mile Island, NA II.

136. Letter from Mitchell Rogovin, Director, NRC/TMI Special Inquiry Group to NRC Chairman Hendrie, Gilinsky, Kennedy, Bradford, Ahearne, November 15, 1979, Series XI: Governor of Pennsylvania, 1979–1987, Subseries 7: Three Mile Island, Box 200, DT Papers, Folder 10, UPSC.

137. Testimony of Jane Lee, Health Resources Planning and Development, Public Hearings: Personal Health Effects of the Three Mile Island Accident, Sheraton-Harrisburg Inn, New Cumberland, Pennsylvania, May 24, 1979, 7–15, RG 220, Central Files, Box 307, unfiled, Papers of the President's Commission on the Accident at Three Mile Island, NA II. Jane Lee is also interviewed in Del Tredici, *The People of Three Mile Island*, 87–88.

138. J. Robert Heckman, PhD, Elizabethtown College, "Low Level Radiation and Genetic Mutations," Prepared for House Select Committee on TMI, Public Hearing, Bainbridge, PA, May 31, 1979, Beverly Hess Papers, Box 5, Folder 5, TMIC, DCASC.

139. Both of these testimonies come from Health Resource Planning and Development, Public Hearing, Middletown, PA, May 24, 1979, RG 220, Central Files, Box 307, unfiled, Papers of the President's Commission on the Accident at Three Mile Island, NA II.

140. Quoted in Walsh, *Democracy in the Shadows*, 39.

141. See, for example, letters to commission from Nikki Naumann and Mary M. Wertman, RG 220, Central Files, Box 307, unnamed folder, Papers of the President's Commission on the Accident at Three Mile Island, NA II.

142. "TMI Mothers Anxiety Still Above Normal," *Harrisburg Evening News*, November 12, 1982.

143. "Three Years Later: Middletown Remembers," *Harrisburg Evening News*, April 2, 1982.

144. "TMI: For Many, Legacy of Fear Lives," *Harrisburg Patriot*, March 25, 1984.

145. Letter from Charlotte Drennen to NRC, May 24, 1979, RG 220, Central Files, Box 307, unfiled, Papers of the President's Commission on the Accident at Three Mile Island, NA II.

146. On Nilsson, see Eric Goldscheider, "Fetal Positions," *Boston Globe*, August 10, 2003. The publication of the series in *Life* was timed to come out around the time of Nillson's book *A Child Is Born*. The fetuses he photographed were actually corpses. See Sara Dubow, *Ourselves Unborn: A History of the Fetus in Modern America* (New York: Oxford University Press, 2010). See also Luc Boltanski, *The Foetal Condition: A Sociology of Engendering and Abortion* (London: Polity, 2013).

147. "The Weighty Responsibility of Drinking for Two," *New York Times*, November 29, 2006.

148. Laury Oaks, "Smoke Filled Wombs and Fragile Fetuses: The Social Politics of Fetal Representation," *Signs* 26, no. 1 (Autumn 2000): 63–108.

149. Mary Segers and Timothy Byrnes, *Abortion Politics in American States* (New York: M. E. Sharpe, 1995).

150. See Planned Parenthood Association of Pennsylvania, *Money, Power, and the Radical Right in Pennsylvania* (Darby, PA: Diane, 1996).

151. Quoted in Faye Ginsburg, *Contested Lives: The Abortion Debate in an American Community* (Berkeley: University of California Press, 1988), 104.

152. I did not find many direct references to abortion politics in my primary sources on the accident, which frankly surprised me. However, this may have been a tactical decision on the part of local women who might not have wanted to call attention to the tension between their nominal opposition to abortion rights and the fact that some of them apparently considered the procedure after the accident. But this is only a hypothesis on my part. The sources do not offer much in the way of clues.

153. PANE newsletter (undated), Folder 2, PANE Newsletter Collection (unprocessed), TMIC, DCASC. See also "TMI: Anxiety, Apathy Live Side by Side at Middletown," *Pittsburgh Press*, March 25, 1984.

154. Ginsburg, *Contested Lives*, 9.

155. "No Evidence of Increases of Cancer Near TMI Plant," *Pittsburgh Post-Gazette*, September 6, 1985.

156. Bethany Moreton, *To Serve God and Walmart: The Making of Christian Free Enterprise* (Cambridge: Harvard University Press, 2010); Moreton argues that the rise of the conservative Christian Right was haunted by the nightmare of "vulnerable human life tossed out as refuse." Jerry Falwell recalled his awakening to a prolife position, Moreton writes, by invoking "a dumpster in Los Angeles overflowing with the dismembered remains of 1,700 fetal bodies and a trash incinerator in Wichita sending up hundreds more in smoke, like the victims of Auschwitz" (120).

157. "Helen Caldicott's Many Lives: Pediatrician, Mother, Activist," *New York Times*, May 25, 1979.

158. Walsh, *Democracy in the Shadows*, 58.

159. Letter to commission from Mary Wertman, May 20, 1979, RG 220, Central Files, Box 7, unnamed folder, Papers of the President's Commission on the Accident at Three Mile Island, NA II.

160. Public Hearing, Middletown, Pennsylvania, May 22, 1979, RG 220, Central Files, Box 9, unnamed folder, Papers of the President's Commission on the Accident at Three Mile Island, NA II.

161. Letter from Carolyn Walborn to Barb Jorgensen, June 14, 1979, RG 220, Central Files, Box 7, unnamed folder, Papers of the President's Commission on the Accident at Three Mile Island, NA II.

3. CREATING A COMMUNITY OF FATE AT THREE MILE ISLAND

1. "TMI Protester Tells Court of Radiation Effects in '79," *Harrisburg Patriot*, August 9, 1984; and "Defendant Alleges TMI Radiation," *Philadelphia Inquirer*, August 9, 1984.

2. For a helpful analysis of this term, see Peter Baehr, "Social Extremity, Communities of Fate, and the Sociology of SARS," *European Journal of Sociology* 46, no. 2 (2005): 179–211.

3. Lawrence Buell, *Writing for an Endangered World: Literature, Culture, and Environment in the US and Beyond* (Cambridge: Harvard University Press, 2001), 31; and Ursula Heise, *Sense of Place and Sense of Planet: The Environmental Imagination of the Global* (New York: Oxford University Press, 2008).

4. On the restart, see J. Samuel Walker, *Three Mile Island: A Nuclear Crisis in Historical Perspective* (Berkeley: University of California Press, 2004), 232–234.

5. Quoted in Edward J. Walsh, *Democracy in the Shadows: Citizen Mobilization in the Wake of the Accident at Three Mile Island* (New York: Greenwood, 1988), 162.

6. TMIA Timeline, Series XI: Governor of Pennsylvania, 1979–1987, Subseries 8: Office of Policy Development, Three Mile Island, Box 223, Folder 4, Dick Thornburgh Papers (hereafter referred to as DT Papers), University of Pittsburgh Special Collections (hereafter referred to as UPSC).

7. On these litigation efforts, see Walsh, *Democracy in the Shadows*.

8. Ibid.

9. "Middletown Remains Concerned by TMI," *Harrisburg Patriot*, February 8, 1985, Series XI: Governor of Pennsylvania, 1979–1987, Subseries 8: Office of Policy Development, Three Mile Island, Box 218, Folder 12, DT Papers, UPSC.

10. Transcript, National Nuclear Debate, the Pennsylvania State University Capitol Complex, Series XI: Governor of Pennsylvania, 1979–1987, Subseries 7: Three Mile Island, Box 197, Folder 5, DT Papers, UPSC.

11. Letter from Patricia Longnecker to Don Hewitt, 60 Minutes, April 21, 1980, Beverly Hess Papers, Box 1, Folder 2, Three Mile Island Collection (hereafter referred to TMIC), Dickinson College Archives and Special Collections (hereafter referred to as DCASC).

12. Susan Stranahan, *Susquehanna, River of Dreams* (Baltimore: Johns Hopkins University Press, 1995), 207–208.

13. "Middletown Remains Concerned by TMI."

14. Robert Del Tredici, *The People of Three Mile Island* (San Francisco: Sierra Club, 1980), 48.

15. Ibid., 48–49.

16. Interview with College Administrator No. 8, August 7, 1979, LMOHI, TMIC, DCASC. Resource Center of threemileisland.org, www.threemileisland.org/resource/item_detail.php?item_id=00000222.

17. Interview with business employee and spouse, August 20, 1979, LMOHI, TMIC, DCASC. Resource Center of threemileisland.org, www.threemileisland.org/resource/item_detail.php?item_id=00000222.

18. Interview with Teacher No. 2, undated, LMOHI, TMIC, DCASC. Resource Center of threemileisland.org, www.threemileisland.org/resource/item_detail.php?item_id=00000231.

19. "TMI Coalition: Prospectus for a Three Mile Island Legal Fund," February 29, 1980, Beverly Hess Papers, Box 2, Folder 1, TMIC, DCASC.

20. "Thoughts on Stress," Faye Forwood, *Susquehanna Valley Alliance Newsletter* (hereafter referred to as SVA Newsletter), March 1980, Beverly Hess Papers, Box 1, Folder 12, TMIC, DCASC.

21. "The Fears Over TMI Cannot Be Smokescreened," *Philadelphia Inquirer*, March 28, 1980.

22. Leaflet: Stop the Restart at Three Mile Island, Series XI: Governor of Pennsylvania, 1979–1987, Subseries 7: Three Mile Island, Box 196, Folder 8, DT Papers, UPSC.

23. John Kemeny, *Accident at Three Mile Island: The Need for Change, the Legacy of TMI* (Oxford: Pergamon, 1979), 13, 138.

24. See Transcript of William Scranton, February 26, 1970, Box 196, Folder 7, Series XI: Governor of Pennsylvania, 1979–1987, DT Papers, UPSC; additional materials about the restart and cleanup can be found in Series XI: Governor of Pennsylvania, 1979–1987, Subseries 13: Office of General Counsel, Box 354, Folder 9, DT Papers, UPSC.

25. On race, class, and toxic waste, see Andrew Szasz, *Ecopopulism: Toxic Waste and the Movement for Environmental Justice* (Minneapolis: University of Minnesota Press, 1994); and Julie Sze, *Noxious New York: The Racial Politics of Urban Health and Environmental Justice* (Boston: MIT Press, 2006).

26. *SVA Newsletter*, November 1980, Beverly Hess Papers, Box 1, Folder 12, TMIC, DCASC.

27. On venting, see Walker, *Three Mile Island*, 225–232.

28. Ibid., 226.

29. "Candle Vigil Flares to Verbal Clenched Fists," *Harrisburg Evening News*, March 28, 1980, Series XI: Governor of Pennsylvania, 1979–1987, Subseries 8: Office of Policy Development, Three Mile Island, Box 210, Folder 14, DT Papers, UPSC.

30. Walsh, *Democracy in the Shadows*, 113.

31. Letter from State Representative Steven Reed to President Jimmy Carter, March 20, 1980, Records of the Office of the Staff Secretary, Box 156, Folder 3/27/80, Jimmy Carter Presidential Library (hereafter referred to as JCPL).

32. Del Tredici, *The People of Three Mile Island*, 47–48. On the meeting on March 19, 1980, see Walker, *Three Mile Island*, 226–227. The meeting was also covered at length in the *Philadelphia Bulletin* (March 21–23, 1980) and the *Philadelphia Inquirer* (March 22–23, 1980).

33. Transcription, William Scranton, February 26, 1980, Box 196, Folder 7, Series XI: Governor of Pennsylvania, 1979–1987, DT Papers, UPSC.

34. Deposition of Richard Thornburgh, 88–89, RG 220, Central Series, Box 30, Papers of the President's Commission on the Accident at Three Mile Island, NA II.

35. "What Have We Learned from TMI Over the Last Year?," Statement of Susan Shetrom, Etters, Pennsylvania, Beverly Hess Papers, Box 6, Folder 3, TMIC, DCASC.

36. Letter from Carl Morton to Ivan Smith, March 4, 1981, Edwin Charles Collection, Box 1, Folder 18, TMIC, DCASC.

37. PANE Newsletter, August 1983, Series XI: Governor of Pennsylvania, 1979–1987, Subseries 8: Office of Policy Development, Three Mile Island, Box 217, Folder 18, DT Papers, UPSC.

38. Quoted in "We Don't Want to Live with TMI," *Philadelphia Daily News*, May 23, 1985.

39. Letter from Concerned Mothers and Women to Linda Chavez, the White House, September 8, 1985, Box 201, Folder 12, Series XI: Governor of Pennsylvania, 1979–1987, Subseries 8: Office of Policy Development, Three Mile Island, DT Papers, UPSC.

40. For example, see Walsh, *Democracy in the Shadows*, 66.

41. Letter from Mary Wertman to Cara Marrett, May 20, 1979, RG 220, Central Series, Box 7, unnamed folder, Papers of the President's Commission on the Accident at Three Mile Island, NA II.

42. Letter from Joan Hamme to Ivan Smith, NRC, March 24, 1981, Edwin Charles Collection, Box 1, Folder 21, TMIC, DCASC.

43. "What's Venting at TMI Is Frustration and Fear," *Philadelphia Inquirer*, March 23, 1980.

44. "68% in Poll Say Danger of Radiation Is Great," *New York Times*, April 5, 1979; "Polls Show Sharp Rise Since '77 in Opposition to Nuclear Plants," *New York Times*, April 10, 1979.

45. Henry M. Vyner, Background Paper for the Three Mile Island Public Health Fund's Workshop on the Psychosocial Effects of the Invisible Environmental Contaminants, Beverly Hess Papers, Box 3, Folder 1, TMIC, DCASC.

46. PANE Newsletter, undated, PANE Newsletter Collection (unprocessed), TMIC, DCASC.

47. "Concerned Mothers and Women of Three Mile Island," Beverly Hess Papers, Box 4, Folder 20, TMIC, DCASC.

48. Quoted in PANE Newsletter, undated, PANE Newsletter Collection, Folder 2, unprocessed, TMIC, DCASC.

49. Letter from Mary Wertman to Kemeny Commission, May 20, 1979, and to Russell Peterson, May 20, 1979, RG 220, Central Series, Box 7, unnamed folder, Papers of the President's Commission on the Accident at Three Mile Island, NA II.

50. "They'd Rather Fight Than Switch," *Washington Post*, undated, Beverly Hess Papers, Box 3, Folder 27, TMIC, DCASC.

51. Letter from Beverly Hess to Joseph Taylor, August 22, 1979, Beverly Hess Papers, Box 1, Folder 7, TMIC, DCASC.

52. Letter to Kemeny Commission from Charlotte Dennan, RG 220, Central Series, Box 307, unfiled, Papers of the President's Commission on the Accident at Three Mile Island, NA II.

53. Letter from Linda Braasch to NRC Commissioners, January 21, 1981, Edwin Charles Collection, Box One, Folder 15, TMIC, DCASC.

54. Sermon of Karl Fike, Jr., Pastor, Church of the Brethren, Elizabethtown, Pennsylvania, April 1, 1979, Beverly Hess Papers, Box 2, Folder 6, TMIC, DCASC.

55. "The Springtime of Our Discontent: Lessons from TMI," Sermon of Wallace Fisher, Senior Pastor, Trinity Lutheran Church, Lancaster, Pennsylvania, November 18, 1979, Text: Romans 8:28, Beverly Hess Papers, Box 4, Folder 25, TMIC, DCASC.

56. Bishop Paul Moore, Jr., "Sermon for Anniversary of Three Mile Island," Beverly Hess Papers, Box 4, Folder 21, TMIC, DCASC.

57. See undated letter from PIRC to Pennsylvania Council of Churches, Beverly Hess Papers, Box 1, Folder 21, TMIC, DCASC. On interfaith services, see Beverly Hess Papers, Box 4, Folder 8, TMIC, DCASC. These included the Pennsylvania Council of Churches, the Central Pennsylvania Synod, the Pennsylvania Central Conference, and the Bishop of the Roman Catholic Diocese of Harrisburg, as well as synods of the United Church of Christ, the Lutheran Church, and the United Methodist Church.

58. "Message to the Churches on the TMI Experience," York County Council of Churches, approved on June 13, 1979, Beverly Hess Papers, Box 4, Folder 33, TMIC, DCASC.

59. See undated letter from PIRC to Pennsylvania Council of Churches, undated, Beverly Hess Papers, Box 1, Folder 21, TMIC, DCASC. On interfaith services, see Beverly Hess Papers, Box 4, Folder 8, TMIC, DCASC.

60. "Message to the Churches on the TMI Experience," York County Council of Churches, approved on June 13, 1979, Beverly Hess Papers, Box 4, Folder 33, TMIC, DCASC.

61. "The Springtime of Our Discontent."

62. "What Have We Learned from TMI Over the Last Year?"

63. See interview with Mrs. Reigle in "Communities: Meeting, Listening, Protesting," in Del Tredici, *The People of Three Mile Island*, 47–50.

64. See "3 Mile Island: No Health Impact Found," *New York Times*, April 15, 1980.

65. See Walker, *Three Mile Island*, 235–236. See also "The Social and Economic Effects of the Accident at Three Mile Island," Study prepared for the Nuclear Regulatory Commission by Mountain West and Social Impact Research, Series XI: Governor of Pennsylvania, 1979–1987, Subseries 8: Office of Policy Development, Three Mile Island, Box 197, Folder 1, DT Papers, UPSC.

66. Interview with Judith Johnsrud, in Del Tredici, *The People of Three Mile Island*, 59–60; US Congress, House of Representatives, *Hearing Before the Subcommittee on Natural Resources and Environment of the Committee on Science and Technology*, Testimony of Dr. Chauncey Kepford, Environmental Coalition on Nuclear Power, 96th Cong., 1st sess., June 2, 1979, 3; Statement of Joseph Califano, Secretary of Health, Education, and Welfare, TMI Nuclear Accident, 1979 in US Congress, Senate, *Hearing Before the Subcommittee on Health and Scientific Research of the Committee on Labor and Human Resources*, 96th Cong., 1st sess., April 4, 1979, 84–88.

67. Walsh, *Democracy in the Shadows*, 171.

68. Philip Starr, Public Hearing Statement, RG 220, Central Series, Box 307, unfiled, Papers of the President's Commission on the Accident at Three Mile Island, NA II.

69. Phil Brown, "Popular Epidemiology and Toxic Waste Contamination: Lay and Professional Ways of Knowing," *Journal of Health and Social Behavior* 33 (September 1992): 267–281.

70. "Innocence Lost," *Pennsylvania Illustrated*, August 1979, Series XI: Governor of Pennsylvania, 1979–1987, Subseries 8: Office of Policy Development, Three Mile Island, Box 200, Folder 1, DT Papers, UPSC; "Fear Itself"; and Del Tredici, *The People of Three Mile Island*, 15.

71. Del Tredici, *The People of Three Mile Island*, 31.

72. Rough Draft of presentation by Mitsuri Katagiri and Aileen Smith Katagiri, March 3, 1983, Beverly Hess Papers, Box 5, Folder 6, TMIC, DCASC.

73. Interview with Engineer and Wife, August 28, 1979, LMOHI, TMIC, DCASC. Resource Center of threemileisland.org, www.threemileisland.org/resource/item_de tail.php?item_id=00000222. See also Beverly Hess Papers, Box 5, Folders 4 and 6; Box 6, Folder 3 in TMIC, DCASC.

74. Interview with Engineer and Wife, August 28, 1979, LMOHI, TMIC, DCASC. Resource Center of threemileisland.org, www.threemileisland.org/resource/item_de tail.php?item_id=00000267.

75. "Fear Itself."

76. "Boy George Corn: Another Agricultural Oddity of the Season," *Lancaster Intelligencer Journal*, October 1984, accessed in Beverly Hess Papers, Box 5, Folder 7, TMIC,

DCASC. On corn's significance as a symbol of fertility and fecundity in rural communities, see Gabriel Rosenberg, *The 4-H Harvest: Sexuality and the State in Rural America* (Philadelphia: University of Pennsylvania Press, 2016), 21–23, 34–35, 37, 39, 42–43.

77. "Fear Itself."

78. Letter from Charles and Helen Hockers to the NRC, Etters, Pennsylvania, January 22, 1981, Edwin Charles Collection, Box 1, Folder 14, TMIC, DCASC.

79. "Neighbors Find TMI a Strain," *Philadelphia Inquirer*, December 8, 1982; and "Fear Itself." See also Public Hearing, RG 220, Central Series, Box 307, Unfiled, Papers of the President's Commission on the Accident at Three Mile Island, NA II. On animals, see Affidavit of Robert Weber, Veterinarian, Records of the Office of the Staff Secretary, Box 38, Folder: Nuclear Issues (and TMI), JCPL; "What Have We Learned from TMI Over the Last Year?"; Testimony of Jane Lee, Nuclear Regulatory Licensing Board, April 23, 1981, Edwin Charles Collection, Box One, Folder 23, TMIC, DCASC; TMI Coalition: Prospectus for a Three Mile Island Legal Fund"; and Marjorie Aamodt, "The Three Mile Island Accident: An Investigation of the Effect on the Health of Residents and Flora in Three Areas NW and SW of TMI," Beverly Hess Papers, Box 5, Folder 4, TMIC, DCASC.

80. See Affidavit 6, Beverly Hess Papers, Box 5, Folder 4, TMIC, DCASC.

81. Editorial cartoon is reproduced in PANE Newsletter, June 1983, 4, Newsletters from PANE, Series XI: Governor of Pennsylvania, 1979–1987, Subseries 8: Office of Policy Development, Three Mile Island, Box 217, Folder 8, DT Papers, UPSC.

82. Del Tredici, *The People of Three Mile Island*, 87.

83. Ibid.

84. The Caldicott quotation comes from Transcript, National Nuclear Debate, Penn State Capitol Complex, moderated by Jim Lehrer, Report on the One-Year Anniversary, Series XI: Governor of Pennsylvania, 1979–1987, Subseries 7: Three Mile Island, Box 197, Folder 5, DT Papers, UPSC.

85. Walsh, *Democracy in the Shadows*, 55. For another example, also see "Crisis: Three Mile Island," *Washington Post*, Series XI: Governor of Pennsylvania, 1979–1987, Subseries 7: Three Mile Island, Box 200, Folder 1, DT Papers, UPSC.

86. Del Tredici, *People of Three Mile Island*, 31. For another example of guinea pig metaphor, see "What Have We Learned from TMI Over the Last Year?"

87. Del Tredici, *People of Three Mile Island*, 23.

88. "Fear Itself."

89. Del Tredici, *The People of Three Mile Island*, 64–66. On disappearing animals, see also Nakao Hajime, "TMI: The Language of Science and People's Reality, Part II," *Kyoto Review*, Spring 1981, Beverly Hess Papers, Box 5, Folder 11, TMIC, DCASC; and "What Have We Learned from TMI Over the Last Year?"

90. "What Have We Learned from TMI Over the Last Year?"

91. On the state's Department of Agriculture, see Box 199, Folder 13, DT Papers, UPSC; also see "Nuclear Fabulists," *New York Times*, April 18, 1980.

92. Del Tredici, *The People of Three Mile Island*, 70.

93. Letter from Charlotte Drennan to Kemeny Commission, May 24, 1979, Box 307, unfiled, RG 220, Central Series, Papers of the President's Commission on the Accident at Three Mile Island, NA II.

94. Joseph Masco, *Nuclear Borderlands: The Manhattan Project in Post–Cold War New Mexico* (Princeton: Princeton University Press, 2006), 32–33.

95. See Statement of Beverly Hess, Town Meeting, Lancaster, Pennsylvania, January 5, 1984, Beverly Hess Papers, Box 2, Folder 6, TMIC, DCASC. My italics.

96. Del Tredici, *The People of Three Mile Island*, 22. For another example, see "A Young Mother's Story: Three Mile Island Happened to Us," *Redbook*, April 1980.

97. Appendix D, Table D.3 Percent employed in Agriculture, Forestry, Fishing, and Hunting Industries; Percent Employed in Manufacturing Industry; and Percent Urban, in Renee Lamis, *The Realignment of Pennsylvania Politics Since 1960: Two Party Competition in a Battleground State* (University Park: Pennsylvania State University Press, 2009), 359–360; David Walbert, *Garden Spot: Lancaster County, the Old Order Amish, and the Selling of Rural America* (New York: Oxford University Press, 2002); and TMI Population Registry, Jane Lee Papers, Box 1, Folder 23, TMIC, DCASC.

98. On these symptoms, see "They're Moving But Still Fight TMI Restart," *Pittsburgh Post-Gazette*, February 15, 1985; "We Don't Want to Live With TMI," *Philadelphia Daily News*, May 23, 1985, 3; "Fear Itself"; and Del Tredici, *The People of Three Mile Island*, 48, 93.

99. "Fear Itself."

100. On the Aamodts, see "No Evidence of Increases of Cancer Near TMI Plant," *Pittsburgh Post-Gazette*, September 6, 1985; "Another 43 File Claims Against TMI," *Patriot*, August 21, 1985; "Cancer Study Debunks Link to TMI Mishap," *Harrisburg Evening News*, September 5, 1985, accessed in Subsection: Newspaper Clippings, Three Mile Island, DT Papers, UPSC; Series XI: Governor of Pennsylvania, 1979–1987, Subseries 8: Office of Policy Development, Three Mile Island, Box 202, Folder 14, DT Papers, UPSC; Walsh, *Democracy in the Shadows*, 174; SVA Newsletter, February 1985, Beverly Hess Papers, Box 1, Folder 13, TMIC, DCASC; "A Decade of Delay, Deceit and Danger: TMI 1979–1989," a Retrospective Published by TMIA, Beverly Hess Papers, Box 4, Folder 9, TMIC, DCASC; Marjorie Aamodt, "The Three Mile Island Accident: An Investigation of the Effect on the Health of Residents and Flora in Three Areas NW and SW of TMI," Beverly Hess Papers, Box 5, Folder 4, TMIC, DCASC; John Murdoch Papers, Box 1, Folder 5, TMIC, DCASC; and Press Release: NRC Charged with Cover-up of Cancer Deaths at Three Mile Island, PIRC Collection, Box 2, Folder 12, TMIC, DCASC.

101. See Walker, *Three Mile Island*, 237–239, on the ways that Chernobyl actually lent credence to this theory.

102. Press Release: NRC Charged with Cover-Up of Cancer Deaths at Three Mile Island, PIRC Collection, Box 2, Folder 12, TMIC, DCASC.

103. Quoted in Walker, *Three Mile Island*, 174.

104. "They're Moving But Still Fight TMI Restart," *Pittsburgh Post-Gazette*, February 15, 1985.

105. Ibid.

106. Letter from Helen Hockers to Jimmy Carter, April 3, 1980, Edwin Charles Collection, Box 1, Folder 1, TMIC, DCASC.

107. Memo from Les Francis to Frank Moore regarding suggested response to Harrisburg Plant Crisis, March 31, 1979, Records of the Office of the Staff Secretary, Box 38, Folder: Nuclear Issues (and TMI), JCPL.

108. Walsh, *Democracy in the Shadows*, 190–191.

109. "The Nuclear Fabulists," *New York Times*, April 18, 1980.

110. Del Tredici, *The People of Three Mile Island*, 67. See also Bruce Moholt, "Just a Little Radiation? Don't Believe It," SVA Newsletter, March 1980, Beverly Hess Papers, Box 1, Folder 12, DCASC.

111. Del Tredici, *The People of Three Mile Island*, 54. See also Interview with Teacher #1, 28 September 1979, LMOHI, TMIC, DCASC. Resource Center of threemileisland .org, www.threemileisland.org/resource/item_detail.php?item_id=00000215.

112. Statement of Patty Anonia, Public Hearing, RG 220, Central Series, Box 307, unnamed folder, Papers of the President's Commission on the Accident at Three Mile Island, NA II.

113. "What Have We Learned from TMI Over the Last Year?"

114. Del Tredici, *The People of Three Mile Island*, 123–125.

115. Statement of John Gofman, Public Hearning, RG 220, Central Series, Box 8, Unnamed Folder, 4, Papers of the President's Commission on the Accident at Three Mile Island, NA II.

116. See, for example, Interview with College Student #2, August 6, 1979; Interview with Government Agency Employee, July 24, 1979; Interview with Homemaker #1, August 1, 1979; Interview with Newspaper Employee #2, undated; Interview with Secondary School Teacher, June 6, 1979; Interview with Secretary #6, June 21, 1979; Interview with College Professor #1, August 7, 1979. LMOHI, TMIC, DCASC. Resource Center of threemileisland.org, www.threemileisland.org/resource/index.php?aid=00024.

117. Baylor University Editorial Cartoon collection, Box 56, File 1564, Baylor Collections of Political Materials, Baylor University.

118. The editorial cartoon can be found in PANE Newsletter, June 1983, Series XI: Governor of Pennsylvania, 1979–1987, Subseries 8: Office of Policy Development, Three Mile Island, Box 217, Folder 8, DT Papers, UPSC.

119. Phil Brown writes that popular epidemiology is largely a woman's project, because women are "the most frequent organizers of lay detection because they are the chief health arrangers for their families, and partly because they are more concerned than men with local environmental issues." See again Brown, "Popular Epidemiology and Toxic Waste Contamination."

120. "Fear Itself."

121. "Determined Woman Vows to Seek Mishap Answers," *New York Times*, April 13, 1979.

122. See Brown, "Popular Epidemiology and Toxic Waste Contamination."

123. Spencer R. Weart, *Nuclear Fear: A History of Images* (1989; Cambridge: Harvard University Press, 2012), 323–333; Stuart Leslie, *The Cold War and American Science: The Military-Industrial-Academic Complex at MIT and Stanford* (New York: Columbia University Press, 1994); and Michael Egan, *Barry Commoner and the Science of Survival: The Remaking of American Environmentalism* (Cambridge: MIT Press, 2009).

124. "Painful Truth About TMI," TMIA Alert, May 1983, TMIA 1.4.3.4, TMIC, DCASC.

125. Pamphlet of the Union of Concerned Scientists, "The Nuclear Power Controversy," RG 220, Central Series, Box 224, Folder 11, Papers of the President's Commission on the Accident at Three Mile Island, NA II.

126. "TMI Anniversary Crowd Stern," *Harrisburg Patriot*, March 28, 1980.

127. "Health Studies in the Three Mile Island Area," Box 194, Folder 21, DT Papers, UPSC. See also Kemeny, *Accident at Three Mile Island*, 12.

128. "Health Studies in the Three Mile Island Area," Box 194, Folder 21, DT Papers, UPSC. "The Social and Economic Effects of the Accident at Three Mile Island," Study prepared for the Nuclear Regulatory Commission by Mountain West and Social Impact Research, Box 197, Folder 1, DT Papers, UPSC; and Evelyn Bromet et al., "Three Mile Island: Mental Health Findings," Department of Health and Human Services, National Institute of Mental Health, Disaster Assistance and Emergency Mental Health Section, October 1980, Section XI: Governor of Pennsylvania, 1979–1987, Subseries 8: Office of Policy Development, Three Mile Island, Box 218, Folder 12, DT Papers, UPSC.

129. TMIA Press Release, May 17, 1980, Section XI: Governor of Pennsylvania, 1979–1987, Subseries 7: Three Mile Island, Three Mile Island, Box 197, Folder 9, DT Papers, UPSC.

130. "Health Studies in the Three Mile Island Area," Box 194, Folder 21, DT Papers, UPSC; "The Social and Economic Effects of the Accident at Three Mile Island"; Study prepared for the Nuclear Regulatory Commission by Mountain West and Social Impact Research, Section XI: Governor of Pennsylvania, 1979–1987, Subseries 7: Three Mile Island, Box 197, Folder 1, DT Papers, UPSC; "TMI Still Frightens Neighbors," *Pittsburgh Press*, March 28, 1982; and "Neighbors Find TMI a Strain."

131. Kemeny, *Accident at Three Mile Island*, 13.

132. TMI Alert Press Update, "The Sixth Anniversary of the Three Mile Island Accident," March 28, 1985, Beverly Hess Papers, Box 4, Folder 9, TMIC, DCASC.

133. Letter from Joanne Doroshow of TMIA, to Richard Thornburgh, August 20, 1982, Section XI: Governor of Pennsylvania, 1979–1987, Subseries 8: Office of Policy Development, Three Mile Island, Box 223, Folder 4, DT Papers, UPSC.

134. Advertisement calling for March on Harrisburg: "Have you forgotten about Three Mile Island? We haven't," Section XI: Governor of Pennsylvania, 1979–1987, Subseries 8: Office of Policy Development: Three Mile Island, Box 201, Folder 13, DT Papers, UPSC.

135. Interview with Richard Thornburgh, Section XI: Governor of Pennsylvania, 1979–1987, Subseries 7: Three Mile Island, Box 196, Folder 10, DT Papers, UPSC; Letter from Richard Thornburgh to the NRC, June 22, 1979, Box 201, Folder 13, DT Papers, UPSC; Letter from Richard Thornburgh to Joseph Hendrie, June 22, 1979 re: restart of Unit 1, Box 217, Folder 8, DT Papers, UPSC. Boxes 201 and 217 are both in Section XI: Governor of Pennsylvania, 1979–1987, Subseries 8: Office of Policy Development, Three Mile Island.

136. Letter from Mary Wertman to Kemeny Commission, RG 220, Central Series, Box 7, unnamed folder, 20 May 1979, Papers of the President's Commission on the Accident at Three Mile Island, NA II.

137. "We Don't Want to Live with TMI," *Philadelphia Daily News*, May 23, 1985, 3.

138. "Neighbors Find TMI a Strain."

139. Quoted in Walsh, *Democracy in the Shadows*, 109.

140. On the Agent Orange comparison, see S. V. Kasl, R. F. Chisholm, and B. Eskenazi, "The Impact of the Accident at the Three Mile Island on the Behavior and Well Being of Nuclear Workers, Part I and Part III," *American Journal of Public Health* 71 (1981): 472–495.

141. "Neighbors Find TMI a Strain."

142. On the hostage crisis, see David Farber, *Taken Hostage: The Iran Hostage Crisis and America's First Encounter with Radical Islam* (Princeton: Princeton University Press, 2006); Melani McAlister, *Epic Encounters: Culture, Media, and US Interests in the Middle East, 1945–2000* (Berkeley: University of California Press, 2001); and Gary Sick, *All Fall Down: America's Tragic Encounter with Iran* (New York: Penguin, 1986).

143. "Candle Vigil Flares to Verbal Clenched Fists," *Evening News*, March 28, 1980, Section XI: Governor of Pennsylvania, 1979–1987, Subseries 8: Office of Policy Development, Three Mile Island, Box 201, Folder 13, DT Papers, UPSC.

144. Del Tredici, *The People of Three Mile Island*, 54.

145. "Crisis: Three Mile Island," *Washington Post Special Report*, Section XI: Governor of Pennsylvania, 1979–1987, Subseries 7: Three Mile Island, Box 200, Folder 1, DT Papers, UPSC.

146. "TMI Area Mother Tells of Her Life of Fear," *Harrisburg Patriot*, March 25, 1982, Subseries: News Articles Collection, DT Papers, UPSC.

147. "TMI Has Made Stress a Fact of Life," Letter to the Editor from Mel Clouser, Middletown Resident, *Harrisburg Patriot*, March 15, 1982, Subseries: News Articles Collection, DT Papers, UPSC.

148. "Fear Itself."

149. "TMI and the Politics of Public Health," Lecture Prepared for Physicians for Social Responsibility, Gordon MacLeod, November 22, 1980, Beverly Hess Papers, Box 5, Folder 6, TMIC, DCASC.

150. "Three Years Later, Middletown Remembers," undated, Section XI: Governor of Pennsylvania, 1979–1987, Subseries 8: Office of Policy Development, Three Mile Island, Box 223, Folder: Untitled Event, DT Papers, UPSC.

151. "Lancastrian Urges Shutdown of TMI," *Harrisburg Patriot*, March 31, 1980, Box 201, Folder 13, DT Papers, UPSC.

152. "Middletown Remains Concerned by TMI."

153. Interview with Guidance Counselor, May 25, 1979, LMOHI, TMIC, DCASC. Resource Center of threemileisland.org, www.threemileisland.org/resource/item_de tail.php?item_id=00000193.

154. Associated Press Article, TMI Plus Four, March 27, 1983, Box 197, Folder 6, DT Papers, UPSC.

155. Letter from Barbara Kunder to Richard Thornburgh, February 5, 1982, member of Friends and Family of TMI, Section XI: Governor of Pennsylvania, 1979–1987, Subseries 8: Office of Policy Development, Three Mile Island, Box 207, Folder 1, DT Papers, UPSC.

156. "A Middletowner's Comments," John Chubb, *Insights*, April 1979, Section XI: Governor of Pennsylvania, 1979–1987, Subseries 8: Office of Policy Development, Three Mile Island, Box 207, Folder 1, DT Papers, UPSC.

157. US Congress, *Joint Hearings of Subcommittee on Nuclear Regulation of the Senate Committee on Environment and Public Works and the Subcommittee on Energy and the Environment of the House Committee on Interior and Insular Affairs*, Supplemental View by Anne D. Trunk, Report of the Presidential Commission on the Three Mile Island Accident, 96th Congress, 1st sess., October 31, 1979, 77.

158. Mary Bradley, Harrisburg Evening News, RG 220, Central Series, Box 472, no folders named, Public Information Task Force, Interviews of Reporters, NA II. On

Germany, see Interview with Engineer and Wife, August 28, 1979, LMOHI, Three Mile Island Collection, DCASC. Resource Center of threemileisland.org, www.three mileisland.org/resource/item_detail.php?item_id=00000222. On comparisons between local and national news reporting, see Interview with Attorney, July 7, 1979; Interview with College Administrator #9, August 29, 1979; Interview with College Professor #1, July 8, 1979; Interview with College Professor #2, June 6, 1979; Interview with Cumberland County Coordinator, August 8, 1979; and Interview with Homemaker #2, August 9, 1979, LMOHI, TMIC, DCASC. Resource Center of threemileisland.org, www .threemileisland.org/resource/index.php?aid=00024.

159. Interview with Jeff Blitzer, WHP-TV, Harrisburg local television/CBS affiliate, RG 220, Central Series, Box 472, no folders named; Public Information Task Force Interviews of Reporters, Papers of the President's Commission on the Accident at Three Mile Island, NA II. On the crucial role of local media in the context of disasters, see Eric Klinenberg, *Fighting for Air: The Battle to Control America's Media* (New York: Metropolitan, 2007).

160. David Salisbury, *Christian Science Monitor*, RG 220, Central Series, Box 472, no folders named; Public Information Task Force Interviews of Reporters, Papers of the President's Commission on the Accident at Three Mile Island, NA II.

161. "Innocence Lost."

162. Rebecca Solnit, *A Paradise Built in Hell: The Extraordinary Communities That Arise in Disaster* (New York: Viking, 2009), 118.

163. *Synopsis of US Court of Appeals Decision*, Opinions Filed, May 14, 1982; US Court of Appeals, September 1981, PANE Versus the Nuclear Regulatory Commission, Section XI: Governor of Pennsylvania, 1979–1987, Subseries 8: Office of Policy Development, Three Mile Island, Box 218, Folder 12, DT Papers, UPSC.

164. Ibid.

165. Ibid.

166. Quoted in "Justices to Rule on TMI," *Philadelphia Inquirer*, November 2, 1982.

167. *Synopsis of US Court of Appeals Decision.*

168. Ibid.

169. Ibid.

170. "High Court Rejects TMI Stress Issue," *Philadelphia Inquirer*, April 20, 1983, Section XI: Governor of Pennsylvania, 1979–1987, Subseries 8: Office of Policy Development, Three Mile Island, Box 223, Folder: Untitled Event, DT Papers, UPSC.

171. Ibid.

172. Michael Kinsley, "Mental Cases," *Harper's*, July 1982, Section XI: Governor of Pennsylvania, 1979–1987, Subseries 8: Office of Policy Development, Three Mile Island, Box 218, Folder 13, DT Papers, UPSC.

173. Quoted in Walker, *Three Mile Island*, 169.

174. Ibid., 195.

175. On the centralization of the nuclear industry, see Christian Joppke, *Mobilizing Against Nuclear Energy: A Comparison of the United States and Germany* (Berkeley: University of California Press, 1993), 23–36.

176. On these abuses, see Kay Pickering and R. R. Smedley, TMIA Letter, February 1984, Beverly Hess Papers, Box 4, Folder 4; and Box 5, Folder 7, TMIC, DCASC; and PIRC Collection, Box 1, Folder 19; Box 2, Folder 8; Box 3, Folders 8 and 19, TMIC, DCASC.

177. "Nuclear Fallout: High Technology Age Causes New Problems in Coverage by Media," *Wall Street Journal*, August 24, 1983, Section XI: Governor of Pennsylvania, 1979–1987, Subseries 8: Office of Policy Development, Three Mile Island, Box 223, Folder: Untitled Event, DT Papers, UPSC.

178. SVA Newsletter, February 1985, Beverly Hess Papers, Box 1, Folder 13, TMIC, DCASC.

179. "Fears Caused by Three Mile Island Endure," *New York Times*, November 11, 1982, Section XI: Governor of Pennsylvania, 1979–1987, Subseries 8: Office of Policy Development, Three Mile Island, Box 223, Folder: Untitled Event, DT Papers, UPSC.

180. Letter from Joan Olsavsky to the Nuclear Regulatory Commission, August 22, 1981, Edwin Charles Collection, Box 1, Folder 12, TMIC, DCASC.

181. Walsh, *Democracy in the Shadows*.

4. THE SECOND COLD WAR AND THE EXTINCTION THREAT

1. Nicholas Meyer, dir., *The Day After*, 1983, ABC Television.

2. Jonathan Schell, "The Abolition I: Defining the Great Predicament," *New Yorker*, January 2, 1984, 2.

3. "Hollywood Is Hoping Nuclear Drama Isn't a Box-Office Bomb," *Wall Street Journal*, July 19, 1983.

4. See, for example, Congress of the United States, the Office of Technology Assessment, *The Effects of Nuclear War*, May 1979; Helen Caldicott, *Nuclear Madness: What You Can Do* (New York: Bantam, 1978); Jonathan Schell, *The Fate of the Earth* (New York: Knopf, 1982). Other texts they used included Nigal Calder, *Nuclear Nightmares: An Investigation Into Possible Wars* (New York: Penguin, 1981); Committee for the Compilation of Materials on Damage Caused by the Atomic Bombs in Hiroshima and Nagasaki, *Hiroshima and Nagasaki: The Physical, Medical, and Social Effects of the Atomic Bombings* (New York: Basic, 1981); and Arthur Katz, *Life After Nuclear War* (New York: Ballinger, 1982).

5. Richard Barnet, "Fantasy, Reality, and the Arms Race: Dilemmas of National Security and Human Survival," *American Journal of Orthopsychiatry* 52, no. 4 (October 1982): 582–589.

6. "Fallout Over 'The Day After,'" *Newsweek*, October 24, 1983.

7. Ibid.

8. "Fallout from a TV Attack," *Time*, December 5, 1983, 40.

9. The "coitus interruptus" phrase comes from Kim Newman, *Apocalypse Movies: End of the World Cinema* (New York: St. Martin's, 2002), 231. On the made-for-TV movie as a genre and its relation to melodrama more generally, see Laurie Schulze, "The Made-for-TV Movie: Industrial Practice, Cultural Form, Popular Reception," in *Hollywood in the Age of Television*, ed. Tino Balio (New York: Routledge, 2013), 351–376; Lynne Joyrich, "All That Television Allows: TV Melodrama, Postmodernism, and Consumer Culture," *Camera Obscura* 6, no. 1 (January 1988): 128–153; and Todd Gitlin, *Inside Prime Time* (Berkeley: University of California Press, 2000). On *The Day After* specifically, see Gregory Waller, "Re-Placing the Day After," *Cinema Journal* 26, no. 3 (Spring 1987): 3–20; and Deron Overpeck, "Remember! It's Only a Movie: Expectations and Receptions of *The Day After*," *Historical Journal of Film, Radio, and*

Television 32, no. 2 (June 2012): 267–292. On the film's reception at the time, see "TV's Nuclear Nightmare," *Newsweek*, November 21, 1983, 70.

10. On the presidency of Ronald Reagan and the place of the Cold War revival within it, see Gil Troy, *Morning in America: How Ronald Reagan Invented the 1980s* (Princeton: Princeton University Press, 2005); Robert Collins, *Transforming America: Politics and Culture in the Reagan Years* (New York: Columbia University Press, 2007); Sean Wilentz, *The Age of Reagan: A History, 1974–2008* (New York: Harper, 2008); James T. Patterson, *Restless Giant: The United States from Watergate to Bush v. Gore* (New York: Oxford University Press, 2005); and Doug Rossinow, *The Reagan Era: A History of the 1980s* (New York: Columbia University Press, 2015).

11. The directive itself can be accessed at www2.gwu.edu/~nsarchiv/nukevault/ebb390/. On the directive, see William Burr, "How to Fight a Nuclear War," *Foreign Policy* (September 14, 2012), www.foreignpolicy.com/articles/2012/09/14/how_to_fight_a_nuclear_war.

12. Interview with George Bush by Robert Sheer in *Los Angeles Times*, January 23, 1980, SO 454, Box 5, Folder: National Committee, March-June 1982, National Nuclear Weapons Freeze Collection, the State Historical Society of Missouri, University of Missouri at St. Louis (hereafter referred to as SHSM).

13. Quoted in Lawrence Wittner, *Toward Nuclear Abolition: A History of the World Disarmament Movement, 1971–Present* (Stanford: Stanford University Press, 2003), 119. See also David S. Meyer, *A Winter of Our Discontent: The Nuclear Freeze and American Politics* (New York: Praeger, 1990).

14. William Chipman, Director of Civil Defense Division, FEMA, quoted in *Los Angeles Times*, January 16, 1982. SO 454, Box 5, Folder: National Committee, March-June 1982, National Nuclear Weapons Freeze Collection, SHSM.

15. Ibid.

16. *Rejoinders, a Handbook: Facts and Authorities for Doubters about the Bilateral Nuclear Arms Freeze*, by Harold and Edith Waterhouse, plus excerpts from questions and answers on the Soviet threat and national security, all indexed together for use by Californians for a Bilateral Nuclear Weapons Freeze, SO 454, Box 5, Folder: Opposition/Criticism, May 1981–March 1982, National Nuclear Weapons Freeze Collection, SHSM.

17. Quoted in "Does Reagan Expect a Nuclear Armageddon?," *Washington Post*, April 8, 1984.

18. Ibid. Quotation originally appeared in the *Atlanta Journal Constitution*, October 29, 1983.

19. Quoted in Robert Scheer, *With Enough Shovels: Reagan, Bush, and Nuclear War* (New York: Random House, 1982), 3.

20. T. K. Jones, Deputy Undersecretary of Defense for Strategic and Nuclear Forces, Interview with Robert Scheer, *Los Angeles Times*, January 15, 1982, SI 454, Box 5, Folder: National Committee, March–June 1982, National Nuclear Weapons Freeze Collection, SHSM. Quotation also appears in Edward M. Kennedy and Mark O. Hatfield, *Freeze! How You Can Prevent Nuclear War* (New York: Bantam, 1982), 94; and Schell, "The Abolition I."

21. "The Dirt on TK Jones," *New York Times*, March 19, 1982. On Reagan's civil defense, see Kennedy and Hatfield, *Freeze!*; and Scheer, *With Enough Shovels*. See also SO 660, Box 1, Folder: Civil Defense, Physicians for Social Responsibility Collection (hereafter referred to as PSR Collection), SHSM.

22. Randall Forsberg, "Call to Halt the Nuclear Arms Race: Proposal for a Mutual US-Soviet Nuclear-Weapon Freeze." https://livingwiththebomb.files.wordpress.com /2013/08/call-to-halt-arms-race.pdf.

23. Quoted in Wittner, *Toward Nuclear Abolition*, 194, 225; On the freeze movement, see also David Meyer, *A Winter of Our Discontent: The Nuclear Freeze and American Politics* (New York: Praeger, 1990); Bradford Martin, *The Other Eighties: A Secret History of America in the Age of Reagan* (New York: Hill and Wang, 2011), 3–24; and Michael Foley, *Front Porch Politics: The Forgotten Heyday of American Activism in the 1970s and 1980s* (New York: Hill and Wang, 2013).

24. On the place of futurology in the Cold War national security state, see Matthew Connelly, Matt Fay, Giulia Ferrini, Micki Kaufman, Will Leonard, Harrison Monsky, Ryan Musto, Tauton Paine, Nicholas Standish, and Lydia Walker, "General, I Have Fought Just as Many Nuclear Wars as You Have: Forecasts, Future Scenarios, and the Politics of Armageddon," *American Historical Review* 117, no. 5 (December 2012): 1431–1460.

25. Schell, *The Fate of the Earth*, 21.

26. Ibid., 227.

27. Quoted in Carl Sagan, "The Nuclear Winter," brochure published by Council for a Livable World Education Fund, SO 660, Box 4, Folder: Nuclear Winter, PSR Collection, SHSM.

28. Jennifer Leaning, MD, "Civil Defense in the Nuclear Age: What Purpose Does It Serve and What Survival Does It Promise?," National Executive Committee and Board, Physicians for Social Responsibility, SO 660, Box 1, Folder: Civil Defense, "Civil Defense in the Nuclear Age: What Purpose Does It Serve and What Survival Does It Promise?," PSR 1982, PSR Collection, SHSM.

29. Schell, *The Fate of the Earth*, 85.

30. "The Nuclear Threat to San Francisco," SO 660, Box 6, Folder: Public Health Booklets, Marin Co/Mass Department of Health, PSR Collection, SHSM.

31. "How Doctors Hope to Stop Nuclear War," *Wall Street Journal*, November 28, 1980.

32. Herbert Leiderman and Jack Mendelsohn, "Some Psychiatric and Social Aspects of the Defense Shelter Program," *New England Journal of Medicine* (May 31, 1962): 18. On the medical effects of a nuclear war, see Schell, *The Fate of the Earth*; Helen Caldicott, *Nuclear Madness*; and Ruth Adams and Susan Cullen, eds., *The Final Epidemic: Physicians and Scientists on Nuclear War* (Chicago: University of Chicago Press, 1981); H. Jack Geiger, "Addressing Apocalypse Now: The Effects of Nuclear Warfare as a Public Health Concern," *American Journal of Public Health* 70, no. 9 (September 1980): 958–961; Kevin Lewis, "The Prompt and Delayed Effects of Nuclear War," *Scientific American* 241, no. 1 (July 1979): 35–47; PSR pamphlet, Medical Aspects of Nuclear War, SO 454, Box 2, Folder: *The Day After*, November 1983–February 1984, National Nuclear Weapons Freeze Collection, SHSM; Physicians for Social Responsibility, *The Last Epidemic: The Medical Consequences of Nuclear Weapons and Nuclear War* (Santa Cruz: Resource Center for Non-Violence, 1980); Special Report: Medical Problems of Survivors of Nuclear War, *New England Journal of Medicine* 305, no. 20 (November 12, 1981): 1226–1232.

33. Schell, *The Fate of the Earth*, 46.

34. Schell, "The Abolition I."

35. Robert Jay Lifton, "In a Dark Time," in Adams and Cullen, *The Final Epidemic*, 7.

36. Quoted in "Anatomy of a Nuclear Protest," *New York Times*, July 11, 1982. Large numbers of physicians throughout the country were compelled by the argument, and PSR grew rapidly between 1979 and 1984, from a few hundred to over thirty thousand members. By December 1982, there were 125 PSR chapters in forty-seven states. The following year, the PSR House of Delegates endorsed four planks: support for a bilateral freeze, support for a comprehensive test ban; opposition to destabilizing first strike weapons; and opposition to civil defense planning for a nuclear attack. On PSR, see Adams and Cullen, *The Final Epidemic*; Bernard Lown, "Nuclear War and the Public Health," *Journal of Public Health Policy* 3, no. 1 (March 1, 1982): 12–21; Bernard Lown, Eric Chivian, James Muller, and Herbert Abrams, "Nuclear Arms Race and the Physician," *New England Journal of Medicine* 304, no. 12 (March 19, 1981): 726–729; See also Christine Cassel and Andrew Jameton, "Medical Responsibility and Thermonuclear War," *Annals of Internal Medicine* 97, no. 3 (September 1982): 426–432; Herbert Abrams and William E. Von Kaenel, "Special Report: Medical Problems That Would Confront Survivors," *New England Journal of Medicine* (November 12, 1981); Bernard Lown, "Physicians and Nuclear War," *Journal of the American Medical Association* 246, no. 20 (November 20, 1981): 2331–2333; "Physicians Warn of Nuclear Risks," *New York Times*, December 10, 1981; J. E. Coggle and Patricia Lindop, "Medical Consequences of Radiation Following a Global Nuclear War," *Ambio: A Journal of the Human Environment* 11, no. 2/3 (1982): 106; "How Doctors Hope to Stop Nuclear War," *Wall Street Journal*, November 28, 1980; and Howard Hiatt, "Preventing the Last Epidemic," *Journal of the American Medical Association* 244, no. 20 (November 21, 1980): 314–315.

37. Quoted in "Physicians Warn of Nuclear Risks," *New York Times*, December 10, 1981.

38. "Physicians for Social Responsibility Gain Respectability," *New Physician* 31, no. 5 (1982), SO 660, Box 4, Folder: *New Physician*, PSR Collection, SHSM.

39. See, for example, Leaning, "Civil Defense in the Nuclear Age." Adams and Cullens, *The Final Epidemic*, 150; and PSR Statement on Civil Defense, 1983, SI 454, Box 5, Folder: PSR, 1982–1986, National Nuclear Weapons Freeze Collection, SHSM.

40. Physicians for Social Responsibility, *The Last Epidemic*, 1981.

41. On the inadequacy of shelters, see S. Warren, "You, Your Patients, and Radioactive Fallout," *New England Journal of Medicine* 266, no. 31 (May 1962): 1123–1125; V. W. Sidel, H. Jack Geiger, and Bernard Lown, "The Physician's Role in the Post-Attack Period," *New England Journal of Medicine* 266 (May 31, 1962): 1137–1145; Kevin Lewis, "The Prompt and Delayed Effects of Nuclear War," *Scientific American* 241, no. 1 (July 1979): 35–47; and Physicians for Social Responsibility, *The Last Epidemic*, 1981.

42. Leaning, "Civil Defense in the Nuclear Age."

43. Ibid., 35.

44. See SI 454, Box 5, Folder: PSR, 1982–6, National Nuclear Weapons Freeze Collection, SHSM; "The Nuclear Threat to San Francisco," SO 660, Box 6, Folder: Public Health Booklets, Marin Co/Mass Department of Health, PSR Collection, SHSM; and Jeannie Peterson, *The Aftermath: The Human and Ecological Consequences of Nuclear War* (New York: Pantheon, 1983).

45. Bernard Lown, Eric Chivian, James Muller, and Herbert Abrams, "Nuclear Arms Race and the Physician," *New England Journal of Medicine* 304, no. 12 (March 19, 1981): 726–729.

46. Sidel, Geiger, and Lown, "The Physician's Role in the Post-Attack Period," 1137–1145.

47. Brochure: Civil Defense Planning for Nuclear War: Security or Illusion?, SO 660, Box 1, Folder: Arsenic Pills for Civil Defense, PSR Collection, SHSM; "Physicians Warn of Nuclear Risk," New York Times, December 10, 1981; and Leaning, "Civil Defense in the Nuclear Age."

48. Arnold Relman, "Physicians, Nuclear War, and Politics," New England Journal of Medicine 308, no. 6 (September 16, 1982): 744–745.

49. Ibid.

50. Letter dated September 1, 1981, from Kathryn Bennett, Medical Staff President, Health Services Department, Contra Costa County to John H. Moxley, Department of Defense, SO 660, Box 1, Folder: Civil Defense, PSR Collection, SHSM. See also Herbert Abrams, "Preparing for the Highest Rate of Casualties in History," Bulletin of Atomic Scientists 39, no. 6 (June 1983): 11S–16S.

51. Letter to the Editor in Lancet, April 25, 1981, SO 660, Box 1, Folder: Civil Defense, PSR Collection, SHSM.

52. "Coast Doctors Rebuff Pentagon on Plan for War," New York Times, October 27, 1981.

53. Jay Bisgard, "The Obligation to Care for Casualties," Hastings Center Report 12 (April 1982): 15–17. For other critiques of PSR's position, see Howard Maccabee, Doctors for Disaster Preparedness, "A Medical and Ethical Argument," Emergency Management Review, Winter 1984. See SO 660, Box 2, Folder: Geiger/Maccabee 2/6/84, PSR Collection, SHSM.

54. Arnold Relman, "Physicians, Nuclear War, and Politics," New England Journal of Medicine (September 16, 1982): 744–745.

55. H. Jack Geiger, "Why Survival Plans Are Meaningless," Hastings Center Report 12 (April 1982): 17–19.

56. Randall Kehler Congressional testimony, March 22 1982, 1, SO 454, Box 3, Folder: Freeze Forum, National Nuclear Weapons Freeze Collection, SHSM.

57. Schell, "The Abolition I."

58. Patrick Caddell, "The State of American Politics," October 25, 1983, Draft: confidential, Cambridge Survey Research, SO 454, Box 3, Folder: Freeze Activists for Presidential Campaigns of 1984, October 1983–October 1984, National Nuclear Weapons Freeze Collection, SHSM.

59. Rejoinders, a Handbook.

60. See SO 454, Box 7, Folder: Strategy Committee, Jan–March 1981, National Freeze Strategy, 1/3/81, National Nuclear Weapons Freeze Collection, SHSM.

61. Ibid.

62. "Professional Approach to Peace," Nuclear Times, August/September 1983, SO 454, Box 5, Folder: Nuclear Times, Jan–Dec 1983, National Nuclear Weapons Freeze Collection, SHSM.

63. "Anatomy of a Nuclear Protest."

64. "A Physician's View on Nuclear War: An Interview with Helen Caldicott," SO 660, Box 1, Folder: Helen Caldicott, PSR Collection, SHSM.

65. "On Women and War: Interview with Joanne Woodward," Common Cause Magazine, November/December 1983, SO 454, Box 5, Folder: News Clippings, March 1974–December 1983, National Nuclear Weapons Freeze Collection, SHSM.

66. "Will Gender Gap Become a Gulf?," *Nuclear Times*, April 1984, SO 454, Box 5, Folder: *Nuclear Times*, Jan-Apr 1984, National Nuclear Weapons Freeze Campaign, SHSM.

67. See SO 454, Box 5, Folder: Peace/Disarmament, 1984–5, National Nuclear Weapons Freeze Campaign, SHSM.

68. "Will Gender Gap Become a Gulf?"

69. Quoted in "A Matter of Life and Death," *Newsweek*, April 26, 1982, 20–25.

70. Quoted in Press Release, Presbyterian Church USA, June 4, 1984, SO 454, Box 5, Folder: Peace/Disarmament, 1984–5, National Nuclear Weapons Freeze Campaign. SHSM.

71. See Meyers, *A Winter of Our Discontent*, 104–109.

72. www.usccb.org/upload/challenge-peace-gods-promise-our-response-1983.pdf.

73. "Bishops Endorse Stand Opposed to Nuclear War," *New York Times*, May 4, 1983.

74. See "Anti-Bomb Equals Anti-Choice," *Nuclear Times*, February 1984, Box 5, Folder: *Nuclear Times*, Jan-Apr 1984, National Nuclear Weapons Freeze Campaign. SHSM.

75. See "A Matter of Life and Death," *Newsweek*, April 26, 1982, 20–25; see also "Four Proposals Concerning Political Aspects of the Freeze," SO 454, Box 7, Folder: Strategy Committee, Jan-March 1984, National Nuclear Weapons Freeze Campaign. SHSM.

76. Four Proposals Concerning Political Aspects of the Freeze, SO 454, Box 7, Folder: Strategy Committee, Jan-March 1984, National Nuclear Weapons Freeze Campaign, SHSM.

77. "Anatomy of a Nuclear Protest."

78. "What About the Children?," publication of Parents and Teachers for Social Responsibility, SO 660, Box 3, Folder: Kids and Nuclear War, PSR Collection, SHSM.

79. Warning, Peace Marchers Flyer, paid for by the Alliance to Halt the Advance of Marxism in the Americas, SO 454, Box 5, Folder: Opposition/Criticism, Apr-Aug 1982, National Nuclear Weapons Freeze Campaign, SHSM.

80. Letter from Jerry Falwell to members of the Moral Majority, June 17, 1982, 1, SO 454, Box 5, Folder: Opposition/Criticism, Apr-Aug 1982, National Nuclear Weapons Freeze Campaign, SHSM.

81. See Interchange Memorandum Re: Anti-Freeze Initiatives/Report #2, January 20, 1983, SO 454, Box 5, Folder: Opposition/Criticism November 1982-Feb 1983, National Nuclear Weapons Freeze Campaign, SHSM. See also Secretary of Defense Casper Weinberger, remarks to the Massachusetts Medical Society, May 19, 1982, Shattuck Lectures, *New England Journal of Medicine*, September 16, 1982, 765–768; and "Nuclear Freeze Crusade: Gaining or Waning," *US News and World Report*, April 25, 1983.

82. Letter from Vinton Heuck to David Riley, Co-Chair, Freeze Campaign, April 12, 1984, SO 454, Box 2, Folder: The Day After Organizer's Kit, November 1983, National Nuclear Weapons Freeze Campaign, SHSM.

83. Memo from Mark Niedergang, November 1982, SO 454, Box 7, Folder: Strategy Committee, National Nuclear Weapons Freeze Campaign, SHSM.

84. Letter from Beverly Woodward, Coordinator of International Seminars on Training for Nonviolent Action, December 5, 1981, SO 454, Box 1, Folder: Correspondence, Jan 1981-Mar 1982, National Nuclear Weapons Freeze Campaign, SHSM.

85. Ibid.

86. Judith Butler, *Precarious Life: The Powers of Mourning and Violence* (London: Verso, 2006).

87. Quoted in "The Movement in Black and White," *Nuclear Times*, August/September 1983, SO 454, Box 5, Folder: Nuclear Times, Jan-Dec 1983, National Nuclear Weapons Freeze Campaign, SHSM.

88. Letter from Patricia Williams to Randy Kehler, May 3, 1984, SO 454, Box 4, Folder: Minorities Outreach Program, 1984, National Nuclear Weapons Freeze Campaign, SHSM.

89. H. Jack Geiger had been a civil rights activist before helping to found PSR. He was a member of the Medical Committee for Human Rights (MCHR), an interracial group of physicians and other healthcare providers who sent volunteers to Mississippi in the summer of 1964. Geiger remained there after the voting drive was over in order to address the medical needs of the African American community. See Jennifer Nelson, *More Than Medicine: A History of the Feminist Women's Health Movement* (New York: New York University Press, 2015), 1–6.

90. "Depolarizing Disarmament Work: Twelve Guidelines to Help Us Reach New People," by Wendy Mogey, The New Manhattan Project, SO 660, Box 2, Folder: "How to Do Its," PSR Collection, SHSM.

91. Assessment, Nuclear Weapons Freeze Campaign, Kearney, Nebraska, SO 454, Box 5, Folder: Political Consultant Meeting, January 20, 1983, National Nuclear Weapons Freeze Campaign, SHSM.

92. Schell, *The Fate of the Earth*, 70.

93. See, for example, J. E. Coggle and Patricia Lindop, "Medical Consequences of Radiation Following a Global Nuclear War," *Ambio: A Journal of the Human Environment* 11, no. 2/3 (1982): 59.

94. "What About the Children?"

95. Sidel, Geiger, and Lown, "The Physician's Role in the Post-Attack Period," 1144.

96. Carol Amen, dir., *Testament* (PBS, 1983).

97. Adams and Cullen, *The Final Epidemic*, 130.

98. On social reproduction, see Johanna Brenner and Barbara Laslett, "Gender, Social Reproduction, and Women's Self-Organization: Considering the US Welfare State," *Gender and Society* 5, no. 3 (September 1991): 311–333; and Evelyn Nakano Glenn, "From Servitude to Service Work: Historical Continuities in the Racial Division of Paid Reproductive Labor," *Signs* (Autumn 1992): 1–43.

99. H. Jack Geiger, "Addressing Apocalypse Now: The Effects of Nuclear Warfare as a Public Health Concern," *American Journal of Public Health* 70, no. 9 (September 1980): 960.

100. "The Nightmare Comes Home," *Time*, October 24, 1983.

101. *The Day After* is discussed at length in SO 454, Box 5, Folder: *Nuclear Times*, Jan-Dec 1983; Box 5, Folder, *Nuclear Times*, Jan-Apr 1984; Box 2, Folder: *The Day After*, Aug-Oct 1983; and Box 2, Folder: *The Day After*, November 1983-February 1984, all in the National Nuclear Weapons Freeze Campaign, SHSM. Markey is quoted in "ABC Film Depicting Consequences of Nuclear War," *New York Times*, October 6, 1983.

102. See, for example, R. P. Turco, O. B. Toon, T. P. Ackerman, J. B. Pollack, and Carl Sagan, "Nuclear Winter: Global Consequences of Multiple Nuclear Explosions," *Science* 222, no. 4630 (December 23, 1983): 1283–1292 (this became known as the

TTAPS study); Paul Ehrlich et al., "Long-Term Biological Consequences of Nuclear War," *Science* 222, no. 4630 (December 23, 1983): 1293–1298; Carl Sagan, "Nuclear War and Climatic Catastrophe: Some Policy Information," *Foreign Affairs* (Winter 1983/1984): 257–292; Curt Covey, Stephen Schneider, and Starley Thompson, "Global Atmospheric Effects of Massive Smoke Injections from a Nuclear War: Results from General Circulation Model Simulations," *Nature* (March 1984): 21–25; Barry Pittock, "The Effects on the Atmosphere of a Major Nuclear Exchange," *Environment* 27, no. 3 (April 1985): 25; Peterson, *The Aftermath*; Anne Ehrlich, "Nuclear Winter," *Bulletin of the Atomic Scientists* 40, no. 4 (April 1984): 1S–14S; National Research Council, *Long-Term Worldwide Effects of Multiple Nuclear War Detonations* (Washington DC: National Academy of Sciences, 1975); and Paul Crutzen and John Birks, "The Atmosphere After a Nuclear War: Twilight at Noon," *Ambio* 11, no. 2/3 (January 1, 1982): 114–125. For an illuminating overview of the nuclear winter debate, see Lawrence Badash, *A Nuclear Winter's Tale: Science and Politics in the 1980s* (Cambridge: MIT Press, 2009).

103. Interestingly, NW theory simultaneously anticipated current geoengineering schemes that have been proposed as potential remedies for rising global temperatures, including releasing stratospheric sulfates in order to cool things down. For a discussion of this, see Stewart Brand, *Whole Earth Discipline: Why Dense Cities, Nuclear Power, Transgenic Crops, Restored Wildlands, and Geoengineering Are Necessary* (New York: Penguin, 2010).

104. Sagan, *The Nuclear Winter*.

105. See Sagan, "Nuclear War and Climatic Catastrophe," 273; John Harte is quoted in Anne Ehrlich, "Nuclear Winter," *Bulletin of the Atomic Scientists* 40, no. 4 (April 1984): 1S–14S.

106. Ehrlich, "Nuclear Winter."

107. H. Jack Geiger, "The Meaning of Nuclear Winter: Scientific Evidence and the Human Spirit," speech delivered at fourth congress of IPPNW, Helsinki, Finland, June 5, 1984, SO 660, Box 4, Folder: Nuclear Winter, PSR Collection, SHSM.

108. Sagan, "Nuclear War and Climatic Catastrophe," 264.

109. Ehrlich, "Nuclear Winter," 1S–14S.

110. On this intuitive model of disaster, see H. Jack Geiger, "The Illusion of Survival," in Adams and Cullen, *The Final Epidemic*, 174.

111. Geiger, "The Meaning of Nuclear Winter."

112. On the history of the concept of extinction, see Elizabeth Kolbert, *The Sixth Extinction: An Unnatural History* (New York: Holt, 2014), 23–69. My discussion here is wholly indebted to her history of extinction.

113. Luis W. Alvarez, Walter Alvarez, Frank Asaro, and Helen Michel, "Extraterrestrial Cause for the Cretaceous-Tertiary Extinction," *Science* 208, no. 4448 (June 6, 1980): 1095–1108.

114. Ehrlich, "Nuclear Winter," 1S–14S.

115. Herbert Abrams, "Infection and Communicable Diseases," in Adams and Cullen, *The Final Epidemic*, 201.

116. Charles Darwin, *The Origin of Species*, 150th anniversary ed. (New York: Signet, 2003), 150. See also Rebekah Sheldon, *The Child to Come: Life After the Human Catastrophe* (Minneapolis: University of Minnesota Press, 2016).

117. Schell, *The Fate of the Earth*, 166.

118. Robert Jay Lifton, "Beyond Psychic Numbing: A Call to Awareness," *American Journal of Orthopsychiatrics* 52, no. 4 (October 1982): 626.

119. Schell, *The Fate of the Earth*, 115.

120. Ibid., 115.

121. Ibid., 118.

122. Ibid., 116.

123. Ibid., 144.

124. Ibid., 140.

125. Ibid., 146, 162.

126. Ibid., 160.

127. Jerome Shapiro, *Atomic Bomb Cinema: The Apocalyptic Imagination on Film* (New York: Routledge, 2002), 185.

128. Office of Technology Assessment, *Nuclear Power in an Age of Uncertainty* (Washington, DC: US Congress, Office of Technology Assessment, OTA-E-216, February 1984).

129. "Nuclear Follies," *Forbes Magazine*, February 11, 1985.

130. See Nuclear Public Relations Campaign in US Congress, House of Representatives, *Hearings Before the Subcommittee on Energy Conservation and Power of the House Committee on Energy and Commerce*, 98th Cong., 1st sess., June 30, 1983.

131. US Congress, House of Representatives, *Hearings Before the Subcommittee on Energy Conservation and Power of the House Committee on Energy and Commerce*, 98th Cong., 1st sess., May 23, 1983, 156. See also US Congress, House of Representatives, *Hearings Before the Subcommittee on Energy Research and Production of the House Committee on Science and Technology*, 97th Congress, 1st sess., December 15, 1981, 5.

132. *Nuclear Public Relations Campaign* in US Congress, House of Representatives, *Hearings Before the Subcommittee on Energy Conservation and Power of the House Committee on Energy and Commerce*, 98th Cong., 1st sess., May 23, 1983, 191–197.

133. Ibid.

134. Quoted in *The Legacy of Chernobyl: Health and Safety Twenty Years Later*, in US Congress, *Hearing Before the Commission on Security and Cooperation in Europe*, 109th Cong., 2nd sess., April 25, 2006, 25. On Chernobyl, see Adriana Petryna, *Life Exposed: Biological Citizens After Chernobyl* (Princeton: Princeton University Press, 2003).

135. Cassandra Koerner, "Media, Fear, and Nuclear Energy: A Case Study," *Social Science Journal* 51 (2014): 240–249.

136. Quoted in "Chernobyl Causes Big Revisions in Global Nuclear Power Policies," *New York Times*, October 27, 1986.

137. Hans A. Bethe, "Chernobyl: It Can't Happen Here," *New York Times*, May 2, 1991.

138. Quoted in "Chernobyl Causes Big Revisions in Global Nuclear Power Policies," *New York Times*, October 27, 1986.

139. "Chernobyl Reconsidered: The Disaster Reflected a Society in Decline," *New York Times*, April 26, 1996.

140. Letter from Edwin Markey to Anatoly Mayorets, Minister of Power and Electrification, and Genadi Veretenikov, April 29, 1986, in *Soviet Nuclear Accident at*

Chernobyl, reprinted in US Congress, House of Representatives, *Briefing and Hearing Before the Subcommittee on Energy Conservation and Power of the House Committee on Energy and Commerce*, 99th Cong., 2nd sess., May 1 and 7, 1986, 52.

141. Naomi Klein, *This Changes Everything: Capitalism vs. the Climate* (New York: Simon and Schuster, 2014), 73; Bill McKibben, *The End of Nature* (Norwell, MA: Anchor, 1989); "Endangered Earth," *Time*, January 2, 1989.

142. Rep. George Miller, American Energy Council Congressional Information, February 1989, *Future of Nuclear Power*, in US Congress, House of Representatives, *Oversight Hearing Before the Subcommittee on Energy and the Environment of the House Committee on Interior and Insular Affairs*, 101 Cong., 2nd sess., May 10, 1990, 21.

143. *The U.S. Nuclear Energy Industry's Strategic Plan for Building New Nuclear Power Plants*, Executive Summary, May 1998, http://lobby.la.psu.edu/051_Nuclear_Waste/Organizational_Statements/NEI/NEI_Strategic_Plan.pdf.

144. See "Greenwash!," *Mother Jones* (March/April 1991), 38–41, 88; *Future of Nuclear Power*, 80; and Diane Farsetta, "The Campaign to Sell Nuclear Energy," *Bulletin of the Atomic Scientists* 64, no. 4 (September/October 2008): 38–41.

145. US Congress, Senate, *Hearing on Radiological Contamination in the United States Before the Senate Committee on Governmental Affairs*, 102 Cong., 2nd sess., April 9, 1992, 2.

146. Statement of Michael Mariotte, Executive Director, Nuclear Information and Resource Center, *Future of Nuclear Power*, 96.

CONCLUSION

1. The quotation comes from Charles Maier. See Niall Ferguson, Charles Maier, Erez Manela, and Daniel Sargent, eds., *The Shock of the Global: The 1970s in Perspective* (Cambridge: Harvard University Press, 2011), 44.

2. Naomi Klein, *This Changes Everything: Capitalism vs. the Climate* (New York: Simon and Schuster, 2014).

3. Joni Adamson, Mei Mei Evans, and Rachel Stein, eds., *The Environmental Justice Reader: Politics, Poetics, and Pedagogy* (Tucson: University of Arizona Press, 2002); Robert Bullard, *Dumping in Dixie: Race, Class, and Environmental Quality* (Boulder: Westview, 2000); Melissa Checker, *Polluted Promises: Environmental Racism and the Search for Justice in a Southern Town* (New York: New York University Press, 2005); Jennifer Clapp, *Toxic Exports: The Transfer of Hazardous Waste from Rich to Poor Countries* (Ithaca: Cornell University Press, 2001); Rob Nixon, *Slow Violence and the Environmentalism of the Poor* (Cambridge: Harvard University Press, 2011); David Naguib Pellow, *Garbage Wars: The Struggle for Environmental Justice in Chicago* (Cambridge: MIT Press, 2004); Julie Sze, *Noxious New York: The Racial Politics of Urban Health and Environmental Justice* (Cambridge: MIT Press, 2006); Dorceta Taylor, *Toxic Communities: Environmental Racism, Industrial Pollution, and Residential Mobility* (New York: New York University Press, 2014); and Carl Zimring, *Clean and White: A History of Environmental Racism in the United States* (New York: New York University Press, 2016).

4. Klein, *This Changes Everything*, 423–434.

5. The contemporary Black Lives Matter movement and the writings of Ta-Nehisi Coates build upon this earlier politicization of the black body. See Coates, *Between the World and Me* (New York: Spiegel and Grau, 2015).

6. See, for example, Kevin Kruse, *White Flight: Atlanta and the Making of Modern Conservatism* (Princeton: Princeton University Press, 2005); Kevin Kruse and Thomas Sugrue, eds., *The New Suburban History* (Chicago: University of Chicago Press, 2006); Matthew Lassiter, *The Silent Majority: Suburban Politics in the Sunbelt South* (Princeton: Princeton University Press, 2012); Lisa McGirr, *Suburban Warriors: The Origins of the New American Right* (Princeton: Princeton University Press, 2002); and Robert Self, *American Babylon: Race and the Struggle for Postwar Oakland* (Princeton: Princeton University Press, 2005).

7. Courtney Jung, *Lactivism: How Feminists and Fundamentalists, Hippies and Yuppies, and Physicians and Politicians Made Breastfeeding Big Business and Bad Policy* (New York: Basic, 2015).

8. Jackie Orr, *Panic Diaries: A Genealogy of Panic Disorders* (Durham: Duke University Press, 2006), 12.

9. On the history of neoliberalism, see David Harvey, *A Brief History of Neoliberalism* (New York: Oxford University Press, 2007); and Wendy Brown, *Undoing the Demos: Neoliberalism's Stealth Revolution* (Cambridge: Zone, 2015).

10. For a recent example of how this palliative mode works vis-à-vis ecological threats, see Natasha Zaretsky, "Trusting the Water Again: Understanding the West Virginia Chemical Spill," *Tikkun*, April 9, 2014. During the chemical spill in West Virginia in January 2014, the state government could provide no guarantee that the water supply was safe. Instead, the governor told the local population that the question of water consumption was "their choice" and that they should only drink the water if they felt "comfortable."

11. Polling suggested that the industry's rebranding as a clean, green technology was working. One Gallup poll conducted in January 2014 found that 62 percent of the public favored nuclear power (up from 46 percent in 2001), and an NEI commissioned poll placed the approval figure even higher at 70 percent.

12. On the nuclear renaissance, see "A US Nuclear Future?," *Nature* 467 (September 23, 2010): 391–393; Alvin Weinberg, "New Life for Nuclear Power," *Issues in Science and Technology* 19, no. 4 (Summer 2003): 60–62; Paul Joskow and John Parsons, "The Economic Future of Nuclear Power," *Daedalus* 138, no. 4 (Fall 2009): 45–59; Federation of American Scientists, *The Future of Nuclear Power in the United States* (Lexington: Washington and Lee University, 2012); and the Massachusetts Institute of Technology, *The Future of Nuclear Power: An Interdisciplinary Study*, 2003, updated in 2009. The issue of *Daedalus* from fall 2009, titled "On the Global Nuclear Future," was devoted to the theme.

13. Richard Lester and Robert Rosner, "The Growth of Nuclear Power: Drivers and Constraints," *Daedalus* 138, no. 4 (Fall 2009): 19–30; and Paul Joskow and John Parsons, "The Economic Future of Nuclear Power," *Daedalus* 138, no. 4 (Fall 2009): 45–59. As of early 2009, there were forty-four new nuclear units under global construction: eleven in China, eight in Russia, six in India, and five in South Korea. See Jose Goldemberg, "Nuclear Energy in Developing Countries," *Daedalus* 138, no. 4 (Fall 2009): 71–80.

14. See Harold Feiveson, "A Skeptic's View of Nuclear Energy," *Daedalus* 138, no. 4 (Fall 2009): 60–70.

15. Stephanie LeMenager, *Living Oil: Petroleum Culture in the American Century* (New York: Oxford University Press, 2014). Compared to this "cheap" energy, nuclear power is expensive. This is partly because while the nuclear industry is required to pay for its own waste disposal, there is no fee for disposing of the principle waste produced by carbon-based fuels, carbon dioxide. As a result, the true cost of carbon is artificially suppressed. If the staggering social and environmental costs of carbon emissions were ever internalized (through a carbon tax, for example), nuclear power might look more competitive. In making this argument, I do not mean to imply that the current crisis can be remedied through the free market and its capacities for self-correction. Instead, I agree with sociologist Jason Moore when he writes: "calls for capital to pay the 'true costs' of resource-use . . . are to be welcomed, because such calls directly contradict capital's fundamental logic. To call for capital to pay its own way is to call for the abolition of capitalism." See Jason W. Moore, *Capitalism in the Web of Life: Ecology and the Accumulation of Capital* (London: Verso, 2015), 145.

16. Robert Stone, dir., *Pandora's Promise* (CNN Films, 2013).

17. Evan Osnos, "The Fallout: Letter from Fukushima," *New Yorker*, October 17, 2011, 46.

18. See Julia Adeney Thomas, "History and Biology in the Anthropocene: Problems of Scale, Problems of Value," *American Historical Review* 119, no. 5 (December 2014): 1587–1607; Steve Kroll Smith and Worth Lancaster, "Bodies, Environments, and a New Style of Reasoning," *Annals of the American Academy of Political and Social Science* 584 (November 2002): 203–212; Michelle Murphy, "Chemical Regimes of Living," *Environmental History* 13, no. 4 (October 2008): 695–703; Barbara Allen, "Environment, Health and Missing Information," *Environmental History* 13, no. 4 (October 2008): 659–666; Sarah Vogel, "From 'The Dose Makes the Poison' to 'The Timing Makes the Dose': Conceptualizing Risk in the Synthetic Age," *Environmental History* 13, no. 4 (October 2008): 667–673; and Vogel, "The Politics of Plastics: The Making and Unmaking of Bisphenol A 'Safety,'" *American Journal of Public Health* 99, no. S3 (September 3, 2009): 559–566; Linda Nash, "Purity and Danger: Historical Reflections on Environmental Regulations," *Environmental History* 13, no. 4 (October 2008): 651–658.

19. Andrew Solomon, *Far From the Tree: Parents, Children, and the Search for Identity* (New York: Scribner, 2013), 1.

BIBLIOGRAPHY

ARCHIVAL SOURCES

Association of Religious Data Archives. www.thearda.com/mapsReports/reports
/counties/42043_1980.asp
Baylor University Editorial Cartoon Collection, Waco, Texas
Beverly Hess Papers
Clamshell Alliance
Dick Thornburgh Papers
Editorial Cartoons—Nuclear Power
Edwin K. Charles Papers
Jane Lee Papers
Jimmy Carter Presidential Library, Atlanta, Georgia
John H. Murdoch Papers
Lonna Malmsheimer Oral History Interviews
National Archives II, University of Maryland, College Park
National Nuclear Weapons Freeze Collection
Papers of the President's Commission on the Accident at Three Mile Island
Physicians for Social Responsibility Collection
Public Interest Resource Center Papers
Records of the Office of the Staff Secretary
SANE, Inc. Records
Shad Alliance Records, 1978–1983
State Historical Society of Missouri, University of Missouri at St. Louis
Swarthmore College Peace Collection, Swarthmore, Pennsylvania
Three Mile Island Alert Papers
Three Mile Island Collection, Dickinson College Archive and Special Collections, Carlyle, Pennsylvania
University of Pittsburgh Special Collections

GOVERNMENT PUBLICATIONS

"Atoms for Peace." Address by Dwight D. Eisenhower to the 470th plenary meeting of the United Nations General Assembly, December 8, 1953. Reprinted in *Public Papers of the Presidents of the United States, Dwight D. Eisenhower: Containing the Public Messages, Speeches, and Statements of the President, January 20, 1953 to January 20, 1961,* 813–822. Washington, DC: US Government Printing Office, 1958–1961.

"Mental Health Aspects of the Peaceful Uses of Atomic Energy: Report of a Study Group." No. 151, World Health Organization, Technical Paper, Geneva, 1958.

Nuclear Regulatory Commission, Special Inquiry Group. *Three Mile Island: A Report to the Commissioners and to the Public.* Washington, DC: Government Printing Office, 1980.

US Congress. *Hearing Before the Commission on Security and Cooperation in Europe.* 109th Cong., 2nd sess., April 25, 2006.

US Congress, House of Representatives. *Briefing and Hearing Before the Subcommittee on Energy Conservation and Power of the House Committee on Energy and Commerce.* 99th Cong., 2nd sess., May 1 and 7, 1986.

US Congress, House of Representatives. *Hearings Before the Subcommittee on Energy Conservation and Power of the House Committee on Energy and Commerce.* 98th Cong., 1st sess., May 23, 1983.

US Congress, House of Representatives. *Hearings Before the Subcommittee on Energy Conservation and Power of the House Committee on Energy and Commerce.* 98th Cong., 1st sess., June 30, 1983.

US Congress, House of Representatives. *Hearings Before the Subcommittee on Energy Research and Production of the House Committee on Science and Technology.* 97th Congress, 1st sess., December 15, 1981.

US Congress, House of Representatives. *Hearing Before the Subcommittee on Natural Resources and Environment of the Committee on Science and Technology.* 96th Cong., 1st sess., June 2, 1979.

US Congress, House of Representatives. *Oversight Hearing Before the Subcommittee on Energy and the Environment of the House Committee on Interior and Insular Affairs.* 101 Cong., 2nd sess., May 10, 1990.

US Congress, House of Representatives, Committee on Science and Technology. *Hearings Before the Subcommittee on Natural Resources and the Environment.* 96th Cong., 1st sess., June 2, 1979.

US Congress, House of Representatives, Subcommittee on Natural Resources and Environment of the Committee on Science and Technology. *Research on Health Effects of Nonionizing Radiation.* 96th Cong., 1st sess., July 12, 1979.

US Congress, Joint Hearings. *Joint Hearings of Subcommittee on Nuclear Regulation of the Senate Committee on Environment and Public Works and the Subcommittee on Energy and the Environment of the House Committee on Interior and Insular Affairs.* 96th Cong., 1st sess., October 31, 1979.

US Congress, Joint Hearing, Special Subcommittee on Radiation of the Joint House and Senate Committee on Atomic Energy. *Fallout from Nuclear Weapons Tests.* 86th Cong., 1st sess., June 1959.

US Congress, Joint Hearings, Subcommittee on Nuclear Regulation of the Senate Committee on Environmental and Public Works, and the Subcommittee on Energy and the Environment of the House Committee on Interior and Insular Affairs. *Report of the Presidential Commission on the Three Mile Island Accident*. 96th Cong., 1st sess., October 31, 1979.

US Congress, Joint Hearings, Subcommittee on Oversight and Investigations of House Committee on Interstate and Foreign Commerce, and Health and Scientific Research Subcommittee of the Senate Labor and Human Resources Committee and Committee on the Judiciary. *Health Effects of Low-level Radiation, Volume 1*. 96th Cong., 1st sess., April 19, 1979.

US Congress, Office of Technology Assessment. *The Effects of Nuclear War*. Washington, DC: Government Printing Office, 1979.

US Congress, Senate. *Hearings Before the Subcommittee on Energy, Nuclear Proliferation, and Federal Services of the Committee on Governmental Affairs*. 96th Cong., 1st sess., 1979.

US Congress, Senate. *Hearing on Radiological Contamination in the United States Before the Senate Committee on Governmental Affairs*. 102 Cong., 2nd sess., April 9, 1992.

US Congress, Senate, Subcommittee on Health and Scientific Research of the Committee on Labor and Human Resources. *Three Mile Island Nuclear Accident, 1979*. 96th Cong., 1st sess., April 4, 1979.

"You Can Understand the Atom." Washington, DC: Atomic Energy Commission, 1951.

PERIODICALS

Ambio
American Journal of Orthopsychiatry
American Journal of Public Health
Annals of Internal Medicine
Bulletin of Atomic Scientists
Christian Science Monitor
Common Cause Magazine
Daedalus
Emergency Management Review
Esquire
Forbes
Harper's Magazine
Harrisburg Evening News
Harrisburg Patriot News
Hastings Center Report
Health Physics
Issues in Science and Technology
Journal of Public Health Policy
Journal of the American Medical Association
Lancaster Intelligencer Journal

Lancet
Las Vegas Sun
Los Angeles Review of Books
Los Angeles Times
McCall's
Mother Jones
Nature
New England Journal of Medicine
New Physician
New Republic
Newsweek
New Yorker
New York Times
Nuclear Times
Pennsylvania Illustrated
People Magazine
Philadelphia Bulletin
Philadelphia Daily News
Philadelphia Inquirer
Philadelphia Magazine
Pittsburgh Post-Gazette
Pittsburgh Press
Redbook
Rolling Stone
Saturday Evening Post
Science
Scientific American
Social Science Journal
Time Magazine
US News and World Report
Wall Street Journal
Washington Post

PUBLISHED SOURCES

Ackland, Len. *Making a Real Killing: Rocky Flats and the Nuclear West*. Albuquerque: University of New Mexico Press, 1999.

Adam, Barbara. *Timescapes of Modernity: The Environment and Invisible Hazards*. London: Routledge, 1998.

Adams, Ruth, and Susan Cullen, eds. *The Final Epidemic: Physicians and Scientists on Nuclear War*. Chicago: University of Chicago Press, 1981.

Adamson, Greg. *We All Live on Three Mile Island Now: The Case Against Nuclear Power*. Sydney: Pathfinder, 1981.

Adamson, Joni, Mei Mei Evans, and Rachel Stein, eds. *The Environmental Justice Reader: Politics, Poetics, and Pedagogy*. Tucson: University of Arizona Press, 2002.

Alaimo, Stacey. *Bodily Natures: Science, Environment and the Material Self.* Bloomington: Indiana University Press, 2010.

Allen, Barbara. "Environment, Health and Missing Information." *Environmental History* 13, no. 4 (October 2008): 659–666.

Allen, Michael J. *Until the Last Man Comes Home: POWs, MIAs, and the Unending
Vietnam War.* Chapel Hill: University of North Carolina Press, 2011.

Alonso, Harriet Hyman. "Mayhem and Moderation: Women Peace Activists During
the McCarthy Era." In *Not June Cleaver: Women and Gender in Postwar America,
1945–1960,* edited by Joanne Meyerowitz, 128–150. Philadelphia: Temple University
Press, 1994.

——. *Peace as a Women's Issue: A History of the U.S. Movement for World Peace and
Women's Rights.* Syracuse: Syracuse University Press, 1993.

Amen, Carol, dir. *Testament.* PBS, 1983.

Arendt, Hannah. "Lying in Politics: Reflections on the Pentagon Papers." In *Crises of
the Republic.* New York: Harcourt Brace Jovanovich, 1972.

Badash, Lawrence. *A Nuclear Winter's Tale: Science and Politics in the 1980s.* Cambridge: MIT Press, 2009.

——. "Radium, Radioactivity, and the Popularity of Scientific Discovery." *Proceedings
of the American Philosophical Society* 122 (1978): 145–154.

Baehr, Peter. "Social Extremity, Communities of Fate, and the Sociology of SARS." *European Journal of Sociology* 46, no. 2 (2005): 179–211.

Ball, Howard. *Justice Downwind: America's Atomic Testing Program in the 1950's.* Oxford: Oxford University Press, 1986.

Balogh, Brian. *Chain Reaction: Expert Debate and Public Participation in American
Commercial Nuclear Power, 1945–1975.* Cambridge: Cambridge University Press,
1991.

Beck, John. *Dirty Wars: Landscape, Power, and Waste in Western American Literature.*
Lincoln: University of Nebraska Press, 2009.

Bedford, Henry. *Seabrook Station: Citizen Politics and Nuclear Power.* Amherst: University of Massachusetts Press, 1990.

Beers, Paul. *City Contented, City Discontented: A History of Modern Harrisburg.* Harrisburg: Midtown Scholar, 2011.

Bell, Daniel, ed. *The Radical Right: The New American Right.* New York: Doubleday, 1963.

Berger, Dan. *The Hidden 1970s: Histories of Radicalism.* New Brunswick, NJ: Rutgers
University Press, 2010.

Blum, Elizabeth. *Love Canal Revisited: Race, Class, and Gender in Environmental Activism.* Lawrence: University Press of Kansas, 2008.

Boltanski, Luc. *The Foetal Condition: A Sociology of Engendering and Abortion.* London: Polity, 2013.

Borstelmann, Thomas. *The 1970s: A New Global History from Civil Rights to Economic
Inequality.* Princeton: Princeton University Press, 2013.

Bourke, Joanna. *Fear: A Cultural History.* Berkeley: Counterpoint, 2007.

Boyer, Paul. *By the Bomb's Early Light: American Thought and Culture at the Dawn of
the Atomic Age.* Chapel Hill: The University of North Carolina, 1994.

——. *Fallout: A Historian Reflects on America's Half-Century Encounter with Nuclear
Weapons.* Columbus: Ohio State University Press, 1998.

——. "From Activism to Apathy: The American People and Nuclear Weapons, 1963–1980." *Journal of American History* 70, no. 4 (March 1984): 821–844.

Brand, Stewart. *Whole Earth Discipline: Why Dense Cities, Nuclear Power, Transgenic Crops, Restored Wildlands, and Geoengineering Are Necessary*. New York: Penguin, 2010.

Brenner, Johanna, and Barbara Laslett. "Gender, Social Reproduction, and Women's Self-Organization: Considering the US Welfare State." *Gender and Society* 5, no. 3 (September 1991): 311–333.

Briggs, Laura. *Reproducing Empire: Race, Sex, Science, and US Imperialism in Puerto Rico*. Berkeley: University of California Press, 2002.

——. *Somebody's Children: The Politics of Transracial and Transnational Adoption*. Durham: Duke University Press, 2012.

Brown, Kate. *Plutopia: Nuclear Families, Atomic Cities, and the Great Soviet and American Plutonium Disasters*. New York: Oxford University Press, 2013.

Brown, Phil. "Popular Epidemiology and Toxic Waste Contamination: Lay and Professional Ways of Knowing." *Journal of Health and Social Behavior* 33 (September 1992): 267–281.

Brown, Wendy. *Undoing the Demos: Neoliberalism's Stealth Revolution*. Cambridge: Zone, 2015.

Buell, Lawrence. *Writing for an Endangered World: Literature, Culture, and Environment in the US and Beyond*. Cambridge: Harvard University Press, 2001.

Bullard, Robert. *Dumping in Dixie: Race, Class, and Environmental Quality*. Boulder: Westview, 2000.

Burr, William. "How to Fight a Nuclear War," *Foreign Policy* (September 14, 2012). www.foreignpolicy.com/articles/2012/09/14/how_to_fight_a_nuclear_war.

Butler, Judith. *Precarious Life: The Powers of Mourning and Violence*. London: Verso, 2006.

Calder, Nigal. *Nuclear Nightmares: An Investigation into Possible Wars*. New York: Penguin, 1981.

Caldicott, Helen. *Nuclear Madness: What You Can Do*. New York: Bantam, 1978.

——. *Nuclear Power Is Not the Answer*. New York: New Press, 2006.

Campos, Luis. "The Birth of Living Radium." *Representations* 97 (Winter 2007): 1–27.

——. *Radium and the Secret of Life*. Chicago: University of Chicago Press, 2015.

Cannon, Walter. *The Wisdom of the Body*. New York: Norton, 1932.

Carson, Rachel. *Silent Spring*. New York: Houghton Mifflin, 1962.

Caufield, Catherine. *Multiple Exposures: Chronicles of the Radiation Age*. Chicago: University of Chicago Press, 1990.

Chakrabarty, Dipesh. "The Climate of History: Four Theses." *Critical Inquiry* 35, no. 2 (Winter 2009): 197–222.

Checker, Melissa. *Polluted Promises: Environmental Racism and the Search for Justice in a Southern Town*. New York: New York University Press, 2005.

Clapp, Jennifer. *Toxic Exports: The Transfer of Hazardous Waste from Rich to Poor Countries*. Ithaca: Cornell University Press, 2001.

Clarke, Lee. *Worst Cases: Terror and Catastrophe in the Popular Imagination*. Chicago: University of Chicago Press, 2005.

Coates, Ta Nehisi. *Between the World and Me*. New York: Spiegel and Grau, 2015.

Collins, Robert. *Transforming America: Politics and Culture in the Reagan Years*. New York: Columbia University Press, 2007.

Committee for the Compilation of Materials on Damage Caused by the Atomic Bombs in Hiroshima and Nagasaki. *Hiroshima and Nagasaki: The Physical, Medical, and Social Effects of the Atomic Bombings*. New York: Basic, 1981.

Connelly, Matthew, Matt Fay, Giulia Ferrini, Micki Kaufman, Will Leonard, Harrison Monsky, Ryan Musto, Tauton Paine, Nicholas Standish, and Lydia Walker. "General, I Have Fought Just as Many Nuclear Wars as You Have: Forecasts, Future Scenarios, and the Politics of Armageddon." *American Historical Review* 117, no. 5 (December 2012): 1431–1460.

Corburn, Jason. *Street Science: Community Knowledge and Environmental Health Justice*. Cambridge: MIT Press, 2005.

Cowie, Jefferson. *Stayin' Alive: The 1970s and the Last Days of the Working Class*. New York: New Press, 2012.

Cutter, Susan. *Living with Risk: the Geography of Technological Hazards*. New York: Wiley, 1995.

Darwin, Charles. *The Origin of Species*. 150th anniversary ed. New York: Signet, 2003.

Davis, Kathy. *The Making of Our Bodies, Ourselves: How Feminism Travels Across Borders*. Durham: Duke University Press, 2007.

de Baecque, Antoine. *The Body Politic: Corporeal Metaphor in Revolutionary France, 1770–1880*. Stanford: Stanford University Press, 1997.

de Chadarevian, Soraya. "Mice and the Reactor: The Genetics Experiment in 1950s Britain." *Journal of the History of Biology* 39 (2006): 707–735.

de La Pena, Carolyn. *The Body Electric: How Strange Machines Built the Modern American*. New York: New York University Press, 2005.

Delgado, James. *Nuclear Dawn: The Atomic Bomb from the Manhattan Project to the Cold War*. Oxford: Osprey, 2009.

DeLillo, Don. *White Noise*. New York: Penguin, 1986.

Del Tredici, Robert. *The People of Three Mile Island*. San Francisco: Sierra Club, 1980.

Divine, Robert A. *Blowing on the Wind: The Nuclear Test Ban Debate, 1954–1960*. New York: Oxford University Press, 1978.

Douglas, Mary. *Purity and Danger: An Analysis of Concepts of Pollution and Taboo*. New York: Taylor, 2002.

Dower, John. *Cultures of War: Pearl Harbor/Hiroshima/9-11/Iraq*. New York: Norton, 2011.

Dubow, Sara. *Ourselves Unborn: A History of the Fetus in Modern America*. New York: Oxford University Press, 2010.

Dunaway, Finis. "Gas Masks, Pogo, and the Ecological Indian: Earth Day and the Visual Politics of American Environmentalism." *American Quarterly* 60, no. 1 (March 2008): 67–99.

——. *Seeing Green: The Use and Abuse of American Environmental Images*. Chicago: University of Chicago Press, 2015.

Dunlap, Thomas. *DDT, Silent Spring, and the Rise of Environmentalism*. Seattle: University of Washington Press, 2008.

Easton, Robert. *Black Tide: The Santa Barbara Oil Spill and Its Consequences*. New York: Delacorte, 1972.

Echols, Alice. *Daring to Be Bad: Radical Feminism in America, 1967–1975.* Minneapolis: University of Minnesota Press, 1989.

Edelman, Lee. *No Future: Queer Theory and the Death Drive.* Durham: Duke University Press, 2004.

Egan, Michael. *Barry Commoner and the Science of Survival: The Remaking of American Environmentalism.* Cambridge: MIT Press, 2009.

Ehrlich, Paul. *The Population Bomb.* San Francisco: Sierra-Ballantine, 1971.

Epstein, Barbara. *Political Protest and Cultural Revolution: Non-Violent Direct Action in the 1970s and 1980s.* Berkeley: University of California Press, 1991.

Epstein, Steven. *Impure Science: AIDS, Activism, and the Politics of Knowledge.* Berkeley: University of California Press, 1996.

Erikson, Kai. *A New Species of Trouble: The Human Experience of Modern Disasters.* New York: Norton, 1995.

Farber, David. *Taken Hostage: The Iran Hostage Crisis and America's First Encounter with Radical Islam.* Princeton: Princeton University Press, 2006.

Federation of American Scientists. *The Future of Nuclear Power in the United States.* Lexington: Washington and Lee University, 2012.

Ferguson, Frances. "The Nuclear Sublime." *Diacritics* 14, no. 2 (Summer 1984): 4–10.

Ferguson, Niall, Charles Maier, Erez Manela, and Daniel Sargent, eds. *The Shock of the Global: the 1970s in Perspective.* Cambridge: Harvard University Press, 2011.

Ferlund, Kevin, ed. *The Cold War American West.* Albuquerque: University of New Mexico Press, 1998.

Foley, Michael. *Front Porch Politics: The Forgotten Heyday of American Activism in the 1970s and 1980s.* New York: Hill and Wang, 2013.

Foner, Eric. *The Story of American Freedom.* New York: Norton, 1999.

Gaard, Greta. "Toward a Feminist Postcolonial Milk Studies." *American Quarterly* 65, no. 3 (September 2013): 595–619.

Gaonkar, Dilip Parameshwar. "Toward New Imaginaries: An Introduction." *Public Culture* 14, no. 1 (Winter 2002), 1–19.

Gerhard, Jane. *Desiring Revolution: Second Wave Feminism and the Rewriting of American Sexual Thought, 1920–1982.* New York: Columbia University Press, 2001.

Gerstle, Gary. *American Crucible: Race and Nation in the Twentieth Century.* Princeton: Princeton University Press, 2002.

Gibbs, Lois Marie. *Love Canal and the Birth of the Environmental Health Movement.* Washington, DC: Island, 2010.

Ginsburg, Faye. *Contested Lives: The Abortion Debate in an American Community.* Berkeley: University of California Press, 1988.

Gitlin, Todd. *Inside Prime Time.* Berkeley: University of California Press, 2000.

Glenn, Evelyn Nakano. "From Servitude to Service Work: Historical Continuities in the Racial Division of Paid Reproductive Labor." *Signs* (Autumn 1992): 1–43.

Gordon, Linda. *Woman's Body, Woman's Right: Birth Control in America.* Rev ed. New York: Penguin, 1990.

Gottlieb, Robert. *Forcing the Spring: The Transformation of the American Environmental Movement.* Washington, DC: Island, 2005.

Gould, Debra. *Moving Politics: Emotion and ACT-UP's Fight Against AIDS.* Chicago: University of Chicago Press, 2009.

Graebner, William. *The Age of Doubt: American Thought and Culture in the 1940s*. New York: Twayne, 1991.

Gusterson, Hugh. "(Anti)nuclear Pilgrims," *Anthropologiska Studier* 62–63:61–66.

——. "Nuclear Tourism." *Journal for Cultural Research* 8, no. 1 (2004): 23–31.

Hacker, Barton. *The Dragon's Tail: Radiation Safety in the Manhattan Project, 1942–1946*. Berkeley: University of California Press, 1987.

Hagelin, Sarah. *Reel Vulnerability: Power, Pain, and Gender in Contemporary American Film and Television*. New Brunswick, NJ: Rutgers University Press, 2013.

Hamblin, Jacob. *Arming Mother Nature: The Birth of Catastrophic Environmentalism*. New York: Oxford University Press, 2013.

——. "A Dispassionate and Objective Effort: Negotiating the First Study on the Biological Effects of Atomic Radiation." *Journal of the History of Biology* 40, no. 1 (Spring 2007): 147–177.

——. *Oceanographers and the Cold War: Disciples of Marine Science*. Seattle: University of Washington Press, 2005.

——. *Poison in the Well: Radioactive Waste in the Oceans at the Dawn of the Nuclear Age*. New Brunswick, NJ: Rutgers University Press, 2009.

Haraway, Donna. *Staying with the Trouble: Making Kin in the Chthulucene*. Durham: Duke University Press, 2016.

Harper, Peter. *A Short History of Medical Genetics*. New York: Oxford University Press, 2007.

Harris, Jonathan Gil. *Foreign Bodies and the Body Politic: Discourses of Social Pathology in Early Modern England*. Cambridge: Cambridge University Press, 2006.

Hartman, Andrew. *A War for the Soul of America: A History of the Culture Wars*. Chicago: University of Chicago Press, 2015.

Harvey, David. *A Brief History of Neoliberalism*. New York: Oxford University Press, 2007.

Hayes, Christopher. *Twilight of the Elites: America After Meritocracy*. New York: Broadway, 2012.

Hecht, Gabrielle. *Being Nuclear: Africans and the Global Uranium Trade*. Cambridge: MIT Press, 2012.

Hecht, Selig. *Explaining the Atom*. New York: Viking, 1947.

Heise, Ursula. *Sense of Place and Sense of Planet: The Environmental Imagination of the Global*. New York: Oxford University Press, 2008.

Hersey, John. *Hiroshima*. New York: Knopf, 1946.

Hofstadter, Richard. *The Age of Reform: From Bryan to FDR*. New York: Random House, 1955.

Houser, Heather. *Ecosickness in Contemporary US Fiction: Environment and Affect*. New York: Columbia University Press, 2014.

Iverson, Kristin. *Full Body Burden: Growing Up in the Shadow of Rocky Flats*. New York: Crown, 2012.

Jacobs, Meg. *Panic at the Pump: The Energy Crisis and the Transformation of American Politics in the 1970s*. New York: Hill and Wang, 2016.

James, William. "On a Certain Blindness in Human Beings." In *Talks to Teachers on Psychology and to Students on Some of Life's Ideals*. New York: Holt, 1915.

Jeffords, Susan. *Hard Bodies: Hollywood Masculinity in the Reagan Era*. New Brunswick, NJ: Rutgers University Press, 1993.

Joppke, Christian. *Mobilizing Against Nuclear Energy: A Comparison of the United States and Germany*. Berkeley: University of California Press, 1993.

Joskow, Paul, and John Parsons. "The Economic Future of Nuclear Power." *Daedalus* 138, no. 4 (Fall 2009): 45–59.

Joyrich, Lynne. "All That Television Allows: TV Melodrama, Postmodernism, and Consumer Culture." *Camera Obscura* 6, no. 1 (January 1988): 128–153.

Jung, Courtney. *Lactivism: How Feminists and Fundamentalists, Hippies and Yuppies, and Physicians and Politicians Made Breastfeeding Big Business and Bad Policy*. New York: Basic, 2015.

Kantorowicz, Ernst. *The King's Two Bodies: A Study in Medieval Political Theology*. Princeton: Princeton University Press, 1958.

Katz, Arthur. *Life After Nuclear War*. New York: Ballinger, 1982.

Katz, Milton. *Ban the Bomb: A History of SANE, 1957–1985*. Westport, CT: Greenwood, 1986.

Kemeny, John. *Accident at Three Mile Island: The Need for Change, The Legacy of TMI*. Oxford: Pergamon, 1979.

Kennedy, Edward M., and Mark O. Hatfield. *Freeze! How You Can Prevent Nuclear War*. New York: Bantam, 1982.

Kinder, John. *Paying with Their Bodies: American War and the Problem of the Disabled Veteran*. Chicago: University of Chicago Press, 2015.

Kinsella, William J., and Jay Mullen. "Becoming Hanford Downwinders: Producing Community and Challenging Discursive Containment." In *Nuclear Legacies: Communication, Controversy, and the US Nuclear Weapons Complex*, edited by Bryan C. Taylor, William Kinsella, Stephen Depoe, and Meredith Metzler, 73–108. Lanham, MD: Lexington, 2007.

Klein, Naomi. *This Changes Everything: Capitalism vs. the Climate*. New York: Simon and Schuster, 2014.

Kline, Wendy. *Bodies of Knowledge: Sexuality, Reproduction, and Women's Health in the Second Wave*. Chicago: University of Chicago Press, 2012.

Klinenberg, Eric. *Heatwave: A Social Autopsy of Disaster in Chicago*. Chicago: University of Chicago Press, 2002.

Kolbert, Elizabeth. *The Sixth Extinction: An Unnatural History*. New York: Holt, 2014.

Krupar, Shiloh R. *Hot Spotter's Report: Military Fables of Toxic Waste*. Minneapolis: University of Minnesota Press, 2013.

Kruse, Kevin. *White Flight: Atlanta and the Making of Modern Conservatism*. Princeton: Princeton University Press, 2005.

Kruse, Kevin, and Thomas Sugrue, eds. *The New Suburban History*. Chicago: University of Chicago Press, 2006.

Kuletz, Valerie. *The Tainted Desert: Environmental Ruin in the American West*. New York: Routledge, 1998.

Lamis, Renee. *The Realignment of Pennsylvania Politics Since 1960: Two Party Competition in a Battleground State*. University Park: Pennsylvania State University Press, 2009.

Langston, Nancy. *Toxic Bodies: Hormone Disrupters and the Legacy of DES*. New Haven: Yale University Press, 2011.

Lassiter, Matthew. *The Silent Majority: Suburban Politics in the Sunbelt South*. Princeton: Princeton University Press, 2012.

Lehman, Peter, ed. *Masculinity: Bodies, Movies, Culture*. New York: Routledge, 2001.

LeMenager, Stephanie. *Living Oil: Petroleum Culture in the American Century.* New York: Oxford University Press, 2014.

Leslie, Stuart. *The Cold War and American Science: The Military-Industrial-Academic Complex at MIT and Stanford.* New York: Columbia University Press, 1994.

Lieven, Anatol. *America Right or Wrong: An Anatomy of American Nationalism.* New York: Oxford University Press, 2004.

Lifton, Robert Jay. *Death in Life: Survivors of Hiroshima.* Chapel Hill: University of North Carolina Press, 1991.

Lindee, Susan. *Suffering Made Real: American Science and the Survivors at Hiroshima.* Chicago: University of Chicago Press, 1997.

Lytle, K. Hamilton. *The Gentle Subversive: Rachel Carson, Silent Spring, and the Rise of the Environmental Movement.* New York: Oxford University Press, 2007.

Malley, Marjorie. *Radioactivity: A History of a Mysterious Science.* New York: Oxford University Press, 2011.

Malm, Andreas. "The Anthropocene Myth." *Jacobin*, March 30, 2015. www.jacobinmag .com/2015/03/anthropocene-capitalism-climate-change/.

——. "The Geology of Mankind? A Critique of the Anthropocene Narrative." *Anthropocene Review* 1, no. 1 (April 1, 2014): 62–69.

Marinacci, Barbara, and Ramesh Krishnamurthy, eds. *Linus Pauling on Peace: A Scientist Speaks Out on Humanism and World Survival.* Los Altos: Rising Star, 1998.

Martin, Bradford. *The Other Eighties: A Secret History of America in the Age of Reagan.* New York: Hill and Wang, 2011.

Masco, Joseph. "Bad Weather: On Planetary Crisis." *Social Studies of Science* 40, no. 1 (February 2010): 7–40.

——. *Nuclear Borderlands: The Manhattan Project in Post–Cold War New Mexico.* Princeton: Princeton University Press, 2006.

——. "Nuclear Technoaesthetics: Sensory Politics from Trinity to the Virtual Bomb in Los Alamos." *American Ethnologist* 31, no. 3 (2004): 349–373.

Massachusetts Institute of Technology. *The Future of Nuclear Power: An Interdisciplinary Study.* 2003, updated in 2009.

McAlister, Melani. *Epic Encounters: Culture, Media, and US Interests in the Middle East, 1945–2000.* Berkeley: University of California Press, 2001.

McGirr, Lisa. *Suburban Warriors: The Origins of the New American Right.* Princeton: Princeton University Press, 2002.

McKibben, Bill. *Eaarth: Making a Life on a Tough New Planet.* New York: St. Martin's, 2011.

——. *The End of Nature.* Norwell, MA: Anchor, 1989.

Menand, Louis. *The Metaphysical Club.* New York: Farrar, Straus and Giroux, 2001.

Meyer, David S. *A Winter of Our Discontent: The Nuclear Freeze and American Politics.* New York: Praeger, 1990.

Meyer, Nicholas, dir. *The Day After.* ABC Circle Films, 1983.

Moore, Jason W. *Capitalism in the Web of Life: Ecology and the Accumulation of Capital.* London: Verso, 2015.

Moreton, Bethany. *To Serve God and Walmart: The Making of Christian Free Enterprise.* Cambridge: Harvard University Press, 2010.

Morgen, Sandra. *Into Our Own Hands: The Women's Health Movement in the United States, 1969–1990.* New Brunswick, NJ: Rutgers University Press, 2002.

Mukherjee, Siddhartha. *The Emperor of All Maladies: A Biography of Cancer*. New York: Scribner, 2011.

Murphy, Michelle. "Chemical Regimes of Living." *Environmental History* 13, no. 4 (October 2008): 695–703.

Nash, Linda. "Purity and Danger: Historical Reflections on Environmental Regulations." *Environmental History* 13, no. 4 (October 2008): 651–658.

National Research Council. *Long-Term Worldwide Effects of Multiple Nuclear War Detonations*. Washington, DC: National Academy of Sciences, 1975.

Nelkin, Dorothy, and Michael Pollak. *The Atom Besieged: Anti-Nuclear Movements in France and Germany*. Cambridge: MIT Press, 1982.

Nelson, Alondra. *Body and Soul: The Black Panther Party and the Fight Against Medical Discrimination*. Minneapolis: University of Minnesota Press, 2011.

Nelson, Jennifer. *More Than Medicine: A History of the Feminist Women's Health Movement*. New York: New York University Press, 2015.

——. *Women of Color and the Reproductive Rights Movement*. New York: New York University Press, 2003.

Newman, Kim. *Apocalypse Movies: End of the World Cinema*. New York: St. Martin's, 2002.

Newman, Richard. *Love Canal: A Toxic History from Colonial Times to the Present*. New York: Oxford University Press, 2015.

Nixon, Rob. *Slow Violence and the Environmentalism of the Poor*. Cambridge: Harvard University Press, 2011.

Nye, David. *American Technological Sublime*. Cambridge: MIT Press, 1994.

Oaks, Laury. "Smoke Filled Wombs and Fragile Fetuses: The Social Politics of Fetal Representation." *Signs* 26, no. 1 (Autumn 2000): 63–108.

Office of Technology Assessment. *Nuclear Power in an Age of Uncertainty*. Washington, DC: US Congress, 1984.

Oliver, Kelly. *Witnessing: Beyond Recognition*. Minneapolis: University of Minnesota Press: 2001.

Orr, Jackie. *Panic Diaries: A Genealogy of Panic Disorders*. Durham: Duke University Press, 2006.

Overpeck, Deron. "Remember! It's Only a Movie: Expectations and Receptions of *The Day After*." *Historical Journal of Film, Radio, and Television* 32, no. 2 (June 2012): 267–292.

Pachirat, Timothy. *Every Twelve Seconds: Industrial Slaughter and the Politics of Sight*. New Haven: Yale University Press, 2011.

Patterson, James. *The Dread Disease: Cancer and American Culture*. Cambridge: Harvard University Press, 1989.

——. *Restless Giant: The United States from Watergate to Bush v. Gore*. New York: Oxford University Press, 2005.

Peacock, Margaret. *Innocent Weapons: The Soviet and American Politics of Childhood in the Cold War*. Chapel Hill: University of North Carolina Press, 2014.

Peiss, Kathy, and Christina Simmons, eds. *Passion and Power: Sexuality in History*. Philadelphia: Temple University Press, 1989.

Pellow, David Naguib. *Garbage Wars: The Struggle for Environmental Justice in Chicago*. Cambridge: MIT Press, 2004.

Peluso, Nancy Lee, and Michael Watts, eds. *Violent Environments*. Ithaca: Cornell University Press, 2001.

Perlstein, Rick. *Nixonland: the Rise of a President and the Fracturing of America*. New York: Scribner, 2009.

Perrow, Charles. *Normal Accidents: Living with High Risk Technologies*. New York: Basic, 1984.

Peterson, Jeannie. *The Aftermath: The Human and Ecological Consequences of Nuclear War*. New York: Pantheon, 1983.

Petryna, Adriana. *Life Exposed: Biological Citizens After Chernobyl*. Princeton: Princeton University Press, 2003.

Physicians for Social Responsibility. *The Last Epidemic: The Medical Consequences of Nuclear Weapons and Nuclear War*. Santa Cruz: Resource Center for Non-Violence, 1980.

Pittock, Barrie. "The Effects on the Atmosphere of a Major Nuclear Exchange." *Environment* 27, no. 3 (April 1985): 25–28.

Planned Parenthood Association of Pennsylvania. *Money, Power, and the Radical Right in Pennsylvania*. Darby, PA: Diane, 1996.

Proctor, Robert. *Cancer Wars: How Politics Shapes What We Know and Don't Know About Cancer*. New York: Basic, 1995.

Purdy, Jedediah. *After Nature: A Politics for the Anthropocene*. Cambridge: Harvard University Press, 2015.

Pursell, Carroll. *Technology in Postwar America*. New York: Columbia University Press, 2007.

Quarantelli, Enrico. "Conventional Beliefs and Counterintuitive Realities." *Social Research* 75, no. 3 (Fall 2008): 873–904.

Reagan, Leslie. *Dangerous Pregnancies: Mothers, Disabilities, and Abortion in Modern America*. Berkeley: University of California Press, 2012.

Rodgers, Daniel. *Age of Fracture*. Cambridge: Harvard University Press, 2011.

Rogin, Michael. *The Intellectuals and McCarthy: The Radical Specter*. Cambridge: MIT Press, 1967.

Rome, Adam. *The Bulldozer in the Countryside: Suburban Sprawl and the Rise of American Environmentalism*. New York: Cambridge University Press, 2001.

——. *The Genius of Earth Day: How a 1970 Teach In Unexpectedly Made the First Green Generation*. New York: Hill and Wang, 2014.

Rosenberg, Gabriel. *The 4-H Harvest: Sexuality and the State in Rural America*. Philadelphia: University of Pennsylvania Press, 2016.

Rossinow, Doug. *The Reagan Era: A History of the 1980s*. New York: Columbia University Press, 2015.

Sagan, Carl. "Nuclear War and Climatic Catastrophe: Some Policy Information." *Foreign Affairs* (Winter 1983/1984): 257–292.

Sandman, Peter M., and Mary Paden. "At Three Mile Island." *Columbia Journalism Review* (July/August 1979): 43–58.

Savran, David. *Taking It Like a Man: White Masculinity, Masochism, and Contemporary American Culture*. Princeton: Princeton University Press, 1998.

Scheer, Robert. *With Enough Shovels: Reagan, Bush, and Nuclear War*. New York: Random House, 1982.

Schell, Jonathan. *The Fate of the Earth*. New York: Knopf, 1982.

Schulman, Bruce J. *The Seventies: The Great Shift in American Culture, Society, and Politics*. New York: Da Capo, 2002.

Schulman, Bruce J., and Julian Zelizer, eds. *Rightward Bound: Making America Conservative in the 1970s*. Cambridge: Harvard University Press, 2008.

Schulze, Laurie. "The Made-for-TV Movie: Industrial Practice, Cultural Form, Popular Reception." In *Hollywood in the Age of Television*, edited by Tino Balio, 351–376. New York: Routledge, 2013.

Schweitzer, Albert. *The Rights of the Unborn and the Peril Today: Statement with Reference to the Present Nuclear Crisis in the World*. Chicago: Albert Schweitzer Education Foundation, 1958.

Scranton, Roy. *Learning to Die in the Anthropocene*. San Francisco: City Lights, 2015.

Segers, Mary and Timothy Byrnes. *Abortion Politics in American States*. New York: M. E. Sharpe, 1995.

Self, Robert. *All in the Family: The Realignment of American Democracy Since the 1970s*. New York: Hill and Wang, 2012.

——. *American Babylon: Race and the Struggle for Postwar Oakland*. Princeton: Princeton University Press, 2005.

Shapiro, Jerome. *Atomic Bomb Cinema: The Apocalyptic Imagination on Film*. New York: Routledge, 2002.

Sheldon, Rebekah. *The Child to Come: Life After the Human Catastrophe*. Minneapolis: University of Minnesota Press, 2016.

Shermer, Elizabeth. *Sunbelt Capitalism: Phoenix and the Transformation of American Politics*. Philadelphia: University of Pennsylvania Press, 2013.

Sherry, Michael. *In the Shadow of War: The United States Since the 1930s*. New Haven: Yale University Press, 1997.

Sick, Gary. *All Fall Down: America's Tragic Encounter with Iran*. New York: Penguin, 1986.

Silverman, Joshua. "Nuclear Technology." In *A Companion to American Technology*, edited by Carroll Pursell, 298–320. Malden, MA: Blackwell, 2005.

Silverman, Kaja. *Male Subjectivity at the Margins*. New York: Routledge, 1992.

Skloot, Rebecca. *The Immortal Life of Henrietta Lacks*. New York: Broadway, 2011.

Smith, Michael L. "Advertising the Atom." In *Government and Environmental Politics: Essays on Historical Development Since World War Two*, edited by Michael J. Lacey, 233–262. Baltimore: Johns Hopkins University Press, 1991.

——. "'Planetary Engineering': The Strange Career of Progress in Nuclear American." In *Possible Dreams: Enthusiasm for Technology in America*, edited by John L. Wright, 111–123. Dearborn, MI: Henry Ford Museum and Greenfield Village, 1992.

Smith, Rogers M. *Civic Ideals: Conflicting Visions of Citizenship in U.S. History*. New Haven: Yale University Press, 1999.

Smith, Steve Kroll, Phil Brown, and Valerie J. Gunter, eds. *Illness and the Environment: A Reader in Contested Medicine*. New York: New York University Press, 2000.

Smith, Steve Kroll, and Worth Lancaster. "Bodies, Environments, and a New Style of Reasoning." *Annals of the American Academy of Political and Social Science* 584 (November 2002): 203–212.

Smith-Howard, Kendra. *Pure and Modern Milk: An Environmental History Since 1900*. New York: Oxford University Press, 2013.

Solnit, Rebecca. *A Paradise Built in Hell: The Extraordinary Communities That Arise in Disaster*. New York: Viking, 2009.

Solomon, Andrew. *Far from the Tree: Parents, Children, and the Search for Identity.* New York: Scribner, 2013.

Sontag, Susan. *Illness as Metaphor.* New York: McGraw-Hill, 1977.

Stein, Judith. *Pivotal Decade: How the United States Traded Factories for Finance in the Seventies.* New Haven: Yale University Press, 2010.

——. *Running Steel, Running America: Race, Economic Decline, and the Decline of Liberalism.* Chapel Hill: University of North Carolina Press, 1998.

Stoll, Steven. *US Environmentalism Since 1945: A Brief History with Documents.* New York: Bedford St. Martin's, 2007.

Stone, Robert, dir. *Pandora's Promise.* CNN Films, 2013.

Stranahan, Susan. *Susquehanna, River of Dreams.* Baltimore: Johns Hopkins University Press, 1995.

Swerdlow, Amy. *Women Strike for Peace: Traditional Motherhood and Radical Politics in the 1960s.* Chicago: University of Chicago Press: 1993.

Szasz, Andrew. *Ecopopulism: Toxic Waste and the Movement for Environmental Justice.* Minneapolis: University of Minnesota Press, 1994.

Sze, Julie. *Noxious New York: The Racial Politics of Urban Health and Environmental Justice.* Cambridge: MIT Press, 2006.

Taylor, Charles. *Modern Social Imaginaries.* Durham: Duke University Press, 2003.

Taylor, Dorceta. *Toxic Communities: Environmental Racism, Industrial Pollution, and Residential Mobility.* New York: New York University Press, 2014.

Thomas, Julia Adeney, "History and Biology in the Anthropocene: Problems of Scale, Problems of Value." *American Historical Review* 119, no. 5 (December 2014): 1587–1607.

Tone, Andrea. *The Age of Anxiety: A History of America's Turbulent Affair with Tranquilizers.* New York: Basic, 2011.

Troy, Gil. *Morning in America: How Ronald Reagan Invented the 1980s.* Princeton: Princeton University Press, 2005.

US Nuclear Energy Industry's Strategic Plan for Building New Nuclear Power Plants. Executive Summary, May 1998. http://lobby.la.psu.edu/051_Nuclear_Waste/Organizational_Statements/NEI/NEI_Strategic_Plan.pdf.

Vanderbilt, Tom. *Survival City: Adventures Among the Ruins of Atomic America.* Princeton: Princeton Architectural Press, 2002.

van Wyck, Peter C. *Signs of Danger: Waste, Trauma, and Nuclear Threat.* Minneapolis: University of Minnesota Press, 2005.

Vogel, Sarah. "From 'The Dose Makes the Poison' to 'The Timing Makes the Dose': Conceptualizing Risk in the Synthetic Age." *Environmental History* 13, no. 4 (October 2008): 667–673.

——. "The Politics of Plastics: The Making and Unmaking of Bisphenol A 'Safety.'" *American Journal of Public Health* 99, no. S3 (September 3, 2009): 559–566.

von Eschen, Penny. "Duke Ellington Plays Baghdad: Rethinking Hard and Soft Power from the Outside In." In *Contested Democracy: Freedom, Race, and Power in American History*, edited by Manisha Sinha and Penny Von Eschen, 279–300. New York: Columbia University Press, 2007.

Walbert, David. *Garden Spot: Lancaster County the Old Order Amish, and the Selling of Rural America.* New York: Oxford University Press, 2002.

Walker, J. Samuel. *Permissible Dose: A History of Radiation Protection in the Twentieth Century*. Berkeley: University of California Press, 2000.

——. *Three Mile Island: A Nuclear Crisis in Historical Perspective*. Berkeley: University of California Press, 2004.

Waller, Gregory. "Re-Placing the Day After." *Cinema Journal* 26, no. 3 (Spring 1987): 3–20.

Walsh, Edward J. *Democracy in the Shadows: Citizen Mobilization in the Wake of the Accident at Three Mile Island*. New York: Greenwood, 1988.

Weart, Spencer R. *Nuclear Fear: A History of Images*. 1989; Cambridge: Harvard University Press, 2012.

Weinberg, Alvin. "New Life for Nuclear Power." *Issues in Science and Technology* 19, no. 4 (Summer 2003): 60–62.

Weiner, Jon. *How We Forgot the Cold War: A Historical Journey Across America*. Berkeley: University of California, 2012.

Wellock, Thomas. *Critical Masses: Opposition to Nuclear Power in California, 1958–1978*. Madison: University of Wisconsin Press, 1998.

Welsome, Eileen. *The Plutonium Files: America's Secret Medical Experiments in the Cold War*. New York: Dial, 1999.

Wilentz, Sean. *The Age of Reagan: A History, 1974–2008*. New York: Harper, 2008.

Williams, Hill. *Made in Hanford: The Bomb That Changed the World*. Pullman: Washington State University, 2011.

Williams, Terry Tempest. *Refuge: An Unnatural History of Family and Place*. New York: Vintage, 1991.

Wills, Garry. *Bomb Power: The Modern Presidency and the National Security State*. New York: Penguin, 2011.

Wittner, Lawrence. *Toward Nuclear Abolition: A History of the World Disarmament Movement, 1971–Present*. Stanford: Stanford University Press, 2003.

Yoneyama, Lisa. *Hiroshima Traces: Time, Space, and the Dialectics of Memory*. Berkeley: University of California Press, 1999.

Zaretsky, Eli. *Why America Needs a Left: A Historical Argument*. London: Polity, 2012.

Zaretsky, Natasha. *No Direction Home: The American Family and the Fear of National Decline, 1968–1980*. Chapel Hill: University of North Carolina Press, 2007.

——. "Radiation Suffering and Patriotic Body Politics." *The Journal of Social History* 48:3 (Spring 2015), 487–510.

Zimring, Carl. *Clean and White: A History of Environmental Racism in the United States*. New York: New York University Press, 2016.

ACKNOWLEDGMENTS

This book took me a decade to write, and its completion would not have been possible without the sustenance of many students, colleagues, friends, and family members. I am grateful to my colleagues in the history department at Southern Illinois University, who have helped make our sweet town such a supportive and nurturing place to live and work. I also owe a debt to my students, many of whom have arrived at the university against the cumulative odds created by poverty and geographical isolation. They inspire me every day with their intuitive smarts and basic decency and remind me why teaching matters. I was incredibly fortunate to have Kay Carr as a department chair in the years that I was finishing this manuscript. At a time of great pressure and strain in public higher education, chairs like her, who aim to empower and protect their faculty members no matter what, are unsung heroes.

While conducting my research, I benefited from several archivists who helped me navigate their rich collections. I am especially grateful to Nancy Collins Watson at the University of Pittsburgh Special Collections and Jim Gerencser at the Dickinson College Archives for their assistance. At SIU's Morris Library, Anna Xiong helped me to track down census data. A big thank-you to Matthew Schneider Mayerson, Finis Dunaway, Rebecca Onion, Roy Scranton, Rodney Taveira, and Clare Corbould for organizing conference panels, talks, and roundtables, where I had the opportunity to share my ideas and learn from others. One of the exciting parts of this project was venturing into the vibrant interdisciplinary fields of environmental and energy humanities. The environment and culture caucus of the American Studies Association and Rice University's Center for Energy and Environmental Research in the Human Sciences provided space for rich intellectual exchange. I am also grateful to Eric Epstein and Mary Osborne, who shared with me their memories of the accident.

A few institutions and individuals deserve special mention. SIU's College of Liberal Arts gave crucial support along the way. Likewise, in the summer of 2016, I had the good fortune of being a visiting research fellow at the University of Sydney's United States Studies Centre, a beautiful and congenial place to work. I am grateful to the staff and faculty there, and especially to Rebecca Sheehan, whom I am proud to call a friend and feminist co-conspirator. When this book was still in its infancy, historian Samuel Walker generously shared with me his writings and insights about Three Mile Island. His blow-by-blow account of the accident proved invaluable to me as I sought to tell a different version of the same story. Sandra Beth Levy, Colin Fannon, Mike Fiala, and Sandy Stevens all helped me keep body, mind, and soul together. Ellen Wiesen is the most delightful, supportive mother-in-law one could ask for. At an early stage in the project, Ramzi Fawaz encouraged me to think more boldly and imaginatively about the meaning of mutation. The halls of academe shine more brightly because of him. Meghann Pytka and Kelsey Kretschmer read and responded to an early incarnation of my book proposal, and further down the line, indefatigable historian Nathan Brouwer read the manuscript and provided terrific feedback. At just the right moment, Jacob Haubenreich arrived at SIU and asked where the writing groups were. My gratitude goes out to him, as well as to Laurel Frederickson and Joe Shapiro, for filling the void.

I have caught many lucky breaks in my professional career, but at the very top of the list was landing at a university where the faculty is unionized. During the hundreds of hours that I was working on this book, a small group of dedicated colleagues were tirelessly volunteering their time and energy on behalf of workplace rights. In this case, saying thank you does not seem nearly enough. I am especially indebted to my dear friends George Boulukos and Rachel Stocking, who in the fall of 2011 taught me what solidarity can achieve, even against considerable odds.

I am deeply grateful to Columbia University Press and to editor Philip Leventhal, who saw this book's potential early on. Shortly after I secured a contract, Philip passed the editorial reins to Bridget Flannery-McCoy. A change in editorship midstream can be stressful for a writer, but Bridget has been a wonderful successor. I thank her for shepherding the manuscript to completion and for encouraging me to pursue my vision. Likewise, whenever I emailed them with a question about an illustration or copyright, Ryan Groendyk and Christian Winting got back to me right away. Two anonymous reviewers provided incisive and thoughtful feedback that made the book better by forcing me to clarify my arguments and be more forthright about the book's status as a work of cultural history. I could not have asked for a more wonderful interlocutor than Jeremy Varon, who was an enthusiastic reader and trenchant critic. His commitment to both rigorous intellectual work and political activism is awesome.

My parents are not just generous people, but brilliant thinkers and editors as well. My father Eli Zaretsky and my stepmother Nancy Fraser read the entire manuscript and encouraged me to tease out the connections between this project and my prior scholarly work, which improved this book immeasurably and, no less important, helped me make sense of my own intellectual journey. Having my ideas filtered through their sharp minds feels like a ridiculous home-court advantage. My mother, Linda Zaretsky, has been my staunchest, proudest champion. Her anger at injustice and her empathy toward suffering are an inspiration. All three of my parents were and remain movement people. Among many things, this book is a love letter to their younger selves. If it makes even a modest contribution to honoring the enormity of what their generation accomplished, then I will consider the last ten years time well spent.

Researching and writing this book required delving into material that was at times frightening and sad. Yet the years that I have worked on this project have been the happiest of my life, because I have gotten to share them with my two children, Daniel and Julian. I thank them for their dependency on me and for needing to be clothed, fed, sheltered, and hugged. Those demands reeled me away from atomic nightmares and planted me back in the routine world of daily living. I bristle when parents say that their children give them hope for the future, as I suspect those comments are not so much for the benefit of children, but rather to relieve parental anxieties and guilt about the fractured world that we are leaving behind.

Yet I would be lying if I did not say that my children's capacities for kindness and reflection do help me look toward the future with expectation, curiosity, and, yes, even hope.

Finally, I must thank my mensch of a husband, Jonathan Wiesen, whom I have taken to referring to as my secret weapon. He has read every word of this book more than once and brought his own considerable talents as a historian and writer to bear on it. He has stood by my side through many a "meltdown" and then had me laughing about it soon after. Again, I bristle at the aspiration of "having it all"—a pipedream, if ever there was one, for men and women alike. But any success I have had with balancing work, marriage, parenting, and health can be credited to Jonathan, who lives his feminism every day through his devotion to my career and to our family. What got me to this book's finish line was imagining this very moment, when I could dedicate it with love to him.

INDEX

Aamodt, Marjorie, 120–21, 142

Aamodt, Norman, 120

Abortion: in atomic age, 38–39; conservative Christian Right and, 230*n*156; disarmament and, 167–68; fetal health and, 95–96, 173; freeze movement and, 167–68; nuclear war and, 167–68; politics and, 96–98; religion and, 96–98; rights of unborn and, 39–40, 167–68; TMI and, 84–85, 92–93, 97, 122, 230*n*152; women's rights and, 84–85, 96–99, 167–68

Abstraction, of military, 19

Accidental activists, 53

Acquired immune deficiency syndrome (AIDS), 206*n*15

AEC. *See* Atomic Energy Commission

Africa, 21–22

Agent Orange, 91, 133

Agriculture, 62, 90, 119–20

AIDS. *See* Acquired immune deficiency syndrome

Alcohol, 95–96

American Century, 193

ANGRY. *See* Anti-Nuclear Group Representing York

Animals, 93, 116–20, 127–28, 181–82

Anthropocene, 2–3, 72–73, 192, 204*n*3

Anti-Nuclear Group Representing York (ANGRY), 104

Antinuclear movement, xv–xvi, 17; accidental activists, 53; antiwar activists and, 55, 106–7; body and, 49–51, *51*; Cold War and, 52–53, 55; freeze movement, 151–73, 244*n*36; Invisible Violence and, 54; on ionizing radiation, 49–51, *51*; maps by, 46–49, *49*, 53–54; nuclear power plants and, 45–51; physician activists, 154–60; politics and, 46–47, 51–56; radiation activists, 51, 55, 218*n*121; religion and, 99–100, 111–13; reluctant activists, 103–13; SANE and, 39–41, *42*; social movements influencing, 45–46, 98–99; on TMI, 61, 104–13; Vietnam War and, 55–56, 106–7; women's health movement and, 54, 98–100; women's rights and, 99–100

Antiwar activists, 55, 64, 106–7

Antiwar movement: freeze movement and, 162–63; patriotic body politics